Critical Essays on
GEORGE SANTAYANA

CRITICAL ESSAYS
ON
AMERICAN LITERATURE

James Nagel, General Editor
Northeastern University

Critical Essays on

GEORGE SANTAYANA

edited by

KENNETH M. PRICE

and

ROBERT C. LEITZ, III

G. K. Hall & Co.
BOSTON, MASSACHUSETTS

Library of Congress Cataloging-in-Publication Data

Critical essays on George Santayana / edited by Kenneth M. Price and
Robert C. Leitz, III.
     p.   cm. — (Critical essays on American literature)
    Includes bibliographical references and index.
    ISBN 0-8161-7303-6
    1. Santayana, George, 1863–1952—Criticism and interpretation.
  I. Price, Kenneth M.   II. Leitz, Robert C.   III. Series.
  PS2773.C75   1991
  811'.52—dc20   91-3281

The paper used in this publication meets the minimum requirements
of American National Standard for Information Sciences—Permanence
of Paper for Printed Library Materials, ANSI Z39.48-1984.♾️™

Printed and bound in the United States of America

Contents

◆

General Editor's Note

♦

This series seeks to anthologize the most important criticism on a wide variety of topics and writers in American literature. Our readers will find in various volumes not only a generous selection of reprinted articles and reviews but also original essays, bibliographies, manuscript sections, and other materials brought to public attention for the first time. *Critical Essays on George Santayana* is the most comprehensive collection of essays ever published on one of the most important writers in American literature. It contains both a sizable gathering of early reviews and a broad selection of more modern scholarship. Among the authors of reprinted articles and reviews are Newton Arvin, Ellen Glasgow, Malcolm Cowley, Adrienne Koch, Joel Porte, and Daniel Aaron. In addition to a substantial introduction by Kenneth M. Price and Robert C. Leitz, III, there are also three original essays—by William G. Holzberger, Herman J. Saatkamp, Jr., and Peter Conn—commissioned specifically for publication in this volume. We are confident that this book will make a permanent and significant contribution to the study of American literature.

JAMES NAGEL

Northeastern University

Publisher's Note

◆

Producing a volume that contains both newly commissioned and reprinted material presents the publisher with the challenge of balancing the desire to achieve stylistic consistency with the need to preserve the integrity of works first published elsewhere. In the Critical Essays series, essays commissioned especially for a particular volume are edited to be consistent with G. K. Hall's house style; reprinted essays appear in the style in which they were first published, with only typographical errors corrected. Consequently, shifts in style from one essay to another are the result of our efforts to be faithful to each text as it was originally published.

Introduction

◆

KENNETH M. PRICE
ROBERT C. LEITZ, III

George Santayana held that a philosopher's "vision of things" ought to be endowed "with all the force, colour, and scope" possible. Then, even if the "the truth of Nature" is missed, a work of imagination will result.[1] Santayana's career is unusually rich because of his contributions in philosophy and in a wide range of literary genres. He has been primarily regarded as a philosopher, however, leaving his literary achievement obscured and his cultural impact only partially understood. This collection of critical essays, by bringing together much of the best commentary on Santayana, should help clarify his place in American letters.

The standard bibliography of writings by and about Santayana is *George Santayana: A Bibliographical Checklist, 1880–1980,* compiled by Herman J. Saatkamp, Jr. and John Jones.[2] It treats primary sources, secondary sources, and manuscript holdings at the four major repositories of Santayana papers: Butler Library of Columbia University, Clifton Waller Barrett Library of the University of Virginia, the Humanities Research Center of the University of Texas at Austin, and the Houghton Library of Harvard University. *Overheard in Seville: Bulletin of the Santayana Society* (1983–), edited by Saatkamp and Angus Kerr-Lawson, provides a forum for work on Santayana and updates the *Bibliographical Checklist.*

THE POET

Santayana was careful not to claim too much for his poetry. He once asserted that his poetry was "simply my philosophy in the making." He added: "Of impassioned tenderness or Dionysiac frenzy I have nothing, nor even of that magic and pregnancy of phrase—really the creation of a fresh idiom—which marks the high lights of poetry. Even if my temperament had been naturally warmer, the fact that the English language (and I can write no other with assurance) was not my mother-tongue would of itself preclude any inspired

1

use of it on my part; its roots do not quite reach to my centre."[3] Nonetheless, reviews of Santayana's *Sonnets and Other Verses* (1894), *A Hermit of Carmel* (1901), and *Poems by George Santayana* (1923) ranged from the respectful to the admiring. Some of the most interesting notices followed the appearance of the last of these volumes. Newton Arvin judged Santayana's finest achievement to be in the sonnet sequences. He admired the "unusual solicitude" for form, the power of his philosophical thought, and the candor and lucidity of his verse. Phillip Littel praised him for standing apart from a modern "generation . . . which prefers fullness to wholeness, and which likes to conceive its universe as too confused and self-contradictory to be reducible to unity by thought."[4] Those reviewers less taken by Santayana's verse generally argued that it was inferior to his criticism, that it lacked the "lyric humanity which is the life-blood of song," that its attempt to attain a classical severity succeeded only in being severe.[5]

Serious critical study of the poetry begins with George W. Howgate's *George Santayana* (1938), the first full-length biography. Howgate analyzes those features Santayana categorized under euphony—meter, rhyme, prosody—and finds him to be a careful and largely successful craftsman. He notes that the poet's manipulation of his favorite form, the Petrarchan sonnet, is strict yet inventive. Predictably, the biographer interprets poems in terms of the life. Thus, for example, he asserts that "Sonnets 34 to 37 are clearly autobiographical and point to a particular young woman as the immediate source of inspiration." He later speculates that Santayana may have been involved with two women because sonnet 24 suggests the consummation of love while sonnet 36 admits that his beloved is not even aware of the love he holds.[6] The speculations of Margaret Munsterberg took another direction: she hinted broadly that Nancy Toy, the wife of Harvard Professor Crawford H. Toy, might have sparked the passion of the sonnets. Douglas L. Wilson, in his dissertation, suggested that it was Susana, Santayana's half-sister, who inspired the love poetry.[7]

Wilson came to his conclusion, in part, because of Santayana's letter to Daniel Cory, his secretary and confidant, explaining the limitations of Howgate's analysis. No biographer, Santayana asserted, could know enough about private emotions to trace the links between life and art. "There is my sister, for instance, certainly the most important influence in my life, psychologically my mother, and one might almost say, my wife. Not that an incestuous idea ever entered my mind or hers; but Freud might have discovered things unsuspected by ourselves."[8] Santayana repeatedly denied that there was a particular woman behind the sonnets, asserting instead that "she" was merely a necessary ingredient of platonic love poetry. He claimed that the emotion of the poems was authentic, though it was based on no single individual or experience.

Still, biographical interpretation retains its fascination. Recent critics, such as Robert K. Martin, stress the importance of Santayana's friendship with Warwick Potter and frequently see the sonnet sequence as prompted by homosexual love.[9] This type of interpretation has much to recommend it. In fact, Santayana implicitly invited homosexual readings of his love poems when he remarked to Cory: "I suppose Housman was really what people nowadays call 'homosexual.' " He continued, "I think I must have been that way in my Harvard days—although I was unconscious of it at the time."[10]

Two other studies of the sonnet sequences, by Douglas L. Wilson and Lois Hughson, offer compelling arguments. In "Santayana's Metanoia: The Second Sonnet Sequence" (1966) Wilson asserts that "these poems are 'sublimated love sonnets,' not in the sense of celebrating a frustrated love affair in which a strong passion is thwarted, but rather in the sense of celebrating a symbolic passion which is transformed by an insight into something more inclusive and more satisfying." He points out that the "great paradox" of the relationship in the sonnets is that the "love is perfectly hopeless." The perfect lover must renounce hope of fulfillment or else love will be doomed to mere temporal satisfaction at best and, therefore, be imperfect.[11]

For Lois Hughson the key to understanding the sonnets is the line "A perfect love is nourished by despair." Her article, "The Uses of Despair: The Sources of Creative Energy in George Santayana" (1971), illustrates how Santayana worked "to project a realm in which he would enjoy compensation for the gratification which experience denied him." She continues: "The price of denying his own rage [stemming from separation from his mother, for three years, beginning at age five] involved the denial of the vast range of possibilities life offers a man of thirty. He cannot see mature sexual relationships or professional fulfillment or any other satisfactions of adult life before him; he sees only loss and frustration." Paradoxically, Santayana's *metanoia* constricted his emotional life and freed the energies of his poetry and his criticism.[12] The *metanoia* was as much affirmation as it was renunciation.

Other critics have discussed the broader theoretical and philosophical issues implicit in Santayana's poetry. In "The Philosopher as Poet and Critic" (1940), Philip Blair Rice contends that Santayana had three handicaps: "he was a philosopher, he was addicted to Platonism, and he lived in the United States at the end of the 19th Century." (The fin de siècle milieu he regards as the gravest handicap of all.) Santayana's curious role is apparent: he was ahead of his time in terms of the type of poetry he called for, yet his own verse "falls below the requirements of his poetic theory not only in scope but in quality."[13] Maurice F. Brown admires Santayana's faith in poetry as a "valid medium of approach to truth." Santayana "attempted to use poetry to break through cultural disintegration to a new ethos. . . . Santayana is very much a contemporary poet, wrestling with those problems of the imagination and the creation of relevant myth." Frederick W. Conner in "*Lucifer* and *The Last Puritan*" (1961) notes that the leading characters in Santayana's two works share similar virtues and possess in a sense special to Santayana "the quality of spirituality." Both "have in high degree the detached and contemplative bent which is characteristic of the life of the spirit."[14]

Students of Santayana's poetry are fortunate to have William G. Holzberger's *The Complete Poems of George Santayana* (1979). In this carefully prepared edition, Holzberger added 84 unpublished poems to the 151 poems previously printed and wrote a lengthy introduction that puts the poetry into biographical and critical context. In addition his article "Unpublished Poems of George Santayana: Some Critical and Textual Considerations" gives special attention to the previously unpublished material he presents.[15]

SANTAYANA THE THEORIST AND CRITIC

Santayana shaped literary tastes in many ways: through his role as one of the founding editors of the *Harvard Monthly,* through his critical essays, through his work on aesthetics, and through his friendships with a wide array of writers.

One of the earliest examinations of Santayana's views on art is John Crowe Ransom's "Art and Mr. Santayana" (1937). Ransom, after comparing him favorably to Emerson, criticizes *Reason in Art* (volume 4 of *The Life of Reason*) for holding that the meaning of the arts is that they are useful and expressive at once. Ransom dismisses as "philosophical rigamarole" Santayana's claim that the artist ought to be concerned with essence rather than matter.[16] Three books have been devoted to Santayana's aesthetics. Willard E. Arnett in *Santayana and the Sense of Beauty* (1955) argues that central to his philosophy is the primacy of aesthetics. He regards Santayana's epistemology, ontology, and moral philosophy as the work of a thinker fundamentally artistic in orientation. Irving Singer's *Santayana's Aesthetics* (1957) attempts both to clarify his philosophy—particularly his philosophy of art and aesthetics—and to suggest a more suitable approach to aesthetics by avoiding the problems of the "intuitionistic tradition to which Santayana and many other philosophers belong" (vii). Jerome Ashmore in *Santayana, Art, and Aesthetics* (1966) argues that "fine art does not occupy a central position in Santayana's aesthetics, that his aesthetic theory is closely associated with psychology, with essences, and with moral goals but not with fine art" (ix).[17] Andrew J. Reck comes to a similar conclusion, holding that "instead of subordinating other activities and values to art and beauty, [Santayana] sought to establish the primacy of morality, to the extent even of maintaining the authority of morality over aesthetics."[18] The audacity of Santayana's *The Sense of Beauty* (1896) is clarified by Arthur Danto in his recent "Introduction" to the work. Against a powerful tradition stemming from Locke, "Santayana's use of the term 'sense' in the title of his book must be satiric, since it is the burden of his argument that if there *is* a sense of beauty, it does not, for all the features it may share with the standard senses, *function* like them at all" (xxi).

Interpretations of Poetry and Religion (1900) made clear that Santayana was both a powerful practical critic and an unorthodox and outspoken thinker regarding poetry and religion. Early reviewers tended to be unpersuaded, if not appalled, by Santayana's argument. Paul Elmer More is typical. He finds the work to be fascinating but finally unconvincing. "No great religion was ever founded unless the prophet believed that the visions he proclaimed were . . . real, and existed outside his own imagination. . . . When religion 'surrenders its illusions,' when faith ceases to be 'the substance of things unseen,' they cease equally to be vital and to be the source of true art."[19] Willard E. Arnett explains in "Santayana and the Poetic Function of Religion" that Santayana was "convinced that the moral—ethical and spiritual—effectiveness of religion depends, for the great majority, on the acceptance of the literal truth of its poetry, myth, and allegory, but that scientifically religion is as irrelevant to the truth as fairy tales that delight imaginative children." Most thinkers who draw this conclusion have insisted on the worthlessness of religion, but he delighted in and cherished perspectives that he regarded as fictions. As Arnett remarks, "It is poetry, then, or expressive creativity, and not the specific beliefs or patterns of a religion, that is native to man; it is the expression and not the petition that is the vital element wherever prayer is appropriate and truly spiritual."[20]

In addition to his writings on aesthetics Santayana produced a considerable body of literary criticism. Q. D. Leavis's "The Critical Writings of George Santayana" and the introduction to Singer's *Essays in Literary Criticism of George Santayana* (1956) provide general assessments of Santayana as a critic. Leavis compares him favorably to Eliot as a critic of Dante. She finds refreshing "the essentially Latin quality of Santayana's criticism" and goes on to assert that his criticism is characterized by "something that for want of a more exact word one can only call wisdom: it is felt in his work pervasively as a mature outlook reinforced by an ancient civilized tradition." Leavis admires his suavity of tone, illuminating metaphors, and epigrammatic style. Singer's "Introduction" to *Essays in Literary Criticism* praises Santayana as a "rare genius who can combine good philosophy with good literary criticism" and who "works out patterns of harmonization between a great many divergent principles."[21]

Santayana's assessments of Shakespeare have stimulated much thought. John M. Major's "Santayana on Shakespeare" (1959) points out that in his criticism of English and American literature Santayana turns most often to Shakespeare among the English and Whitman among the Americans. He further argues that "the Shakespearian criticism of Santayana, for all its shifting about, deserves to be recognized . . . as some of the most interesting our century has produced." F. R. Leavis's "Tragedy and the 'Medium': A Note on Mr. Santayana's 'Tragic Philosophy' " (1944) takes Santayana to task for confusing the speech of Macbeth ("Tomorrow . . .") with Shakespeare's own philosophy.[22] Many critics have been puzzled by Santayana's claim that Shakespeare is inferior to the greatest poets because of his insensibility to religion.[23]

Santayana's most developed single discussion of romanticism is in *Three Philosophical Poets* (1910), a work treating Lucretius, Dante, and Goethe. The essay on Goethe summarizes the criticism of romanticism pervading Santayana's prose. In "Santayana on Romanticism and Egotism" (1966), Maurice Cohen analyzes "the sustained and detailed criticisms of 'egotism' and what for him was its close relative, 'romanticism.' " Santayana held, Cohen explains, that "the greatest single obstacle to . . . achieving a salutary awareness of the inescapable limitations of life is . . . pride or *egotism*—unwillingness to admit the contingency of all existence and the amorality of the cosmos." He finds throughout Santayana's criticism of romanticism the attribution of its origin to self-indulgence.[24]

Santayana's response to individual romantic writers has provoked much commentary. Bertrand Russell thought that Santayana forced himself to express more respect for Goethe than he truly thought he deserved out of respect for his standing. Anthony Woodward, in "Romanticism, Faust, and George Santayana" (1982), points out that Santayana "saw an affinity between Romanticism and the philosophical attitude of German Idealist philosophers." For Santayana, Singer observes, the "saving grace of Goethe . . . is his real and honest attempt to fit romanticism into a framework of classicism."[25] Similarly, Woodward notes that Santayana admired Leopardi because for him "the romantic imagination, that great lamp lighting up the solitary places of the world and suffusing them with sublime relevance to man was *facoltà ingannatrice,* a deceitful faculty."[26]

Despite his aversion to romanticism, Santayana greatly admired Shelley and Keats. Cohen points out that Santayana cites a "certain moral incompetence in [Shelley's] moral intensity" but at heart he is "sympathetic to the Platonic side" of his vision.[27] His overall verdict was typical of the late nineteenth-century American adulation of English romantic poets. Santayana's affinities with Keats are treated by Elkin Calhoun Wilson in *Santayana and Keats* (1980). Wilson's thesis is that "Poetic naturalism appropriately designates Keats's philosophical base; and certainly Santayana is the chief exponent of poetic naturalism in modern philosophy."[28]

Santayana's reaction to the two leading Victorian writers—Robert Browning and Charles Dickens—further clarifies his literary standards. Browning appeared to him a poet who exalted romantic energy at the cost of coherent ideals and classical balance. He explained to William Lyon Phelps his admiration for the novelist and his distaste for the poet: "My disgust at Browning is not because he loves life or has it abundantly, but because he doesn't love it (as Dickens does, for instance) for what is *good* in it, but for what is base, tawdry, and pretentious. I protest against being called a snob; what I love is what is simple, humble, easy, what ought to be common, and it is only the bombast of false ambitions and false superiority, that I abhor."[29] Santayana's essay on Dickens from *Soliloquies in England* (1922) garnered high praise from Phelps, who regarded it as "the finest interpretation I have ever read." And Newton Stallknecht found it to be, along with the essay on Dante, the "masterpiece among [Santayana's] critical writings."[30]

Santayana's reaction to American writers exhibits an even greater complexity and intensity perhaps because he was himself working within this national tradition (despite his Spanish birth). Paul C. Wermuth, in "Santayana and Emerson" (1963), traces the connections between the two thinkers. Santayana, according to Wermuth, sees "the discrepancy between Emerson's conscious beliefs and his inherited presuppositions" as symbolizing "the split throughout the whole of American intellectual life between inherited ideas and habits of thought and the realities of the new American experience." Maurice Brown complements Wermuth's analysis by including a discussion of a previously unpublished Santayana essay, "The Optimism of Ralph Waldo Emerson," written when Santayana was a senior at Harvard. As Brown notes, the "essay is both an analysis of Emerson's philosophical position and an attack." Joel Porte's *Representative Man: Ralph Waldo Emerson* (1979) considers Santayana's "continuing effort to clarify his own philosophy by struggling with Emerson's." He regards *The Last Puritan* as Santayana's engagement with the purification of Puritanism, that is, with an "Ultimate Puritanism . . . equivalent to total disillusionment, the ability to see that what persists through every disappointment and death in a world of incessant and inexorable change, the only reality, is the form or principle that *creates* our illusions."[31]

Santayana was attracted to traditional literary forms, but he was not without appreciation for more revolutionary undertakings. His shifting opinions about Whitman reflect his ambivalence concerning this poet throughout a two decade period, 1890–1911, from "Walt Whitman: A Dialogue" to "The Genteel Tradition in American Philosophy." Certainly Santayana's response to Whitman is complicated and energized by his recognition, at some level, of Whitman's sexual orientation. The literary connection between Whitman and Santayana is treated in Porte's "Introduction" to *Interpretations of Poetry and Religion* and in Kenneth M. Price's *Whitman and Tradition* (1990).[32]

THE NOVELIST

In 1936, Santayana published his bestselling novel, *The Last Puritan*, after having worked on this book for roughly forty-five years. He received a highly favorable review from Ellen Glasgow, who considered him "the greatest contemporary master of English prose." Conrad Aiken deemed the novel to be "the most nearly satisfactory analysis . . . of the New England character" and compared the solidity of the work to that of Fielding and Richardson.[33] For Aiken, Frances W. Knickerbocker, and others, his depiction of a New England mind ranked with the self-portrait of *The Education of Henry Adams*. Although a few readers, such as Richard Church, complained of the "monotone and intellectual sublimity of his rhetoric," most reviewers seemed to be overawed that a serious philosopher had written such a powerful and effective novel.[34] Nonetheless, Santayana was not satisfied. In his own "Preface" to *The Last Puritan,* he complained that commentators underestimated the characters' vital qualities by saying they all sounded like the author himself.[35]

Daniel Aaron's "A Postscript to *The Last Puritan*" (1936) is a brief but powerfully written essay that takes issue with the novel's "social and political gospel." He concludes, "Mr. Santayana, in ridiculing the idealistic and thwarted Oliver, minimizes his scapegoat's rich potentialities and overemphasizes his petty deficiencies. Yet curiously enough, it is Mario who seems dated and old fashioned to us; it is Oliver with whom we are spiritually akin." As Aaron notes, it is difficult to condone Mario's "arrogance, complacency, and selfishness—difficult to appreciate his enthusiastic talk about war and politics which sounds like the gush of a blackshirt fire-eater."[36]

In 1966 James C. Ballowe published "*The Last Puritan* and the Failure of American Culture," arguing that Santayana's point is "to describe the conditions underlying the failure of American youth of high promise." Ballowe nicely states the dilemma of Santayana's protagonist: "Oliver's puritan conscience demands that he participate in the world. As he does so, his conscience wars against itself. For if his duty is to take part in the contemporary world, the conditions of that world force him to give up puritanism."[37]

More recent criticism has often been fascinated by the connections linking biography and fiction. Anthony Woodward rightly perceives that "a bit of Santayana himself is in several of the characters in the novel." He finds, in Mario, Santayana's "fantastic wish-fulfilling symbol of ebullient worldliness and manly sportiveness; those were the terms on which the spectacle of earthly existence was most palatable." Yet he also detects "a degree of identification between Santayana and his hero," noting that "he was always pleased when somebody wrote sympathetically about Oliver."[38]

Peter Conn, in an essay prepared for this volume, points out that "studies of *The Last Puritan* have seldom attempted to situate the book in the context of the nation's depression-era culture." Instead of seeing the novel as an allegory clarifying the author's argument with the genteel tradition, he explores Santayana's relationship with his father and his troubling responses to fascism. In short, for Conn, "*The Last Puritan* recapitulates a contest over authority in terms particularly relevant to the 1930s, using puritanism as a mechanism to investigate the problematic nature of America's patriarchal politics and mythology."[39]

William Holzberger's "The Significance of the Subtitle of Santayana's

Novel: *The Last Puritan: A Memoir in the Form of a Novel,*" links Peter Alden, the father of the protagonist, with facts from Santayana's own life. Holzberger's use of unpublished letters reveals the riches still to be mined in manuscript materials and suggests that the publication of Santayana's collected letters will be a major event in literary scholarship.[40] (Currently only about 250 of 2,500 letters have been published.) It is worth recalling that Lionel Trilling once judged Santayana's letters to be of "classic importance"—the best since Keats's.[41]

THE AUTOBIOGRAPHER

Santayana's autobiography was a public success and a personal frustration. The book sold well and was favorably reviewed, but because of World War II, the manuscript had to be smuggled out of Rome where Santayana was living when hostilities broke out. Santayana had no chance to read page proofs, and he was dissatisfied with the American spellings (he preferred English), with the lack of marginal notations, and with the excision of controversial passages. Moreover, the autobiography was published piecemeal: *Persons and Places: The Background of My Life* (1944), *The Middle Span* (1945), and *My Host the World* (1953).

Philip Blair Rice, in a review entitled "Salt, Pepper, and Pity for Mankind," greeted the first volume of *Persons and Places* with favorable notice in the *Kenyon Review*. He notes that the autobiography could be read as the record of an interesting life, or for "information about the influences which shaped one of the great philosophical systems of our time, or as a critical commentary, by a kind of Henry James in reverse, on the relation of New World culture to the Old. But his life is so much of a piece that these all come to very much the same thing." Another review by Adrienne Koch in *Sewanee Review* laments the "over-appreciation of his 'young' Harvard friends (who are essentially boring) and . . . the under-appreciation of academic colleagues (who must have been more than he allows them)." There is, perhaps, a veiled acknowledgment here of Santayana's homosexual leanings. "Rarely has a philosopher sympathized so bloodlessly and with such cunning knowledge with the motives of the women he knew."[42] Insofar as Santayana's sexual inclinations fostered misogynist attitudes, she is on strong ground.

In "Santayana on Autobiography" (1969), James Ballowe points out that Santayana's reaction to the autobiography of his friend Logan Pearsall Smith clarifies what he intended to achieve in his own memoir. Santayana criticized Smith's *Unforgotten Years* (1937) for offering no details of Harvard and Oxford and of Smith's friends. Moreover, the work seemed "too gentle, too affectionate, too fulsome." Santayana, in contrast, believed that reality "requires a satirist, merciless but just."[43]

In "Fiction, Philosophy, and Autobiography: Santayana's *Persons and*

Places," Herman Saatkamp builds on discoveries made in the course of editing the autobiography to debunk several myths that have developed about Santayana's life. Saatkamp's essay complements Joel Porte's much earlier essay, "Santayana at the 'Gas House' " (1962), which asks: "Was Santayana's withdrawal from Harvard life as radical and simple as the pattern of Platonic renunciation and ultimate flight which he draws in his . . . autobiography would suggest?" Santayana sometimes claimed that Harvard had nothing to offer him after 1897, but Porte shows how deeply involved he was with the Delphic Club. Even after the mild scandal of Charles Macomb Flandrau's *Harvard Episodes* (in which a teacher—obviously resembling Santayana— gives a student an unearned "C"), Santayana did not altogether shirk undergraduate society.[44]

THE CULTURAL CRITIC

Ambivalence gives edge to Santayana's cultural criticsm. As namer and definer of the "genteel tradition," he was a major force in the transformation of literary values that brought about the modernist canon. His importance in this regard is hard to overemphasize. His European credentials made the criticism of the genteel tradition all the more powerful for Americans who still looked to Europe for intellectual legitimization. (He is one in a long line of foreign observers who have helped us understand ourselves.) Santayana's critique carried edge also because he spoke from the inside, despite his Spanish background. He had institutional power by virtue of his position at Harvard, and, curiously, despite his criticism of the genteel tradition, he had impeccable genteel qualifications of his own. As a mentor for both the relatively traditional Harvard poets—George Cabot Lodge, William Vaughn Moody, and Trumbull Stickney—and for modernists such as T. S. Eliot, Conrad Aiken, and Wallace Stevens, Santayana serves as an intriguing transitional figure. Yet, for all his brilliance, his analysis of American life and literature seems partial. In " 'Noble Shit': The Uncivil Response of American Writers to Civil Religion in America," Leo Marx points out that he seems not to have been aware of the experiments in fiction of writers such as Dreiser, Norris, and Crane.[45]

Douglas L. Wilson's "Introductory" stresses that Santayana "never accepted America or its culture as his own; he was truly an alien right from the time his father brought him to the United States at the age of eight." Wilson is convinced that neither Boston nor Harvard was "congenial to his Spanish temperament."[46] Yet such a formulation probably overstates the case. Santayana, in both *Persons and Places* and in *The Last Puritan,* cultivated the role as outsider. As Stefan Collini observes, many social critics emphasize their roles by claiming "marginal" status. This type of claim "need not be taken as an accurate piece of social description: it serves functions of its own, including that of legitimizing the criticisms by indicating the critic's access to some standard of authority denied to those blinkered by or imprisoned in the assumptions of their own society."[47]

Although Santayana adopted the pose of the detached observer, his emotional involvement in his assertions is detectable. Personal slights and private frustrations certainly contribute to the bite his comments have whenever he discusses the genteel tradition of Boston. Unlike de Tocqueville, a visitor who undertook a systematic study of American society as a whole, Santayana was embedded in a particular place: the Cambridge-Boston community. Thus his vision of America, though focused and penetrating, was limited. In a letter to his sister he claimed that speaking in Berkeley (on the occasion of the "Genteel Tradition" address) had been liberating: "When I am here [Cambridge] in the midst of a dull round, a sort of instinct of courtesy makes me take it for granted, and I become unconscious of how much I hate it all: otherwise I couldn't have stood it for *forty years*."[48] Yet Santayana's own account obscures how much he was a participant and approved member in the genteel culture he analyzed and criticized.

The editors of *The Dial*, when they sought a reviewer for Harold Stearns's *Civilization in the United States* (1922), turned to Santayana, famed critic of the genteel tradition, to evaluate a book whose contributors repeatedly invoked the word "genteel" to describe the backwater culture they were rebelling against. Yet to the surprise of many, Santayana was anything but impressed. Wilfred M. McClay remarks that Santayana thought the book's "social criticism . . . merely reflected the authors' personal maladaptations: their conclusions revealed more about their palpitating doubts than about American civilization."[49] The review for the *Dial* was as shrewd a piece of intellectual history as his lecture at Berkeley. Kenneth Lynn reminds us that the intellectuals who buried the genteel tradition were actually its sons, in the sense that they were as much given to fanciful delusions about American life as their predecessors had been.[50]

Daniel Aaron's "George Santayana and the Genteel Tradition" points out that for Santayana *genteel* was a descriptive, not an abusive, term. It "connoted propriety, correctness, dogmatism, and conservatism—and flaccidness, passivity, and complacence as well." Piecing together Santayana's various remarks and asides concerning the genteel tradition, Aaron formulates the "consecutive story" of its "birth, dominion, and decline."[51] Santayana's "identification of the genteel tradition with a predominantly feminine sensibility" is worth consideration. Martin Green, in *The Problem of Boston,* notes that Santayana, Bernard Berenson, Henry James, and Henry Adams shared certain traits, including anglophilic tendencies, an aesthetic idealism, a preference for a community of select spirits, an attraction to Roman Catholicism, and a feminine sensibility.[52]

Santayana engaged in a memorable battle with the New Humanists. Q.D. Leavis comes down on the side of Santayana in comparing him with

Babbitt: his procedure "is as different as possible from the pusillanimous literary criticism of an Irving Babbitt which censors in the interests of a conventional morality."[53] Santayana's complaint against Babbitt and the New Humanists was that they enshrined a canon of European masterworks, granting them universal status, in an attempt to establish a criterion of morals and taste. In doing so, they lost sight of the peculiarities of individual cultures. Santayana, however, recognized that each country had its own enterprises compatible with its own conditions. Thus, he concluded, "The more different [America] can come to be, the better; and we must let it take its own course, going a long way around, perhaps, before it can shake off the last trammels of alien tradition, and learn to express itself simply, not apologetically, after its own heart."[54]

Joel Porte, in "Santayana's Masquerade," points out that "Santayana's claim to have surveyed experience from the point of view of the 'impersonal and universal,' largely justified as it may have been, was also and necessarily flawed, and it frequently masked a sharp individual perspective, especially . . . with regard to questions of race and religion." Porte observes that McCormick's biography and the new edition of *Persons and Places* reveal a much more disturbing side of Santayana: in places "the naked fact of anti-Semitism glares from the page." Santayana stared with "less than dispassionate regard at elements of change which must have seemed. . . much more threatening than the innocuous gentility on which he had originally vented his Spanish spleen."[55]

INFLUENCE

There has been great scholarly interest in Santayana's influence on other writers. The roll call of brilliant students—from George Cabot Lodge and Conrad Aiken to T. S. Eliot and Wallace Stevens—only begins to tell the story. Through his correspondence and his books he evoked responses from such writers as Ezra Pound and Robert Lowell. Lois Hughson's *Thresholds of Reality: George Santayana and Modernist Poetics* (1977) describes Santayana as "a formidable bridge from the late Anglo-American Victorian world to modernist literary culture." She argues that for Santayana, the "creation of poetry itself became the explicit paradigm for every individual's creation of the world from the flux of his immediate experience. Here was announced the theme of much of the poetry and fiction of the early twentieth century: the poet as a maker, both of meaning and myth, who descends into the chaos underlying convention to emerge with materials for a world of his own making, a world symbolic of his experience but removed from it." She detects in Stevens, Yeats, and Eliot a similar relationship between a "fragmented experience and a powerful and productive imagination."[56]

Many critics have noted Eliot's debts to Santayana. B. R. McElderry,

Jr.'s "Santayana and Eliot's 'Objective Correlative' " considers the possible sources of Eliot's famous term (Santayana, rather than Pound or Washington Allston, seems most likely). Henry Wasser, in "A Note on Eliot and Santayana," observes yet another borrowing. The final lines of Eliot's "The Hollow Men" ("This is the way the world ends / Not with a bang but with a whimper") apparently derive from Santayana's comment on the world of Dante in *Three Philosophical Poets*: "And it all ends, not with a bang, not with some casual incident, but in sustained reflection, in the sense that it has not ended, but remains by us in its totality, a revelation and a resource forever."[57]

The Stevens-Santayana criticism is too extensive to itemize here, though there seem to be recurring observations throughout these studies. Most critics stress their early connection at Harvard, philosophical similarities, and the brilliance of Stevens's "To an Old Philosopher in Rome." David P. Young, for example, provides a helpful analysis in "A Skeptical Music: Stevens and Santayana." Young observes that Stevens's willingness to mix philosophy and poetry—his concern to write an apology for poetry in a scientific and skeptical era—owes much to Santayana. Both men were "connoisseurs of chaos, and for neither was the discovery of an irrational universe a signal for despair or even pessimism." Daniel Fuchs's "Wallace Stevens and Santayana" contends that Santayana's poetry "offers a thematic analogy to what Stevens was doing in some of his earlier work." The prose works, Fuchs adds, strengthens the case for influence. Martha Strom argues in "Wallace Stevens' Revisions of Crispin's Journal: A Reaction Against the 'Local' " that Stevens and Santayana possessed a similar sense of the comic. Moreover, she holds that two of Santayana's essays—"The Comic Mask" and "Carnival"— can be linked to Stevens's major comic poem, "The Comedian as the Letter C." Stevens's indebtedness is both in "general attitude" toward the subject and in "particular rhetorical borrowings."[58]

Alan Filreis in "Wallace Stevens and the Crisis of Authority" (1984) and "Wallace Stevens and the Strength of the Harvard Reaction" (1985) notes that "a considerable minority of the faculty at Harvard College felt uneasy teaching under Charles W. Eliot's long regime of liberal reform (1869–1909). The seat of Unitarian optimism and untroubled positivism, Eliot's Harvard had ratified and acclaimed an easy truce between Protestantism and science." Stevens, torn between the values of his father and those of Santayana, was ultimately more influenced by the antiliberal reaction and by its antimodern attitudes than by those who "backed the curriculum that trained him to be successful in his father's terms."[59]

A. Walton Litz points out that "in the late 1940's Stevens' interest in the old philosopher began to quicken, an interest . . . based on . . . his exemplary role as a poet-philosopher." Litz believes that Stevens saw Santayana as an "alter ego" when he wrote his English Institute essay, "Imagination as Value." (Fuchs calls "Imagination and Value" in part "literally a tribute to Santayana.")[60]

Lucy Beckett's chapter "Imagination as Value" (from her book *Wallace Stevens*) explores the connections between Santayana and both T.S. Eliot and Wallace Stevens. She credits Santayana with giving Eliot "a toughness, an intellectual rigour in thought about poetry and an unwillingness to tolerate emotional self-indulgence." The "challenge that Santayana formulated for the modern poet, more cogently and carefully than Arnold had done, though less optimistically, was essentially post-Christian." For Stevens the figure of Santayana came to suggest "the saving goodness, the emblematic victory over life, that in another age would have been represented by the figure of a saint."[61]

Studies of Santayana and Ezra Pound touch frequently on the difficult question of these writers links to fascism. John McCormick in "George Santayana and Ezra Pound" (1982) stresses that biographers working with Pound sources have conveyed the erroneous impression that these two writers were of one mind about social and political questions. McCormick regards the allegation of Santayana's fascism and anti-Semitism to be understandable but ultimately "unjust." Anthony Woodward's "Pound and Santayana" (1984) contrasts the activist Pound with Santayana's preference for the "contemplative exercise of pure thought." Woodward points out that "that aspect of Greek thought to which Santayana was most drawn in his later years, namely that contemplative aspect which has links with Eastern spirituality," provoked Pound's deep mistrust.[62]

There has recently been an explosion of interest in Santayana. John Mc-Cormick's biography, *George Santayana*, surpasses Howgate's as the best available biography. Providing a sympathetic but by no means uncritical account, McCormick advances understanding of Santayana in many ways. He is unwilling to accept the conclusion that Santayana was a significant poet, finding instead that his verse is marred by stale diction. Like Porte, moreover, he delves into the problem of Santayana's anti-Semitism in a chapter entitled "Moral Dogmatism: Santayana as Anti-Semite." Woodward's *Living in the Eternal* provides an urbane and incisive intellectual portrait. Intriguingly, he ends his study with an analysis of *The Last Puritan*, arguing that it contains, as Santayana remarked in a letter, "all my experience of human life and character." John Lachs's *George Santayana*, though it does not treat literary matters directly, is a sound introduction to Santayana's philosophy and thus a good starting point for grasping his literary opinions. What seems surprising in this otherwise excellent book, so often carefully laudatory of Santayana, is that it never confronts his problematic attitudes on race and women.[63]

One of the most notable events in recent Santayana studies is the publication of an edition of the first volume of the *Collected Writings of George Santayana*, approved by the Center for Scholarly Editions. In editing *Persons and Places*, Saatkamp and Holzberger have restored many lost passages and have annotated the overall work. Volume 2, *The Sense of Beauty* and volume 3, *Interpretations of Poetry and Religion*, appeared in 1988 and 1989, respectively, and volume 4, *The Last Puritan,* is currently in press.[64] Twenty volumes will eventually make up the critical edition.

Much remains to be done in Santayana scholarship. Of primary importance is the continued publication of reliable texts of his works and a complete and annotated edition of his letters. A second fundamental need is a good overall assessment focusing on his literary career. Of course, more specialized inquiries would also reward further work. For example, Santayana's reaction to German thought deserves consideration: from his dissertation on Lotze to *Egotism in German Philosophy* to *Three Philosophical Poets* to *The Last Puritan* (with its German nursemaid given to reciting Goethe), he showed a fascination with German writers. A fuller understanding of his reaction to German idealism would clarify his indictment of romanticism. No doubt, Santayana's role as a pivotal figure in the movement from the genteel to the modern will continue to attract commentators. Though often treated, more good work is possible on this topic, particularly if the studies become more particularized concerning his circumstances at Harvard. In recent years Santayana's importance has been coming more clearly into focus. Given current interests in interdisciplinary studies and literary theory, and given Santayana's range, acuity, and stylistic brilliance, he promises to engage critical attention for the foreseeable future.

Notes

1. Santayana, *The Realm of Essence* (New York: Scribner's, 1927), xvi.
2. Herman J. Saatkamp, Jr., and John Jones, *George Santayana: A Bibliographical Checklist, 1880–1980* (Bowling Green: Bowling Green State University Press, 1982).
3. Santayana, preface to *Poems: Selected by the Author and Revised* (New York: Scribner's, 1923), xii, vii–viii.
4. Newton Arvin, "Ex Libris," *Freeman* 7 (28 March 1923): 71; and Phillip Littel, "Books and Things," *New Republic,* 21 March 1923, 102.
5. These reviews are quoted in George W. Howgate, *George Santayana* (Philadelphia: University of Pennsylvania Press, 1938), 74–75.
6. Howgate, 58.
7. For an account of the various biographical interpretations of the sonnet sequences, see William G. Holzberger, introduction, *The Complete Poems of George Santayana* (Lewisburg: Bucknell University Press; London: Associated University Presses, 1979), 49–52.
8. Daniel Cory, *Santayana, The Later Years: A Portrait with Letters* (New York: George Braziller, 1963), 210.
9. Robert K. Martin, *The Homosexual Tradition in American Poetry* (Austin: University of Texas Press, 1979), 109–14.
10. Quoted in Holzberger, introduction, 52.
11. Wilson, "Santayana's Metanoia: The Second Sonnet Sequence," *New England Quarterly* 39 (March 1966):19–20.
12. Hughson, "Uses of Despair: The Sources of Creative Energy in George Santayana," *American Quarterly* 23 (1971):728.

13. Rice, "The Philosopher as Poet and Critic" in *The Philosophy of George Santayana,* ed. Paul Arthur Schilpp (Evanston: Northwestern University Press, 1940), 265, 267.

14. Brown, "Santayana's Necessary Angel," *New England Quarterly* 36 (December 1963):436; and Conner, *"Lucifer* and *The Last Puritan," American Literature* 33 (1961):2, 7.

15. Holzberger, "Unpublished Poems of George Santayana: Some Critical and Textual Considerations," *Southern Review* 11 (1975):139–55.

16. See Arthur Danto, introduction to George Santayana, *The Sense of Beauty,* ed. Herman J. Saatkaamp, Jr., and William G. Holzberger (Cambridge: MIT Press, 1988), xv–xxviii; and John Crowe Ransom, "Art and Mr. Santayana," *Virginia Quarterly Review* 13 (1937):420–36.

17. See, in order, Willard E. Arnett, *Santayana and the Sense of Beauty* (Bloomington: Indiana University Press, 1955); Irving Singer, *Santayana's Aesthetics: A Critical Introduction* (Cambridge: Harvard University Press, 1957); and Jerome Ashmore, *Santayana, Art, and Aesthetics* (Cleveland: The Press of Western Reserve University, 1966).

18. Reck, "The Authority of Morality over Aesthetics in Santayana's Philosophy," *Southern Journal of Philosophy* 10 (Summer 1972):150. Reck's essay appears in a special issue devoted to Santayana.

19. More, "Santayana's 'Poetry and Religion,' " *Harvard Graduate's Magazine* 9 (1900):21.

20. Arnett, "Santayana and the Poetic Function of Religion," *Journal of Philosophy* 53 (1956):773–87.

21. Leavis, "The Critical Writings of George Santayana," *Scrutiny* 4 (1935):281, 289; and Singer, *Essays in Literary Criticism of George Santayana* (New York: Scribner's; Toronto: Saunders, 1956), ix, xii.

22. See Major, "Santayana on Shakespeare," *Shakespeare Quarterly* 10 (Autumn 1959):470; F. R. Leavis, "Tragedy and 'Medium': A Note on Mr. Santayana's 'Tragic Philosophy,' " *Scrutiny* 12 (1944):249–60.

23. See, for example, Irving Singer, "Introduction," *Essays in Literary Criticism of George Santayana,* xi.

24. Maurice Cohen, "Santayana on Romanticism and Egotism," *Journal of Religion* 46 (1966):264, 273.

25. See Russell, "Santayana's Philosophy" in *The Philosophy of George Santayana,* 474; and Woodward, "Romanticism, Faust, and George Santayana," *English Studies in Africa* 25, no. 1 (1982):4; and Singer, Introduction, xix.

26. Woodward, "Romanticism, Faust, and George Santayana," 8.

27. Cohen, "Santayana on Romanticism and Egotism," 275.

28. Elkin Calhoun Wilson, *Santayana and Keats* (Birmingham, Ala.: Commercial Printing Co., 1980), 2.

29. *The Letters of George Santayana,* ed. Daniel Cory (New York: Scribner's, 1955), 187.

30. See William Lyon Phelps, *Autobiography with Letters* (New York: Oxford University Press, 1939), 349; and Newton P. Stallknecht, "George Santayana and the Uses of Literature," *Yearbook of Comparative and General Literature* 15–16 (1966–1967):12.

31. Wermuth, "Santayana and Emerson," *Emerson Society Quarterly* 31 (1963):38; Brown, "Santayana on Emerson: An Unpublished Essay," *Emerson Society Quarterly* 37 (1964):60–70; and Porte, *Representative Man: Ralph Waldo Emerson in His Time* (New York: Oxford University Press, 1979), 22.

32. Porte, Introduction, to George Santayana, *Interpretations of Poetry and Religion,* ed. Herman J. Saatkamp, Jr., and William G. Holzberger (Cambridge: MIT Press, forthcoming); and Price, *Whitman and Tradition: The Poet in His Century* (New Haven: Yale University Press, 1990), 129–35.

33. Glasgow, "George Santayana Writes a 'Novel,' " *New York Herald Tribune,* books section, 2 February 1936, 1; Aiken, "The New England Animal," *New Republic,* 5 February 1936, 5.

34. Knickerbocker, "Epitaph on Puritanism," *Sewanee Review* 44 (April–June 1936):246–49; and Church, "Review of *The Last Puritan*," *Criterion* 15 (1936):524–27.

35. Santayana, preface, *The Last Puritan*, Triton Edition, (New York: Scribner's, 1937), vii.

36. Aaron, "A Postscript to *The Last Puritan*," *New England Quarterly* 9 (1936):683–86.

37. Ballowe, "*The Last Puritan* and the Failure in American Culture," *American Quarterly* 18 (1966):123–35.

38. Anthony Woodward, *Living in the Eternal: A Study of George Santayana* (Nashville: Vanderbilt University Press, 1988), 138, 133, 146.

39. Peter Conn, "Paternity and Patriarchy: *The Last Puritan* and the 1930s," appearing in this volume, 000–00.

40. William G. Holzberger, "The Significance of the Subtitle of Santayana's Novel: *The Last Puritan: A Memoir in the Form of a Novel*," appearing in this volume.

41. Trilling, " 'That Smile of Parmenides Made Me Think,' " in *A Gathering of Fugitives* (London: Secker & Warburg, 1957), 153.

42. Rice, "Salt, Pepper, and Pity for Mankind," *Kenyon Review* 6 (Summer 1944):455; and Koch, "Baroque-Rococo," *Sewanee Review* 53 (Autumn 1945):678, 679.

43. James Ballowe, "Santayana on Autobiography," *American Literature* 41 (May 1969): 219–30.

44. Saatkamp, "Fiction, Philosophy, Autobiography: Santayana's *Persons and Places*," appearing in this volume, 000–00; and Porte, "Santayana at the 'Gas House,' " *New England Quarterly* 35 (1962):338–39, 341.

45. Douglas L. Wilson, "Introductory," *The Genteel Tradition: Nine Essays by George Santayana* (Cambridge: Harvard University Press, 1967), 1–25; and Leo Marx, " 'Noble Shit': The Uncivil Response of American Writers to Civil Religion in America," *Massachusetts Review* 14 (1973):713.

46. Wilson, "Introductory," 2. "Speaking from Somewhere," *Times Literary Supplement*, 15–21 April 1988:427

47. Stefan Collini, as quoted by Daniel Aaron, "George Santayana and the Genteel Tradition," appearing in this volume.

48. Quoted in Wilson, "Introductory," 4.

49. Wilfred M. McClay, "Two Versions of the Genteel Tradition: Santayana and Brooks," *New England Quarterly* 55 (1982):369.

50. Kenneth S. Lynn, "Santayana and the Genteel Tradition," *Commentary* 73 (March 1982), 83.

51. Daniel Aaron, "George Santayana and the Genteel Tradition," appearing in this volume.

52. See Wilson, "Introductory"; Aaron, "George Santayana and the Genteel Tradition"; and Martin Green, *The Problem of Boston* (New York: Norton, 1966), 142–63.

53. Q. D. Leavis, "The Critical Writings of George Santayana," *Scrutiny* 4 (1935):290.

54. *The Letters of George Santayana*, 194.

55. Porte, "Santayana's Masquerade," *Raritan* 7 (Fall 1987):141, 131, 142.

56. Hughson, *Thresholds of Reality: George Santayana and Modernist Poetics* (Port Washington, N.Y.: Kennikat Press, 1977), ix, xi.

57. McElderry, "Santayana and Eliot's 'Objective Correlative,' " *Boston University Studies in English* 3 (1957):179–81; and Wasser, "A Note on Eliot and Santayana," *Boston University Studies in English* 4 (1960):125–26.

58. See, in order, Young, "A Skeptical Music: Stevens and Santayana," *Criticism* 7 (1965):263, 266; Fuchs, "Wallace Stevens and Santayana" in *Patterns of Commitment in American Literature*, ed. Marston La France (Toronto: University of Toronto Press, 1967), 135–64; Strom, "Wallace Stevens' Revisions of Crispin's Journals: A Reaction Against the 'Local,' " *American Literature* 54 (1982):262.

59. Filreis, "Wallace Stevens and the Crisis of Authority," *American Literature* 56 (December 1984):560–78; and Filreis, "Wallace Stevens and the Strength of the Harvard Reaction," *New England Quarterly* 58 (1985):27, 28.

60. Litz, *Introspective Voyager: The Poetic Development of Wallace Stevens* (New York: Oxford University Press, 1972), 277, 279; Fuchs, "Wallace Stevens and Santayana," 146–47.

61. Beckett, *Wallace Stevens* (Cambridge, England: Cambridge University Press, 1974), 28, 31.

62. John McCormick, "George Santayana and Ezra Pound," *American Literature* 54 (October 1982):413–33; and A. G. Woodward, "Pound and Santayana," *South Atlantic Quarterly* 83 (Winter 1984):80–90.

63. McCormick, *George Santayana: A Biography* (New York: Knopf, 1987); Woodward, *Living in the Eternal,* 130; and Lachs, *George Santayana* (Boston: Twayne, 1988).

64. Santayana, *Persons and Places: Fragments of Autobiography,* Critical Edition, ed. William G. Holzberger; and Herman J. Saatkamp, Jr. (Cambridge: MIT Press, 1986); and Santayana, *The Sense of Beauty,* Critical Edition, ed. William G. Holzberger and Herman J. Saatkamp, Jr. (Cambridge: MIT Press, 1988).

ESSAYS

♦

[*Interpretations of Poetry and Religion*]

PAUL E. MORE

A good deal of courage was required of Prof. Santayana, we fancy, to publish his "Interpretations of Poetry and Religion," for he must have known that the outspoken Catholic tone of the volume would offend many of his readers, and that his criticism of Shakespeare and Browning and Emerson would arouse righteous indignation among the worshipers of these literary idols. Further than that, his setting of measure and repose and inner significance above stress and passion must seem perilously near effeminacy to many believers in Anglo-Saxon force. Let us make haste to say that to one reader at least this book of essays has seemed the wisest and most fascinating work in constructive criticism that has appeared in English for several years; and this judgment we would maintain, although the determining thought of the whole cannot be acceptable to us.

Every paragraph in the closing chapter, where the author sums up his interpretation of poetry and religion, is the product of long and subtle reflection. To follow him in the ascending climax, as he shows how "poetry rises from its elementary and detached expressions in rhythm, euphuism, characterization, and story-telling, and comes to the consciousness of its highest function, that of portraying the ideals of experience and destiny," to read his acute and often profound observations on the nature and office of each of these elements, is to acquire a new faculty for the understanding and enjoyment of the poets. Such criticism is constructive in the true sense of the word; and withal the language employed is so clear and sensuous, and the emotional interest of the author in his ideas is so manifest and contagious, that the expression would seem to need only the addition of rhythm to be itself poetry. Yet at the last, when he comes to his final generalization, we are brought face to face with a note of unreality which runs as an undercurrent through the whole book, and does much, as it appears to us, to conceal the true wisdom of most of his critical work. "This higher plane," he says in conclusion, "is the sphere of signficant imagination, of relevant fiction, of idealism become the interpretation of the reality it leaves behind. Poetry raised to its highest power is then identical with religion grasped in its inmost truth; at their point of union both reach their utmost purity and

Reprinted from "Santayana's 'Poetry and Religion,' " *Harvard Graduate's Magazine* 9 (1900–1901): 19–23.

beneficence, for then poetry loses its frivolity and ceases to demoralize, while religion surrenders its illusions and ceases to deceive."

To understand these "illusions" which religion surrenders we must turn to the first chapter, where the author unfolds the philosophic theory lying at the base of his criticisms. Now we shall not presume to argue with Prof. Santayana on the philosophic question at issue, being but indifferent metaphysicians ourselves. We are concerned with his views only as they bear upon the conduct of life, and consequently upon the validity of literature; we are concerned to find why, in the critical slang of the day, his essays, despite the beauty of their language and the subtlety of their thought, fail to "convince." His philosophy is based on that peculiar phase of mind when active faith, as the world commonly understands the word, has disappeared, and in its stead is left a sort of aesthetic faith such as may be found in many of the earlier Romantic writers. Beyond perception and reason stands the imagination building up its own beautiful or monstrous world out of material afforded by the lower faculties. "The imagination, therefore, must furnish to religion and to metaphysics those large ideas tinctured with passion, those supersensible forms shrouded in awe, in which alone a mind of great sweep and vitality can find its congenial objects." Nor is this realm of the imagination an indifferent one; though it has nothing to do with reality in the ordinary sense of the word, yet it has everything to do with the values of life. When considered apart from the conduct of life this ideal world is the sphere of poetry, when related to conduct it is religion. A beautiful theory no doubt and one that deserves to be decked out in all the flowers of rhetoric; it may be true in metaphysics; but to the unmetaphysical reader there is in the end something hollow and unsatisfying about it. No great religion was ever founded unless the prophet believed that the visions he proclaimed were as real, and existed outside his own imagination as absolutely, as does a stock or a stone to popular perception. And in so far as poetry is related to religion, no great poem was ever composed whose author did not have equal faith in the reality of the ideal world. And the greatest of philosophers has been a living force in the world largely for the very reason that ideas existed for him objectively and with a reality which the world of phenomena does not possess. When religion "surrenders its illusions," when faith ceases to be "the substance of things unseen," they cease equally to be vital and to be the source of true art.

Prof. Santayana's attitude toward that other world which is the home of faith is shown most clearly in his treatment of mysticism. If there is a faculty by which man may grasp or at least approach a region beyond the reason, then mysticism may be a positive activity; if there exists no such faculty, then mysticism is, as our author maintains, a mere progressive negation of the categories of thought. In the end the mystic reaches, as Prof. Santayana affirms, a state of Nirvana, or complete negation. Now we cannot refrain from pointing out here that Nirvana was never admitted by Buddha to be a state of nihilism, nor can we conceive that any great religion should have arisen which made such a negation its ultimate goal. The point is important enough to be insisted upon. There is in one of the Buddhist books a curious discussion between the disciple Vaccha and the Master, wherein the disciple seeks for an elucidation of the doctrine of Nirvana. After repeated answers to the disciple's questions Gotama at last cries out: "Enough, O Vaccha! Be not at a loss what to think in this matter, and be not greatly confused. Profound, O Vaccha, is this doctrine, recondite, and difficult of comprehension, good, excellent, and not to be reached by mere reason, subtile, and intelligible only to the wise. . . . The saint, O Vaccha, who has been released from what is styled form, is deep, immeasurable, unfathomable, like the mighty ocean. To say that he is reborn would not fit the case. To say that he is not reborn would not fit the case. To say that he is both reborn and not reborn would not fit the case. To say that he is neither reborn nor not reborn would not fit the case."[1] Now we do not pretend to be one of the wise to whom this doctrine is intelligible, nor do we think it will be intelligible to many persons to-day in the western world; but we do maintain that it conveys something very different from a complete negation, and is in fact a positive statement of transcendental faith. And we do maintain that when faith ceases to be or to seem to be the apprehension of an objective reality and becomes a work of the imagination dealing with the values of life, immediately religion becomes poetry in quite a different sense from that which is upheld in the present volume, while poetry itself is cut off from its vital source.

We have dwelt so long on this essential question that little space is left to comment on the chapters of individual criticism wherein, as we think, Prof. Santayana has displayed a judgment no less bold than it is discriminating and profound. At first reading it may seem somewhat audacious to criticise so severely the lack of specific religious doctrine in Shakespeare, yet after being sickened by the indiscriminate laudation commonly bestowed on the great Elizabethan, it may be wholesome now and then to dwell for a moment on the defects of his work. Certainly the present essay does much to explain a curious mental phenomenon we have ourselves often observed. While reading Shakespeare we are always carried away by the intensity of his passion and the manifold wonders of his genius, but for some reason his plays do not dwell in the mind and arouse reflection on the great problems of life as do the tragedies of ancient Greece or the great epics of literature. It is wholesome at times to have our minds withdrawn from the admiration of exuberant force and wilful fancy to dwell on the orderly development of a more organic view of life.

To this same desire to set orderly thought and spiritual significance above force and license may be ascribed the criticism of Walt Whitman and Browning, the coupling of whose names together will, we opine, seem to many Browningites little less than presumptuous blasphemy. Yet so keen and consummately wise an estimate of Browning's work we do not remember ever to have read. Only in the chapter on Emerson, it seems to us that the note of disparagement is somewhat too strongly emphasized. "The source of his [Emerson's] power," we read, "lay not in his doctrine, but in his temperament, and the rare quality of his wisdom was due less to his wisdom than to his imagination." And farther on: "But his mind was endowed with unusual plasticity, with unusual spontaneity and liberty of movement—it was a fairyland of thoughts and fancies." We suspect that Emerson's power was due not so much to his imagination as to that principle of faith which, in effect at least, is quite a different faculty.

Note

1. Translated by Henry C. Warren.

[Poems: Selected by the Author and Revised]

NEWTON ARVIN

Mr. Santayana's is the poetry of a recluse and a thinker. . . . [W]hat is extraordinary about Mr. Santayana is that in spite of his monastic life he is capable of writing poetry that is only in small part bloodless. In the preface to this new selection of his poems, he speaks of them as being "mental and thin" in texture; and as applied to his "Odes" and some of the "Various Poems" those adjectives are not inappropriate. At his least felicitous, Mr. Santayana is literary and somewhat otiose, but he is at his least felicitous in a surprisingly small proportion of the verses that he has reprinted. It would be nearer the truth to say that his best poetry has the sobriety of reflectiveness than to say it is "mental and thin." There is a sense in which all poetry is posthumous, and, as expression, comes after the stress of the emotion itself has died away: these poems of Mr. Santayana's have, more than most poetry, the quality of a record and even of a reminiscence, but that is in no marked degree a limitation.

The best of Mr. Santayana's work is the two series of sonnets, fifty in all, which stand at the beginning of this volume. Like all good poetry, they spring from the marriage of emotion with thought, and can not spring from either alone; yet he himself calls them his "philosophy in the making," and there is no injustice in interpreting them in that light. They are the utterance, then, of a kind of priestly Platonism, steeped in melancholy and regret; a Platonism into which the formulas of the schools have not entered and could not enter. Like every brooding spirit, Mr. Santayana is oppressed with the insufficiency of human wisdom, the inaccessability of the ideal:

> Our knowledge is a torch of smoky pine
> That lights the pathway but one step ahead
> Across a void of mystery and dread.

He speaks of himself as "a homeless mind," and there is the stamp upon all these poems of an infinite spiritual forlornness, the nostalgia of a sensitive and other-worldly spirit.

Reprinted from "Ex Libris," *Freeman* 7 (1923): 71.

If it were not for that other-worldliness as a background, there would be in his celebration of beauty and love something almost too insubstantial for poetry. To Mr. Santayana, beauty is not what it is for most poets, a thing to be sensuously enjoyed in itself, but an embodiment of the ideal, a "proof of heaven"; and it is not the ecstacy and turmoil of love that he sings, but its abstergent action, its power to set the soul free from the bondage of reality. As an aspiration towards perfection is the key to the thought of these poems, so a struggle for perfection shows itself in their formal finish: Mr. Santayana handles the sonnet with a precision which is as complete as is, on the whole, Blunt's negligence. He says himself that his sonnets lack perfect grace and naturalness because the English tongue is not, originally, his own: "its roots do not quite reach to my centre." Yet surely the shade by which these lines fail of the purest idiomatic quality, is an elusive and even unreal one:

> How liberal is beauty that, but seen,
> Makes rich the bosom of her silent lover!
> How excellent is truth, on which I lean!
> Yet my religion were a charmed despair,
> Did I not in thy perfect heart discover
> How beauty can be true and virtue fair.

That is the kind of lucidity and candour for which the word classic must be reserved, and the purity of his phrasing is sustained everywhere by the combined exactitude and flexibility of his structure; it is his constant success in keeping on that level that makes one wonder whether English verse has ever been written as excellently as Mr. Santayana has written it, by anyone else to whom the English language was not native.

[*The Genteel Tradition at Bay*]

Lewis Mumford

The battle between the New Humanists and their foes is over. There are signs of the conflict all over the Acropolis. Here is Professor Babbitt's clay foot, broken off from the eloquent marble; there is Mr. Frank Jewett Mather's knightly armor, battered and tarnished as much by the embraces of his enemies as by the horrified attacks of his friends; in the shadow of the Museion lies the golden book of humanistic wisdom, compiled directly from the oracles by Mr. Norman Foerster, which bears the evidence on its broken covers of more strenuous usage than its unthumbed pages might indicate. Huddled in a corner of this fantastic Acropolis, the Anti-Humanists have already begun to quarrel among themselves: Mr. Allen Tate would claim the Humanist spoils for theology; Mr. Hartley Grattan demands them for science.

Enter Mr. George Santayana. A faintly amused smile, too ripe for malice, plays over his lips; and as he walks about slowly, picking up a broken lance or turning over a helmet with the point of his toe, he soliloquizes on the old Humanism, the three R's of the modern world, the Renaissance, the Reformation, and the Revolution, and the more ancient R of Romance; takes note of the importance of the supernatural as a logical foundation for the moral absolutism or provinciality of the New Humanists, and ends with an exposition of the moral adequacy of Naturalism. This is the reverie of a harmonious and disinterested mind, picking its own path amid the debris of a controversy: in its very allusiveness, its lack of direction, its refusal to follow the line of battle or even to perform any tender offices for the dead and wounded that are lying about the field, it achieves that sense of intellectual liberation which is the better part of philosophy.

Reprinted from "Enter Mr. Santayana," *New Republic*, 8 April 1931, 214.

[*The Last Puritan*]

ELLEN GLASGOW

In his preface to "Character and Opinion in the United States" Mr. Santayana reminds us of Spinoza's saying that other people's ideas of a man are apt to be a better expression of their nature than of his. And if this wise observation applies to a man, certainly it would seem to apply quite as appropriately to a book—especially to such a book as "The Last Puritan."

To know what a reader thinks of this remarkable memoir in the form of a novel would give me a finer understanding of his mental or moral susceptibilities than I could gather from a casual acquaintance of many years. For one either enjoys or does not enjoy this book according to one's natural bias of mind. Like a feeling for rhythm or a sense of humor, the perceptive faculty is there or it is not there. As a philosophical narrative, "The Last Puritan" possesses every merit, if I except the breath of the body or the pulse of the heart; yet for this very reason no doubt, I should hesitate to recommend it to the confirmed reader of fiction. I should hesitate, in particular, to offer it to an adherent of any one of the flourishing cults in recent American letters—to the sentimental conservative, the new barbarian, or the earnest believer in social regeneration through literary violence. On the contrary, I should heartily recommend it to all those who prefer to think while they read, who relish a deep inward irony, who are interested more in the drama of ideas than in the play of conditioned or unconditioned reflexes.

For we have here, at the rare, right moment, an analysis of our civilization by the only modern philosopher (as all true lovers of "The Life of Reason" will maintain) who has been able to make philosophy into an art. "I am an ignorant man, almost a poet," Mr. Santayana confesses blandly; and he is also, though he does not confess it, the greatest contemporary master of English prose. It does not matter whether one accepts or rejects, or accepts only in part, Mr. Santayana's system. It scarcely matters whether or not one is able to distinguish lucidly between essences and platonic ideas. For this novel is what philosophy so often is not, and that is literature. As literature, therefore, and as literature alone, we may scrutinize its theme and its structure.

We watch, then, in a slightly frigid yet golden air, the conflict of intelligence with a universe that remains indifferent or actually hostile.

Reprinted from "George Santayana Writes a 'Novel,' " *New York Herald Tribune* books section, 2 February 1936, 1–2.

28

Inevitably, I suppose, this book will be compared with "Marius the Epicurean." It will be compared, not because the two books are alike, but because each, in its separate and lonely field, is unlike any other work in prose fiction. Both are novels not so much of life as of dialectic, although in "The Last Puritan" one may miss, perhaps, the antique harmony of "Marius," that luminous curve of reason which transcended, when it could not redeem the Age of the Antonines. Still, if the form of Mr. Santayana's novel appears less symmetrical, the substance is spiced with wit or tinctured with irony, and the clear and tranquil prose is eloquent with its own rhythms.

Unlike any other work in prose fiction, I have said; yet this, of course, is only a partial truth. Since, unhappily, comparison leads to comparison, I may admit that, in my first absorbed reading of "The Last Puritan," I tried to trace a subtle family resemblance to the treasured features of "The Way of All Flesh." We may recognize, I told myself, the same flickering sardonic smile which casts a sudden light in the mind. Ernest and Oliver may be distant cousins in satire; but in the treatment of poor Ernest both his creator and destiny are more savage; and the malicious insight of Samuel Butler is subdued to the cutting edge of truth by Mr. Santayana's urbane manner.

Surely this is well. Surely it is well to be urbane, to be impartial, to be scrupulously exact. Nevertheless, I find myself asking: Is it that malicious insight or that savage temper which made the characters in "The Way of All Flesh" so dangerously human? For the many persons in "The Last Puritan" act as human beings act, and yet are never quite human. They will appeal most strongly to those reflective readers who are satisfied to enjoy abstractions in art, without demanding that the symbol shall be made flesh or the incorruptible put on corruption. These symbols are not what we call "real" characters; yet, in some miraculous way, they live and move in the brilliant air of the mind. They live and move with that singular vividness which is the best, if not the only, substitute for reality. The illumination is so intense that it appears to deepen the intellectual twilight in our novels.

To many of us nowadays, the contemporary novel seems to have wandered into a blind labyrinth, where it must either break down the decaying barriers we know as "naturalism" or else destroy itself in an endless maze of futility. And so we may still regard the creation of living character as the chief glory of the novel, and yet welcome with enthusiasm a re-examination of ideas. Whether we look for understanding of life or for emotional and intellectual excitement, we are content to let the novelist select his own material and pattern. All we require of him, indeed, is that he shall conform, as thinker and artist, to his inner vision, that he shall obey the laws of his own universe. To banish soliloquy and speculation from the vast area of fiction appears to us as unreasonable as to decree that only humanity in the roots or consciousness at the source offers a fair transcript of life. The world of "The Last Puritan" is a complicated and highly organized world, and the author has dissected its nature with unerring integrity.

In an earlier work, written immediately before the war, Mr. Santayana has diagnosed those diseases of culture which have afflicted not only our novels, but our whole civilization and even ourselves.

> "Trustful faith in evolution," he wrote in his essay on the Intellectual Temper of the Age, "and a longing for intense life are characteristic of contemporary sentiment; but they do not appear to be consistent with that contempt for the intellect which is no less characteristic of it. Human intelligence is certainly a product, and a late and highly organized product, of evolution; it ought apparently to be as much admired as the eyes of molluscs or the antennae of ants. And if life is better the more intense and concentrated it is, intelligence would seem to be the best form of life. But the degree of intelligence which this age possesses makes it so very uncomfortable that, in this instance, it asks for something less vital, and sighs for what evolution has left behind. Finding their intelligence enslaved, our contemporaries suppose that intelligence is essentially servile; instead of freeing it, they try to elude it. . . . Having no stomach for the ultimate, they burrow downwards towards the primitive. But the longing to be primitive is a disease of culture: It is archaism in morals. To be so preoccupied with vitality is a symptom of anaemia.

I have quoted this passage because it describes the age and the moral climate in which Oliver Alden, the last puritan, suffered defeat. Seldom in fiction, or even in biography, has a life been so completely recorded, or a character so scrupulously examined. In spite of Mr. Santayana's incurable antipathy to puritanism, he has held the balance fairly between an idea and a universe.

> "I am afraid" [the narrator remarks in the Prologue to "The Last Puritan"] "I am afraid that there will always be puritans in this mad world. Puritanism is a natural reaction against nature.
> "But in Oliver puritanism worked itself out to its logical end. He convinced himself, on puritan grounds, that it was wrong to be a puritan.
> "And he remained a puritan notwithstanding.
> "That was the tragedy of it. . . . He kept himself for what was best. That's why he was a true Puritan.
> "His puritanism had never been mere timidity or fanaticism or calculated hardness. It was a deep and speculative thing; hatred of all shams, scorn of all mummeries, a bitter merciless pleasure in the hard facts. . . . I don't prefer austerity for myself as against abundance, against intelligence, against the irony of ultimate truth. But I see that in itself, as a statuesque object, austerity is more beautiful, and I like it in others."

For there are, we must remember, two logical attitudes toward experience. We may seize it as an essence, this perfume of the moment, this "transcript of the immediate," or we may reject the life of nature, and refuse, like the true puritan, to "accept anything cheaper or cruder than our own conscience." It is "a petrified conscience, a moral cramp," protested Oliver's father, Peter Alden, who had escaped from puritanism after committing murder with the college Bible. But to Oliver the whole of life is "either the truth or nothing," and, as Mr. Santayana has remarked elsewhere, to covet truth is a very distinguished passion.

In this disintegrating world, then, in this age, in this dry New England atmosphere, Oliver Alden was born of adequate, if not irreproachable, ancestry. We are first introduced to him in prenatal darkness, at the crucial instant when "his little organism long before birth, had put aside the soft and drowsy temptation to be a female. It would have been so simple for the last pair of chromosomes to have doubled up like the rest, and turned out every cell in the future body complete, well-balanced, serene and feminine." But no. Instinctively and inevitably, before he was formed, Oliver made his first unconscious and characteristic choice: "One intrepid particle decided to live alone, unmated, unsatisfied, restless and masculine." And some years after that great refusal, when Mario, his cousin from Europe, a joyful hedonist, inquired: " 'I say, Oliver, were you brought up on the bottle or did you have a wet nurse?' Oliver laughed at the idea of a wet nurse. Fancy Miss Tirkettle in that capacity! Nobody had a wet nurse in America. Of course, he was brought up on the bottle. 'I thought so!' Mario exclaimed triumphantly, 'You don't know what a woman is.' "

Our popular fiction, ably assisted by Freudian psychology, has accustomed us to dark views of our ancestors. We are used to seeing the old Puritan portrayed as a hypocritical rogue hiding our sinister inheritances beneath a sanctimonious exterior. It is, therefore, surprising, it is even startling, to find that Oliver's sincerity was his sole point of offense. Unlike so many other puritans in modern American novels, Oliver met disaster, not because he was a hypocrite, but because he was not one. He suffered the terrible fate of being consumed by his virtue.

While he continues to exist and agonize (somewhere, I think, Mr. Santayana has called Calvinism "an expression of the agonized conscience"), we know him thoroughly. We know him, not perhaps as a fellow being, but as we know the works of a clock that we have taken apart and put together again. We share in his infancy, his childhood, his school hours, his college years, his predispositions and antipathies, his frustrated loves and his more vital friendships. "Women were rather a difficulty to him. He thought he liked them and they thought they liked him; but there was always something wanting. He regarded all women as ladies, more or less beautiful, kind, privileged and troublesome. He never discovered that all ladies are women."

The book is crowded with characters, and each character has some significant relation to the whole; each character means something more than itself. Not only a life but an era unrolls before us. Although the greater part of the scene is placed in New England, my difficulties arise when I try to think of "The Last Puritan" as an American novel. In spite of the publishers' label, this for me is an impossible act of thought; and I recall Mr. Santayana's avowal that only an American can speak for the heart of America, that he has tried to understand it as a family friend may who has a different temperament. Understand us, I think he does, so far at least as we are composed of mind and conscience; but the quality I feel in him—it may be, as he implies, the mellow tone of Catholic tradition—has no place in that "long Arctic night" of the Nordics. He might be, indeed, some brilliant and dispassionate observer from another, and a more civilized, planet.

Nevertheless, we must admit that the figures in this novel are to be found, without too wide or diligent a search, in America. Some few may have wandered from an older society; but beyond their upright outlines even when they are in Europe, we seem to see the spiritual horizon of New England. All are here, and all are recognizable—the conscript mind, the rebel mind, the old Puritan, the new Epicurean, the casual Christian, the sincere sensualist and the myth of woman ancient and modern, with "something wanting." For the rest, what and where is the true, the "real," America? What American has understood more of it than the fact or fiction of his own particular time and place?

In the end we receive the indelible impression of a way of life called Oliver Alden, of a way of life which was defeated and yet vaguely triumphant. Nothing, we think, could be more bitterly ironic than Oliver's death. "We have dedicated ourselves to the truth," he reflects, "to living in the presence of the noblest things we can conceive." So he goes into the war, impelled by duty, "to fight the Germans whom I like, on the side of the French whom I don't like." And with one last satirical twist of unreason for the reasonble, he is denied even the right death because he dies at the wrong moment.

> "Whatever the Germans may be guilty of," Mario said, "they didn't kill Oliver, and in a literal sense there was no question of blood in his case. It was several days after the armistice. All firing had ceased, but the troops were advancing rapidly; and somebody on a motor-bicycle, who thought all danger was over, came round a curve without warning on the wrong side of the road. Oliver, in trying to avoid a collision, ran into a milestone. His car turned turtle; he was caught under it and his neck was broken. There were no external injuries, hardly a bruise. . . . It was possible to take a photograph. I have one here."
>
> "You were always taking his photograph," Rose interposed coldly, as she continued to pour out the tea. Oliver had loved her; he had wanted to marry her; he had left her a legacy. But Rose continued to pour out the tea.

Thus appropriately, it appears, Oliver, who had always made the right choice, died because somebody else was on the wrong side of the road. Beneath this catastrophe to good intentions, to virtue out of touch with its age, there may be, or there may not be, a symbolical irony. But, strangely enough, there is, in literature as in life, a deeper irony than the creator's and that is the futile and unconscious irony of the creature. For when we have turned the last page of this extraordinary novel, when we pause and look back over the animated scenes to the vanishing point in the long perspective, we discover that, not only as a statuesque object, but even as a state of mind, austerity may be more beautiful than prodigality. Among all the human beings, wise or foolish, that people this hard-hearted yet soft-minded world, poor Oliver, the tenderly despised puritan, is the only one who proved himself to be capable of a genuine passion for reality, of a bitter merciless pleasure in the hard facts.

But even so: "When life is over, and the world has gone up in smoke, what realities might the spirit in us still call its own without illusion save the form of those very illusions which have made up our story?"

[*The Last Puritan*]

Richard Church

Perhaps the best way to present the nature of this book would be to compile an anthology of humane profundities from it. The harvest would be rich, for here is a writer who, after a lifetime of exploring the Bergsonian doctrine of the possibility of purposively exploiting the intuition, now puts precept into practice. In this work, therefore, the philosopher becomes the artist. The critic has to discover whether the two are incompatible, or whether they are one. The discovery that they are one is still inconclusive, for the suspicion then follows that the unity is not expressly shown in this work of art, beautiful and sensuous as it is, but rather in the tendency of Mr. Santayana's philosophical beliefs. For the book is heavily loaded with them, both directly and indirectly stated, and it would sink were they not what they are, the codification of an artist's instincts.

The philosopher being therefore so isolated, so experimental, the story should be restless and urgent, especially as it takes for symbol the revolt from the special and exaggerated form of Puritanism which gripped New England during the writer's formative years, his years of revolt.

Yet it is not so. Its keynote is serenity; a sort of evening, Thomas-Gray-like serenity, with that day's-death light which Leonardo de Vinci said always brought the sitter's soul into the gleam of eye and lip. The book therefore evokes wonder in the reader, and that is the deepest possible response. Wonder at the diversity of characterization and the further diversity and subtlety in the development of each individual. This is the first reception of the story. Afterwards one realizes how deliberately this multi-form, this social interplay, is developed from a simple, almost rigid, framework of idea, and how it is drawn back again at the end into that simple idea or rather spiritual attitude. And the realization makes one gratefully conscious that here is the novel being seriously used as an art-form, which is the device of poetry for expressing human life so far as it is a period of pilgrimage. In his epilogue, Mr. Santayana says, "perhaps, while life lasts, in order to reconcile mankind with reality, fiction in some directions may be more needful than truth." And again, "fiction is poetry, poetry is inspiration, and every word should come from the poet's heart, not out of the mouths of other people."

Some readers will object that the people in this story are not stupid

Reprinted from "Review of *The Last Puritan*," *Criterion* 15 (1936): 524–27.

enough; that they are supernaturally lit up by their author, who makes them, even in their destructive re-actions from his central conception of virtue, too conscious of their aims or lack of aims, and too voluble in their expression even of their spiritual dumbness. But the answer to this objection is in the *medium* in which the story floats, that pervasive rhetoric which is the author himself, richly alive in thought, and in that intuition which the tendency of his philosophic training has given a logical expression hardly to be differentiated from the technique of a poet. I say hardly, because there is a slight difference in the result. If we compare, for instance, this book with the *Divine Comedy* (both of them fully conscious in their philosophic scheme) we shall see that the philosopher turned poet is not the same as the poet turned philosopher (or pehaps I should say as the poet turned poet). Dante is *living;* Santayana is *looking* at life; he is almost too coherent, his puritanism as a composite portrait of spiritual disease is too astonishingly articulated. It becomes idealized into the author's own philosophic attitude, and in the end the hero, the Last Puritan, emerges into a solitude that is really an exile, stepping into the sterile inheritance of his own pride of spirit (that death-trap of Protestantism).

But all this is remote, the ulterior drag of the author's serene pessimism (for he is a Stoic, the nearest approach to Epicureanism to which a post-Reformation thinker can come). He knows the danger of any form of fixity of vision (that condition which we call inspiration). "So far from guiding us wisely," he says, "inspiration cheats us with some mirage. If we were moving in the right direction, where reality might fulfil our hopes, we shouldn't need any visionary ideals to beckon us. Events would open out before us congenially, and would call forth our innocent interest and delight, gradually, concretely, in ways odder and more numerous than we expected. Why, then, is this not so? Why does experience leave us so desolate, so puzzled, so tired, that like Plato and Plotinus and the Christian saints we must look to some imaginary heaven or some impossible utopia for encouragement and for peace?"

Such being his attitude to the very power by which he creates his universe, he has no reason to subdue a sardonic element, a cruel kindness, that chills the warmest and embitters the sweetest passages of the story. This heaven of "divine despair," so novel in Matthew Arnold's day, is more familiar to us now than is an all-trusting faith. As Santayana says, 'This is a dark age for the spirit, an age of secret preparation'. That secret preparation is the 'plot' of this novel. We are made to watch it with excitement, for it contains a hopefulness, the author's belief that "all the materialism that now distracts us from salvation will later be consecrated to salvation." The plot is centered in the soul of the hero, Oliver Alden, a rich young New Englander reared by a negative-minded puritanical mother. His father, a queer cosmopolitan Ishmael, rescues him and is the means of introducing him to the fleshpots of intellectual curiosity. But he finds no appetite for them.

Their only effect is to stimulate his spiritual pride, which he uses as a talisman to protect himself from sexual love (he makes two futile attempts to marry), and to sublimate his relationships with other men; men who are complementary to him, the pagan, the amorist, the mystic, the saint, the athlete. He ends by taking a little from each of them, but not enough to change his rock-bare personality, or to prevent him from passing out of life into a solitude hardly distinguishable from that which he has known in this world. It is strange, therefore, that at the end of this pilgrimage of expurgation, we are left with a sense of victory, of glory, though fully aware that it is an illusion.

The confession explains the serenity of the book: it explains also the convention adopted by the writer, his assimilation of all his material into the monotone and intellectual sublimity of his rhetoric. That rhetoric here is a valuable medium, fully conscious, in which the characters, incidents, and all the warring realities are set and unified. Life is thus determined into a form, but the medium of that determination being so transparent, so fully deliberate, the life elements lose none of their surprise and variety. Thus within the simplicity of the whole we have a full-blooded confusion of the common stuff of humanity, nature, and metaphysics. Man fighting his environment, man cheating his conscience, and in turn cheated by the impulses of his own blood, all these factors of conflict are lavishly introduced by an author whose capacity for living is hearty and humorous. His appetite for the moment, his rich historical sense of proportion, his ability to distil a conclusion from a large mass of evidence, and his power for collecting that evidence in such fullness; these gifts fill the story, giving it persuasive easiness and movement. It moves as life moves, not mechanically, but by means of natural will, by the urge of characters in growth, and by the seeming accidents which are really the manifestations of those characters in the conflict of development.

[*The Last Puritan*]

Conrad Aiken

It is surely a choice piece of irony that "The Last Puritan," the most nearly satisfactory analysis, in fiction, of the New England character, should have been written by a Catholic and a Latin. But perhaps, just the same, there is nothing surprising in it—perhaps Santayana's unique opportunity for a vision that should be at once detached and kindly, lay precisely in these accidents of difference. If the American has the advantage over the European that he can *become* European, the European has—and more often uses!—the same advantage over the American. During his years at Harvard, first as undergraduate and then as a professor of Philosophy, it is now obvious that Santayana "became" a New Englander, in the sense of realizing what it was to *be* one, more accurately and consciously than any other novelist of New England manners one can think of. James touched on this ground repeatedly, it is true, and saw it as itself a theme of the first importance, notably in some of the short stories: but he never got round to working it exhaustively. Santayana has worked it exhaustively—the thing is done, for good and all. "The Last Puritan" is as complete, in its way, as that New England autobiography of which it is the perfect companion-piece: "The Education of Henry Adams."

Adams described New Englanders as "sane and steady men, well balanced, educated, and free from meanness or intrigue—men whom one liked to act with, and who, whether graduates or not, bore the stamp of Harvard College . . . as a rule, the New Englander's strength was his poise, which almost amounted to a defeat. He offered no more target for love than for hate; he attracted as little as he repelled; even as a machine, his motion seemed never accelerated." It is this sort of New Englander whom with a miracle of tenderness, Santayana proceeds to destroy. His little twentieth-century Henry Adams, a bundle of inhibitions, an incarnated sense of duty, a skeptical awareness of which perhaps the first principle is an inherited fatigue, combined with that strangest of all paradoxes, a democratic sense of *noblesse oblige*—this unhappy creature serves only too admirably as the personification of the principles—or should we say obsessions—which Santayana so urbanely and cunningly attacked in his "Skepticism and Animal Faith": the esurient negativism, the denial of life itself, implicit in any complete tran-

Reprinted from "The New England Animal," *New Republic*, 5 February 1936, 372.

scendentalism. It is as if he said, "This kind of self-destructive soul-searching and skepticism and conscientiousness can only grow in a moral atmosphere such as this, and from a thin soil like this." And it is as if he added, "It is a kind of uprooted refinement of which the inevitable ends are sterility and death." His Oliver Alden, born tired, child of a loveless and joyless marriage, austere, self-controlled, beautifully schooled and regimented, was doomed to remain a mere spectator in life, incapable of contact or immersion, incapable of animal faith. He might, and did, *will* a contact or immersion: but only to perceive at once, with tragic clearness, that this was by no means the same thing. "He convinced himself, on puritan grounds, that it was wrong to be a puritan. . . . Thought it his clear duty to give puritanism up, but couldn't." Once dedicated to the vision, there was somehow no surrendering it, no possibility of finding any adequate substitute.

It may be objected that Santayana has a little unnecessarily loaded the dice against his tragic young man, made his inheritance, the congenital predicament, too complete. One hardly needs, in order to account for Oliver, the opium-fiend neurasthenic father, and perhaps the whole background is a shade overdrawn. But to this the answer is that Santayana has made the father, like every other character in the book, astonishingly and delightfully real. The process is leisurely, little or nothing happens, as in life itself things seldom seem to arrange themselves in scenes or dramatic actions; but if it is all placid and uneventful it is also everywhere vivid and rich and true. Unashamedly old-fashioned in its method, and in its quiet thoroughness, "The Last Puritan" makes the average contemporary novel, even the best, look two-dimensional by contrast. It has the solidity of a "Tom Jones" or "Clarissa Harlowe," and does for the New England scene, or a part of it, what those novels did for eighteenth-century England, and with the same air of easy classic completeness. Nor is it quite fair, either, to call it old-fashioned: for Santayana's employment of a kind of soliloquy-dialogue is an extremely interesting invention technically, and very skillfully done.

But the whole book is a delight, so richly packed with perceptions and wisdoms and humors, not to mention poetry, that it can be read and reread for its texture alone. It might be of himself that Santayana speaks when he says: "The odds and ends of learning stuck pleasantly in his mind, like the adventures of a Gil Blas or a Casanova; it was the little events, the glimpses of old life, like the cadences of old poetry, that had the savor of truth. Perhaps there were no great events: a great event was a name for our ignorance of the little events which composed it." Or again: "To him the little episodes painted in the corners were often the best of the picture: they revealed the true tastes of the artist and the unspoken parts of life." "The Last Puritan" is full of such intriguing corners—perhaps inevitably, since it is the work of the kindliest of living philosophers.

[*The Last Puritan*]

FRANCES W. KNICKERBOCKER

Twenty-four years after his departure from us, Santayana has revisited in memory the land of his long sojourn. *The Last Puritan* is not a revised version of *Character and Opinion in the United States,* that penetrating diagnosis of the American mind; it is an interpretation, a work of art wrought of piercing perceptions, compassionate irony, word melody. Santayana, inheritor of the classic and Catholic traditions, American only by association, ever an alien in our midst, has yet given us an imaginary portrait of a New England mind that ranks with the self-portrait of *The Education of Henry Adams.*

Nor need we wonder that this distinguished philosopher, this master of English prose, should, like Pater and Melville and many another, have used the novel as a "fable," a medium for reflection upon life. For in telling us, in his "Brief History of my Opinions," "My pleasure was rather in expression, in reflection, in irony," Santayana had already described the very quality of this "memoir in the form of a novel."

A novel with a difference indeed. For Santayana has here used the soliloquy, that sensitive instrument of his earlier philosophic musings, to express his characters and even at times to carry the narrative. Hence, his orchestration is monotonous—like a symphony scored for the solo clarinet. Moreover, as he disarmingly admits in his Epilogue, his men and women all speak his own exquisite and subtle language; they are all incredibly articulate and clairvoyant. But, replies Santayana, fiction is poetry, and all the resources of a poet's language are needed to convey, not the actual speech of his personages, but their real feelings. And indeed with some of them he does achieve a reality that transcends realism. Though most of his women seem images, of the hero's desire or their creator's ironic vision, his men live with a two-fold intensity, self-revealing and revealed.

Oliver Alden, the "last Puritan," is the child of a thin-spun race, a ferocious Calvinist grandfather and an elderly, weary, drug-haunted father. From this heritage springs his inner conflict. His fearless mind, refusing the narrow puritanism of superstition and sham, hypocrisy and hate, (Oliver, like Santayana, was "never afraid of disillusion") vows itself to integrity and understanding. Yet his inborn sense of duty keeps him submissive to outer

Reprinted from "Epitaph on Puritanism," *Sewanee Review* 44 (April–June 1936): 246–49.

compulsions, conscience-bound, root-entangled, unable at moments of choice "to reshape his duty in a truer harmony with his moral nature." Rejecting puritanism, he remained a puritan. And so, dutiful, dedicated, unfulfilled, he yields to the last hated duty of war, and dies in a needless accident after the armistice.

Over against Oliver are set his two friends: "Lord Jim," with his frank animal manliness clothed in those fair outward English ways that Santayana in the *Soliloquies in England* has so lovingly depicted; and the sunlit worldling Mario, moulded by his Catholic heritage and his Eton education of the English gentleman. The Mario of the Epilogue survives to enrich the future with the grand tradition of the past. Embodying the living forces of nature, "blood within and sunlight above," he represents the good life according to Santayana: the harmony of reason, the happiness of each after his own heart. But the Mario of the novel, with his easy charms and butterfly loves, leaves us cold; it is Oliver of the austere beauty and frustrated passion for perfection who moves us at moments, as he must have moved his creator.

Here, says Santayana, is the tragedy of the puritan: the spirit that seeks to govern and is not content to understand, that rebels against nature and animal faith and demands some absolute sanction for love. But the tragedy of Oliver was deeper than this. Your true puritans, who through faith subdued kingdoms, wrought righteousness, stopped the mouths of lions, were men and women of ardors, even gaiety. Oliver was the child of a dead faith, of a marriage without love and a home without laughter. And so he could neither believe in any cause nor laugh at himself nor forget himself in love. Santayana has portrayed not the tragedy but the death of puritanism.

Again, as in the last chapters of *Character and Opinion in the United States,* one aspect of the American scene is depicted with devastating clarity: that homely, hurried, mechanical life, with its optimism (now dimmed), its mediocrity and compulsions, its "perpetual football match." Santayana knows only "the great emptiness of America"; its richness and its promise he cannot discern. And again the Harvard of his own day, that golden age of philosophy in America of which he was so great a part, is glimpsed, not as his pupils have celebrated it, but as an age of intellectual innocence and earnestness with its "slight smell of brimstone." The superbly satiric sketch of the old Boston of Beacon Hill and King's Chapel is woven partly of his own boyhood memories. But the lonely, tragic beauty of New England, so poignantly rendered in Wolfe's *Of Time and the River,* is to Santayana only meagre and desolate: "there was nothing," he has said, "in which the spirit of beauty was deeply interfused." For beauty charged with passion and discipline he turns to Oxford, described in a passage of haunting melody that belongs with those other deathless tributes to that place of recollection and fidelity.

These judgments on America, with the yet sterner judgment of Santayana's withdrawal from us, are not new. What *The Last Puritan* leaves with us is not a verdict but an epitaph on a vanished era. If we cannot look to Santayana for guidance toward a fuller life of reason for America that shall also be a life of justice for all, we can be very grateful for a book of remembrance that is so wise, so tender, and so beautiful.

George Santayana:
The Philosopher as Poet

PHILIP BLAIR RICE

$\mathbf{M}$r. Santayana began his poetic career with three handicaps which he did not entirely overcome: he was a philosopher, he was addicted to Platonism, and he lived in the United States at the end of the 19th Century. These handicaps were greater, I suspect, than the one on which he himself lays most emphasis, that English was not his mother-tongue, that he "never drank in in childhood the homely cadences and ditties which in pure spontaneous poetry set the essential key," that he knew "no words redolent of the wonder-world, the fairy-tale, or the cradle." This circumstance would bar to him a certain kind of lyricism, but I cannot believe that such a master of English prose as Santayana has suffered severely from the linguistic difficulty. The chief defects that show in his poetry are defects of perception and imagination.

A profound acquaintance with philosophy is not necessarily detrimental to a poet; in fact Santayana argues persuasively that the greatest poetry is philosophical. Yet each pursuit has its exacting craft; and though the whole mind is enlisted in both cases, the emphasis, the method and the daily discipline are radically different. If the philosopher is addicted to Platonism, even with Santayana's reservations, the handicap is more serious. In *The World's Body* John Crowe Ransom has argued, with plausibility, that it was a kind of Platonism, conscious or unconscious, that set English poetry on a wrong track, late in the 17th Century, from which it has not altogether returned to the main highway. If this view is correct, then Santayana's Platonism was simply a part of his third handicap, his time and place. In suggesting that to write poetry in English at the end of the 19th Century was the gravest handicap of all, I am assuming the fundamental soundness of the revolution in the conception of poetry that has occurred in the last twenty or twenty-five years. Like most revolutions, this one has consisted partly in a return to an earlier state of affairs, real or imagined, and consequently in the repudiation of a vested heresy. Recent critics have written voluminously on the subject, but I shall summarize the latest and one of the most brilliant (although not perhaps the most judicious) treatments of it, Cleanth Brooks's

Reprinted from *Kenyon Review* 2 (Winter 1940): 460–75.

in his book *Modern Poetry and the Tradition*. The heresy in question, as Brooks argues with documentation, was shared in greater or less degree by all the leading arbiters of poetic taste since and including Dryden: by Addison, Pope, Dr. Johnson, Wordsworth, Coleridge, Arnold, and latterly A. E. Housman. Its central assumption is that metaphor or imagery in a poem is primarily an illustration or an ornament. That is to say, that metaphor is not an integral structural part of the poem. The core of the poem, according to this view, consists in its "subject," which may be a Platonic idea, a moral direction, or an emotion. But in any of these cases the imagery is merely instrumental: it explains the idea, or renders the moral teaching palatable and persuasive, or sets the emotion vibrating.

In opposition to this conception of poetry, the moderns have returned to the faith of the Elizabethans and the 17th Century "metaphysicals" in the structural character of metaphor. As Mr. Brooks put it, "We cannot remove the comparisons from their [the metaphysicals'] poems, as we might remove ornaments or illustrations attached to a statement, without demolishing the poems. The comparison *is* the poem in a structural sense."

I shall try to show that Santayana, in his theory of poetry, was ahead of, or, if you prefer, in a certain sense behind, his time; that with his wide knowledge of literature and his sure taste, he perceived many of the errors in the prevailing conception of poetry. If this were all, his writings would be of merely historical interest. But I believe that Santayana's statement of his poetics, despite certain omissions and mistaken emphases, is in many respects superior to those now current, and possesses the further advantage of being firmly grounded in his general philosophy. And finally I shall try to show that in his poetry he was less able to escape the limitations of his time, and that, as he is well aware, his verse falls below the requirements of his poetic theory not only in scope but in quality.

Santayana's theory of poetry was given its most summary statement in the essay, "The Elements and Functions of Poetry," published as Chapter X of *Interpretations of Poetry and Religion* (1900). The elements or functions of poetry are classified as four: "euphony," "euphuism," what we may call experiential immediacy, and what we may call rational imagination. Euphony is the most rudimentary and indispensable element; but poetry rises in the scale of value as it progressively incorporates the other three.

Euphony is defined as "the sensuous beauty of words and their utterance in measure." *The Sense of Beauty* treated the aesthetic object as an organic whole analyzable into the three aspects of material, form and expression. Euphony consists of the intrinsic pleasingness of the material of poetry, sound, but of sounds in relation to each other. That is to say, it is dependent on "form" as well as "material." And the form itself, as we shall see, is conditioned by the "expression."

It may be rather surprising that Santayana should dignify as a second element what he calls euphuism, "the choice of colored words and rare and elliptical phrases." His own verse is not markedly precious, especially when it is compared with that of his contemporaries. That he should single out this quality is nevertheless revealing. Pope's verse, he says, although euphonious is not euphuistic; the Symbolists, on the other hand, exploited this element almost exclusively. He is reflecting here the highly attenuated version of Symbolism which flourished in England during the late eighties and nineties and became the aesthetic fashion among the more advanced young men in Boston and New York. As it was then understood, the chief aim of Symbolism, a continuation of one of the main currents of Romanticism, was to heighten and purify the emotional quality of poetry, and the emotion most prized was the "sense of mystery." The symbol, that is the concrete imagery of the poem, was not an end in itself nor a structural factor in the poem; its function, like that of the Imagination according to Wordsworth, was to suggest "the plastic, the pliant, and the indefinite." Euphuism, as Santayana defined it, would appear to be a purely verbal quality. It is evident, however, that Santayana is associating it with the Wordsworthian-Symbolist conception of the imagination when he goes on to say that euphuism takes us "out of the merely verbal into the imaginative region."

Verse that is compacted of euphony and euphuism has its charm, according to Santayana, but it is poetry at rather a low level. It is in part his emphasis on the third element, which I have called experiential immediacy, that makes his conception of poetry akin to that of the better Symbolists, the metaphysicals and their 20th Century disciples. Poetry "has body; it represents the volume of experience as well as its form." Whereas scientific prose seeks to establish and use conventional symbols, poetry "breaks up the trite conceptions designated by current words into the sensuous qualities out of which these conceptions were originally put together." It seeks "the many living impressions which the intellect rejected," and labors with the "nameless burden of perception." "Our logical thoughts dominate experience only as the parallels and meridians make a checker-board of the sea. . . . Sanity is a madness put to good uses; waking life is a dream controlled. Out of the neglected riches of this dream the poet fetches his wares. He dips into the chaos that underlies the rational shell of the world and brings up some superfluous image, some emotion dropped by the way, and reattaches it to the present object; he reinstates things unnecessary, he emphasizes things ignored, he paints in again into the landscape the tints which the intellect has allowed to fade from it. If he seems sometimes to obscure a fact, it is only because he is restoring an experience."

This element is similar to the *raisonné dérèglement* of Rimbaud, the dissociation preached by Rémy de Gourmont. It enriches the affective qualities of the poem, and on occasion can correct the partial perspective of the scientific vision. But it does not represent the highest organization of which poetry is capable. The unifying factor at this level is feeling: "the poet's art is to a great extent the art of intensifying emotions by assembling the scattered objects that naturally arouse them. . . . By this union of disparate things having a common overtone of feeling, the feeling is itself evoked in all its strength; nay, it is often created for the first time."

The ultimate end of poetry is more than the accomplishment of a mystical disintegration, which would be its tendency if it remained here. The poet's analysis of experience into its immediate elements is for the sake of creation. Santayana's discussion of the fourth element, which I have called rational imagination, is not wholly satisfactory; the essentials of a complete theory are here, but they are not fully developed, and he includes so many things under this function that the result is a certain confusion. His definition of it is: "to repair to the material of experience, seizing hold of the reality of sensation and fancy beneath the surface of conventional ideas, and then out of that living but indefinite material to build new structures, richer, finer, fitter to the primary tendencies of our nature, truer to the ultimate possibilities of the soul."

This element includes two, or perhaps three, aspects of poetry which are not wholly separable but which it is useful to distinguish more explicitly than Santayana does. One we may call imaginative structure, in a sense in which it is an element of any fully realized poem. The second is the logical structure; the third is the moral or ideal import, which only the prophetic kind of poetry possesses in high degree.

Santayana is saying here that poetry can have more structure than is supplied by a unity of feeling. The differentiation of the feelings themselves "depends on the variety of the objects of experience,—that is, on the differentiation of the senses and of the environment which stimulates them." Feeling and imagination must be fed by sense-experience, and they remake their materials into a form that is as concrete as sense-experience itself. The glorious emotions with which a child or a poet bubbles over "must at all hazards find or feign their *correlative objects*." The phrase which I have italicized will at once remind the reader who is versed in contemporary criticism of T. S. Eliot's rather barbarous key phrase (which he may very well have adapted from Santayana's better one), the "objective correlative" of an emotion; to find this is the chief business of poetry as poetry. The poem possesses full structural unity only when it has been achieved.

Such a notion is required by Santayana's definition of beauty or aesthetic value in *The Sense of Beauty:* "value positive, intrinsic and objectified. Or, in less technical language, Beauty is pleasure regarded as the quality of a thing." The important word here is "objectified"; the questionable one is "pleasure" or "value." I am not questioning primarily the equation of value with pleasure; Santayana's developed theory of value makes many of the necessary qualifications. The disputable point is whether it is exclusively the pleasure (or value) that is objectified. If so, we are landed in a Romantic-Symbolist theory of art; art is the expression of feeling. By objectification Santayana means this: although the pleasure exists only in the act of perception, it exists as if in the object. Later in the same book the author presents a somewhat different and better view of what is objectified. This is explained in his theory of "expression," the third ingredient of the aesthetic object in addition to material and form. Santayana makes a very important distinction between "expressiveness" and "expression." He uses "expressiveness" to designate all the capacity of association or suggestion possessed by an idea or symbol; as such it is not a differentiating function of aesthetic experience. "Expression," on the other hand, is limited to those suggestions or associations which are "incorporated in the present object." It includes values, but more, for it includes other elements of meaning together with their values. Such meanings must be compressed into the immediate experience if the object is an aesthetic one rather than the occasion for a sentimental reverie.

What, then, is the aesthetic object in the case of a poem? Santayana's essay on the elements and functions of poetry gives us some clues, although not a developed theory. The correlative object, at rather a low level of invention, consists of the characters of the poem; at a somewhat higher level, of the figures against their physical and historical background, or the cosmic landscape; the poem is still more highly organized when it has a plot, when the characters belong to an imagined society, and move within a dramatic situation, implied or enacted. There are other possibilities before we go on. Santayana might have put in somewhere in this list a single physical object, such as Keats's Grecian urn or Marvell's garden, which focuses the poem and supplies a structure through its ramifications for experience. It is such imagined referents of the significant sounds in the poem, I believe, that constitute the phenomenal world, or segment of a world, recreated in the experience of the poem. The referent of the poem, in a famous one by Yeats, is at most a pseudo-Byzantium, and it may not copy very closely any real Byzantium that ever existed; but it should have the same *kind* of structure for experience as a real city, or it does not have the characteristically poetic structure. This is the gist of the distinction between poetry and music. Music in its sound patterns objectifies nothing if not the structure and quality of an emotional experience itself. Poetry, on the other hand, projects at a psychic distance an imaginatively reconstructed, particular referent—the garden, the urn, the pseudo-Byzantium, the court of Elsinore, Dante's whole imagined universe yearning for its imagined creator—in which the sounds and feelings have their locus. In a certain sense, poetry is an "impure" art: the poetic object is not, like the musical object, a mere pattern of sounds with their incorporated feelings. It contains two kinds of sensory elements, the sounds and the non-auditory images of which they are the signs. The non-auditory imagery constitutes the primary object, but it retains and fuses with the sounds themselves, which are not mere signs but enter reflexively into the complex referent. The poet's success in reinforcing the imagery with the sound is the measure of his success in exploiting his medium.

The "poetic object," or complex referent, must embody the logical implications or moral attitudes or socio-political directions of the poem, when it has any of these. The poem, we can say, may refer to universals as well as particulars, but the universals must exist *in re,* in the concrete experience of the poem, and not merely *ante rem* in the intention of the poet or *post rem* in the reflection of the reader.

It is through the act of the imagination, so conceived, that poetry may achieve its ideal function. The poet becomes a prophet, Santayana holds, when he "portrays the ideals of experience and destiny." But this function is not accomplished exclusively through imagining Utopias, or even feasible enhancements of the existing reality. Tragedy gives us a "glimpse into the ultimate destinies of our will;" through its invocation of a cosmic order, it creates the "sense of a finished life, of the will fulfilled and enlightened." At its highest reaches poetry is metaphysical or religious in character: "The imagination . . . must furnish to religion and to metaphysics those large ideas tinctured with passion, those supersensible forms shrouded in awe, in which alone a mind of great sweep and vitality can find its congenial objects." So far as their rational function is concerned, poetry and religion at their final limit of development become identical. And both are best when they are true as well as imaginative: "The highest ideality is the comprehension of the real."

Santayana's theory must have been influenced by his poetic practice, as well as by his reading of other poets and by his general philosophy. Since he is a conscious artist, his poems in turn must have been subjected to scrutiny in the light of his principles. No genuine poet writes poems to exemplify a theory, but his theory can modify his attitude toward experience, can exercise suasion over the process of revision, can determine which poems he will publish and which he will withhold.

Within limits, Santayana is a skillful workman in respect of all that he includes under euphony—meter, rhyme, prosody. His language is always at least "felicitous," in the better sense of that word, and his joinery is neat. His formalism, however, often leads him to pad his lines with superfluous adjectives and phrases. While his phrasing never becomes in a high degree creative, it is usually precise. He uses words that poets have used before, or that one feels they might have used, and the context rarely elicits new or unexpected shades of meaning from them. Within the limits of a vocabulary that is almost completely bookish—that draws nothing from colloquial usage or linguistic experimentation—his language is free from the imitativeness of the dull poet; the phrase strikes one as hackneyed less often than its component words.

His musical effects rarely achieve more than well-patterned simple melody. They are varied enough to save the poem from monotony, and there is some degree of internal alliteration, assonance and consonance, although not enough to produce a strong illusion of musical counterpoint. His limitations are not primarily defects of euphony and euphuism but of experiential immediacy and imaginative structure. This can best be shown by confronting the poetry itself. I shall choose Sonnet I from his longest sequence:

> I sought on earth a garden of delight,
> Or island altar to the Sea and Air,
> Where gentle music were accounted prayer,
> And reason, veiled, performed the happy rite.
> My sad youth worshipped at the piteous height
> Where God vouchsafed the death of man to share;
> His love made mortal sorrow light to bear,
> But his deep wounds put joy to shamèd flight.
> And though his arms, outstretched upon the tree,
> Were beautiful, and pleaded my embrace,
> My sins were loth to look upon his face.
> So came I down from Golgotha to three,
> Eternal Mother; let the sun and sea
> Heal me, and keep me in thy dwelling-place.

This is one of Santayana's most interesting sonnets, although not one of his most nearly perfect. The intellectual content is more important than in many better poems. The "gentle music" of the first quatrain is itself appropriate to the theme; and in the last line the tonal quality and the repetition of the long vowel "e," with the resultant slowing of the rhythm, bring the poem to the kind of consummation that the thought demands.

Suppose, however, that one should come back to it immediately after reading these lines from Donne's third Satyre:

> On a huge hill,
> Cragged, and steep, Truth stands, and he that will
> Reach her, about must, and about must goe;
> And what the hills suddennes resists, winne so;

If this is compared with the second quatrain of the sonnet, the two are perceived to have certain similarities. In both, the theme is the search for religious faith, the "correlative object" is a hill, and the hill of Golgotha (for Donne is talking about the Truth of the Christian religion). The most striking difference in treatment is that Santayana tells us about the hill: Donne takes us there. We fall in behind him and try to climb it with him. The words "huge hill" themselves confront us with an obstacle; "Cragged, and steep, Truth stands" gives us its topography and its toilsomeness; the next line sets us at the obdurate ascent, not only by its rhythm but through the dramatic suggestions condensed in the words "about must, and about must": the attitude is that of a weary but determined man. The phrase "And what the hills suddennes resists" likewise gives us the *object as experienced.* The tempo quickens at the beginning of the line, only to check us with the two stressed syllables "hills sud-" and to jolt us on the three following short syllables, bringing us up finally at the syllable "-sists," the whole managed with as much lashing by sibilants and grinding by double and triple consonants as we can bear. These effects would not give the line its power, if they were not fused with the dramatic suggestions of the word "suddennes." This is not the most exact word to describe literally the object as it is in itself— "steepness" or "sheerness" would be scientifically more accurate—but it is the right word to describe the hill for us; and its very unexpectedness creates the shock of coming up against a blank wall of stone. Donne has conveyed the body of experience here;

> . . . . . e la presente
> E viva, e il suon di lei.

The shortcoming of Santayana's poem does not consist in a failure to find concrete symbols for the experience. The garden, the hill, and the seashore are at least potentially appropriate images here, even though their particular qualities are not fully elicited. But the structural use that is made of them is somewhat confusing. In a Petrarchan sonnet, one expects the principal structural units, as set by the rhyme scheme, to be the octet and sestet. So strongly does the convention of the Petrarchan form, as well as its logic, establish this expectation, that when I first read the sonnet I took the first quatrain, in conjunction with the second, to refer to a kind of aesthetic Christianity, whereas, of course, even a slightly less casual reading shows that the "garden" of the first quatrain is the pagan paradise by the sea of the last tercet. The structure of the poem, both logical and imaginative, divides therefore not 8–6 like the rhyme scheme but 4–7–3, with lines 1–4 and 12–14 forming a unit contrasted with lines 5–11. This defect is not explained away by the fact that the poem is the introductory one in a sequence of twenty, and that the first quatrain states the theme of the entire sequence. So I cannot overcome the conviction that the sonnet would have been better organized if the poet had been able to make lines 5–11 into the octet, and had put the rest into the sestet.

Although the structure is imperfect, the "correlative object"—the descent from Golgotha to the sea—is valid for the ideas of the poem. That the poem is an adequate representation of Santayana's own spiritual experience is unlikely. I do not believe that the lines "But his deep wounds put joy to shamèd flight" and "My sins were loth to look upon his face" report accurately Santayana's rejection of Christianity, which was not an act of moral evasion. His true spiritual autobiography might have been more valuable, but apparently he could not find imaginative terms for it, or else found the form Procrustean, and so he let the poem follow its own process of growth. A little later I shall suggest what may be the fundamental reason for the inadequacy of Santayana's poetry to his philosophy.

Although experiential immediacy is wanting generally in his poems, a very large proportion of them have a structural use of the correlative object. Sonnet II, for example, achieves the specific organization of the Petrarchan sonnet. The prosody here is also more consistently fused with the other elements than in the first sonnet.

The connections between the poems, as usually and tolerably in a sonnet sequence, are loose. The sequence is given some semblance of organization, however, in addition to the logical connections, by the motif of the descent, and by such thematic repetitions as in these lines from X, with their reference to the imagery of Sonnet I:

> Doth the sun therefore burn, that I may bask?
> Or do the tirèd earth and tireless sea,
> That toil not for their pleasure, toil for me?

The best poems of this sequence, along with "Cape Cod," "Avila," "King's College Chapel," "Sybaris," and the third and fifth of the Sapphic odes, represent the peaks of Santayana's achievement. But the crucial question concerning the relation between Santayana's poetry and his philosophy is best treated by examining his second sonnet sequence, XXI–L, from which I shall select sonnet XXIV:

> Although I decked a chamber for my bride,
> And found a moonlit garden for the tryst
> Wherein all flowers looked happy as we kissed,
> Hath the deep heart of me been satisfied?
> The chasm 'twixt our spirits yawns as wide
> Though our lips meet, and clasp thee as I list,
> The something perfect that I love is missed,
> And my warm worship freezes into pride.
> But why—O waywardness of nature!—why
> Seek farther in the world? I had my choice,
> And we said we were happy, you and I.
> Why in the forest should I hear a cry,
> Or in the sea an unavailing voice,
> Or feel a pang to look upon the sky?

This illustrates the principal theme of the sequence, which is dominated by Santayana's "Platonism," whereas the first sequence was primarily an expression of his paganism or naturalism. The sequence as a whole is more derivative and artificial than the first sequence, echoing the Italian poets whom he was reading at that time. It is also less adequate to its philosophical theme. The Platonic tradition, with its distrust of the senses, its worship of the abstract, is fundamentally anti-poetic; and Plato was quite consistent, great poet though he was, in excluding the poets from his ideal state.

Now Santayana's own philosophy is only metaphorically Platonic. His essences are not existences (except when they are embodied) but mere possibilities. And values or ideals for him belong only incidentally to the realm of essence. During the time when he wrote these sonnets, he was engaged in working out his theory of value, which is closer to Spinoza than to orthodox Platonism (if one excepts the *Philebus* and *Statesman* from orthodoxy). Values, as Santayana conceives them, are expressions of the living preferences of the organism. They are grounded in our irrational impulses, and represent an organization, purification and projection by reason and imagination of our spontaneous interests. The "things eternal" that Santayana celebrates in his poetry are sometimes mere essences—any characters whatever seen under the form of eternity—and sometimes the reflections of moral ideals in the realm of essence. In his philosophy we are constantly reminded of the foundation of values in the realm of matter or nature. It is, in fact, precisely his explanation of the emergence of the ideal from the natural that constitutes the great originality of his theory of value, and the great superiority of his system to most other naturalisms and idealisms. In the sonnets, however, this natural basis of the ideal, and the irony and wonder of the emergence of values, are almost completely ignored. Instead of finding images that would express the dialectical intricacies of his own system, he is content to use the vehicles of traditional literary Platonism. The semantic scheme of poetry then is as follows: the imagery of the poem symbolizes traditional Platonism, and traditional Platonism in turn symbolizes Santayana's heretical Platonism. This will not do. In philosophical poetry, as in all poetry, the symbol must take us directly to its referent.

Santayana indeed never felt altogether at home with the Platonizers. In the original version of his essay, *Platonism in the Italian Poets,* there is a revealing passage which was unhappily omitted when the essay was reprinted in *Interpretations of Poetry and Religion:*

> As for me, when I read the words of those inspired men and try to understand the depths of experience which is buried in them as in a marble tomb, I feel, I confess, very far away from them. I wonder if all their exaltation is not the natural illusion of a hope too great for any man; but at the same time I remember the story of Ruth and how she was impressed by that so strange and so passionate Jewish race into which she had come—a race that lived on prophecy and hope, and believed in its transcendent destiny—and I envy her that she found it in her heart to say, what I would gladly say to the family of Plato, "Let thy people be my people and thy God my God."

But Santayana himself, unlike Ruth, always remained amid alien corn.

Especially conspicuous in his poetry is the absence of a quality that pervades his prose writings: irony. This consideration can supply, I believe, the principal answer to the question why Santayana's poetic vision is not as full and just as his philosophic vision. Cleanth Brooks, in the book I have cited, takes irony, or its synonym wit (these terms he uses in a very special sense), to be the essential quality of metaphysical poetry. Metaphysical poetry, through its exploration of all the ramifications of its object, achieves a synthesis of the most discordant and heterogeneous qualities. A mature apprehension of those things which we prize includes a recognition of their partial absurdity, ugliness and evil. These aspects are included in and heighten the total effect of the experience, just as an adult love includes, is even given an edge by, a full consciousness of the lady's blemishes. Santayana, however, turned away from his not wholly satisfactory bride to a heavenly one. The dominant tradition of the 18th and 19th Centuries excluded the trivial and tainted aspects of experience from serious and ideal poetry, relegating them to the inferior sphere of "fancy," and recommending that the poetic imagination select an unqualifiedly beautiful or noble subject matter. (Plato here, as so often elsewhere, was better than the Platonists: in the *Parmenides* he makes fun of the young Socrates for refusing to admit Ideas of hair and filth.) In this respect Santayana's poetry is very much limited by its time. I am surprised to find no mention anywhere in Santayana of the English metaphysicals, since the quality of his own mind, as exhibited in his prose, is so much akin to theirs. It is agreeable to fancy how Donne or Marvell would have made this essentially poetic insight into a poem: "Scepticism is the chastity of the intellect, and it is shameful to surrender it too soon or to the first comer: there is nobility in preserving it coolly and proudly though a long youth, until at last, in the ripeness of instinct and discretion, it can be safely exchanged for fidelity and happiness." Or this: "The tight opinionated present feels itself inevitably to be the center and judge of the universe; and the poor human soul walks in a dream through the paradise of truth, as a child might run blindly through a smiling garden, hugging a paper flower."

The first quotation is from *Scepticism and Animal Faith,* the second from *The Realm of Truth.* Since such passages bloom everywhere in his later writings, I can only conclude that Santayana's poetic imagination became fully developed long after he had ceased to write verse. For his philosophic vision is also a poetic vision.

[*Persons and Places*]

NEWTON ARVIN

The philosopher who is also his own biographer—the metaphysician as memorialist—is not a familiar figure, not a classic type, in the history of literature; there are, of course, John Stuart Mill and Herbert Spencer, but unless Rousseau is a kind of exception, it is not very easy to think of others. Time was when one might have generalized against the possible union in one mind of a genius for dialectics and the autobiographer's gift of self-revelation; the editors of a recent series—the "Library of Living Philosophies"—have been undeterred by any such doubts, and the introductory personal essays in these volumes by men like Whitehead and G. E. Moore would seem to vindicate their confidence, for these essays are full of juice. In a similar volume, Irwin Edman's excellent edition of "The Philosophy of Santayana," there appeared A Brief History of My Opinions by Santayana himself, a vigorous fragment of autobiography which made one wonder what Epicurus or Spinoza would have done with a similar assignment; and now comes, by mysterious messengers from Rome, the first volume of what is apparently to be a very full memoir by Santayana—the story, this, of his childhood, boyhood, and college years.

It is an extraordinarily rich and delicate piece of writing: Santayana turns out to be a memorialist in the great tradition. The form, unlike that of the novel, is one in which he moves comfortably and with grace, and the qualities one failed to find in "The Last Puritan"—itself "A Memoir in the Form of a Novel"—qualities of vitality, of spontaneity, of naturalness and charitable humor—are abundantly here. In "The Last Puritan," one felt, Santayana was paying off too many old scores: they are paid now, presumably, and his spirit is free to expatiate over the past without acrimony, or with only the mild infusion of acrimony needful to give such a work savor and character. There was an awkward disequilibrium in his novel between the writer's senses and his sentiments, between his perceptions of the outer world and his habitual abstractions; here, on the contrary, the two are polarized as they ought to be, and Santayana moves back and forth with an effortless irony and tenderness between the rather Goyaesque drawings he makes of Avila in his childhood and the "feeling" story of his early religiosity; between the jerry-built Back Bay of the seventies and the youthful origins of his pessimism,

Reprinted from "Santayana's Memoirs," *Nation,* 29 January 1944, 131–32.

between a handed-down dress of his sister Susana's ("elaborate with a looped over-skirt, yellow satin bow-knots, and scalloped edges") and the handed-down culture, as he saw it, of the Boston into which he was so traumatically flung at the very risky age of eight.

There is no doubt that it *was* a trauma, this shock of transplantation from his father's impecunious but slow-paced Old World household in Castilian Avila to the raw new mansions of Beacon Street and the improved methods of Miss Welchman's Kindergarten. The rather violent conflicts of direction and attachment that it produced have given poignancy and a rather stately pathos to all of Santayana's life as well as to his philosophy; a loss was suffered which he himself does not blink: "There was a terrible moral disinheritance involved," he says, "an emotional and intellectual chill, a pettiness and practicality of outlook and ambition, which I should not have encountered amid the complex passions and intrigues of a Spanish environment." But he adds that if his fate had been in one sense happier, and Spain or southern Europe his permanent home, he would not have been "the person that I am now"; he would certainly not have been the writer he ended by being, and the unique interest of his work as a philosopher—its curious, ambiguous, Mediterranean-Yankee unity in disparity—would have been replaced by something more acceptably uniform, perhaps, but surely less complex, less various, less vitally paradoxical. It was the tension between Santayana's Spanish heritage, his Spanish infancy, and that sensationally contrarious world of the Boston Latin School and Harvard under President Eliot that made possible "The Life of Reason" and "Realms of Being." We might have profited less from a more coherent philosopher: we have after all, to that end, Unamuno—or William James.

Except for William James, as he remarked in "A Brief History," Santayana's thought would never have taken just the turn it did, and one cannot read this new book without feeling in how many ways the discomforts, the antagonisms, even the denials of Santayana's long life in this country kept his senses on the alert and his wits on the stretch: perhaps the all but literally Portuguese Jew Spinoza gained some such good from Amsterdam and The Hague. It is true that, from Santayana's point of view, America had a mainly negative and astringent value for him, and a deep-rooted American will not feel that either "The Last Puritan" or "Persons and Places" does justice to what was most creative in America even in the years they cover—to that perfection which, as Santayana says here and elsewhere, every form of life has in its own fashion. He missed rather more than he saw, or he would hardly have thought J. S. Sargent one of "the two most creditable living Americans." What he missed is perhaps, as Henry James once put it, the American's secret—"his joke, as one may say"—and during this dark night of the European soul, with the spectacle of Europe's tragic failure and ruin before us, we can be neither vainglorious nor cringing on that score. American readers of these books can make their own reservations, mainly in silence, and meanwhile there is much to be learned from them. No one but Santayana could have seen just what he saw in the New England of the Age of Howells: his memories of those decades have a fictional sharpness, a precision of imagery, a piercing psychological quality that one finds in few comparable American autobiographies.

[Persons and Places:
The Background of My Life]

MALCOLM COWLEY

Jorge Agustín Nicolás Ruiz de Santayana—as I think his name appears on
his still Spanish passport—was born in Madrid on December 16, 1863. Less
than nine years later he reached Boston, as the result of several unlikely and
even preposterous events that he describes at length in his autobiography.[1]
Imagine that his mother met Don Agustín de Santayana when they were the
only two Europeans on a little island in the Philippines. Imagine that a year
or two later she married a New England merchant named George Sturgis, on
a British frigate in Manila harbor. Imagine that Sturgis died in the midst of a
disastrous business venture and that she transported her four children to
Boston, losing one of them on the way. And there were other curious events
to follow. Mrs. Sturgis went to Spain for a visit, met Don Agustín again and
married him. When little Jorge, the child of this second union, was five years
old, she traipsed back to Boston with her Sturgis children. Jorge was sent to
follow them three years later, because a series of family misfortunes had left
his father alone in the house and unable to care for him. All these accidents—
or in philosophical terms, these inevitabilities—were the necessary background of Santayana's career.

If he had remained in Spain, I cannot imagine that he would have
become a distinguished philosopher. He would have gone into government
service like his father, and he would have written rather florid verse—for his
early style showed a tendency toward softness, toward decoration, and in
Spain it would have lacked the discipline furnished by writing in a foreign
language. There was nothing essentially new in his principles. He said in the
fifty-year report of his Harvard class—it was '86—"I think I have changed
very little in opinion or temper. I was old when I was young, and I am young
now that I am old." Intellectually he was almost two thousand years old
when he entered college: he was a Roman of the early empire, a disciple of
Lucretius and Democritus. His philosophy was the common sense of the
Mediterranean world, which is very different from common sense in New
England. Essentially it was a philosophy of submission—first of all to nature, then to the weaknesses of the human body and mind, then finally to

Reprinted from "Santayana at Harvard," *New Republic,* 17 January 1944, 88, 90.

constituted governments, even if they are evil, and to the recognized church, even if it is based on a myth.

Although Spain is only in part a Mediterranean country, there are thousands of Spanish intellectuals who agree at heart with these ideas. In Spain, lacking opposition, Santayana might never have bothered to express his common sense as a systematic philosophy. In Boston he seemed a rank heretic, and so he talked and wrote and philosophized to defend his position. Idealism had begun to grow morbid in Boston, and Santayana's pagan ideas were a valuable tonic. They flourished like many importations to a new continent; almost like rabbits and foxes in Australia.

And Santayana himself flourished at Harvard. He was poor but brilliant, handsome in a not too foreign way and socially vouched for by his Sturgis relatives. As a sophomore, he played the leading lady in Institute theatricals. His class records show that he was on the staff of The Lampoon; that he helped to found The Harvard Monthly; that he belonged (in alphabetical order) to the Art Club, the Chess Club, the Everett Athenaeum, Hasty Pudding, the Institute of 1770, the O. K. Society, Phi Beta Kappa, the Philosophical Club (president) and the Shakspere Club. Apparently he joined almost everything open to undergraduates—except Porcellian, which was not in reach of his pocketbook, the Christian Brethren and the Total Abstinence League, from both of which he was barred by his principles. He was graduated *summa cum laude,* with honors in philosophy; he received a traveling fellowship and, in due time, he was given a teaching appointment.

During the next ten years, Don Jorge repaid with interest his debt to New England. The 1890's were a dull period there for literature; the great figures had disappeared and nobody had come forward to replace them except genteel imitators; it was what Van Wyck Brooks calls the Age of the Epigoni. Harvard College, however, was in a state of intellectual ferment, to which Santayana contributed more than his share of yeast. Men now in their seventies talk wistfully about the dinners of the O. K. Society, where Santayana often read one of his lighter poems and where his table talk became a legend. Among the younger members of O. K. were Philip Littell, Hutchins Hapgood, Robert Morss Lovett, William Vaughn Moody, Learned Hand, Ellery Sedgwick, Winthrop Ames, Charles M. Flandrau (who gave the best contemporary picture of the period in his "Harvard Episodes"), George Cabot Lodge and Trumbull Stickney. These last two, except perhaps for Moody, had more creative fire than any of their colleagues, but the fire languished and they died very young—"visibly killed," as Santayana said in a letter, "by the lack of air to breathe. People individually were kind and appreciative to them, as they were to me, but the system was deadly, and they hadn't any alternative tradition (as I had) to fall back upon." In spite of the system, Lovett and his college friend Robert Herrick became great teachers of the next generation. The others had less to say, and Santayana could not give them much to supply that deficiency, since his own work is not characterized by vigor or freshness of ideas. What he could and did teach them, chiefly by example, was to talk well and to write in the tone of men used to good conversation. By combining two provincial cultures—for Madrid was even more of a back-water than Boston—he achieved a real cosmopolitanism; and he played somewhat the same role at Harvard that Pater had been playing at Oxford. Then, in 1912, he went back to Europe and eventually settled in Rome, the capital and shrine of the Mediterranean mind.

This first volume of "Persons and Places," which carries Santayana's story down to his graduation from Harvard, contains not a hint or a personal reflection to show that it was written during the present war; even the style is detached, ironic and, in its manner, perfect. Indeed, the coolness of the book is a little ostentatious. It is almost as if someone had asked him, "What should writers do in war-time?" and as if, instead of giving a theoretical answer—a manifesto or a call to arms—Santayana had produced this volume which might have been written at any time, at any place, but only by a stylist and a man of wisdom.

Because of its contrast with the shoddy literature that we are being given today, one is tempted to exaggerate the merits of Santayana's prose. "Persons and Places," judged by this first volume, is an admirable work that is far from being the greatest autobiography of our time; it has the art but not the human complexity of Yeats's story. It seems as cold, bare and drafty as a Venetian palace in winter. Santayana warns us that he has "a very short memory, except for such things as I absorb and recast in my own mind." A few of his anecdotes are unforgettable, especially those dealing with his father, who was deaf, skeptical and a hypochondriac. Once, when convinced that he was dying, he was assailed at the same moment by hunger; and his voice boomed through the house as he tried to whisper, "*La Unción y la gallina!*"—"Extreme Unction and a boiled chicken." Santayana's mother refused to join the Roxbury Plato Club on the ground that she had no time. "What do you *do?*" asked the persistent visitor. "In winter," said the Spanish lady, "I try to keep warm, and in summer I try to keep cool." But there are too few of these revealing episodes (which abound in Yeats) and most of Santayana's characters seem wordless and disembodied.

He has a tendency, in talking about people, to pass rapidly from personality to philosophy, so that we seem to be moving in a realm of abstract essences. Moreover, he shows a disturbing lack of affection. There are only two of his many friends whom he praises unreservedly; he met both of them in the Boston Latin School and hasn't bothered to see them since 1882. About the others he makes curiously niggling comments. It is as if, dwelling among ideas, he greeted the world of men with a limp handclasp and a somewhat chilly eye.

[Persons and Places:
The Background of My Life]

Philip Blair Rice

Mr. Santayana has always professed that his writings were nothing but soliloquies, and in such works as *Character and Opinion in the United States, Soliloquies in England, Dialogues in Limbo* and his novel, they have shaded imperceptibly into memoirs. It is not surprising that now, at the age of eighty, he should overcome the residue of his coyness and give us an undisguised autobiography; and it was to have been expected that autobiography itself should be another medium for the restatement of his philosophy. *Persons and Places* could, then, be read as the record of an interesting person who has known other interesting persons and lived in interesting places, or for information about the influences which shaped one of the great philosophical systems of our time, or as a critical commentary, by a kind of Henry James in reverse, on the relation of New World culture to the Old. But his life is so much of a piece that these all come to very much the same thing.

For his researches into things past, Santayana has the advantage of an extraordinarily sharp and tenacious memory, which recreates his childhood and youth so fully that this first volume, although indeed it does not adhere to a strict chronology, brings us only to the end of his undergraduate days at Harvard. His experiences, too, were such as to create lasting impressions. The first eight years in Spain were stamped into his memory by the clear outlines and rich if tarnished colors of that spectral civilization; and the contrast with New England culture, which may have seemed to itself to have entered upon its Indian summer but looked very young and boisterous to him, set both in bold relief. To these must be added the habits of perception fostered by an early interest in drawing and architecture which under different circumstances might have dedicated him to the visual arts:

> I remember the *sota de copas* or knave of cups in the Spanish cards, with which I was playing on the floor, when I got entangled in my little frock, which had a pattern of white and blue checks; and I can see the corner of our room, our *antesala,* where I was crawling, and the nurse who helped me up. I also remember sitting in my mother's lap, rather sleepy, and playing with a clasp that could run up and down the two strands of her gold chain, made of

Reprinted from "Salt, Pepper, and Pity for Mankind," *Kenyon Review* 6 (Summer 1944): 455–59.

flexible scales; she wore a large lace collar, and had on a silk gown which she called *el vestido de los seis colores,* because the black background was sprinkled with minute six-petalled flowers, each petal of a different color, white, green, yellow, brown, red and blue.

In the impact and persistency of such images, it is not wholly fanciful to see the origin of the philosopher's doctrine of essences.

With a coldness of temperament transmitted from his mother, all the circumstances of his early life collaborated to produce detachment, personal and speculative. Both his father and his maternal grandfather were Liberals, anti-monarchists and anti-clericals, forced to conceal their admiration for Locke, Rousseau and Manchester economics, and to live circumspectly, by their status as petty officials of His Most Catholic Majesty. Young Santayana took over their philosophic enlightenment and their passivity without the suppressed ardor for reform. The long residence of his parents in the Philippines supplied a background of tropical languor, reinforced by dysentery, to the family's outlook on life. Add to these his marginal position as a foreigner and a poor in-law often invited to dinner by Bostonian merchant princes, and as a Catholic aesthete and poetic materialist among the Unitarians, and it is not matter for wonder that his critics should accuse him of holding to a spectator theory of knowledge. His detachment has been, however, an affair of inner detachment and not of monastic withdrawal from the world. He tells us that he has liked to dress well and go out in society; if his closest friendships are candidly admitted to have contained a large element of convenience, he sketches a long gallery of acquaintances, mediocre and great; and he insists that even in old age his mind has not acquired the Olympianism of an elderly Goethe but is seasoned with "salt, pepper and pity for mankind." His Apollonian aloofness, he tells us, has always been tempered by a Dionysian sympathy with the flux of things, which leads him to acknowledge the rightness, relative to their own conditions, of forms of life which he would not care to imitate.

These two tendencies have both enriched his moral philosophy and created contradictions which he has not been able to resolve. The Dionysian or relativistic strain enables him to write appreciatively of the ideals of America and of old Spain alike, though in both cases at a psychic distance, as from the vantage point of a highly instructed tourist. He is impressed by the sporting temper of Americans, their kindliness and their capacity to fulfill their desires through the magic of an elaborate commercial system built on trust. He also justifies the somnambulistic ritual of Spanish provincial life, with its saint days and fiestas, its resignation to poverty and disease:

> How much respect did these grave, disillusioned, limited people of Avila have for their conventions, and in particular for their religion? Not much, I think, at bottom; but nothing else was practically within their range; and if

something else had been possible for them, would it have been better? The more intelligent of them would have doubted this, and resigned themselves to their daily round. What they had and what they thought they had was at least "the custom"; they could live and express themselves on those assumptions. Their inner man, in bowing to usage, could preserve its dignity. In breaking away, as the demagogues and cheap intellectuals wished them to do, they would have fallen into mental confusion and moral anarchy. Their lives would have been no better, and their judgements much worse. They could never, at the time when I knew them, have come to feel at home in a society where nothing was any longer "the custom," either in opinion or in conduct.

But a relativism of this sceptical kind is something that Santayana is unable to maintain consistently. Though each form of life may have its own justification within itself, we cannot evade the temptation, and sometimes the compulsion, to compare the outcome of each, and to assert qualitative preferences between patterns that are equally successful expressions of their respective energies. Lacking any clear principles in his philosophy which would enable him to make a reflective choice, what Santayana falls back upon is a *de gustibus;* scarcely veiled by reference to a "natural ideal":

> I bore "Uncle James" a grudge. In the first place I didn't like him: and the world is rather sharply divided for me into the people I like and the people I don't like. Philosophy and charity counsel me to correct this caprice, and I don't theoretically build on it; but it persists in my inner feeling, and it is not wholly arbitrary. I dislike the people I dislike for some reason; they offend some natural ideal within me. For I do not either like or dislike people interestedly but absolutely disinterestedly, artistically, erotically: and thus their harmony or disharmony with my psychic impulse has its human importance. After all I am a man: what I like and dislike probably is, fundamentally, what any honest reflective person would like or dislike. "Uncle James" never offended me personally or did me any intentional harm; he would have been kind to me, like all the Sturgises, if there had been any occasion; nevertheless I didn't like him. He had a full round beard, and I cannot like that. . . . Moreover, "Uncle James" was cordial. This is the well-meant American substitute for being amiable; but it won't do.

The reference to Uncle James's beard may suggest that this particular application of Santayana's qualitative standards is whimsical, but the method is retained when more momentous judgments are at stake.

Santayana's critics, especially those of the pragmatic persuasion, will attribute this and other *impasses* of his philosophy to his insufficient recognition of the operational or conative side of knowledge. But similar confusions arise in those philosophies which conceive human nature more strenuously, and the same problems of choice confront those ethical systems which conceive the good life to consist in the integration or co-ordination of motor urges. So that his aesthetic detachment is not primarily responsible for this gap in his doctrine, whatever incompleteness it may produce in his view of life as a whole.

The aesthetic or contemplative emphasis was, indeed, less exclusive during the period when Santayana wrote *The Life of Reason* than it has been since he became foot-loose in Europe. *The Life of Reason,* which most of his readers still prefer as the most complete and balanced statement of his philosophy, though not his most brilliant, was written while as a teacher of undergraduates he was forced to participate in some kind of corporate responsibility. American bustle and practicality, and the association with William James, may have influenced Santayana's thinking much more than he is willing to recognize, and have kept him from that absorption in the realm of essence which has generated the philosophy of his last thirty years.

But this may be one of those cases where originality is to be preferred to many-sidedness and completeness. Excessive detachment is not a pole to which American philosophers, or indeed Occidental philosophers in general, have inclined. We may feel in Santayana's case, as in that of other philosophers, that his doctrines need to be corrected and supplemented, without wishing to change him. For he has explored an aspect of living that has not been given its due place by our idealisms and pragmatisms.

As to the rest, he has written about himself frankly and honestly, and he has given us material by which to judge his limitations as well as his excellences:

> The lady who said many years later that she envied me for not having a conscience, didn't altogether misread me. Like my mother I have firmness of character; and I don't understand how a rational creature can be wrong in doing what he fundamentally wishes to be or do. He may make a mistake about it, or about the circumstances; or he may be imperfectly integrated, and tossed between contrary desires, not knowing his own nature or what he really wants. Experience and philosophy have taught me that perfect integrity is an ideal never fully realized, that nature is fluid and chaotic in the last resort, even in the most heroic soul; and I am ashamed and truly repentant if ever I find that I have been dazed and false to myself either in my conduct or in my opinions. In this sense I am not without a conscience; but I accept nobody's precepts traversing my moral freedom.

An heir to the Puritans, at however far remove, will find that the apple is red and round, and has a worm hole. But the hole has not been stopped with plaster and enamelled.

[*The Middle Span*]

Adrienne Koch

Were moral virtues, as commonly understood, part of the story of Mr. Santayana's life, one could wholeheartedly praise the subdued and chastened ego manifested there. Amiable, enthralled and yet cool, his temperament cannot endure the weight of reflexive elation. Not that the ego is neutral to Santayana or to his philosophy. On the contrary, it is ever-present in sense, as sense is in the character of real events, real persons and places. In each outward sign, the ego has earlier taken hold and cried, "Halt"; in each trance of the memory—aesthetically recreating the incompletely lived past—the ego drinks a deeper draft of evanescent experience, appearing the while oblivious of itself. Self and not-self, man and the cosmos are thus ideally commingled, and through the record of persons and places Mr. Santayana has artfully suggested himself. This is biography in that moral mode which Santayana has brought to modern philosophy. It is natural and ideal, personal and objective, detached and irrationally devoted, animalism and scepticism in one. The realms of essence and matter (in Santayana's sense of the terms) meet here in poetic preoccupation with personal "truth." At last we find Santayana at home, in a world of his own creating.

It may be because of the loneliness which is the burden of a unique imagination, that *The Middle Span* is haunted by the shadow of a man *déraciné*. In this respect, Santayana, poet laureate among contemporary philosóphers, becomes less than his stylized, professional writings had led his admirers to believe he would be. He seems a little out at the elbow on the Harvard campus. He admits he is baffled by Germany. Intrigued by visits to France, he knows the shallowness of intellectual *causerie* and café-bred impressionism. Attracted by London, he sadly confesses that he is drawn to what is exactly opposite to his own nature, and that in striving to fit in, he can achieve, at best, a second-hand imitation of healthy English dogmatism. Not truly at home, therefore in London, in Boston, or in his native Avila, even the cosmic at-homeness of a stout-hearted stoic is denied to Santayana, for he is too exacting in his knowledgeable tastes to suffer happily the variegated manifestations of the brotherhood of man. Sampling and savoring with lucid restraint, Santayana deserts his finicky critique of men and cities only for the over-appreciation of his "young" friends (who are essentially boring) and for

Reprinted from "Baroque-Rococo," *Sewanee Review* 53 (Autumn 1945): 677–80.

the under-appreciation of academic colleagues (who must have been more than he allows them). Yet even in the midst of enthusiasm or vindictiveness, one is conscious of the author's censor, just barely hidden beneath the surface of each line, and somehow painfully embarrassed at the rude assertion of his own "lower" nature.

Santayana creates the illusion, in this autobiography, of having seen himself in the round, perpetually. He appears to be both more aware of his weaknesses and better able to describe them qualitatively than could any outsider. By thus reversing the usual character of leniency, the unreal interlude between his youth and his age is loosened from conventional moorings. Narrative and chronology, in the ordinary sense, are informally ignored, the better to encourage the reminiscence of a philosophical spirit with "a capacity to worship and a capacity to laugh."

Either for this or other reasons, bafflement comes and goes, between page and chapter, transmitted to the reader sometimes by what is explicitly said, sometimes by what Santayana prefers to leave explicitly unsaid. One hesitates, not quite knowing why, to frame the usual judgments about the lack of pride which permits this poet-philosopher to be bullied, taunted, and used as polite auditor by the extraverted sportsman, the second Earl Russell ("Bertie" Russell's elder brother, now dead). To what ethos should one apply for a sage who once said he would have been the same "no matter under what sky I might have been born"? The usual responses, the usual opinions are equally echoes of a universe not his own. Rarely has a philosopher sympathized so bloodlessly and with such cunning knowledge with the motives of the women he knew, all women of considerable duplicity and style. Yet he is unquestionably not engaged by them, except in their aesthetic and moral individuality, or in their totality, as a distinct sex. Susana, his sister, is placed on the same pitiless surgical table, as is his near-cousin in Spain, who, out of a gentle lassitude, cultivates "designs" on him, as are the Boston "ladies" presented to him as excellent choices for marriage—the latter an idea upon which Santayana hardly comments, except to speculate that were he to have wed, he would have required a wife both Catholic and Spanish in some heterodox way! Finally, in an altogether different direction, how can the stern judge of his own shortcomings permit himself the affected pose of wise discrimination in political affairs—a realm, rightly or wrongly, irrelevant to Santayana's interests, and generative of a heat he is clearly not fitted to survive.

Here and there, between the true deep and cultivated depths of Santayana's introspective musing, are shoals of an alarming shallowness. The reader, likely to tire of gossip about "younger Harvard friends" and the habit of contemplative portraiture applied unsparingly to worthy and unworthy alike, may suddenly realize that the philosopher has put his best life into his books—his great *Life of Reason,* his *Scepticism and Animal Faith,* and parts of the more inbred *Realms of Being.* The flesh and blood of the aesthete, engrafted and circulating in these inspired created beings, are deficient in his autobiography which only breathes fully when passages of insight or reason plagiarize the accents of his own structured philosophical organon.

There is revelation in Santayana's statement that the baroque and rococo cannot be foreign to his "Spanish" nature: "They are profoundly congenial and Quixotic, suspended as it were between two contrary insights: that in the service of love and imagination nothing can be too lavish, too sublime, or too festive; yet that all this passion is a caprice, a force, a contortion, a comedy of illusions." They are indeed the contrary impulses of Santayana's unhappy self, which would celebrate the ritual of love, without loving, and simultaneously stand aside, face averted in the twisted smile of full understanding: that what is nature is not this, and what is not natural is neither rooted nor profound.

[*The Middle Span*]

Malcolm Cowley

The second volume of George Santayana's memoirs—he calls it *The Middle Span*[1]—is shorter than the first, and the substance of it seems thinner, too. He is dealing now with the quarter-century between his graduation from Harvard in 1886 and his sudden resignation as a professor in 1912. This is the ground that he has gone over before: he wrote about some of his students in his one novel, *The Last Puritan,* and about James and Royce, his two great colleagues of the Philosophy Department, in a volume of lectures, *Character and Opinion in the United States.* But there was more to be said concerning his own connection with Harvard in those years, and Santayana has omitted too much of it. He tells us almost nothing, for example, about the young writers who were students in his courses or visitors to his various rooms in the Yard. Some of them would play a considerable part in the abortive renaissance of the 1890's, or in the literature of political protest during the early 1900's, or in the revolt against the genteel tradition that began about 1910. During all three decades, Harvard continued to serve as a nursery for American writers, as it had served in the greater days of New England; and it was not until 1917 or thereabouts that poets and novelists in throngs began to appear from other colleges: first Princeton and Yale, in the war years; then Chicago, Vanderbilt, California, Michigan. . . . As long as Santayana remained at Harvard, he helped to set the tone for writing there, not only by his lectures, which were popular with the literary set, but also by his poems, his poetry readings, his philosophical essays and his legendary conversation at the dinners of the O.K. Society. Yet there is so little mention of literature in his memoirs that at one point he stops to apologize.

"I have commemorated many American friends," he says, "and not one man of letters, not one poet." By way of atonement, he then devotes three lonesome pages to his friend Trumbull Stickney, who might have been a great poet except that he lived in the wrong age and died too soon. There were other poets at Harvard in those years: Edwin Arlington Robinson and Robert Frost, to mention only two; but both of these were poor boys, socially unrecognized, and they were not likely to attract Santayana's attention. As a young instructor, he liked to associate with the college swells. He was pleased when the O.K., which had been started as a literary society, began to

Reprinted from "Santayana in Society," *New Republic,* 30 April 1945, 591–92.

admit athletes and Gold Coast politicians. He said in the first volume of his memoirs: "I liked to feel a spark of sympathy pass from those sound simple active heirs of the dominant class to my secret philosophy: and sometimes the spark did pass, and in both directions." He was a snob in those days, to put the matter bluntly, and later he tried to excuse himself. "It might seem," he said, "that all my life I have been 'sponging' on my rich friends, or even that I have sought rich friends for that purpose. This was not the case: there were plenty of rich people about that I fled from. But with people with whom I was otherwise in sympathy, friendship was naturally more easily kept up and cemented if they had a house where they could ask me to stay, or could invite me to be their guest, partly or wholly, for trips or entertainments that I couldn't afford if left to my own resources." Elsewhere he often praises the simple life—"Anything suffices," he says, "if nothing else is demanded"— and he makes you think of Oscar Wilde's remark that his own tastes were simple, he wanted only the best.

He valued kind hearts, and valued them all the more if they beat under coronets. The highest moment in his undergraduate career was when he received a visit from the second Earl Russell, who had been directed to Santayana's room by one of his rich friends. As the young earl looked out of the window, Santayana says, "at the muddy paths and shabby grass, the elms standing scattered at equal intervals, the ugly factory-like buildings and the loud-voiced youths passing by, dressed like shop assistants, I could well conceive his thoughts, and I said apologetically that after Oxford all this must seem to him rather mean; and he replied curtly, 'Yes, it does.' " Santayana was not in the least offended. He went on to explain, so he says, "our manner of life, our social distinctions, our choice of studies, our sports, our food, our town amusements. He listened politely, obviously rather entertained and not displeased to find that, according to my description, all I described might be dismissed forever without further thought." It was the beginning of a friendship that lasted forty-five years, until John Francis Stanley Russell died and the earldom passed to his younger brother Bertrand, the philosopher. Santayana had only two complaints against his friend. The first was "that being the heir to so many privileges he should appreciate them so little, and should use the strength that he derived from tradition in deriding tradition and destroying it"—in brief, that he joined the Labor Party. The second wasn't that he got himself involved in curious love affairs—with two sisters at once, Santayana implies, and again with a mother and a daughter—but rather that he couldn't keep his wives and mistresses out of court. "A young man with a brilliant career open to him in the world is a fool to flout public opinion," Santayana says, "even if he secretly despises it. Peace with the polite world is all-important for one's comfort and euphoria so long as one lives in the polite world."

Peace with the polite world and the political world and all the reigning powers is a central point in Santayana's philosophy. He describes himself as "a materialist, cynic and Tory."—"Regal and priestly grandeur," he says, "even dimly suggested, has always impressed me." He wept at one of Queen Victoria's processions, and when he first trod the steps of Windsor Castle, it was "not without profound emotion." For all his Anglomania, he also admired the provincial nobility of Boston; and he was even willing, as an instructor, to accept and observe the social judgments of Harvard undergraduates. The proudest moment of his teaching career seems not to have been the publication of *The Sense of Beauty,* his first philosophical work, and neither was it his formal appointment to the faculty; instead of these, it was his election as a graduate member of the Gas House, then the most elegant of the so-called "waiting clubs." In his rooms he used to give poetry readings, chiefly to club members. Once he tried to introduce his friend Trumbull Stickney to these readings—"But no," he says, "it wouldn't do. Julian confidentially informed me that 'the others didn't like him.' Why not? Because he had mentioned the sunset and called it 'gorgeous.' " Santayana bowed to their judgment and excluded the one gifted poet who might have attended their poetry evenings. Their standards were false and foolish, he felt, but it would also be foolish to object to them. Precisely by not objecting, he confirmed and strengthened the false standards. Those were the days when Harvard was afflicted with a multiplicity of caste distinctions: Yard against Gold Coast; clubs against fraternities against the great mass of the unaffiliated and unrecognized. Santayana had nothing to do with founding the system, but in one sense he bears a little of the responsibility for it: that is, he approved it, followed its rules, and gave it the support of his prestige as a philosopher.

That is part of the story he tells between the lines of his memoirs; but besides this comedy of manners there are also hints of a private drama with painful overtones. Apparently the year 1896 marked a crisis in Santayana's life. "My young friends," he says, "had become too young for me and I too old for them; I had made a private peace with all religions and philosophies; and I had grown profoundly weary of polite society and casual gayeties." After taking a year's leave of absence, which he spent at the English Cambridge, he returned to Harvard; but he had lost his belief in teaching together with most of his social ambitions; indeed, he suggests that the next fifteen years were a somnambulistic period in his life and one he would like to forget. On receiving a legacy in 1912, he at once resigned his professorship and sailed for Europe, never to return.

The period that followed will be described in the third volume of his memoirs. On the whole it was happier and more productive than his last years at Harvard; and yet there seems to be something forced and almost inhuman in its serenity. He says: "For the future, I desired nothing fixed, no place in society, no circle of prescribed friends and engagements. . . . For constant company I had enough, and too much, with myself." Again he says: "The intellectual world of my time alienated me intellectually. It was a Babel of false principles and blind cravings, a zoölogical garden of the mind, and I had no desire to be one of the beasts. I wished to remain a visitor, looking in at the cages." Santayana had always regarded himself as a visitor; he had been a Spaniard in America, an American in England, an Englishman in Rome, and even his relatives in Avila, his birthplace, had regarded him as a transatlantic cousin. Now the process of alienation would be carried still further, as he watched the death struggles of Europe with little interest and less understanding. When he mentioned them at all, it would be in the voice of a Martian on earth, or rather—so little likeness do his observations bear to our own picture of events—in the voice of a strayed earthling on Mars.

[*My Host the World*]

ADRIENNE KOCH

My Host the World is Santayana's summation of his later years, in England, and after that, in Rome. The summation is achieved by way of selective recall of the characters of his friends and acquaintances. Santayana is the only contemporary philosopher to present an inner landscape of feeling, reverie, and judgment. The philosophic titans who were his friends—William James, Josiah Royce, Bertrand Russell, and even his old philosophic opponent, John Dewey—were too urgently absorbed by formal philosophic inquiry to venture such an excursion in self-analysis and consolatory memory. Their professional reserve, however, was not binding upon a man like Santayana, who did not fear poetic myth but adored it, and whose imaginative sensibilities were alive to the beauty of human experience as expressed in traditional literary forms.

The book is more, however, than a last look at things and friends. It is a last look at himself, as spectator. The opening chapter puts before us a maturing Santayana, undergoing a "change of heart" that will ultimately free him from the world, from the attempt to conquer it and court its favors. He calls attention to the personal moral quest that led him to become, in his old age, "a sort of hermit," living in the clinic of the Blue Sisters in Rome. It is clear that he deliberately created his solitude and desired this confinement, "not from fear or horror of mankind, but by sheer preference for peace and obscurity." The former Harvard professor, having found teaching a burdensome and hollow pretense, refused new appointments and turned, in late middle age, to the ageless role of philosophic contemplation. It was part of his unpredictable and mysterious personality, however, that he preferred to explore this role at first in the friendly environs of the great British universities, mingling with people of mind and talent, but rarely striking down real roots of friendship. And with increasing age, philosophic contemplation became more and more detached from individualized human beings, although never from the encompassing theme of human nature.

Neither mystic nor monk, Santayana once conceded a friend's characterization of him as a "Castilian monk," because he felt that the word "Castilian" removed all unpleasant suggestions. "The Castilian mystic," he wrote, "is vowed to an unflinching realism about the world and an unsullied alle-

Reprinted from *"My Host the World," Sewanee Review* 62 (Spring 1954): 329–34.

giance to the ideal." This is the road Santayana knew, in late middle age, he would travel. Cultivating imagination, loving it; delicately savoring the world, observing it; travelling, comparing places with places and persons with persons: this provided food for "unflinching realism." On the other hand, keeping free of the oppression of the world, its burdensome possessions, its fever not only to possess things but persons: this was the discipline leading toward the ideal. Nature, Santayana believed, must be muted before spirit can be freed.

With this thematic introduction, Santayana permits the reader to share his frank impressions of persons and places—usually distinguished, or at least intellectual, persons and charming places—although chapter headings steadily invoke a geographical frame of reference, as in "King's College, Cambridge," "Travels," "On the South Downs," "Farewell to England," "Old Age in Italy." Even that final comprehensive and unifying metaphor, "My Host the World," indicates that places are transcended, in the speculative vision of the philosopher, for the world; and concrete persons, with their disillusioning imperfections, for a mythical and poetic essence: "my host."

Before persons are transcended or mythologized, their concrete existences are very strikingly interpreted by Santayana's barbed pen. His marked talent for literary psychology is ruthlessly but triumphantly evident in aphoristic sketches of the character of Bertrand Russell, Lord Acton, Robert Bridges, Lowes Dickinson and many others. For example, of the young Lytton Strachey, a fellow weekend-guest at Lady Ottoline's, Santayana commented: ". . . a caricature of Christ; a limp cadaverous creature, moving feebly, with lank long brown hair and the beginnings of a beard much paled in colour, and spasmodic treble murmurs of a voice utterly weary and contemptuous. *Obscene* was the character written all over him; and his expertness in secret history and in satire expressed that character intellectually." Much of the comment is brilliantly correct; but some is cruel, unjust, gossipy, and twisted out of focus by Santayana's own renunciations or constitutional limitations. One imagines a distressing gestalt of pouts, frowns, and contemptuous glances that may have marred the countenance of a "Castilian monk" pursuing that peace which is "an orchestration of transcended sorrows."

In truth, he cares less for persons and places than for the symbolic occasions they provide to reflect on the morality of man and the world. These symbolic associations dominate the events, or the eventlessness, of his life. Santayana therefore does not present a "life" in the normal sense—he is without love, without country, without real attachments or friendship. His Platonized affections for Avila, the little Spanish town where he was born, for example; or for his sister; or for Harvard and Oxford; or the young and old men, the scholars, writers, and philosophers who were counted as friends on both sides of the Atlantic: to all, Santayana offered a cool heart, overly subdued by his head.

This enigmatic quality of Santayana's is also reflected in the Olympian detachment he maintained from the political crises and turmoils of his and our time. *My Host the World* sums up very succinctly Santayana's contempt for the modern world. "The contemporary world has turned its back on the attempt and even on the desire to live reasonably. The two great wars (so far) of the twentieth century were adventures in enthusiastic unreason. They were inspired by unnecessary and impacticable ambitions; and the 'League' and the 'United Nations' feebly set up by the victors were so irrationally conceived that they at once reduced their victory to a stalemate. What is required for living rationally? . . . First, self-knowledge, the Socratic key to wisdom; and second, sufficient knowledge of the world to perceive what alternatives are open to you and which of them are favourable to your true interests." On Santayana's reading of the score, the modern world has revealed a positively insane abandonment of its true interests. Perhaps the modern world deserves such contempt, and the judgment, while not sufficiently fine, is not substantially wrong. But it is empty of compassion and of the concern which breathes hope and good will into action—and into that commitment that urges men on to the next historic effort.

These observations only furnish fresh proof that it was only to ideal objects that Santayana ever pledged his troth. Rich fruit of that marriage, everlasting fruit, he has left for those who taste apple wine in the shadowy realm of spirit. It is not necessary, therefore, to underline the temperamental defects of passion, action, compassion and love that conditioned this mating. Whatever we can intuit here, Santayana knew and suggested for us infinitely better. This is the reason, he tells us, that Rome, the eternal city, closes the journey and completes the quest. Not because Italy and Rome were a last resort, Santayana says. They were his first choice, "my ideal point of vantage in thought, the one anthropological centre, where nature and art were most beautiful, and mankind least distorted from their complete character." Here Santayana entered upon old age with a joyousness that had not characterized his earlier years. In an unforgettable passage he writes: "Nothing is inherently and invincibly young except spirit. And spirit can enter a human being perhaps better in the quiet of old age and dwell there more undisturbed than in the turmoil of adventure. But it must be solitude. . . . In Rome, in the eternal city, I feel nearer to my own past, and to the whole past and future of the world, than I should in any cemetery or in any museum of relics. Old places and old persons in their turn, when spirit dwells in them, have an intrinsic vitality of which youth is incapable; precisely the balance and wisdom that comes from long perspectives and broad foundations."

The subtle web of beauty which caught the musings and idea-play of George Santayana while he lived and wrote is now spun. Santayana's whole work is, as he would have preferred to think, not a "unity" but "complete." With the possible exception of an intricate translation that absorbed the poetic passion of the aged philosopher's last days, a pastoral poem, "Ambra," by Lorenzo de Medici, there is nothing more to expect—unless one can count the shortened revised edition of his great masterpiece, *The Life of Reason,* as, in some sense, new.

Why did Santayana, in his eighty-seventh year, already very ill, blind in one eye and with eyesight failing in the other, deaf, virtually confined to his room in the nursing home of the Blue Sisters, choose to struggle with forty-eight rhymed stanzas of an old Italian poem, determined to create a parallel English poem, faithful to the Italian form in all its technical complexities? The poem concerns a river-god named Ombron, who is enamored of a virginal dryad, Ambra. Ombron passionately pursues Ambra, but is thwarted, in the near victory of capture, by her appeal to Diana for help. Diana, heeding Ambra's call, transforms her into a granite statue on a little island in the river, where the river-god thenceforth must see her, to his overwhelming sorrow and shame. A few days before Santayana died, he confided to his friend, Daniel Cory, that his only remaining wish was to live to complete the translation of "Ambra."

Was it not because this poem would be sign and symbol, the embodied artistic reality of the truth that Santayana had striven to present, from different vistas, in his life's work? He was primarily a moral philosopher, interested in truth as man sees it and must construct it; and in the limits nature places on what man can pursue, attain, know, and keep. What Santayana valued in thought was what he valued in life: his progress towards truth was always a personal quest for integrity, for completion without fanaticism. The philosophy which he prized was one that entertained myth, corrected by disillusion, and scepticism, by sincerity. The critical work of reason, the preoccupation of what he called the "psyche" with the inexhaustible realm of essences, he took to be the primary activity of moral man. But this reverence for the highest phase of man's development, the pursuit of the ideal, Santayana never freed from its natural setting. And *his* naturalism, unlike other varieties, did not exclude religion: it allowed for it as locally, mythically, poetically true. (It was in this sense that he found his Catholic surroundings attractive and good; literally and technically he had no "belief" whatsoever in Catholicism as the one true religion.) A few days before he died, Santayana turned to his friend Cory and said that he had always tried to take into account two worlds in his philosophy: the natural world, which could be traced in part by science, with its method of controlled observation; and the "other" world of the imagination, "which I personally like the best." The important thing, Santayana concluded, is not to drown yourself in either of these worlds, for both are essential for any philosophy "digne de son nom."

There is something unfailingly moving in a philosopher who knows how to accept old age and knows even better how to die. Santayana's whole long experience can be seen as the odyssey of illuminated reason on that cosmic stage, the world. With affecting charm, Santayana confesses that he has selected from his experience those fragments of life that remain alive in memory, "free glimpses of the world that I could love and could carry away . . . my consolations." These hardened amber tears and glowing pleasures recollected in old age contrast sadly with "the vast obscure inexorable world." The essence of Santayana's humanistic vision is that the world will be host to man although it is not made for him. Much prudence and art are required in living out one's life here, as guest. And just as persons and places "individuate" the world and the psyche projects their ideal phases into the realm of spirit, so a temporary traveller here can work his way to a final emancipation from the egotism and passion of restless living. Death then becomes the liberation of the spirit, the hard-won grant to travel unimpeded among ideal essences. This vision is celebrated in an eloquent prose poem that concludes this book and may be taken as the key to all his work.

"Had it happened in my time (as by chance it did happen) that my landlord should give me notice that he was about to pull down his roof over my head, I might have been a little troubled for a moment; but presently I should have begun to look for other lodgings not without a certain curious pleasure, and probably should have found some (as I did, and better ones) in which to end my days. So, I am confident, will the travelling Spirit do—this ever-renewed witness, victim, and judge of existence, divine yet born of woman. Obediently it will learn other affections in other places, unite other friends, and divide other peoples; and the failure of over-exact hopes and overweening ambitions will not prevent spirit from continually turning the passing virtues and sorrows of nature into glimpses of eternal truth."

Santayana on Shakespeare

JOHN M. MAJOR

During a long and fruitful career devoted chiefly to philosophy, George Santayana found time to produce a considerable body of literary criticism, much of which is now available to the reader in a single volume.[1] As a critic of literature, especially of English and American literature, Santayana possessed unusual qualifications. He was of course primarily a philosopher—a moral philosopher, by his own admission—and in this capacity he would insist, often sternly, that literature and the other arts, since they are created by and for civilized men, must observe those laws of reason and moral health without which a civilization cannot long endure. No work of art may be called great, he asserted, unless it has "substance, sanity, and even a sort of pervasive wisdom" (Singer, p. 187). Elsewhere he explicitly states that "every artist is a moralist, though he need not preach."[2] At times Santayana applies this philosophic touchstone to literature so relentlessly as to impair the value of his judgments; on the whole, however, intellectual severity is balanced by the sympathy, insight, and mastery of literary technique which are proper to a man who was himself poet and novelist.

He is, for example, very much attuned to the sensuous quality of literature, and in dealing with such matters as form and imagery and language he can be as exacting as any critic of our own day. To a young author who had sent him a volume of his poems, Santayana wrote that he objected to "two or three impurities of idiom," and then added: "You will think this hypercritical; but, when I read poetry, I expect 'integras accedere fontes', else I am not satisfied."[3] In one of his early essays we come upon a principle sacred to our contemporary critics: that criticism aims to reach a "total appreciation" of the work of art, that the critic's function "is precisely to feel and to confront all values, bringing them into relation, and if possible into harmony."[4] Not only does Santayana give recognition to this vital principle, but he also for the most part adheres to it in his own critical endeavors.

To be at once a philosopher and a poet ought to be a definite advantage in a literary critic. To have the outlook of a highly sophisticated Latin would seem to be an additional advantage, though some Americans have not thought so.[5] It must be admitted that Santayana's affinities with Mediterranean culture, both ancient and modern, sometimes issue, in his comments on

Reprinted from *Shakespeare Quarterly* 10 (Autumn 1959): 469–79, with the permission of the publisher.

art, in a sterile classicism or a petty prejudice against the barbarian North. His judgments all too often seem to derive from the equation: the art of the South, or classic art, has sanity, idealism, serenity, beauty of form, and ultimate meaning; the art of the North, otherwise called romanticism, and in its worst state, barbarism, is little more valuable than the creations of gifted children—energetic, expansive, primary, and painted in flashing colors, but also turbid, shapeless, fragmentary, unenlightened and unenlightening. It is just here, in this quaint and slightly malicious "regionalism" and in his excessive respect for tradition, that Santayana is weakest as a critic. Still, we of the North can perhaps benefit from having our beliefs challenged and our idols regarded without awe by a brilliant foreigner, who moreover has lived among us and excelled in our language. He can aid in our emancipation, in much the same way as our reading of the classics, Thoreau reminds us, can liberate us from our little surroundings and our brief moment in time.

The excursions of this philosopher-poet-classicist into the alien territory of English and American literature—or that part of it which interested him—are recorded in a series of essays notable for their acuteness, their severity, their perversity, their inconsistency, and their dazzling style. They range from Shakespeare to Robert Lowell; they return most often to Shakespeare among English authors and (odd choice, it may seem) to Whitman among the Americans. In the remarks on Shakespeare one sees illustrated most clearly, perhaps, both the merits and shortcomings of this rarest of twentieth-century American critics. Furthermore, the Shakespearian criticism of Santayana, for all its shifting about, deserves to be recognized, I think, as some of the most interesting our century has produced.

Brief comments on Shakespeare are to be found in the earliest of Santayana's books, *The Sense of Beauty,* published in 1896. In that work he follows Matthew Arnold in observing that Shakespeare excels in ethos, or expression, rather than in plot, and is for that reason (it is plainly implied) inferior to the Greek dramatists. He agrees with Aristotle that plot is "the most important element in the effect of a drama," and he attributes the supremacy of the expressive element in modern drama to "the romantic tendency of modern times." "What the great characterizers, like Shakespeare, do," he concludes, "is simply to elaborate and develope (perhaps far beyond the necessities of the plot) the suggestion of human individuality which that plot contains. . . . This is an ingenious and fascinating invention, and delights us with the clear discovery of a hidden personality; but the serious and equable development of a plot has a more stable worth in its greater similarity to life, which allows us to see other men's minds through the medium of events, and not events through the medium of other men's minds."[6] This belief in the primary significance of plot in drama is akin to another thesis of Santayana's, that "indeterminateness of form is fatal to beauty, and, if extreme, even to expressiveness" (*Sense of Beauty,* p. 143)—a thesis, incidentally, which he never abandoned, and which largely accounts for his hostility to modern art.

In these remarks on Shakespeare from *The Sense of Beauty* one hears the voice of the classicist mainly. When Santayana next passes judgment on the poet, in "The Absence of Religion in Shakespeare," he wears his philosopher's robe, of a rather somber hue. The theme of the book in which this essay appears—*Interpretations of Poetry and Religion* (1900)—is that "poetry raised to its highest power is . . . identical with religion grasped in its inmost truth" (Singer, p. 303). In another essay from the same volume, "The Elements and Function of Poetry," Santayana makes clear what are for him the conditions of the "highest" poetry:

> Where poetry rises from its elementary and detached expressions in rhythm, euphuism, characterisation, and story-telling, and comes to the consciousness of its highest function, that of portraying the ideals of experience and destiny, then the poet becomes aware that he is essentially a prophet, and either devotes himself, like Homer or Dante, to the loving expression of the religion that exists, or like Lucretius or Wordsworth, to the heralding of one which he believes to be possible. Such poets are aware of their highest mission; others, whatever the energy of their genius, have not conceived their ultimate function as poets. They have been willing to leave their world ugly as a whole, after stuffing it with a sufficient profusion of beauties. (Singer, p. 301)

From this short roster of "prophetic poets" the name of Shakespeare is conspicuously absent; and when we read that characterization is only an "elementary" quality in poetry, we recall that in *The Sense of Beauty* Shakespeare was designated merely a "great characterizer." The reasons for Shakespeare's failure to qualify as a supreme poet are given at length in "The Absence of Religion in Shakespeare," but before discussing that essay I should like to point out that the passage last quoted illustrates as well as any other Santayana's strongly philosophic, even moralistic, bias as a critic of literature.[7] To some of us it would appear that his insistence on moral or religious significance in the greatest poetry, while more precisely defined than Arnold's doctrine of "high seriousness," is no less one-sided, exclusive, and even reactionary. However, as we shall see, Santayana gradually outgrew this early doctrinaire attitude toward literature.

One virtue in a critic which Santayana seems always to have possessed in full measure is courage. His devastating attack on the philosophies of Whitman and Browning, which was later to appear as a chapter of *Poetry and Religion,* was originally delivered in person around the year 1900 before the Browning Club of Boston.[8] A like temerity is perhaps shown in "The Absence of Religion in Shakespeare" and a later essay entitled "Hamlet" (1908), since these "were written at a time when a blind Shakespeareolatry was more prevalent than it is now, and when A. C. Bradley was convincing a considerable section of the scholarly public that Shakespeare was a great philosopher."[9] "The Absence of Religion in Shakespeare," after a brief tribute to the poet's many-sided genius, proceeds quickly to the argument that in his plays and sonnets there is an almost complete insensibility to religion, for which reason he must be denied a place among the greatest poets. Homer and Dante, who are types of the greatest poets, "gave us man with his piety and the world with its gods." These poets "live in a cosmos"; their universe is "a total." "Reason and imagination have mastered it completely and peopled it. No chaos remains beyond. . . . They have a theory of human life; they see man in his relations, surrounded by a kindred universe in which he fills his allotted place. He knows the meaning and issue of his life, and does not voyage without a chart." Shakespeare's world, in contrast, "is only the world of human society. The cosmos eludes him; he does not seem to feel the need of framing that idea. He depicts human life in all its richness and variety, but leaves that life without a setting, and consequently without a meaning." The sum of Shakespeare's philosophy of man, called by Santayana positivism, is set forth in Macbeth's grim speech beginning "Tomorrow, and tomorrow, and tomorrow."[10]

Though few would agree that Shakespeare held exclusively the beliefs of any single character of his creation, or that religious certitude is essential to great poetry, many of us would have to admire the skill with which Santayana illustrates his point about the absence of a religious view in Shakespeare and answers objections that might be raised on the grounds that Shakespeare was a dramatist and not an epic poet. On the other hand, when Santayana begins to explain this absence by a theory similar to Arnold's in *Culture and Anarchy*, his argument becomes somewhat blurred. Christianity, he maintains, has never succeeded in expressing itself in any adequate drama because in the Christian (or modern) civilization, art and experience have suffered a separation, culture being drawn from one source, classical antiquity, and religion from another, Christianity itself. In Shakespeare's time and country, moreover, "to be religious already began to mean to be Puritanical; and in the divorce between the fulness of life on the one hand and the depth and unity of faith on the other, there could be no doubt to which side a man of imaginative instincts would attach himself. A world of passion and beauty without a meaning must seem to him more interesting and worthy than a world of empty principle and dogma, meagre, fanatical, and false" (Singer, p. 145). It seems evident from this passage that Santayana had come under the influence of Taine's theory that literature depends upon the race, moment, and milieu that produced it, and is therefore rigorously determined.[11] Thus, although Santayana, as a life-long enemy of Puritanism and genteelism, can fully sympathize with Shakespeare's indifference to a religion based on these values (as Santayana sees it to have been), yet he cannot or will not allow his standards of artistic perfection to yield to the laws that bind the poet to circumstance, and so consigns Shakespeare to the second rank, victim of a faulty age.

At one point in the essay Santayana's regional or racial prejudice asserts itself in a rather unpleasant way. When we think of the "luminous philosophy" and well-digested experience of a Homer or a Dante, he writes, "the silence of Shakespeare and his philosophical incoherence have something in them that is still heathen; something that makes us wonder whether the northern mind, even in him, did not remain morose and barbarous at its inmost core" (Singer, p. 142).

A more serious fault, perhaps, is that in this indictment of Shakespeare for having no religion, the critic seems to forget the view of tragedy which he himself has set forth in a companion essay in the same volume. The essence of tragedy, it is stated there, is "the sense of a finished life, of the will fulfilled and enlightened." This enlightenment "is not a matter of theory or of moral maxims; the enlightenment by which tragedy is made sublime is a glimpse into the ultimate destinies of our will. This discovery need not be an ethical gain—Macbeth and Othello attain it as much as Brutus and Hamlet—it may serve to accentuate despair, or cruelty, or indifference, or merely to fill the imagination for a moment without much affecting the permanent tone of the mind."[12] Consistency, as we shall see more than once, is not one of Santayana's strong points.

In spite of its eccentricities, however, "The Absence of Religion in Shakespeare" remains a brilliantly provocative essay. It shows to advantage what Mrs. Leavis has suggested is Santayana's special usefulness as a critic of English (and American, we might add) literature: his skeptical detachment from the entire "insular Nordic Protestant" system of values.[13]

In Santayana's next important work bearing on literature, *Reason in Art* (1905), Shakespeare fares somewhat better. The ideal held up in this work is "rational poetry," a species which, although not altogether unknown—indeed, in every poet there is some "fidelity to nature"—is nevertheless rare, even the greatest poetry suffering an adulteration from "irrelevant false fancy." The requirements of rational poetry are mastery and idealization: "mastery, to see things as they are and dare to describe them ingenuously; idealisation, to select from this reality what is pertinent to ultimate interests and can speak eloquently to the soul."[14] Homer, according to Santayana, succeeded better than anyone else in writing rational poetry, although even he found it necessary to resort to mythology (one kind of "irrelevant false fancy") in order to express his genius. (Here the critic seems to be guilty of another inconsistency; in *Poetry and Religion* he had declared Homer to be a great poet *because* Homer, like Dante, celebrated the existing religion.) By the side of a Homeric epithet, a Shakespearian metaphor seems to Santayana "violent and crude." Still, Shakespeare is not without his moments. "Shakespeare, too, beneath his occasional absurdities of plot and diction, ennobles his stage with actual history, with life painted to the quick, with genuine human characters, politics, and wisdom" (*Reason in Art,* p. 113). Nothing is said about Shakespeare's ability to idealize; doubtless the lack of that ability, as brought out in "The Absence of Religion in Shakespeare," is what makes him inferior to Homer as a rational poet.

Proceeding chronologically, we come next to an essay on *Hamlet,* first published in 1908 as an introduction to the play for an edition of Shakespeare's works, and reprinted with minor changes as "Hamlet" in *Obiter Scripta* (1936). In "Hamlet" we find some of the old criticisms of Shakespeare repeated, but they are offset to a large extent by Santayana's frank admiration for the particular play. Shakespeare is again said to excel in expression rather than in plot-constructing, and to be unable to interpret the cosmos. Still, within its limits, *Hamlet* is a great work. "This picture of universal madness is relieved by the very finest and purest glints of wit, intelligence, and feeling. It is crammed with exquisite lines, and vivified by most interesting and moving characters in great variety, all drawn with masterly breadth, depth, and precision" (Singer, pp. 130, 132).

Perhaps the most stimulating part of the essay is Santayana's analysis of the character of Hamlet, whom he sees as the perfect representative of the romantic mind, victim of the discord between modern genius and modern culture. A similar idea, as we have noticed, was introduced in "The Absence of Religion in Shakespeare" to account for the failure of a Christian drama.

Toward the end of his discussion of *Hamlet* as a monument to the romantic spirit, Santayana displays a rather unexpected critical tolerance. "So absolute a feat of imagination" as this play, he remarks, "cannot be ranked in comparison with other works, nor estimated by any standard of which it does not itself furnish the suggestion and type." Had the essay ended here, Santayana's readers might have gone away pleased as well as instructed. But what Santayana gives with the one hand, he often takes away with the other. Thus the reader before being dismissed has to be reminded that, after all, *Hamlet* is a modern, romantic tragedy, and therefore deficient in wisdom: "if we care to pass . . . from admiration of the masterpiece to reflection on the experience which it expresses, we see that here is no necessary human tragedy, no universal destiny or divine law. It is a picture of incidental unfitness, of a genius wasted for being plucked quite unripe from the sunny places of the world" (Singer, pp. 135–136).

Soliloquies in England and Later Soliloquies (1922) contains one or two references to Shakespeare that are worthy of being noted. In the essay on Dickens, Shakespeare and Aristophanes are said to be "the very greatest comic poets" (Singer, p. 219); and in "Progress in Philosophy," Santayana declares that Shakespeare is the best poet the English have produced because he was the first:

> There is progress [in poetry] in that new poets arise with new gifts, and the fund of transmitted poetry is enriched; but Homer, the first poet amongst the Greeks, was also the best, and so Dante in Italy, and Shakespeare in England.

When a civilization and a language take shape they have a wonderful vitality, and their first-fruits are some love-child, some incomparable creature in whom the whole genius of the young race bursts forth uncontaminated and untrammelled. What follows is more valuable in this respect or in that; it renders fitly the partial feelings and varying fashions of a long decadence; but nothing, so long as that language and that tradition last, can ever equal their first exuberance. (*Soliloquies*, pp. 208–209)

It is agreeable to find Santayana praising Shakespeare so unreservedly, even though in reality it is not so much Shakespeare as early art that is being praised. We also observe in this passage another instance of Santayana's adherence to Taine in the interpretation of literature.

As the years passed, Santayana continued to read Shakespeare and to be both fascinated and repelled by that genius of the barbaric North. In 1932, when Santayana was in his sixty-ninth year, he wrote to Henry Ward Abbot that it was increasingly hard for him to read poetry. "I relish it only in snatches; as it comes in Shakespeare's plays, for instance. I have got a big edition of Shakespeare—for years I was without a copy—and am reading the whole through systematically. How wonderful! Yet how horribly impure, occasional, only half-lifted out of some vile plot and some ranting theatrical tradition. The best of it is that entrancing fusion of music in language with passion, colour, and homely saturation of every word in the humours of life" (*Letters*, p. 274).

The re-reading of Shakespeare's plays at this time, together with the publication in 1933 of the book *On Reading Shakespeare*, by his friend and correspondent Logan Pearsall Smith, seems to have aroused in Santayana a desire finally to pluck out the heart of Shakespeare's mystery. The conclusions of Smith's book, he writes the author, have set his mind "going furiously," and he must unburden himself of his thoughts "before the ferment dies down." For the most part these are the same thoughts Santayana had been expressing in his earlier formal writings, though they are put more succinctly. Again he is convinced that Shakespeare's chief gift was "a great fluid imagination and an enormous eloquence," and that this gift was "set free, fed, and loosened by the circumstances of the age and by his special craft as an actor and playwright." Again he is both admiring and critical of the poet's romantic wildness. "*Exuberance*," he writes, "seems to me to cover everything, the wealth of genius as well as the contempt for art; and in particular it covers the irrelevant elaboration of language and of characters which, to us, is one of Shakespeare's chief charms."

If there is little in these judgments to surprise us, we may be mildly astonished by what follows. With a splendid disregard for his own earlier pronouncements, Santayana declares to Smith that Shakespeare's philosophy was right and true. And in the bargain, he chides T. S. Eliot for denying that fact!

And this brings me back to your conclusion about his philosophy—that life is a dream. Yes, that is his philosophy: and when T. S. Eliot says that this philosophy (borrowed he thinks from Seneca) is an inferior one, compared with Dante's, I agree if you mean inferior morally and imaginatively: but it happens to be the true philosophy for the human passions, and for a man enduring, without supernaturally interpreting, the spectacle of the universe. It is a commonplace philosophy, the old old heathen philosophy of mankind. Shakespeare didn't create it. He felt it was true, and never thought of transcending it. (*Letters*, pp. 279–280)

On closer examination, Santayana's position may not have changed as radically as appears. He still ascribes to Shakespeare himself, as he had done almost forty years previously, Macbeth's philosophy in the "Tomorrow, and tomorrow, and tomorrow" speech; and he still finds that philosophy inferior "morally and imaginatively." On the other hand, there is a really striking change in his present willingness to admit that "Shakespeare's philosophy" is *dramatically* right, because it is "the true philosophy for the human passions." Thus, without actually surrendering his own beliefs, Santayana has at last arrived at a far more sympathetic, and one might say a far sounder, evaluation of Shakespeare.

The idea touched upon in the letter to Smith is developed at length in an essay entitled "Tragic Philosophy," first published in *Scrutiny* in 1936. Except for one or two occasional references in the letters and autobiography, the comments on Shakespeare in "Tragic Philosophy" are the last Santayana expressed in print. We may therefore probably regard them as the closest thing to his final formal evaluation of the poet. It is all the more gratifying, then, to discover in these comments a considerable increase in warmth, tolerance, and critical balance.

"Tragic Philosophy" begins with a rather caustic rebuke of T. S. Eliot for saying that poetically the "Tomorrow, and tomorrow, and tomorrow" speech from *Macbeth* and a line from the *Paradiso* are equally good, but that the philosophy in Shakespeare is inferior.[15] How, Santayana asks somewhat disdainfully, can one compare different types of poetry written in different languages? And how could one fail to see that a "superior" philosophy would make a poem a superior poem? There is an amusing irony in this new attitude; evidently Santayana has forgotten the occasions, in "The Absence of Religion in Shakespeare" and elsewhere, when he himself was guilty of the same critical fallacies he now blames Eliot for. Yet we are pleased to note the important change in Santayana's own critical viewpoint. For one thing, he has finally come round to distinguishing between "Shakespeare's philosophy" and the philosophies expounded by the characters in Shakespeare's dramas. "Shakespeare was not expressing," he now realizes, "a settled doctrine of his own or of his times. Like an honest miscellaneous dramatist, he was putting into the mouths of his different characters the sentiments that, for the moment, were suggested to him by their predicaments." As for the much-discussed speech of Macbeth's, Macbeth at that point in the action "sees no escape, no alternative; he cannot rise morally above himself; his philosophy is that there is no philosophy, because, in fact, he is incapable of any." To account for the general absence of a shaping philosophy in Shakespeare's plays, Santayana (relying still on the "milieu" theory of literature) offers a strange, one-sided view of the Elizabethan intellectual and spiritual climate. The age needed, he believes, "no mastering living religion, no mastering living philosophy. Life was gayer without them. Philosophy and religion were at best like travels and wars, matters for the adventurer to plunge into, or for the dramatist to describe; never in England or for Shakespeare central matters even in that capacity, but mere conventions or tricks of fancy or moods in individuals."

In discussing the passages from *Macbeth* and the *Paradiso*—which he finds "incommensurable," belonging to "different poetic worlds"—Santayana is at his best, bringing to bear on each that powerful combination of intellectual authority and literary insight that was his special gift. His conclusions show how far he has departed from opinions he held in 1900. Dante is still for him a very great poet, but "for our modern feeling the picture is too imaginative, too visionary, soaked too much in emotion. In spite of the stern historical details, when we rub our eyes and shake off the spell, the whole thing seems childishly unreal." The "disillusioned philosophy" of Shakespeare, on the other hand, and his lack of concern for Christianity are now seen to be entirely appropriate for Shakespeare's dramatic purposes:

> These considerations may help us to understand why Shakespeare, although Christianity was at hand, and Seneca, although a Platonic philosophy was at hand, based like Christianity on moral inspiration, nevertheless stuck fast in a disillusioned philosophy which Mr. Eliot thinks inferior. They stuck fast in the facts of life. They had to do so, whatever may have been their private religious convictions, because they were dramatists addressing the secular mind and concerned with the earthly career of passionate individuals, of inspired individuals, whose inspirations contradicted the truth and were shattered by it. This defeat, together with a proud and grandiloquent acceptance of it, is final for the tragic poet. His philosophy can build only on such knowledge of the world as the world can give. . . . To have allowed religion to shift the scenes, override the natural passions of men, and reverse the moral of the story, would have seemed an intolerable anticlimax. . . . I can think of only one tragedy in which religion might well play a leading part, and that is the tragedy of religion itself.[16]

Although "Tragic Philosophy" is Santayana's last formal and extended discussion of Shakespeare, some occasional remarks in the later letters and the autobiography show that his interest in the great dramatist continued to the end. Less than a year before his death he wrote to Corliss Lamont: "I have often tried to define Shakespeare's 'philosophy,' after noticing the strange absence of religion in him; but perhaps he might be set down for a Humanist or Naturalist of our sect, his ghosts and witches and Ariels being wise, sceptical inclusions of mad dreams actually visiting distressed minds" (*Letters,* p. 425). Thus the last barrier between the critic and the poet has been removed, by the mellowness attending on the critic's old age, perhaps. Shakespeare—all of him, philosopher as well as poet and playwright—is finally granted the long withheld paternal blessing. There is a touching irony in his being welcomed into the very sect that all along has sheltered the old philosopher himself.

The real warmth of Santayana's feeling in his later years for Shakespeare is movingly displayed in a passage from the final volume of his autobiography, *My Host the World,* published posthumously in 1953. He is explaining, rather ruefully, the differences between "my England"—the ideal England of his imagination—and the actual England where he spent a part of his life. For the illusion which was "my England," Shakespeare and Dickens were important sources, "and especially Shakespeare's comedies and comic scenes in the histories and tragedies." In the songs "and in Shakespeare's wit and wistfulness everywhere, I find the spirit of my England purer than in any later poet. He was not puritan, he smacked of the country air and of young blood."[17]

Looking back over this long association between critic and poet, we come to several conclusions. George Santayana in his role of critic of literature was perhaps more deeply and consistently interested in Shakespeare than in any other writer, ancient or modern. Discussions of Shakespeare, of varying length and weight, are to be found in almost everything Santayana wrote on art and literature, from *The Sense of Beauty,* published in 1896, to a letter written in 1951, a year before the philosopher's death. The most important of these discussions are the two essays, "The Absence of Religion in Shakespeare" (1900) and "Tragic Philosophy" (1936). Poles apart in their thinking, between them they illustrate the gradual change that took place in the critic's attitude, from a grudging admiration for some of Shakespeare's qualities, and a near-contempt for others, to a fondness and respect for the author almost without reservation.

This change is all the more remarkable considering Santayana's distaste for what, in his opinion (in his earlier writings, at least), characterized the Northern genius in art: spiritual and philosophic shallowness, lack of restraint, formlessness, and inelegance. Like Voltaire, Santayana thought of Shakespeare as an "inspired barbarian"; but whereas Voltaire's strictures were based on Shakespeare's alleged lack of art and taste, Santayana's derived primarily from Shakespeare's philosophy—or rather, his lack of a philosophy. For a long time Santayana was demanding of great poetry that it have a philosophic wholeness, a cosmic view, a sound morality. Because he did not find these qualities in Shakespeare, he relegated him to an inferior rank among the world's poets. In holding to this position he made the error, surprising in so astute a critic, of attributing to Shakespeare himself the philosophies of certain of Shakespeare's characters, in particular Macbeth.

These rigid views on poetry stood for a number of years, at least through Santayana's most important work on literary criticism, *Three Philosophical Poets* (1910). By 1922, however, the year of publication of *Soliloquies in England,* he had become much less demanding. In an essay from that volume entitled "On My Friendly Critics," he writes what amounts almost to a recantation:

> So anxious was I, when younger, to find some rational justification for poetry and religion, and to show that their magic was significant of true facts, that I insisted too much, as I now think, on the need of relevance to fact even in poetry. Not only did I distinguish good religion from bad by its expression of practical wisdom, and of the moral disicipline that makes for happiness in this world, but I maintained that the noblest poetry also must express the moral burden of life and must be rich in wisdom. Age has made me less exacting, and I can now find quite sufficient perfection in poetry, like that of the Chinese and Arabians, without much philosophic scope, in mere grace and feeling and music and cloud-castles and frolic. (*Soliloquies,* p. 254)

Although this new tolerance is not reflected immediately in the judgments on Shakespeare, by the time of "Tragic Philosophy" (1936) it has grown to the point where Santayana can accept wholeheartedly Shakespeare's philosophy as well as Shakespeare's poetry. The only difficulty (as Irving Singer notes) is that since Santayana never tried to reconstruct his earlier criticism, we cannot be sure how much of it he would have clung to in his later years. Nevertheless, the mere spectacle of an acute critical intelligence gradually reversing itself over the years provides much instruction as well as fascination.

At no point in his career as critic does Santayana have any reservations about Shakespeare's mastery of language, his marvelous exuberance, his skill in creating characters, or his wit and humor.

The relative narrowness and inflexibility of Santayana's earlier Shakespearian criticism may have been partly caused by his attachment to Taine's deterministic theory of literature. This attachment seems gradually to have weakened, as did also his extreme preference for classical values and the culture of the Mediterranean regions.

In summary, from Santayana's fairly extensive writings on Shakespeare, both formal and informal, one learns a great deal about his methods and his development as a critic of literature. From them one also obtains a set of brilliant, original, frank, and erratic opinions on our greatest writer.

Notes

1. George Santayana, *Essays in Literary Criticism,* ed. Irving Singer (New York, 1956). Citations from Santayana in my text are to this work (hereafter referred to as Singer), except for those writings which Singer does not include.

2. George Santayana, "The Censor and the Poet," in *Soliloquies in England and Later Soliloquies* (New York, 1923), p. 158.

3. Letter to Arthur Davison Ficke (October 24, 1910), in *The Letters of George Santayana,* ed. Daniel Cory (New York, 1955), p. 99.

4. George Santayana, "What Is Aesthetics?" (1904), in *Obiter Scripta* (New York and London, 1936), p. 40.

5. See, for example, Ludwig Lewisohn, *Expression in America* (New York and London, 1932), pp. 334–339.

6. George Santayana, *The Sense of Beauty* (New York, 1896), pp. 174–176.

7. R. P. Blackmur (in *The Double Agent,* New York, 1935, pp. 279–281) briefly examines Santayana's essay on Lucretius in *Three Philosophical Poets* (1910) as an example of criticism concerned with the "ulterior purposes" of literature.

8. See "Bibliography of the writings of George Santayana to October, 1940", compiled by Shohig Terzian, in *The Philosophy of George Santayana,* ed. Paul Arthur Schilpp (Evanston, 1940), p. 626.

9. Philip Blair Rice, "The Philosopher as Poet and Critic", in Schilpp, p. 287.

10. Singer, pp. 141–142. On the confusion of esthetic values with philosophic values, with this essay of Santayana's as illustration, see John Dewey, *Art As Experience* (New York, 1934), pp. 319–322.

11. The influence may be seen in much of Santayana's criticism, particularly on American writers. For the vogue of Taine in American literary criticism of the late nineteenth and early twentieth centuries, see William Van O'Connor, *An Age of Criticism, 1900–1950* (Chicago, 1952), pp. 45–51.

12. "The Elements and Function of Poetry" (Singer, p. 298).

13. Q. D. Leavis, "The Critical Writings of George Santayana: An Introductory Note", *Scrutiny,* IV (1935–36), 278–295. Mrs. Leavis' suggestion for the best use of Santayana's critical writings is not exactly flattering to their author. She would have them employed "as a live force to assist in the study of literature at the university stage".

14. George Santayana, *The Life of Reason: Reason in Art* (New York, 1924), pp. 113–115.

15. Santayana must be in error here. I assume he is alluding to Eliot's essay, "Shakespeare and the Stoicism of Seneca". In that essay Eliot compares a line from the *Paradiso* with a passage from *King Lear* ("As flies to wanton boys," etc.), not from *Macbeth*. (See T. S. Eliot, *Selected Essays, 1917–1932,* New York, 1932, pp. 116–117.) Ironically, it is the "Tomorrow, and tomorrow, and tomorrow" speech from *Macbeth* which Santayana himself once quoted (in "The Absence of Religion in Shakespeare") to illustrate the inferiority of Shakespeare's philosophy. Eliot later attempted to clarify his point about the "philosophy" in Shakespeare and Dante. See T. S. Eliot, *The Use of Poetry and the Use of Criticism* (London, 1933), pp. 98–100.

16. Singer, pp. 266–277. Various objections are raised to the arguments in "Tragic Philosophy" by F. R. Leavis, in "Tragedy and the 'Medium': A Note on Mr. Santayana's 'Tragic Philosophy' ", *Scrutiny,* XII (1943–44), 249–260.

17. George Santayana, *Persons and Places: My Host the World* (New York, 1953), p. 97.

Santayana's Necessary Angel

Maurice F. Brown

For contemporary readers and poets alike, Santayana's poems exist, if at all, in a quiet backwater of the main stream of poetry. Divorced from the twentieth-century experimentation with imagery, rhythm, and diction, creating a calm, hermetic world that seems all of a piece, the poems suggest that Santayana, the poet, sprang fully formed from the head of some serene and timeless Apollo. Santayana's diction is austerely conventional and lacks the vigor of colloquialism. If there is uniqueness, it comes from a desire for the quaint dignity of occasional anachronism—there is no interest in the shock of a new word. Neither is there the complex interweaving of image and idea or even the reliance on the poetic image itself which the contemporary reader has come to expect in poetry. Santayana's images, rarely startling or perplexing, usually serve as reinforcement for rhetorical statement. His desire for depersonalized experience combines with his curiously restricted sensitivity to the sensuous and emotional potentialities of language to create a poetic texture which seems to lack immediacy and vitality. The steady, unvaried flow of sound, rhythm, and rhetoric translate the experience into some Olympian sphere, and the poetry relies for its effect on its precision of statement, its epigrammatic genius, its high intellectual caliber, and its perfect control.

This is about as far as literary historians and critics have been able to go with Santayana's poetry, and yet, in the perspective of more recent concerns of literature, it becomes clear that Santayana is perhaps our first and one of our most acute poets to grapple with a major twentieth-century problem— the important shift in the relationship of the contemporary poet to his tradition. The record, poetic and critical, begins with Santayana's rejection of the Victorian aesthetic and his early awareness of what was to be a far-reaching cultural upheaval. Having faith in poetry as a valid medium of approach to truth, Santayana attempted to use poetry to break through cultural disintegration to a new ethos. A search for relevant imaginative modes took him through traditions, both classical and Christian, and further into a dramatic examination of the Christian-humanist tradition itself in his play, *Lucifer*. The record is of particular value because Santayana was perfectly

Reprinted from *New England Quarterly* 36 (December 1963): 435–51, with the permission of the author and publisher.

conscious of the implications of his poetic practice, and the course of his poetic development runs parallel to a group of philosophical considerations of the value and utility of poetry. Limited in some ways as a poet, but always alert and suggestive as a thinker, Santayana is very much a contemporary poet, wrestling with those problems of the imagination and the creation of relevant myth which are central to the work of such poets as Wallace Stevens, who have been forced to build on the unavoidable rocks of Santayana's disillusionment.

Santayana's mature career as a poet began in the nineties, after early experimentation which follows the examples of favorites like Leopardi, Musset, Byron, Shelley, and the later Victorians. As Santayana, the philosopher, matured, he became interested in poetry as a means to insight and control. He views the artist as the most important creator of human values in society, and his aesthetic theory, formulated in his teaching during the early nineties, found its expression in *The Sense of Beauty* in 1896. This book, with its emphasis on form and tradition as the most important elements of art, is a quiet but complete rejection of romantic critical theory.

As early as 1886 Santayana had rejected medieval Christian art on the grounds of "deformity," writing,

> This early Christian art is hideous—poor starved, crooked, cowed creatures, in which the attempt at humanity seems to be about given up. . . . I am of course wrong and anti-Nortonian, but I hate sentimentalism and pre-Raphaelitism with all my soul. It is not true that deformity expresses the soul—it only expresses the sad plight of the spirit that can't express itself.[1]

This passage from a letter signals Santayana's movement from some of his early models to a more classical position. By 1896 one of his objectives in *The Sense of Beauty* is the destruction of the romantic "sublime." The destruction is accomplished in terms similar to those to be used in Santayana's critiques of the formless "barbarism" in Browning and Whitman. Discussing "indeterminateness in art," Santayana writes,

> . . . the artist who is not artist enough, who has too many irrepressible talents and too little technical skill, is sure to float in the region of the indeterminate. He sketches and never paints; he hints and never expresses; he stimulates and never informs. This is the method of the individuals and of the nations that have more genius than art.[2]

And indeterminateness, Santayana maintains, is most fatal in the art of poetry, "for meaning is conveyed by the *form* and order of words, not by the words themselves, and no precision of meaning can be reached without precision of style."[3] Although Santayana does not deny the value of what he calls "expressiveness" in poetry, the prime virtue is clarity of meaning and therefore form. In this aspect of his theory, Santayana approaches a neo-classical point of view which anticipates that of Irving Babbitt. Indeed, he establishes a classical hierarchy of formal values on the basis of physiology at one point in *The Sense of Beauty*.[4]

Nature, for Santayana as for the neo-classical theorist, is both the source and test of art. Santayana sees beauty as that pleasure brought into existence by the creation out of nature of an ideal—a product of the "marriage of the imagination with the reality." There is, for Santayana, beauty of form in the external world, and it is essential that the poet be sensitive to it. But this is not enough. Nature is not an artist, or at least not a human artist, and man's desire for form is greater than and different from nature's. The artist turns natural ideals to human purposes and needs, and creates permanent values in a world which, left to nature, would provide only incomplete ideals in a state of perpetual flux.

Santayana's theory of creation is vigorous and essentially anti-eclectic. Indeed, he assails much of the poetic practice of his time:

> . . . we cannot work out our own style because we are hampered by the beauties of so many others. The result is an eclecticism, which, in spite of its great historical or psychological interest, is without aesthetic unity or perma-nent power to please.[5]

Yet Santayana does not exalt originality, but, like Pope,[6] stresses the impor-tance of the poetic tradition. His theory of "expression" leads him to value traditional "objects, interests, and events," all of which he includes in the term, "things." Things gain expressiveness either through a heightening of their own inherent beauty or through an associative process which makes things that are indifferent in themselves suggestive of beauty. From this line of argument, Santayana proceeds naturally to find the most beautiful objects, modes of human experience, aspirations, and interests to be those which have gained expressiveness through centuries of human idealization. Here, then, is the best material for poetry.[7] Santayana is writing, not only of materials however, but of the importance of formal traditions to the artist. If work in a plethora of styles led to eclecticism, creation outside a tradition was impossi-ble. Beauty is not easy and a long practice is needed, Santayana felt, to produce the most noble ideals and the most significant forms. "The only kind of reform usually possible," he wrote, "is reform from within. . . . Disaster follows rebellion against tradition or against utility, which are the basis and root of our taste and progress." And he encouraged "a more intimate study and more intelligent use of the traditional forms."[8]

To turn one's attention from these strong and perceptive remarks to the poems Santayana was writing in the nineties presents a problem. Santayana experimented with a wide range of forms and stanzaic patterns—the Petrar-chan sonnet, the Spenserian stanza, the Sapphic ode, the irregular ode, and the heroic couplet. He generally not only masters the techniques of the particular styles, but works in the spirit of the traditions as well. Too often, however, in spite of genuine achievement in a number of poems, the body of poetry falls short of the need Santayana sees in *The Sense of Beauty:* a tradition is not revived in the poems and we are left with the flat taste of that eclecticism Santayana deplored. Is a failure in contemporary taste to blame? Only partially. Poetic forcefulness is lost through Santayana's tendency to describe his suffering instead of presenting it through his medium. In addition, the experiences—the personal agonies which Santayana says lie in the poems—are too often presented through a filter which generalizes or universalizes them to such an extent that the sense of human immediacy is lost. This tendency is especially evident in Santayana's second sonnet sequence. In certain poems, where Santayana's personal involvement is greatest, or where he is working closely with specific places or historical material, there is the excitement of a traditional style put to new uses and mastering new material. A tradition is given new life in the first sequence of sonnets, some of the odes, "Avila," "King's College Chapel," "Spain in America," and "Cape Cod."

But a more pervasive difficulty lies in Santayana's use of the traditions to which he is drawn. His mood, his compelling sense of cultural disintegration, overwhelm his attempt to do through poetry what he felt needed doing. Santayana was in the position which Wallace Stevens has identified as that of contemporary man. Commenting on an image from *Phaedrus* in his first essay in *The Necessary Angel,* Stevens observes,

> He [the charioteer] was unreal for Plato as he is for us. Plato, however, could yield himself, was free to yield himself, to this gorgeous nonsense. We cannot yield ourselves. We are not free to yield ourselves.

The traditional poet caught in this situation presents a curious study. Working in Christian and classical traditions, Santayana more often communicates his deep sense of their irrevocable fading than of their eternal validity and vitality. A clear conflict in Santayana's use of mythic material comes in an early poem, "Gabriel." Gabriel's wings, the poet sees as fancy and a lie— Gabriel is only a legend. But the poet continues:

> Yet I mistrust the truth, and partly hold
> Thou art a herald of the upper sky,
> Where all the truth yet lives that seemd to die,
> And love is never faint nor virtue cold.

Santayana's "I . . . partly hold" is a clumsy early statement of the subtle later theory of myth, in which myth is seen as a repository of vision, sanctioned and resanctioned by human experience. Yet there is in all of Santayana's use of ideal forms of the past a wistful withholding of faith that keeps them from poetic life. In sonnet twenty-nine, for example, there is this sort of detached relationship with the forms of ancient faith:

> To me the faiths of old are daily bread;
> I bless their hope, I bless their will to save.
> And my deep heart still meaneth what they said.
> It makes me happy that the soul is brave. . . .

Santayana's detached, almost casual approval of faith, hope, and bravery lacks emotional commitment. A good-natured, well-intentioned judge, he pronounces the blessing, but he is not blessed. The pathos of his personal dilemma and that of his time has overcome the conviction of his reasoned aesthetic.

It seems almost incredible, in the midst of the almost universal eclecticism in the arts which marked the nineties, that Santayana should have been aware of this problem in his poetry. Among thinkers of the period, however, only Henry Adams—with some of the same cultural commitments as Santayana—was dealing with this dilemma with the same degree of awareness. In an early poem, "The Power of Art," Santayana indicates the narrow limits that his cultural situation has placed on the power of the modern poet. The poem was one that Santayana, as theorist, had eventually to reject, but it indicates the reason his poetic practice so often degenerates into eclecticism. The octave of the sonnet is an expansion of the poem's first two lines:

> Not human art, but living gods alone
> Can fashion beauties that by changing live. . . .

The power to create beauty is a power of "living gods"—the living ideal. But in an age of dead gods, new creation of beauty is impossible. In the sonnet's sestet, the poet is seen as able to capture the fleeting moment in art. But Santayana immediately undercuts the Pateresque aesthetic implied here, seeing the poet's greatest power in his ability to

> . . . immortalize the day
> When life was sweet, and save from utter death
> The sacred past that should not pass away.

The driving emotional power behind Santayana's eclecticism is perhaps best expressed in a letter Santayana wrote to William James in 1905. James had mentioned "the tears" he found in Santayana's writing, and Santayana replied:

> Not that I care to moan over the gods of Greece, turned into the law of gravity, or over the stained glass of cathedrals, broken to let in the sunlight and the air. It is not the past that seems to me affecting, entrancing, or pitiful to lose. It is the ideal. It is that vision of perfection that we just catch, or for a moment embody in some work of art, or in some idealized reality; it is the concomitant inspiration of life, always various, always beautiful, hardly ever expressible in its fullness.[9]

The passage catches the energy and passion in Santayana's attitude better than much of his poetry, and it indicates his irritation at the limitation of the scientific imagination in its inability to create human ideals. Intellectually, Santayana would have preferred to move forward to a new form and a new ideal to embody the experience of his time. But the difficulties involved were overwhelming. In a letter of 1911, Santayana wrote that the enemies of the church would win some day and a new form arise. "But," he continued, "we don't know what that new order may some day be, and meanwhile the revolution is destroying everything noble and beautiful which actually exists, or which can exist in our day."[10]

The dilemma of allegiance in which Santayana's poetic imagination was caught even as he was writing the poems of the nineties must finally have seemed inescapable. In spite of the achievement in these poems, they were not the salvation he was seeking. The step Santayana took at the end of the nineties was the necessary one: he moved to an analysis of the problem of his culture in terms of the most powerful imaginative traditions of the western world—the Greek and the Christian. The result was again a set of poetic-philosophical parallels, published in 1899 and 1900—the myth play, *Lucifer,* and the book, *Interpretations of Poetry and Religion.*

The almost unknown play, *Lucifer,* is of extreme interest for a number of reasons. It reaches to the heart of the problem of Santayana's earlier experiments with the poetic tradition, focusing the total problem of culture for the poet in the scope of its historical and dialectical oppositions. While the question is one which is central to Santayana's thought through the first decade of the twentieth century, in *Lucifer* he does as much as he can do as poet. For this reason the play marks the turning point of Santayana's career: it is, in effect, his swan song to poetry. In *Lucifer* he defines the meaning of the Greek and Christian traditions for our time, while rejecting the ultimate possibility of their utility to contemporary man. In a partial inversion of Christian myth— one perhaps stimulated by Santayana's interest in Shelley—Santayana turns from a sometime devil's advocate to cast his lot with the devil and find in Lucifer his necessary angel.

Myth was not a new concern for Santayana in the late nineties, of course. Interest in Christianity stems from his boyhood, and at Harvard the teaching and writing of his Greek professor, Louis Dyer, stimulated Santayana to investigation of the Greek tradition. In addition, the work of John

Fiske, the greatest American popularizer of the work of European students of myth and legend in this period, was known to Santayana as early as 1885. In that year he reviewed Fiske's *The Idea of God as Affected by Modern Knowledge* for the Harvard *Monthly,* finding common belief with Fiske in the "quasi-psychical" nature of God. Both *Interpretations of Poetry and Religion* and the later *Reason in Religion* give evidence of wide study of the Victorian mythologists during the nineties.

But of more significance than a detailed examination of possible individual influences upon Santayana's thought is the ethos which guided the pervasive revival of interest in myth at Harvard in the eighteen eighties and nineties.[11] Three motives—sometimes in conflict—guided the scholarly investigation of mythic materials. There was sometimes re-examination of myth for its religious and philosophical implications, and a tendency to view myth, when its dross had properly been refined away, as elevating moral allegory. Secondly, stimulated by Hegel, or by Spencer, or perhaps by Arnold, Harvard professors turned to the study of comparative mythology, motivated by a desire for humanistic synthesis of the ideals of various Western, or Western and Eastern traditions. Finally, a more scientific approach was taken, one which followed the theory and practice of German work by the Grimm brothers and Max Müller. Myth origins and comparative linguistics were major concerns; myth and legend were treated as early and erroneous explanations for natural causation. A flurry of interest in Greek archaeology came with the founding of the American School in Athens, and this contributed to knowledge of Greek myth and ritual.

The vigor of the movement quickened Santayana's interest and its variety forced a clarification of issues. Santayana's commitment to natural, as opposed to supernatural, religion came early in his career, and it released him from the more doctrinaire approaches to myth that were being attempted. His position, certainly influenced by his reading in Lucretius and Spinoza, is stated in his doctoral thesis on Lotze. He wrote,

> The religion of the pagans was a real religion, and the only sort that is possible if we admit the reality of nature such as she appears to us. All other religions have seen in nature an illusion, a temporary setting for lives that in truth belonged to a different world. . . . Religion is the sanction, not the reversal, of the judgments of the world.[12]

Santayana's insistence on natural religion led him, not to discard myth, but to insist on its intrinsic power and to rebel against its emasculation. In a passage from a letter to William James, Santayana reveals his distaste for the "scientization" or dogmatization of myth, writing that he cannot help but "detest the Absolutes and the dragooned myths by which people try to cancel the passing ideal, or to denaturalize it."[13] And in *Interpretations of Poetry and Religion,* Santayana stresses the need for myth that is neither disguised pantheism nor vapid moral allegory. The value of myth, he felt, lies in its "appeal to our sense of fact."

From the Harvard climate of opinion, Santayana absorbed the method of comparative mythology and became interested in moral and cultural implications of mythology for his time. Yet he held back from the poetic and dramatic experiments in myth synthesis that were being attempted by George Cabot Lodge and William Vaughn Moody at the turn of the century. Neither was there the more recent interest in revitalizing myth by activating it in a contemporary context. And Santayana shared none of that desire to unleash through myth the powerful subconscious and primitive forces of the id or the collective unconscious which has produced some of the most powerful literature of our time. Instead, the play, *Lucifer,* is a denial of the possibility of the kind of poetic synthesis that was being attempted, and a denial of the contemporary utility of the myths it treats.

The action of *Lucifer*[14] centers in the changing relationships of Lucifer with three groups of mythical figures. There are Mephistopheles and his crew of minor devils; the risen Christ, Michael, and the angels; and Hermes and the gods of Olympus. Primarily interested in these figures as imaginative embodiments of human values, Santayana tends to disregard their connection with cosmological explanation and detaches them from their respective frameworks of religious dogma. The play operates on a number of levels. Most obviously, *Lucifer* is a poetic representation of the growth and impending deaths of cultural myths. In his "Invocation," Santayana treats the characters of his drama as representatives of myths that have vanished from the modern world. They are caught in historical process and lost to the modern scientific spirit. Santayana views himself as a pilgrim, an exile from their world, asking that they not mock him. The play, then, presents the naturalism, objectivity, and innocence of Greek vision overcome by the intense subjective moral drama of early Christianity. This stage of development is followed by dissolution of the Christian synthesis into undirected emotional response when Christianity became detached from a philosophical world-view that was accessible to the human understanding. A final stage comes with the maturity of the scientific attitude.

But the historical perspective is not the major one presented in the play. In his unsigned review of *Lucifer* for the Harvard *Monthly,*[15] Santayana wrote that the play is set in the present. The action takes place in the "imagination of this age, given to historical and comparative studies." The setting is the contemporary mind, torn between loyalty to what Santayana identifies as the two facets of the human mind in *Interpretations of Poetry and Religion*—the imagination and the understanding. On this level of interpretation, the figures of the drama become allegorical, representing the ideal forms of conflicting human values. The values involved are, in Santayana's own terms, "nature," which includes the Greek values of happiness, innocence, and

objective clarity; "revelation," including the Christian values of human suffering and selfless love; and that "abstract doubt" which is fundamental to the
desire for a knowledge of reality. Finally, on the level of a dramatic action
itself, the play partakes of the very spirit of myth. Lucifer's quest for self-
knowledge leads him through suffering and renunciation to ritual cleansing
and the acceptance of a new identity.

The first act of the play defines the relationship between Lucifer and
Hermes. In the action, which is set in Lucifer's retreat on a cold star in outer
space, Lucifer's character is established. He is the spirit of "reason" and
"indomitable will," and elsewhere in the play is related through simile to
Prometheus and Herakles. He is disturbed by the lack of justice in the
universe, and this keeps him alert and restless. He and Hermes are seen as
allied spirits, just as Santayana saw possibility of agreement between the
Greek and the scientific world views in *Reason in Religion.* There, he has
written, "Paganism was nearer than Herbraism to the Life of Reason because
its myths were more transparent and its temper less fanatical."[16] Lucifer,
drawn by love for Hermes, agrees to leave his isolated star to cast his lot with
the Greek god.

Act two is a "Walpurgisnacht" scene in which Lucifer detaches himself
from the spirit of the devils and witches who claim to follow him on earth.
Mephistopheles and the major devils are depicted as middle-class business-
men at a convention. Lucifer had left the earth to them after the fanaticism
which followed the birth of Christ. Free from his direct rule, they have
reverted to their essential materialistic and sensual natures. Their spirit is in
distinct contrast to the rational spirit of Lucifer, and he exults in his freedom
from the urges which enslave them. Lucifer finally sees the devils as his foes,
as they plan to overthrow his authority and his purer imagination to further
their own ends.

Lucifer defines his relationship to Christ in act three. Lacking the
essential Christian despair, Hermes, the innocent seeker, cannot enter
Heaven. Lucifer, the disillusioned intelligence, must lead him to Christ. It
becomes evident that Hermes must either die or turn to Christ if he chooses
to venture out of the finite Greek world. The contrast in which Santayana is
interested here is that between the objectivity of the Greek myth, establishing limited ideals in space and nature, and the subjectivity of the Christian,
defining the ideal human drama in time, in history, and in the heart of man.
As the act progresses, Lucifer almost capitulates to Christ and accepts suffering love as the way to knowledge. But he draws back, proclaiming freedom
from Christ achieved through the strength of his will and declaring that he
has come to self-understanding, telling Christ, "I have wholly understood
my fate/ And know there is not in this scheme of things/ Room for my soul."
In a final rebellion, Lucifer sees his release from the Christian framework as a
rebirth and immortality, saying,

"I live by truth, as ye by falsehood die.
The wreck of worlds is my supreme release,
The death of gods mine immortality."

In this scene, the turning point of the drama, Lucifer makes a concession which motivates the play's fall. He agrees to submit to Christ if Hermes can be won to accept a Christian *Weltanschauung*. But he prophesies the failure of a synthesis of traditions, for Christianity "is too gross/ And palpable a fiction, fit for those/ Who dream awake." Christ fails, in act four, to convert the gods of Olympus to his gospel. Zeus, who thinks in terms of external force alone, confuses Christ with a revived Cronos coming for revenge. Although, in a sense, he is correct, Christ's lack of visible power calms Zeus' fears. Athena rejects Christ's "Victory," in favor of "Truth," preferring a value capable of objective verification. Ares knows that to lose one's life is not to save it. Aphrodite is interested because Christ speaks of love, but she quickly rejects a suffering love which involves a loss of all other human values in its attainment. Even Hermes, a seeking spirit, must remain true to a naturalistic system. Synthesis impossible, Christ threatens the Olympians with death, but Zeus counters the threat, rising to the sudden sophistication of a philosopher's argument. Being, he maintains, even for gods, involves eventual nonbeing, and therefore, "Fleeting is the breath/ That saith: I am eternal!"

Back on his star, Lucifer realizes that his own disillusion has been the inadvertent cause of Hermes' death. The innocent soul, he observes, cannot exist in his universe. But Lucifer himself has now escaped the net of time and sends his servant away, saying, "This day/ My soul hath entered on eternity." Lucifer dedicates himself wholly to truth, awaiting "A greater, dearer comforter than he [Christ]," in a final soliloquy. While Lucifer's position excludes the values of commitment to anything but truth, he recognizes a need for love and for other human values for total achievement. He has attained self-knowledge but is unable to fulfill his vision himself. He must await a new myth. In *Interpretations of Poetry and Religion,* as in *Lucifer,* Santayana envisions the total collapse of the Christian myth and sees the need for the same kind of myth Lucifer awaits at the end of the play—one "more disillusioned and not less inspired [than Christianity]" to utter "the ideal meaning of their [men's] life."[17] Ironically, although Santayana has created in Lucifer a figure with the power of myth, through that very creation he rejects the possibility of creating a naturalistic and scientific myth through poetry which will fulfill human needs and create humanistic values in his time.

With this play, Santayana in the person of his hero purged himself of his emotional attachment to myth and turned to the "disillusioned understanding" as the only valid means of approach to his problem. *Reason in Religion,* published in 1905, indicates an important shift in Santayana's attitude. Myth is viewed as an early and inaccurate form of science and must inevitably be replaced by the more accurate scientific outlook. Santayana maintains that myth is a natural prologue to philosophy, since the "love of ideas" is at the root of both systems. From these theses, the rest of Santayana's thought follows easily. Poetry, he writes,

> . . . anticipates science, on which it ought to follow, and imagination rushes in to intercept memory, on which it ought to feed. [18]

Even more destructive to Santayana's earlier hope for poetry is his view of the cultural relevance of myth. Although Santayana had created a myth for his time almost instinctively in Lucifer, he would not accept myth as a medium for creating and synthesizing new experience. He wrote,

> It [myth] is therefore a fruit of experience, an ornament, a proof of animal vitality; but it is no *vehicle* for experience; it cannot serve the purposes of transitive thought or action. [19]

Myth must come in the wake of science, unifying poetically an experience already defined. Scientific thought, Santayana continued, is the only possible "*vehicle*" for experience in a scientific culture.

Santayana's disillusion in *Reason in Religion* is not quite complete, however, for as myth loses its "animal vitality" it evolves for the seeker of truth into forms of moral idealism, and

> it is this submerged idealism which, alone, in an age that should have finally learned how to operate in nature and how to conceive her processes, could still win for religion a philosopher's attention or legislator's mercy. [20]

But to put on the filtering lenses of scientific understanding and accept myth with highly qualified commitment as a repository of moral ideals was to join with those very emasculators of myth Santayana had earlier denounced. Divorced from its sources of power as a vehicle for experience, past and present, it becomes the mausoleum of dead vision, of little relevance to the needs of the present. As Santayana turned from *Poetry and Religion* to *Reason in Religion,* he turned from poetry to philosophy, in search of his elusive answer.

We cannot help admiring the perceptiveness with which Santayana dealt with the problem of his poetry and his courage in reaching conclusions which militated against his fondest hopes. In spite of his insensitivity to uses of myth which later poets have shown to be fruitful, Santayana's conclusions may ultimately be the proper ones. Twentieth-century poetic achievements have come only with drastic restriction of the traditional claims for the poet in his relationship with society. Attempts like Hart Crane's to work toward an unknown "new order" have ended in what even his most ardent admirers recognize as a collection of brilliant fragments. Achievement has been possible for Pound and Yeats, yet the extent of the relation of the first's philosophy of history and the second's semi-personal mythology to the success of their poetry—leaving aside questions of their personal needs—seems slight indeed. Achievement is still possible within the traditions, Christian and classical, which inform the poetry of Frost and Eliot. And yet the contemporary use of tradition for purposes of ironic contrast by so many of our poets is certainly not work within a tradition. Santayana's approach to the relation of poet and society, moreover, would probably preclude all twentieth-century achievement, finding in it only new varieties of romantic decadence or idle anachronism. In terms of the problem as Santayana set it, the work of Wallace Stevens is the only contemporary poetry which moves in a possible direction. But for work like Stevens' to become useful to society in the terms of Santayana's desire, the poet must become mid-wife to the myth for which Lucifer's world waits and in which it will find its own partial ideals fulfilled. Can the poet create the unborn gods which the necessary angel serves? The course of literary history would suggest that it is too much to ask.

Notes

1. Daniel Cory, editor, *The Letters of George Santayana* (New York, 1956), 9–10.
2. *The Sense of Beauty*, 131.
3. *The Sense of Beauty*, 143.
4. *The Sense of Beauty*, 162.
5. *The Sense of Beauty*, 155.
6. In "Apologia pro Mente Sua," Santayana falls back upon a phrase from Pope to describe his own youthful attraction to poetry: "I lisped in numbers for the numbers came."
7. This, incidentally, is the crux of Santayana's quarrel with his critics. In a bitter reply in the "Apologia" to a criticism of his poetry by George W. Howgate, Santayana accuses Howgate of insensitivity to "the poetry of the subject-matter" of his poems. His poetry moves, he feels, in the realm of "things." But Santayana's "things" are those which have gained expressiveness, are divorced from the specific and accidental, and live in a permanent world of human value. The critical confusion lies in the difference between the "thing" of twentieth-century poetry—the "real toads" in Marianne Moore's "imaginary gardens"—and the "thing" in Santayana's aesthetic theory.
8. *The Sense of Beauty*, 167.
9. *The Letters of George Santayana*, 83.
10. *The Letters of George Santayana*, 111.
11. In the foreground of the movement at Harvard were Charles R. Lanman, later teacher of T. S. Eliot, Crawford H. Toy, David G. Lyon, Frederick W. Putnam, Frederic D. Allen, John H. Wright, and Charles Eliot Norton—a group with a wide variety of interests and approaches.
12. *Lotze's System of Philosophy* (1889), Harvard University Archives, 314–315.
13. *The Letters of George Santayana*, 83.
14. Of the two complete editions of the play, the first, *Lucifer; A Theological Tragedy* (Chicago and New York, 1899), is the source of references. A version published in Cambridge, Mass., in 1924, with minor revisions and the addition of a subtitle ("The Heavenly Truce") shows some shift in Santayana's attitude.
15. Volume XXVIII, 210–212 (July 1899).

16. *The Life of Reason; or, the Phases of Human Progress: Reason in Religion* (New York, 1905), 107.

17. *Interpretations of Poetry and Religion*, 116–117.

18. *Reason in Religion*, 24.

19. *Reason in Religion*, 129.

20. *Reason in Religion*, 68.

An Expanding Theme in
The Last Puritan

WILLIAM H. MARSHALL

The Last Puritan may first be regarded as an objectification of ideas and images found elsewhere in Santayana's work. "Puritanism," remarks the narrator to Mario Van de Weyer in the "Prologue," "is a natural reaction against nature." In its full meaning, transcending the limits of particular geographical or historical forms, puritanism represents man's attempt to find perfection in an evolving universe, which at any stage is necessarily imperfect; it results from the endeavor to make experience over so that it might conform to absolute principle, to give existence to the ideal. In Oliver Alden "puritanism worked itself out to its logical end," Mario replies. "He convinced himself, on puritan grounds, that it was wrong to be a puritan." Oliver's tragedy arose because despite all this he remained a puritan, the narrator continues: in what we call a fallen universe "his absolutist conscience remained a pretender, asserting in exile its divine right to the crown."[1]

To regard *The Last Puritan* as merely a fictionalized philosophic tract is to undervalue the novel, however, for it is a work of art, possessing structure and expressing its concern with puritanism through systematically developed themes and symbols. Essentially *The Last Puritan* is constructed upon the principle of duplexity, juxtaposing, for example, the Catholic and Protestant traditions, literal and symbolic truths (even suggested by the subtitle, "A Memoir in the Form of a Novel"), social affirmation and alienation. There are various symbols and symbolic patterns in the novel, but the key to that which appears essential to the thematic expansion is found in the paragraph in which the narrator records the birth of Oliver Alden:

> The child had been born punctually. This first grave and alarming duty of entering into the world was performed not only unflinchingly but with a flourish: for this thoroughly satisfactory child was a boy. His little organism, long before birth, had put aside the soft and drowsy temptation to be a female. It would have been so simple for the last pair of chromosomes to have doubled up like the rest, and turned out every cell in the future body complete, well-balanced, serene, and feminine. Instead, one intrepid particle decided to live

Reprinted from *Personalist* 45 (Winter 1964): 27–40, with the permission of *The Pacific Philosophical Quarterly*.

alone, unmated, unsatisfied, restless, and masculine; and it imposed this unstable romantic equilibrium on every atom of the man-child's flesh, and of the man-child's sinews. To be male means to have chosen the more arduous, though perhaps the less painful adventure, more remote from home, less deeply rooted in one soil and one morality. It means to be pledged to a certain recklessness about the future: and if these risks are to be run without disaster, there should be also a greater buoyancy, less sensitiveness, less capacity for utter misery than women commonly show. (p. 75)

Though perhaps easily overlooked at first or regarded as authorial facetiousness, this passage is actually central both to the meaning of *The Last Puritan* and to the mythic development of that meaning. Throughout the novel scenes occur and observations are made concerning the relationship between male and female. It is of course possible to regard these as literal and descriptive rather than as symbolic, as parts of the narrative rather than as elements in the structure of a work of art. Such a reading places Oliver's behavior in a clinical, not a philosophic, orientation, thereby ignoring the propositions which the narrator makes in the "Prologue" to his life of Oliver Alden.

The male organism is, like the universe in which it exists, incomplete—imperfect though always evolving. Its concomitance with the male principle commits it to a quest, not for the perfect but for reconciliation with the imperfect and thereby momentary self-realization. The female organism, on the other hand, is complete, therefore seemingly "perfect" in an imperfect world; expressing the female principle, that of perfection, it seeks to reduce the world around it to comprehensible order. In the male, sexuality becomes the dominant form of asserting his incomplete nature, of succeeding in his quest.[2] In the female, sexuality is something else, a means of demonstrating that the male is imperfect and the role of the female is to tolerate and guide him, thereby bringing a clearly imperfect world somewhat closer to perfection. Because he is aggressive, constantly seeking self-realization, the male has built societies which the female, because she is self-sufficient, seems to accept but quietly controls. "We women too like to have our own way," Irma remarks in a letter to her sister, "but under cover of some authority, God, or a husband, or at least public opinion" (p. 221). The most striking example of the situation can be found in Peter Alden's image of the clergyman, in this instance reported by Oliver: "they are simply the ladies' oracles putting their delusions into words for them, and painting the universe all pink and blue for them to be comfy in" (pp. 213–214). Mr. Edgar Thornton, the young clergyman who later marries Edith, is an ideal instance, "perfect manliness consciously reconciled with supreme consecration" (p. 491).

But by nature the male does not display such evidence of reconciliation. "It would frighten us to stand alone, but your true man loves it," Irma continues in the same letter to her sister. "Men are so much more romantic than women who, if we must confess the truth, are born domestic animals, whereas men don't become tame until they have lost their youth, or have missed it" (p. 221). The male exults in his imperfection, as Peter Alden, Jim Darnley, or Mario Van de Weyer illustrates. It is of some significance that in those remote days of Peter's youth, with which the narrative begins, the conflict between Peter and his older brother and guardian, Nathaniel, primarily concerns a question of sexual behavior. Essentially Nathaniel has accepted the puritanic view that the world, though coarse and vulgar in its external form, is perfectible in the minds of rational men, ultimately by the exclusion of all that is inconsonant with reason. Nathaniel has achieved "supreme consecration"; Peter never does. After the unfortunate accident in the college chapel and some years of wandering and temporary marital attachments, Peter Alden invades the world, absolutist and perfect, of Harriet Bumstead and Letitia Lamb. In later years Harriet recalls:

'Dr. Alden has proposed, and we are engaged to be married.'
'Harriet Bumstead,' she cried, 'you don't mean it?'
'Yes, Letitia Lamb, I do. It will be for the best.'
'Ah,' she murmured, 'but a *man.*' And how *old* is he?'
'Not *old* at all, for a man,' I replied impressively.' (p. 65).

In time Peter abandons their world and, unreconciled to all others, he spends much of his life in travel and goes voluntarily to death. Jim Darnley accepts the unconventional and makes no pretenses to following the pattern which female society imposes. He remarks that Mrs. Bowler is his "wife—not legally, because there's old Bowler; but she was my first flame and practically it's as if we were married. And Bobby's my son" (p. 262). He later deplores the thought of Minnie Bowler, for he presently favors Bella Iggins, the Cynthia Nevil of his cinema career (p. 368). Through life Jim Darnley is the imperfect and variable factor, necessarily reacting to the constants that attract him. "It was those wicked females that ruined him, Mr. Oliver," Jim's mother remarks after her son's death, "women and gaming-tables abroad, women and the turf and the stockbrokers at home" (p. 533). Nevertheless, Jim becomes a kind of spokesman for male imperfection, his own and all others', frequently bringing together, without knowing the philosophic implications of what he says, various aspects of experience. Thus, described by the narrator as "the oracle of horse sense and manly ignorance," Jim remarks of Caleb Wetherbee: "Haven't you noticed, when he talks to you, he looks as if he would like to make love? Poor chap, he can't make love . . . and he takes to his religion as a substitute. He couldn't just be a Caliban, could he?" (p. 200).

Appearing at nearly the halfway point in the narrative, Mario Van de Weyer, who shares the narrator's understanding of Oliver Alden, is a far more articulate spokesman than Jim Darnley. For the study of Oliver's life Mario serves as the control: he represents the tradition of Catholic humanism, a symbolic and comprehensive view of nature and art, and social affirmation. From the beginning Mario has been aware of his own imperfection and has therefore accepted the resultant restlessness and dependence on woman. "You are not comfortable with women. It's all because you never loved your mother and she never loved you. That makes all the difference" (p. 408). For Mario, the Mother as female establishes the image of the complete, the perfect, toward which the Son as male strives, seeking in other females recapitulation of the Mother and self-realization in a world that remains imperfect though always in process. Such adoration of women, the hanging on their slightest wishes, Mario remarks to Rose Darnley at their meeting after Oliver's death, is the "debt we owe to nature" (p. 592). At the time of Mario's involvement with the young actress Aïda de Lancey, his mother is dying; in his reasons for leaving Harvard the two female forces upon his life are poignantly fused. But because he recognizes his imperfection and can reconcile to each other the kinds of love that he experiences, Mario can integrate the self with art, religion, and the world around him. When the War comes, his response is essentially male, given to cosmic tragedy because in his projectional, his anthropomorphic, view of the world he can both intellectually and emotionally accept the imperfection that he sees there: "Mario seemed transformed, his eyes grown darker, and yet brighter, fixed on the vague distance, as if seeing something invisible. At the same time there was a ripple in him of boyish merriment . . . . He was serious, yet secretly happy, deeply elated, as if never so much alive before. That must be the way he looks, thought Oliver, when he is making love. But those were not thoughts to be uttered, only undercurrents in the mind" (p. 523).

In the foregoing I do not propose that the viewpoint of *The Last Puritan*, embodied in the expanding symbolic and thematic structure, simply enforces the proposition about "the hand that rocks the cradle." Though this would be perfectly consistent with the worldview of Harriet Bumstead Alden, it would be a simplification, resulting only from the confusion of the *ideal* and the *existent*; from the point of view of the novel, only a puritan could make such a generalization. The images of the male and female, in other words, are in no sense to be taken literally; nor are they to be regarded as allegorical, for their recurring use accumulates and complicates meanings, of which an analysis such as this can suggest but a few.

Seen in terms of the male-female myth suggested in the passage recording Oliver's birth, the tragedy of the protagonist, that he is compelled on puritan principles to try vainly to reject puritanism, assumes a dimension which it would not otherwise possess. Oliver is neither of the group to which Edgar Thornton belongs, nor is he of that variously represented by Jim Darnley and Mario. Indeed, his body "had put aside the soft and drowsy temptation to be female," but out of the long Calvinistic heritage, from which all traces of anthropomorphism and dogma have long been lost, there has arisen a mind dedicated to the service of principles, tenaciously believing that ultimately the universe must be proved orderly, comprehensible, and moral: "Philosophy possessed the soul of this child from his first breath" (p. 76). There is imbalance rather than synthesis between impulse and ideation: "All sensation in Oliver was, as it were, retarded; it hardly became conscious until it became moral" (p. 159). In terms of the mythic orientation to which I have pointed, though Oliver's physical being and activities are masculine, his soul possesses the feminine quality of believing perfection possible in himself and in the world; he is primarily mind in a world of matter. Thus, he does not seek beyond mind, for woman or religion or conflict, to achieve self-realization.

Oliver's mother gives to his philosophical mind its initial direction. Regarding the world from the female point of view, as somehow comprehensible and perfectible, Mrs. Alden reverses her terms, describing the norm as masculine. Thus early in Oliver's life she remarks, "I don't think little boys ought to be brought up to sit on *cushions*. It is effeminate . . . . If only Oliver wouldn't fidget, but keep his clothes properly pulled down under him, he would be perfectly comfortable, and wouldn't need to find fault with what is provided for him" (pp. 96–97). And many years later she describes Mario as "effeminate" (p. 346). Self-sufficiency is to be Oliver's: intellectually and spiritually "the last pair of chromosomes [is] to have doubled up like the rest." He soon loses the image of woman which Mario has possessed from his earliest moments:

> Far, far in a dim past, as if it had been another world or in a pre-natal condition, Oliver remembered the long-denied privilege of sitting in his mother's lap. It had been such a refuge of safety, of softness, of vantage: you were carried and you were enveloped in an amplitude of sure protection, like a king on his throne, with his faithful bodyguard many ranks deep about him: and the landscape beyond, with its messengers and its motley episodes, became the most entertaining of spectacles, where everything was unexpected and exciting yet where nothing could go wrong. (p. 104)

Without real affection, Oliver has received only "ideas and prejudices from ladies and clergymen," he himself remarks in reporting Peter Alden's opinions. "For this reason Pa is glad that I cottoned at once to Lord Jim . . . it was such a healthy influence for me, and so timely: because there never was anybody like Lord Jim for dashing off everything in bold black and white" (pp. 213–214). It is Jim who sees and reports the nature of things in that world away from women (that Jim and Oliver are for the most part at sea is significant), stimulating in Oliver the early phase of the process which Mario describes in the "Prologue," the futile attempt from puritan compulsion to break away from puritanism.

So long as Jim offers Oliver facts without emotional import, which are therefore reducible to neat generalizations, there is no difficulty, but the break with puritanism is necessarily emotional and, paradoxically, for the real puritan necessarily unattainable. Thus, at the time that Jim dramatizes his masculine imperfection by revealing the nature of his relation with Mrs. Bowler, Oliver does not cease to be a puritan but, instead Jim ceases to live for Oliver:

> Luckily Oliver still had his hand on the closed gate and could steady himself. Jim's words were in his ear, but he was not thinking of them, nor of Mrs. Bowler or Bobby. No images. Only a sickening blank, as on that first afternoon in the yacht, when Jim had died and seemed never to come up again. Yet there was a strange difference. Now Oliver was not waiting. There was nothing to look for, no future. Only the cold fact, like a gravestone, that Jim had gone under for good.
> They had resumed their walk, and the dead man's voice continued speaking. (p. 262)

Some years later, during the War, when Oliver learns that Jim has been lost at sea, the scene is recapitulated, but now without the emotional struggle against emotional acceptance of a foreign fact: "now he rested his hand heavily on the back of his chair, exactly as seven years before he had clutched the gate of the towpath bridge near Sandford . . . . His head swam in the same way, and he had the same indescribable sensation of collapse, of despair. But that was only in the weak, uncontrolled upper parts of his brain; his hand held firm, his legs didn't give way, and in a moment his head, too, was clear" (p. 528).

Through the years the image of Mrs. Bowler has haunted him, Oliver writes to Rose Darnley toward the end of his life, causing despair but strengthening his own sense of sufficiency, "show[in[2]] me how little hold a thousand female hypocrites or Parisian adventuresses would ever have upon me" (561). Women like Minnie Bowler, Aïda de Lancey, or the Baronne are the objects of what Oliver calls *desire* rather than *love.* Plato "knew nothing about love," for he confused it with desire, Oliver writes in a college essay. "Love is . . . entirely different from desire, and unselfish. It may lead a man to give up his life for others, both by living for them and by dying for them. He may be content to be ignored by those he loves, and be satisfied in knowing that they are noble and happy" (p. 438). In itself desire is, in other words, an admission, in fact a dramatization of man's incompleteness, of his need for another, of the fact that in his cellular structure "one intrepid particle decided to live alone, unmated, unsatisfied, restless, and masculine." But for Oliver love must be comprehensible, an assertion of both man's independence and his usefulness to others in a presumably perfectible world.

The football dominating the middle portions of the narrative points up in Oliver's mind his essential problem, which he begins to understand only too late but can never emotionally accept. "His body might be strong enough, but his soul had been crippled," he thinks at one point during the War. "He was like Cousin Caleb Wetherbee turned inside out" (p. 540). Forced by his physical being and environment to participate in what possesses for his mind no meaning, he accepts duty for its own sake: "Existence was a complication, a commitment, a pose. Of course, to play the game you must follow the rules: but why this game, or these rules? And why play at all? There seemed to be two selves or two natures within him; one, pure spirit, that might play any game and lodge in any animal; the other, this particular human, American, twentieth-century male person called Oliver Alden" (p. 351). The commitment to play is of course without any emotional value. But to fail to play your best, "to keep out of the scrimmage, when you were once in the game, would be a form of self-betrayal . . . . So he led his football squad with a cold heart" (p. 382). In the end the self remains unaffected: "What endures is only this spirit, this perpetual witness, wondering at those apparitions, enjoying one, suffering at another, and questioning them all. . . . Did I turn purple because I wore purple in the football field, or should I turn crimson if I wore crimson on some other day?" (pp. 400–401). Without emotional participation, however, without the synthesis between "love" and "desire," motivation is vapid and attainment is unfelt; the puritan, with the ambivalent awareness of intense success and failure, moves faster along the impasse. Ironically, it is Oliver himself who, trying to give image to a concept for the crew coach Remington, unknowingly points in terms of the male-female myth to the cause for the puritan's dilemma: "The vital centre [in the crew] has got to be in one place . . . . Your jockey can manage so easily, because the vital centre is naturally in him, and his mount is only a mare or a gelding. Your gelding might be as fast, mechanically, as you will; he would never stick to it in a race, without a rider who wasn't a gelding" (421). That Oliver fails here as elsewhere to comprehend the nature of the analogy between life and game is simply the inevitable result of his own emotional alienation.

Significantly, Edith, who is closer than any other to Oliver's female counterpart, comes briefly into Oliver's life after the Williams-Harvard game. His attitude toward the game is close to that toward the marriage he later asks Edith to share with him. "I couldn't refuse to play for Williams," he remarks to her. "They needed me. It would have seemed selfish and effeminate" (p. 397). Although in almost any other situation the puritan can with some success substitute duty for emotional affirmation, in sexual commitment the fact becomes obvious. At the end of the *Rheingold* Oliver "calmly" expresses his "philosophical" admiration for Edith and then accompanies her into the lobby:

> These first impressions seemed to him easily absorbed and mastered. He was adapting himself quickly to the circumstances of Edith's life. Operas,

evening gowns, and ritualistic aunts could be accepted as matters of course. He rather liked them. They came in nicely as a sort of perpetual mild joke to fill in the blank spaces of life. Edith in turn would soon begin to adapt herself to his mind, to his intentions, until the understanding between them was perfect. He would take her for a long drive the next afternoon, and they would have a heart to heart talk. (p. 463)

There is conceptualized love, but no desire and certainly not what is popularly expected. "I daresay I'm not in love . . . if that means turning a kind of lunatic for the time being. But as to caring, as to feeling that you belong to me, as it were, by nature, that I belong to you, I had that feeling in a sort of dream on the first day I saw you," he remarks to Edith during the intended talk. "Yes: and it wasn't absurdly conceited or arrogant in me to imagine that you would find your best life, too, in living with me, and devoting yourself to me" (pp. 476–477). The letter in which Oliver proposes to Edith is entrusted to Tom Piper, who, becoming involved with the extra girl accompanying Josh Burr (clearly a kind of masculine imperfection), accidently drops it and when he finds it soaked with ditch water consciously destroys it. Some days later Edith's own letter arrives, protesting her "unchanged affection" for Oliver but announcing her engagement to Edgar Thornton.

Slowly Oliver Alden is being reduced to self by the loss of father, family, friends, and now Edith. This is the position which the puritan seeks, for he demands only mind for identity. But of course it is unsatisfactory; the journey with Mario around the world "taught Oliver little except how inevitably centred and miserably caged he was in himself" (p. 507). Whereas the admission of ignorance may be the first step toward wisdom, the puritan's intellectual admission of failure leads no place, except perhaps to more intense intellectual activity, for he can never bring emotional support to his admission. Oliver's contemplation at Oxford therefore merely renders his dilemma more apparent and painful.

"In Oliver's philosophy there was no principle, astronomic or volcanic, to mark the particular summer for catastrophe," the narrator remarks. "But that summer happened to be the summer of 1914" (p. 522). Though Mario has contempt for the Allied cause, he goes at once. To Oliver the War remains incomprehensible, for it openly embraces evil and the irrational, for which in his own mind there has been no place. In time he thinks that he recognizes "how exactly war was like football," for despite "all the false reasons" given by "high-minded people," it affects the moral nature of no one (p. 541). And after the United States has entered the War, Oliver brings to the conflict the same attitude with which he entered the Williams-Harvard game: "I have played all their games. I am playing their horrible game now. I am going to fight the Germans whom I like on the side of the French whom I don't like. It's my duty" (p. 582). He remains sickened by what he sees, and his physical system tries to throw off one of the two incompatibles, the puritan mind (with its absolute belief that all the cosmic chromosomes have doubled) or human perception (with its obvious evidence that they have not).

Oliver Alden's last considered act is in providing in his will for the Darnley family, thereby demonstrating what by his own definition is his "love" for Rose. From her rejection of him he emerges the puritan, concluding, "the true lover's tragedy is not being jilted; it is being accepted" (p. 580). Oliver Alden's last unconsidered act is described by Mario, who comes to the Darnley women as executor for Oliver's estate: "It was several days after the armistice. All firing had ceased, but the troops were advancing rapidly; and somebody on a motor-bicycle . . . came round a curve without warning on the wrong side of the road. Oliver, in trying to avoid a collision, ran into a milestone. His car turned turtle; he was caught under it and his neck broken" (p. 585). Though passing uncommited through the War, Oliver is ultimately the victim of accident and matter, the inexplicable.

Toward Oliver's memory Rose Darnley remains cold, for there is no "love"; toward the living Mario she is warm, for there is "desire." After Mario's departure Rose goes to her room and weeps, to be comforted by her mother, for whose last words, unconsciously recalling the key passage near the beginning of his story, the narrator has reserved the final irony: "No need breaking your silly heart over a young man who's dead and gone. Hasn't he left you a pretty penny, and can't you marry somebody else? After all, he was a stranger to us, and no ladies' man. Yet for all that . . . he was a *kind gentleman*" (p. 595).

Essentially Oliver Alden "was played out," as the narrator remarks in this final chapter. "Every human achievement is submerged in the general flood of things, and its issue soon grown ambiguous and untraceable. We must be satisfied to catch our triumphs on the wing, to die continually, and to die content." Oliver himself could never have come to know this, of course, so that, as the narrator continues, "he would have gained nothing by living to a hundred, never would have found better friends, or loved women otherwise. His later years would only have been pallid copies of his earlier ones" (pp. 584–585). Such is necessarily the puritan's lot, for, conceiving only of perfection, he cannot intellectually and emotionally comprehend the possibility of imperfection in the self and of growth therefrom. But those who see puritanism from the outside and essentially understand it become involved in paradox: they cannot make definitive propositions about the puritan and his failure without embracing the absolutism that is essential to the puritan. Thus, the story of the life of Oliver Alden is placed between a "Prologue" and an "Epilogue," in which the narrator himself appears uncertain, conscious of the likelihood of failure in his undertaking. He can find justification in his role only in the belief that he states in the "Epilogue": "Perhaps, while life lasts, in order to reconcile mankind with reality, fiction in some directions may be more needful than truth" (p. 600). In full perspective *The Last Puritan* appears concerned with the narrator's casting his memoir in the form of a novel; the theme with which he has dealt in the life of Oliver Alden can become humanly comprehensible only if it finds embodiment in and expansion through a mythic structure. The narrator has chosen to develop, at the structural center of the novel, the male-female myth, introduced in the passage recording Oliver's birth, because it derives from the core of that material "reality" with which mankind is to be reconciled.

Notes

1. George Santayana, *The Last Puritan, A Memoir in the Form of a Novel* (New York: Charles Scribner's Sons, 1936), p. 6. Hereafter I shall indicate page numbers within parentheses in the text.
2. See chapter I, "Love," *Reason in Society* (New York: Charles Scribner's Sons, 1905).

Santayana's *Metanoia:*
The Second Sonnet Sequence

DOUGLAS L. WILSON

George Santayana began his literary career in poetry and spent his formative years as a practicing and committed poet. The bulk of his poetry, not unsurprisingly, reflects the preoccupations of these formative years—the tensions and anxieties that attended his personal and cultural dislocation. His first poetic effort of any magnitude was the sequence of twenty sonnets which opened his first published book, *Sonnets and Other Verses* (1894), and which contains a number of his best-known sonnets. It represents an attempt to achieve and record a reconciliation of his naturalistic temperament and outlook with his Catholic background and tradition. The importance of these sonnets as an expression of Santayana's life and thought has long been recognized. But two years later, Santayana published, in a new edition of the same book, another sequence which expresses a quite different yet no less important event in his intellectual development. This sequence, properly understood, provides the basis for an understanding of the origin and character of the aspect of Santayana's personality and writings that has most disturbed his critics—his peculiar aloofness and detachment from human concerns.

Unlike the first sequence, which was written over a period of nearly ten years, the second sequence, consisting of thirty sonnets, was written in the relatively short space of about one year.[1] These are the poems that Santayana refers to in later years as his "Platonizing" sonnets. He submits his poetic impulse in these sonnets to the discipline of the highly demanding conventions of Renaissance Platonism, and the result is a remarkable sequence of love sonnets in the Italian Renaissance tradition. This second sequence represents a calculated artistic attempt to bring to formal expression an important transformation in the poet's way of regarding life and the world around him.

I

There has been no full or adequate study of Santayana's poetry, much less the second sonnet sequence, though George Howgate's book contains a useful

Reprinted from *New England Quarterly* 39 (March 1966): 3–25, with the permission of the author and publisher.

survey of the subject.[2] But the student of Santayana's poetic career does not have to proceed very far before discovering the intimate connection between the crucial events in the poet's inner life and his poetry. The early poetry, especially, is devoted to the expression of intensely personal problems. Santayana, in his autobiographical writings, has been quite open about the matter. In fact, the first chapter of the last volume of his autobiography, *My Host the World,* is given over to a rather full discussion of the emotional experience which the second sonnet sequence was intended to express, and it is here that I wish to begin my discussion.

He had written earlier, in the first volume, *Persons and Places,* that his understanding of something that happened in his mother's early life was based on a similar experience in his own.

> She had undergone a veritable conversion, a sweeping surrender of all earthly demands or attachments; she retained her judgments and her standards, but without hope. I am confident of this, because at about the same age I underwent a similar transformation, less obviously, because in my case there were no outer events to occasion it, except the sheer passage of time, the end of youth and friendship, the sense of being harnessed for life like a beast of burden. It did not upset my mother; but it separated the inner self from the outer, and rendered external things comparatively indifferent. I recorded this conversion in my Platonizing sonnets; my mother expressed it silently in the subsequent fifty years of her life.[3]

In *My Host the World,* he returned to that "conversion" in his own life (even though he had actually passed it chronologically in the previous volume) and devoted to it fifteen pages of intensive discussion. Changing the metaphor of "conversion," Santayana employed the Greek word *metanoia,* which means "a change of mind" or "repentance." He apparently had in mind a meaning which lies somewhere between these alternatives, aptly expressed in the title of the chapter, "A Change of Heart."[4] This *metanoia* was a radical philosophical "re-adjustment" to the world of ideas and to ideas of the world.

In the realm of ideas, Santayana tells us that he had early (at the age of about twenty-four) seized upon some lines of Goethe's as "a sort of motto." The lines are from the song of an old soldier which begins:

> Ich hab' mein Sach auf Nichts gestellt . . .
> Drum ist's so wohl mir in der Welt.
>
> [I don't trouble myself about anything,
> but in spite of that, everything goes well
> for me in the world.]

Santayana says that this is "perhaps more cavalier-like and jaunty" than he was at the time, but that his mind and temperament were attuned to the theme, which is expressed in the title: "*Vanitas! vanitatum vanitas!*" He goes on to note that there is an "equivocation in his boast," when at the end of the song the old soldier says,

> Nun hab' ich mein Sach auf Nichts gestellt . . .
> Und mein gehört die ganze Welt.
>
> [And so I don't trouble myself about anything,
> and the whole world belongs to me.]

"The whole world," Santayana says

belongs to me implicitly when I have given it all up, and am wedded to nothing in particular in it; but for the same reason no part of it properly belongs to me as a possession, but all only in idea. Materially I might be the most insignificant of worms; spiritually I should be the spectator of all time and existence. This implication touched the depth of my vital or congenital philosophy, and for that reason doubtless the refrain of his song became a sort of motto for me at that time. Yet more than ten years had to pass before that implication, on the emotional side, came to expression in my Platonizing sonnets. . . .[5]

The relation between Goethe's old soldier's sentiment and Santayana's "congenital philosophy," though somewhat crude, struck the young student with the shock of recognition. Not feeling a part of the things around him (having been unwillingly transplanted from Spain to Back Bay Boston at the age of nine), he came to see that he could "enjoy everything with a free mind."[6] Disillusionment—or as he preferred to call it, "disintoxication"[7]—with the world, with the life around him, could itself become a viable philosophic perspective, because, like the old soldier, if you trouble yourself about nothing, the whole world belongs to you. In this way, as Santayana explains it, he was able to sustain a manageable view of life, and to do so on his own terms.

So much for the realm of ideas. What about the practical business of human affairs? He had been able to clarify his religious problems (in the first sonnet sequence) by learning "to conceive those myths as poetry, [in which] their meaning and beauty, far from being lost, seemed . . . clearer and more profound than ever." But, he says, "The problem was not so easily solved when it came to exorcising the world, and freeing myself from all illusions about it. The world is not a myth, to be clarified by a little literary criticism."[8] Coming to terms with the world, establishing an attitude toward human affairs most consistent with his philosophical temperament, was not so much brought about as facilitated by the conjunction of a number of significant events between 1892 and 1893. He mentions four in "A Change of Heart." The resolution of his religious problem was one. The death of his father was another. But the marriage of his spinster half-sister, Susana, to whom Santayana was closer than any other member of his family or anyone else, was perhaps the most significant of these events which helped to "disintoxicate" his mind. At over forty, she had married a Spanish widower with six children, and Santayana couldn't help regarding the event as one of tragic desperation.

The impact of these events is readily understandable. They are the kinds of events which touch on many human lives and which, by their very unsettling character, generally help to reconstitute and reshape the lives of those who are affected. But more interesting for our discussion, because of its indicative nature, is the fourth event which he mentions—the death of a former student, Warwick Potter.

When Santayana was a rather widely anthologized minor poet, among the poems most often reprinted and admired was the little sequence of four sonnets entitled "To W. P." They were written on the occasion of the death of Warwick Potter, which occurred six months after his graduation from Harvard in 1893, and published in the 1894 volume. The concluding two lines of the first sonnet are the most famous and most memorable:

> Living you made it goodlier to live,
> Dead you will make it easier to die.[9]

But certain lines of the other sonnets, indeed the entire sequence, take on special meaning when seen in the perspective of Santayana's *metanoia*. For if the death of W. P. is taken as a symbolic event in the poet's life, the poems are seen to be about the poet even more than the dead friend. The second sonnet begins:

> With you a part of me has passed away,[10]

and the last one begins very pointedly:

> In my deep heart these chimes would still have rung
> To tell your passing, had you not been dead.[11]

The chimes would have rung to toll his friend's passing even if he hadn't been dead because the event is a symbolic and inevitable one in the life of the poet. Warwick Potter's death was only an accident in time. The inevitable chimes sounded the knell of Santayana's own youth.

The passing of youth had a special significance in the case of Santayana. He had continued to live the life of an undergraduate even after he had taken his Ph.D. and become a teacher. Perhaps, as we have suggested before, this was unavoidable after being thrown into the august Harvard faculty at such an early age. His friends were mostly undergraduates, and he took a regular part in their social and literary activities. He ate at their eating clubs, drank with them at their hangouts, and wrote for their magazines. But by 1893, something had changed. He was thirty, and "For a poet and a lover of youth the age of thirty is itself a ground for *metanoia*."[12] His young friends seemed to him "every year younger and younger, more standardised and generic." They were ceasing to be his friends so much as "boys at the school where I happened to be one of the masters." At that point his love of youth, he believes, was transformed from a personal friendship with his pupils into the love of youth as an ideal. For even though "That chapter had come to an end . . . youth, in the poet's eyes, is perpetual. The platonic transition was therefore at once spontaneous and inevitable, from the many to the one, from the existent but transitory to the ideal and eternal."[13] It is this transition that is the "conversion," the *metanoia,* that is recorded in the "Platonizing" sonnets of 1895, and this is the theme that is prefigured in the sonnets "To W. P."

In "A Change of Heart" he explains that it later became clear to him that the "W. P." sonnets were more about himself than Warwick Potter. For even though Warwick Potter was a

> general favourite . . . there was after all nothing extraordinary about him. The cause of my emotion was in myself . . . I found myself, unwillingly and irreparably, separated from Spain, from England, from Europe, from my youth and from my religion. It was not good simple Warwick alone that inspired my verses about him. It was the thought of everything that was escaping me: the Good in all modes of it that I might have caught a glimpse of and lost.[14]

The sonnets "To W. P.," then, thematically prefigure the "Platonizing" sonnets of the second sequence. For illustration of this, one might examine the third sonnet in which the sestet describes the eternal realm where "all my loves are gathered into one,"[15] the realm of the platonic ideal. The poem is patently about the "platonic transition," which Santayana speaks of in "A Change of Heart," from "the many to the one, from the existent but transitory to the ideal and eternal." Not only this sonnet, but all four of the sonnets to W. P. record, not always indirectly, the change in outlook to which the poet awakened through the death of his young friend. The event enables him to see the transcendent importance of the ideal in a personal, rather than in a merely abstract or philosophical way. And it presents him with an occasion to articulate what is already present but latent in his mind.

But the death of Warwick Potter, like the death of his father and the desperate marriage of his sister, did not force his *metanoia* on him, if we are to credit his later analysis of the situation. "I was driven," he says, "from the temporal to the eternal, not by any one crisis or conjunction of events, but by the very nature of existence, when this had been honestly faced and frankly admitted."[16] These events, it would seem, merely provided occasions for testing and putting into human terms his philosophical viewpoint. The resulting reflection taught him to see things in a new and different light.

Honestly facing the nature of existence was, as he put it in his best-known ode, to "learn to love, in all things mortal, only | What is eternal." With this lesson learned, "The cry of Ecclesiastes, *Vanitas vanitatum,* could be re-echoed, and the motto from Goethe about setting my heart on nothing could be retained; but both in a new spirit."[17] Having "understood and renounced everything," his spirit could say, like La Valliere in the Carmelite convent, "*Je ne suis pas heureuse; je suis contente.* Nature had been muted, but spirit had been freed. In that sense, and under the spell of that profound conviction, I composed the second sequence of my sonnets, using the traditional language and images of love which can render that sentiment best."[18]

II

The form with which Santayana chose to record poetically his *metanoia* was the love sonnet and the platonic conventions of the great Italian Renaissance poets. He had been studying these writings, in the original, at this time and had written an essay on the subject. First delivered as a lecture in Buffalo in 1896 entitled "Platonism in the Italian Poets,"[19] it was later revised and included in *Interpretations of Poetry and Religion* (1900) under the title, "Platonic Love in Some Italian Poets." The aspect of this poetry that particularly interested him was its Platonism and the platonic love conventions of courtly poetry, where he discovered, perhaps quite by accident, a poetic device for symbolizing and recording the *metanoia* that he felt so strongly, and that demanded expression.

In the final version of the essay, we are fortunate in having Santayana's detailed explanation and interpretation of the poetic conventions of the courtly tradition. These conventions centered on "one or two Platonic ideas, ideas which under the often ironical title of Platonic love, are constantly referred to and seldom understood." He defines them for the purposes of his discussion as "the transformation of the appreciation of beautiful things into the worship of an ideal beauty and the transformation of the love of particular persons into the love of God."[20] Santayana emphasizes that the Platonism of these poets was not doctrinal, deriving from Plato himself, but natural. "Their Platonism was all their own: it was all the more genuine for being a reincarnation rather than an imitation of the old wisdom."[21]

Santayana uses Michael Angelo's sonnets as an example of the embodiment of the first idea of platonic love, "the transformation of the appreciation of beautiful things into the worship of an ideal beauty." Michael Angelo, he tells us, was concerned with the goal of art, which he conceived to be perfection. Spirituality, in this view of things, is conceived in aesthetic terms. "The soul, he tells us in effect, is by nature made for God for the enjoyment of divine beauty."[22] The love of beauty is a form of the love of God, since God is perfection or divine beauty. The artist's effort is then a symbolic act, an attempt to achieve perfection, an acknowledgment of the transcendency of perfection, which is God.

To illustrate the other idea of platonic love, "the transformation of the love of particular persons into the love of God," Santayana uses the poetry of Dante and Guido Cavalcanti. Dante's Beatrice and Guido's Giovanna were real women, but at the same time they were symbols and the love they inspired, myths. In them, the poets embodied or symbolized the perfection of love, of which all other loves were necessarily imperfect aspects. Beatrice was an idealization; Dante's lifelong devotion to her was "something purely mental and poetical."[23] She existed for him only as the embodiment of an ideal, an inspiration, and, as she finally appears in the *Comedia,* a symbolic guide to show him the way to paradise.

The function and importance of this kind of idealization for the poet, especially the religious or sacramental poet, who perceives the things of this world as symbols of a transcendent order, becomes clear. "While the object of love is any particular thing, it *excludes* all other; but it *includes* all others as soon as it becomes a general ideal."[24] All forms of love and objects of love point toward, are imperfect representations of, the highest love and the perfect object of love. "All beauties attract by suggesting the ideal and then fail to satisfy by not fulfilling it."[25] The fact that "every mortal passion leaves, as Keats has told us,

> A heart high-sorrowful and cloyed,
> A burning forehead and a parching tongue,"

is proof, for the natural Platonist, that mortal passions are imperfect, and that satisfaction lies only in the perfection of love. Thus the Italian poets, who were natural Platonists because of their tradition and culture, sought to dramatize the relationship between their earthly loves and the heavenly love of God. To do this, they utilized their chivalrous, courtly conventions to create a highly symbolic poetic convention—platonic love. By raising an earthly object of love, a beautiful woman, to a position from which she might be regarded in chaste reverence and self-effacing worship which symbolized perfection, and *ideal* relationship. The object of love thus became a symbol of all that was worthy of earthly aspiration. As Santayana was to write soon after, man creates the ideal, when he does, in order to have something by which to test or judge the real.[26] "All things become to the worshipper of the ideal [the natural Platonist] so many signs and symbols of what he seeks."[27] Or, as he later put it, in true poetry "everything visible is a sacrament—an outward sign of that inward grace for which the soul is thirsting."[28] In this Italian Renaissance poetry, as Santayana apprehends it, earthly love is a sacrament whose meaning lies not in itself, but in its relation to the ideal. This concept of the sacramental character of human love is an important one which we will return to later.

Santayana is of course too much the confirmed naturalist to allow such transcendentalism to pass without comment. He regarded all inspired imaginative efforts as expressive of something profoundly true, though true only in a symbolic sense. The concept of Platonic love and the poetic conventions based upon it are no exceptions. Behind these ideas lies the wisdom of knowing that

> Too much subjection to another personality makes the expression of our own impossible, and the ideal is nothing but a projection of the demands of our imagination. If the imagination is overpowered by too strong a fascination, by the absolute dominion of an alien influence, we form no ideal at all. We must master a passion before we can see its meanings.[29]

III

By 1895 Santayana had seen the meaning of the passion of his thirtieth year. He had understood, as he thought, what had happened to him in 1893. He realized that he had experienced a profound transformation, a "conversion," a *metanoia,* a "change of heart." It remained only to give it expression, and as he was a serious and committed poet, it was inevitable that this expression should be poetic.

The sonnets are ostensibly about a passion that the poet conceives for a woman. It would perhaps be more accurate to say that the poems are about what *happens to* or what *becomes of* the passion that the poet conceives for a woman. But knowing, as we do, what the poet has said of the poetic theory and conventions he has employed, and knowing further something of what the poet was attempting to express, we are able to have a much broader and deeper understanding of these sonnets than would be possible if we had only the poems themselves. Not only what Santayana has said of the poems publicly, but also what he has written to private correspondents, informs our understanding of his motives and his methods.

Broadly speaking, the sequence tells of a transformation of the poet's passion for a woman from a physical and unsatisfying state to a spiritual and completely satisfying one. It records a discovery of the *discipline* rather than the *doctrine* of Platonic love. This discipline leads to the achievement of contentment in love, to security and peace (Sonnet 50). It involves the recognition that the physical passion called love is merely the "hunger for love," a material symptom or manifestation of the imperfection of love, ideally considered (Sonnet 23). And it also involves the recognition of the affinity of all forms of love—a brother's, a lover's, a friend's, a hermit's (Sonnet 31). The individual sonnets embody the progressive stages and moments of discovery or insight; the general movement is from anguish and despair to serenity and peace.

George Howgate has divided the sonnets up into fairly acceptable groupings, and has identified the principal moods and tonal shifts.[30] These become clear when one studies the sequence closely. Sonnets 21–26 record the poet in a state of unhappiness because of an unsatisfying, physical love. Sonnets 27–29 record the turning point, as the poet discovers, with the help of Petrarch, the way out of his despair. In this connection, Howgate is close to the truth when he says that the quotation from Petrarch in Sonnet 28 is the "keystone in the arch of his sonnet sequence,"[31] for these lines introduce the "platonic transition" that is central to the meaning of the sequence. The remaining sonnets, except 34–37 which I shall discuss later, record further insights into the new "platonic" relationship and celebrate its superiority as a mode of love.

In order to see the sonnets as a revelation and expression of Santayana's *metanoia,* we must bear in mind that the Platonism of the sonnets is a consciously employed myth, as Santayana himself testifies. Platonism was not natural to him, though he had a strong sympathy for it, but he was often impatient with those who would dismiss it out of hand without seeing that it was, as he thought, expressive of something true in the nature of man and of human aspirations. Still, he was not, and did not want to appear to be, a Platonist himself. In a passage that formed a part of the original Buffalo lecture, he makes this quite clear:

> As for me, when I read the words of these inspired men [Italian poets] and try to understand the depths of experience which is buried in them as in a marble tomb, I feel, I confess, very far away from them. I wonder if all their exaltation is not the natural illusion of a hope too great for any man; but at the same time I remember the story of Ruth and how she was impressed by that so strange and so passionate Jewish race into which she had come,—a race that lives on prophecy and hope, and believed in its transcendental destiny—and I envy her that she found it in her heart to say, what I would gladly say to the family of Plato, "Let thy people be my people and thy God, my God."[32]

Although he later excised this passage, it survives in the earlier version as a useful reminder that Santayana, so platonic in the sonnets, is no platonist at heart, and that (to return to our point) the platonism of the sonnets is a convenient framework, an expressive myth, borrowed for a specific purpose from the Italian poets.

The lady is a centrally important and fascinating aspect of these "Platonizing" sonnets. So far as is known, by Santayana's own account and those of his close friends, there was no romantic love interest in his life. Yet these sonnets unblushingly relate a most passionate attachment. This state of affairs led one of his Harvard friends, Henry Ward Abbott, to write Santayana many years later and ask him whether or not the lady of the sonnets might be a certain person, whom he named. This provoked an illuminating response:

> . . . in my old age [he was 60], I have become far more sentimental and even benevolent. I couldn't write now those sublimated love sonnets, nor Lucifer . . . ; they were a perfectly sincere *conviction,* but they were not an actual experience; they were an evasion of experience, on the presumption (quite just when you are young and on a high horse) that experience would be a ghastly failure. The lady of the sonnets, far from being the one you absurdly mention, is a myth, a symbol: certainly she stands for Somebody, not always the same Somebody, and generally for a hint or suggestion drawn from reason rather than for any specific passion; but the enthusiasm is speculative, not erotic: I had been convinced by Plato and the Italian Platonists: I had not been obliged to make the Pilgrim's progress in person. [33]

That they record "an evasion of experience," in the sense of not going through with an actual love affair, the sonnets themselves suggest very strongly. Yet the sonnets also suggest that "Somebody" was the Beatrice of these poems, or perhaps, as Howgate suggests (and Santayana's letter, in one way, tends to bear out), two "Somebodies." [34] Sonnets 34 to 37 make it seem that the poet has in mind, not only a symbolic lady, but a real lady who has actually read the sonnets and who remarks only, "I like the verses; they are written well." [35] A number of points in these four sonnets are indicative of specifically personal involvement on the part of the poet. For example, in Sonnet 34 the poet says that they were

> . . . far divided in our birth
> By nature's gifts and half the planet's girth,
> And speech, and faith, and blood, and ancient wars. [36]

The facts of Santayana's Spanish birth and American residence disincline one to regard this as mere literary realism, and Sonnet 35 fairly well clinches it:

> We needs must be divided in the tomb,
> For I would die among the hills of Spain
> And o'er the treeless melancholy plain
> Await the coming of the final gloom.
> But thou—O pitiful! will find scant room
> Among thy kindred by the northern main . . . [37]

The genuine anguish of the next sonnet, when the poet anticipates the rebuff he would receive if he ventured to tell the lady that she was his "torment" and his "rapture too," further suggests the lady's actual existence. And the rebuff itself is of singular interest. The poet imagines what would have happened if, after reading his verses to the lady and hearing her response about liking them, he had

> . . . knelt confessing "It is you,
> You are my torment and my rapture too."
> I should have seen you rise in flushed disdain:
> "For shame to say so, be it false or true!"
> And the sharp sword that ran me through and through,
> On your white bosom too had left a stain.[38]

The next sonnet, the last of this seemingly autobiographical group, records that the poet was silent, instead of venturing in this fashion, and that it is better so. But one can hardly read the episode without wondering exactly why the lady would think it shameful for the poet to speak so. Is it merely that she would think it *gauche* or lacking in *savoir faire?* If so, the gravity of tone, especially in the concluding image, is ridiculously overdone. Still, the lady does not say that it is shameful for the poet to love her, but that it is shameful *to say so,* "be it false or true." Apparently it is all right to love her and to write poems about it, but not to tell her as much. This at least is what the poet anticipates, and why he doesn't say what he is thinking. Apparently also, the possibility of an actual, physical, reciprocal love affair is out of the question, though we are not told why.

Every indication is that the love is perfectly hopeless in any but a platonic sense. This might be because she is married, biographically a strong possibility because Santayana had many married women as friends, cultured Boston ladies such as Harvard faculty wives, who cultivated the society of the charming young poet. This may be the best explanation from a biographical point of view, though certain things in the poems taken along with Santayana's known devotion for his sister Susana, foster the irrepressible suggestion that the inspiration of the sonnets might have been she. Daniel Cory's recent book on Santayana contains evidence which strongly supports this suggestion. In what Cory calls "one of his longest and most revealing letters."[39] Santayana discusses Howgate's treatment of his poetry and only partial understanding of his work. He says that this is necessarily so, because it is impossible for anyone to know enough about his life to understand him completely. To illustrate this, he writes:

> There is my sister, for instance, certainly the most important influence in my life, psychologically my mother, and one might almost say, my wife. Not that an incestuous idea even entered my mind or hers; but Freud might have discovered things unsuspected by ourselves. She was once a novice in a Carmelite convent, and I much admired her resolution to turn her back so completely on Boston, on the family, and on me. When later she was married, I didn't like it, nor her husband, although he was an admirable person in his way.[40]

Having said this by way of confession and example, as something he obviously wants Cory (his potential biographer) to know, he concludes: "Such things are obscure and unpleasant; but they give body to sentiments that, verbally, might seem unsubstantial."[41] The "Platonizing" sonnets might well be taken as such sentiments.

There is no need to labor a point which is perhaps academic and inconclusive, but the fact that Susana might have served as the inspiration of Santayana's "Platonizing" sonnets puts the inner experiences which the sonnets are designed to express in a significant light. For these poems are "sublimated love sonnets," not in the sense of celebrating a frustrated love affair in which a strong passion is thwarted, but rather in the sense of celebrating a symbolic passion which is transformed by an insight into something more inclusive and more satisfying.

IV

The great paradox of the relationship in the sonnets between the poet and the lady, and what later becomes for the poet the great beauty of it, is that this love is perfectly hopeless. In fact, the phrase "perfectly hopeless" has a profound aptness. For the lesson that the poet learns in the course of the sequence is that the only truly satisfying love, perfect love, is not physical and real but imaginative and ideal. The first line of Sonnet 33 is "A perfect love is nourished by despair."[42] In discussing the significance of the sequence in "A Change of Heart," Santayana wrote that this line was "the key to the whole," but he significantly misremembered the line and quoted it as "A perfect love is *founded on* despair."[43] Perfect love must be founded on despair because "The perfect lover must renounce pursuit and the hope of passion."[44] Otherwise, the love is doomed to be unsatisfying (or only temporarily satisfying) and therefore *im*perfect.

In formulating the concept of perfect love in "A Change of Heart," Santayana employs Stendhal's grammar of terms in *De L'Amour*. Stendhal, Santayana observes, posits four kinds of love: *l'amour physique, l'amour vanité, l'amour goût,* and *la grande passion.* "The first two," Santayana says, "are obviously imperfect and impure: they include craving, jealousy, cruelty, fear, folly, and self-degradation."[45] But *la grande passion* transforms "physical lust and jealousy" into "absolute devotion, heroism and suicide," and *l'amour goût* is "more playful and turns the vital element into laughter and delight . . . Combine these two elements, the tragic and the lyrical, and you have turned love into a rapture and an adoration which seems to me its perfection."[46]

Such is the nature of the perfect love, the discovery of which the second sonnet sequence records. But his love, like the lady, is symbolic; it constitutes, as Santayana believed of all platonic forms, a myth. Moreover, as

Santayana confessed to Howgate, the whole effort was "somewhat of a literary exercise," in which "his mind if not his heart was touched."[47] Similarly, one of the first things he told Cory was that "there was no 'dark lady' to be identified in his sonnets: it was all an idealization of conventional themes."[48] The most important question, then, is not what lady might have served as the inspiration of the sonnets, but what the symbolic lady and the mythical love are expressive of. It seems reasonable, in light of Santayana's deliberate and earnest testimony, that the sequence must be taken as the expression of what he calls a *metanoia*. And this *metanoia* would seem to be, in large part, the common experience at a certain age of all reflective people, namely, the "agonizing reappraisal" which becomes necessary when the perspective of youth must finally be abandoned. The world must be construed in somewhat different terms, and a spiritual "readjustment" must be effected. The study of the Platonism of the Italian Renaissance poets provided Santayana with the means of expressing his spiritual "re-adjustment."

It may seem strange that a relatively modern poet should conceive and execute such a poetic scheme, but Santayana's view of the poet and his function, once we understand it, is seen to inspire just such imaginative activity as this. To draw on a tradition and set of poetic conventions no longer used or even understood did not seem to him an artistic liability, for as he said later, "To say that what was once good is good no longer is to give too much importance to chronology."[49] The emotional experience that he wished to record demanded a poetic form that would properly express it. "What I felt when I composed those verses," he later wrote, "could not have been rendered in any other form."[50] That a philosophical *metanoia,* an "intellectual emotion," should be symbolized by a mythical love affair was a natural effect of his view of poetry and its dramatic and emotional nature:

> The substance of poetry is, after all emotion; and if the intellectual emotion of comprehension and the mimetic one of impersonation are massive, they are not so intense as the appetites and other transitive emotions of life; the passions are the chief basis of all interests, even the most ideal, and the passions are seldom brought into play except by the contact of man with man.[51]

Thus, a dramatic situation involving the passions is required to express the emotion properly, and the poet's role is to invent one that is suitable, or as Santayana puts it: "to imagine occasions in which these feelings may manifest all their inward vitality is the poet's function. . . ."[52] The poet must find "an appropriate theatre" in which to dramatize his impulses, and "the glorious emotions with which he bubbles over must at all hazards find or feign their correlative objects."[53] Like the derivative formulation of his student, T. S. Eliot, Santayana's theory holds that the poet must invent a "set of objects, a situation, a chain of events" capable of evoking the emotion he wishes to express. Hence, the mythical love affair and the symbolic beloved.

Why are these suitable correlative objects for evoking the emotion of a *metanoia?* The question is not so difficult as it appears when we first confront it. Love between man and woman, at least as Santayana presents it, is a transitory emotion. It promises or prefigures what it cannot achieve. In the grammar of Platonism, this is because it is imperfect. Perfection in love, as in all things, belongs to the transcendent realm of the ideal. In Santayana's own life, the discovery that his youth had passed, a discovery largely prompted by the four events referred to in "A Change of Heart," brought home dramatically and personally the realization that all things in life are transitory. The flux of experience that offered things of value also took them away. He was learning, with the help of Spinoza, to see all things *sub specie aeternitatis,*[54] so as not to be "taken in" by their transitory nature; he was learning "to love in all things mortal, only │ What is eternal." Love was an appropriate metaphor for the transitory, and platonic love was a particularly appropriate convention for expressing his *metanoia* and what it had taught him.

Love in the second sonnet sequence is a sacrament. That is, it is an earthly activity with transcendent significance, a symbol of something beyond itself. As we have noted earlier (and the notion pervades Santayana's religious and poetic theory), he thought that, for the true poet, everything in the visible world is a sacrament, "the outward sign of that inward grace for which the soul is thirsting." This is at the center of his idea that religion and poetry are "identical in essence." In the sonnets, the lady becomes an object of holy adoration, and the poet's love becomes worship. Far from the sensual anguish and frustration that attends physical love, the relationship that the poet achieves confers upon him a grace, a religious peace. In Sonnet 39, he anticipates the reaction of the world at large:

> The world will say, "What mystic love is this?
> What ghostly mistress? What angelic friend?"
> Read, masters, your own passion to the end,
> And tell me then if I have writ amiss.
> When all loves die that hang upon a kiss,
> And must with cavil and with chance contend,
> Their risen selves with the eternal blend
> Where perfect dying is their perfect bliss.
> And might I kiss her once, asleep or dead,
> Upon the forehead or the globed eyes,
> Or where the gold is parted on her head,
> That kiss would help me on to paradise
> As if I kissed the consecrated bread
> In which the buried soul of Jesus lies.[55]

Here, the poet's love is explicitly treated as a parallel to the Christian sacrament. This continues in Sonnet 44, in which the poet says that everything in the world now takes its meaning through the lady. All of this is in line with Santayana's idea that the ideal is postulated by man to order and give meaning to the real, thereby perfecting and transcending it. The sestet reads:

> For thee the labour of my studious ease
> I ply with hope, for thee all pleasures please,
> Thy sweetness doth the bread of sorrow leaven;
> And from thy noble lips and heart of gold
> I drink the comforts of the faiths of old
> And thy perfection is my proof of heaven.[56]

In Sonnet 45 he compares his meditation before her image with the worship of the crucifix, and in Sonnet 47 he refers to her as the "shade of Him." Finally in the last poem, Sonnet 50, the poet confesses that he will not be disappointed if heaven does not follow death. The sequence ends:

> Hath not my grief the blessed joy of thee?
> Is not the comfort of these singing hours,
> Full of thy perfectness, enough for me?
> They are not evil, then, those hidden powers:
> One love sufficeth an eternity.[57]

One love suffices an eternity if it is an ideal love, self-forgetful in its conception and hopeless in its material ends. Such a love is perfectly expressive, as a symbol, of the "intellectual emotion" of Santayana's *metanoia.* Disillusioned with life and what it offered a young man so unfortunately situated as he was, Santayana came at the age of thirty to view the world in a new perspective. Just as the poet discovers, in the second sonnet sequence, that physical love, which promises so much, is a transitory and unsatisfying experience, so Santayana discovered that youth and the warm fellowship it afforded him, were transitory and irretrievable. His relationship with his sister was seriously altered by her marriage; his father was dead; his religion had proved false. But a shift in perspective, in the way of assigning value to things, "separated the inner self from the outer." The outer self belonged to the temporal flux of experience, but the inner, myth-making, idealizing self could be attuned to the realm of the eternal. This separation, in which both elements are reconciled, provided Santayana with a tenable vision of experience, focused in such a way as to see all things "under the form of eternity." This "re-adjustment," as I have been calling it, this *metanoia,* expressed by the highly stylized conventions of his second sonnet sequence, goes a long way toward explaining the origin and nature of the aloofness and detachment which Santayana's critics have long noted in his work.

Notes

1. In the 1923 edition of his selected *Poems,* the first sequence (Sonnets 1–20) is given the title "Sonnets 1883–1893"; the second sequence (Sonnets 21–50) is given the title "Sonnets 1895," referring not to the date of publication (1896), but presumably to the period of composition.

2. *George Santayana* (Philadelphia, 1938), 40–86. Intelligent observations on Santayana's poetry can also be found in Philip Blair Rice's contribution to *The Philosophy of George Santayana,* edited by Paul Arthur Schilpp (Evanston and Chicago, 1940), 265–291; Horace Gregory and Marya Zaturenska, *A History of American Poetry* (New York, 1940), 67–78; Carlin Kindilien, *American Poetry in the Eighteen Nineties* (Providence, 1956), 113–119; Daniel Hoffman, *American Poetry and Poetics* (Garden City, 1962), xliv–xlv.

3. *Persons and Places: The Background of My Life* (New York, 1944), 51–52.

4. First published separately in *The Atlantic Monthly,* CLXXXII, 52–56 (December, 1948).

5. *My Host the World* (New York, 1953), 5. Actually, at most nine years could have passed between his first year in Germany (1886–1887), where he says he read the lines in Goethe, and 1895.

6. *My Host the World,* 6.

7. He used this word in similar contexts in *Platonism and the Spiritual Life, The Works of George Santayana* (New York, 1936–1940), x, 179; and "A Brief History of My Opinions," *Works,* II. The word is a particularly apt coinage because it points up the salient feature of this "sobering" experience.

8. *My Host the World,* 6.

9. *Works,* I, 241.

10. *Works,* I, 242.

11. *Works,* I, 243.

12. *My Host the World,* 7.

13. *My Host the World,* 8.

14. *My Host the World,* 8.

15. *Works,* I, 242.

16. *My Host the World,* 11.

17. *My Host the World,* 11.

18. *My Host the World,* 14.

19. The occasion was an address given to the Contemporary Club in February, 1896. The lecture, presumably as delivered, was printed privately in Buffalo.

20. *Works,* II, 87.

21. *Works,* II, 87.

22. *Works,* II, 95.

23. *Works,* II, 88.

24. *Works,* II, 91; italics mine.

25. *Works,* II, 91.

26. "Preface," *Interpretations of Poetry and Religion, Works,* II, 6.

27. "Platonic Love in Some Italian Poets," *Works,* II, 92.

28. "The Elements and Functions of Poetry," *Works,* II, 198.

29. "Platonic Love," *Works,* II, 94.

30. *George Santayana,* 58–61.

31. *George Santayana,* 64.

32. This is quoted by Philip Blair Rice in his contribution to the Schilpp volume, 282. He adds perceptively, "Santayana himself always remained amid alien corn."

33. *The Letters of George Santayana,* edited by Daniel Cory (New York, 1955), 208.

34. Though Santayana himself, in a letter to Daniel Cory, hooted at Howgate's suggestion that there seemed to be two ladies involved [see Daniel Cory, *Santayana: The Later Years* (New York, 1963), 209], his inference is reasonable on the evidence of the sonnets. Sonnet 24 presumably tells of kissing the lady, whereas in Sonnet 36 the poet says that he would be severly reproached if he even mentioned his love to the lady. This suggests the possibility of there being two ladies: one kissable, one not.

35. Sonnet 36, *Works,* I, 232.

36. Sonnet 36, *Works,* I, 231.

37. Sonnet 36, *Works,* I, 232.

38. Sonnet 37, *Works,* I, 232.

39. *Santayana: The Later Years,* 208.

40. *Santayana: The Later Years,* 210.

41. *Santayana: The Later Years,* 210.

42. *Works,* I, 251.

43. *My Host the World,* 14; italics mine.

44. *My Host the World,* 14.

45. *My Host the World,* 14.

46. *My Host the World,* 15.

47. Howgate, 57.

48. Cory, 17.

49. "Preface," *Poems, Works,* I, 211; this preface was first published in the selected edition of his *Poems* in 1923.

50. *Poems, Works,* I, 210.

51. "Elements and Function of Poetry," *Works,* II, 192.

52. "Elements and Function of Poetry," *Works,* II, 192.

53. *Works,* II, 192. The verbal similarity to T. S. Eliot's famous "objective correlative" is no accident. Santayana's idea would appear to be nothing less than its source, for, far from being an accidental similarity of phrasing, the two theories ("correlative object" and "objective correlative") are almost identical in substance. Compare Eliot's celebrated formulation: "The only way of expressing emotion in the form of art is by finding an 'objective correlative'; in other words, a set of objects, a situation, a chain of events which shall be the formula of that particular emotion; such that when the external facts, which must terminate in sensory experience, are given, the emotion is immediately evoked." From "Hamlet and his Problems," *Selected Essays* (New York, 1932), 124–125.

54. This phrase usually appears in Santayana's writings as "under the form of eternity."

55. *Works,* I, 234.

56. *Works,* I, 236.

57. *Works,* I, 239.

The Last Puritan and the
Failure in American Culture

JAMES C. BALLOWE

I

The crux of George Santayana's criticism of America has been summed up by George W. Howgate: America has had a dichotomous development of the Will and the Intellect; and it might find a more harmonious life by acknowledging the natural grounds for morality, by being dedicated to reason, and by harboring a pure and disillusioned idealism.[1] The precise emphasis of this criticism has been best understood by Lionel Trilling, who writes,

> Santayana was ill at ease everywhere in America, but what offended his soul was New England, especially Boston, especially Cambridge. For the America of raw energy, the America of material concerns, the America that he could see as young and barbaric and in the line of history he had a tolerance and affection that were real and not merely condescending.[2]

In a letter to Van Wyck Brooks, Santayana restates his continued optimism for the materialistic gush and go of America and his growing distaste for the minds which hoped to tame this vital energy. He noted that the "petering out" of Randolph Bourne and other American intellectuals was due to their practice of *"applied culture"*: "Instead of being interested in what they are and what they do and see," he wrote, "they are interested in what they think they would like to be and see and do. . . ." On the other hand,

> A certain degree of sympathy and assimilation with ultra-modern ways in Europe or even Asia may be possible, because young America is simply modernism undiluted: but what Lewis Mumford calls "the pillage of the past" (of which he thinks I am guilty too) is worse than useless. I therefore think that art, etc, has a better soil in the ferocious 100% America than in the Intelligentsia of New York. It is veneer, rouge, aestheticism, art museums, new theatres, etc. that make America impotent. The good things are football, kindness, and jazz bands.[3]

Reprinted from *American Quarterly* 18 (Summer 1966): 123–35, with the permission of the American Studies Association; © 1966, American Studies Association.

It must not be thought, however, that Santayana's materialism resembles the valueless, anti-intellectual sort common to vitalistic America. His materialism, he insists, is really naturalism; but not the "*romantic* naturalism like Goethe's . . . or that of Bergson. Mine" he says, "is the hard, non-humanistic naturalism of the Ionian philosophers, of Democritus, Lucretius, and Spinoza."[4] It is this pre-Platonic materialism which allows him to stand aloof from both sides of America, criticizing the one for having cut off the intellect and the spirit from their natural basis and smiling rather benevolently on the other for returning to the primitive state in which a new intellect and spirit may arise.

II

In *The Last Puritan: A Memoir in the Form of a Novel* (1935) Santayana gives flesh and blood to his criticism of American culture. If this criticism appears less academic or less authoritative in fiction than it does in his essays, it remains nonetheless clear and consistent. But in the world of people and events, time and space, the abstractions become concrete, the hypotheses become dramatically credible. Imperfection in characters tempers the criticism with irony. The novel records what Santayana discovered about his young acquaintances who were bred in the ethos of the genteel tradition at the end of the century. Yet the novel gives a more mature criticism than it might have had it been written in the 1890s. As it is, the narrative benefits from all he had to say about America from his own undergraduate days at Harvard to *The Genteel Tradition at Bay* (1931). Even so, it retains the freshness and simplicity of an early avowed purpose: to describe the conditions underlying the failure of American youth of high promise.[5]

It is just this singleness of purpose which led Henry Seidel Canby to remark that Santayana's novel was an undergraduate view of America, lacking in complete perspective.[6] In a way, this is correct. Santayana hardly mentions the physical side of American life. His own excuse for this is that he himself was not in the main stream of that life. But in an answer to Canby he points out that he did try to show it in peripheral figures such as Mr. James Van de Weyer, Senator Lunt, Edith Van de Weyer and the Rev. Edgar Thornton—all successful participants in a progressive society.[7] Actually, in failing to describe in detail the American Will, Santayana has subtly emphasized the hiatus existing between the two Americas. In the novel, members of the genteel tradition ignore, disdain or fear the world outside. When modernism shows itself, there seems to be a feeling that it can be kept in check by denying its existence. Just as sacrosanct Boston no doubt sensed the presence of an impending and vital physical world, the rock-ribbed puritans of the novel are made uncomfortable by its persistent nudging from the background. Nathaniel Alden attempts to shut out the encroachments of teeming South Boston by pulling the blinds of his house and by turning his indiscreet and susceptible half-brother Peter from his doors. Harriet Bumstead Alden, Peter's wife, refuses to allow their son Oliver, "the last puritan," to associate with the unhygienic family of her gardener, lies about the mother-child relationship Oliver once sees on his way into Great Falls, Connecticut, and discourages the apothecary's son from becoming Oliver's friend. Ironically, Oliver, who desires a place in the world, is indignant when his cousin Edith Ven de Weyer actually arranges an opportunity for him in business. Santayana's depiction of modernism in the novel is solely from the point of view of the genteel tradition.

But the New England genteel tradition is itself of wide variety. Santayana did not live in proximity with it for forty years without noticing its capacity for producing strong as well as weak minds. In Caleb Wetherbee, Oliver Alden's eccentric, elderly cousin, the genteel tradition has returned again to supernaturalism, following Santayana's advice that this is the only way it could gain sanctions for its moral absolutism.[8] Caleb's sermon to Oliver encouraging him to live in Boston and attend Harvard is Santayana's admission that Cambridge remains the intellectual mecca for America. Caleb tells Oliver that in Boston he "might almost escape the scramble outside, the low boasts, the ugly language, the aggressive commonness of modern life, and its idiotic pleasures," by way of quietness, books, music and sympathy. But the intellectual can benefit Boston, too. Boston and Harvard, Caleb adds, "are becoming too much like the rest of the country, choked with big business, forced fads, and merely useful knowledge." Having only "Charley Copeland and Barrett Wendell and William James" among its radicals, it needs new minds which will break away from professionalism, standard opinion, "the dulcet mendacity of the pulpits," and weak political rulers. Caleb's view of Boston as a place in which one can ignore the optimism, worldliness and mediocrity of the physical world while refurbishing the intellectual is a rationale that Peter Alden (and Santayana) cannot accept. It renounces humanity for an illusion. Peter is Santayana the materialist—an interested spectator in the present and a prophet of change in the future. He tells Caleb that the intellectual illusions of absolutists mean little in the overall scheme of things. "Let the world . . . have its fun," he says to Caleb.

> "Let it cook in its own broth; and let those whose nerves are tougher than yours and mine enjoy the bustle of unregenerate America and make the whole world whiz faster and faster with one identical deafening infernal roar. What an experience for mankind and what a subject afterwards for the moralist!"[9]

Those puritans who unlike Caleb did not lock themselves in a monastery and adopt a supernatural view found vitalistic America more difficult to avoid. Nathaniel Alden succeeds best because he has been able to secrete himself behind family name, fortune, and routine. For his moral sanctions

Nathaniel has retained the hard liberalism of the mid-century. By sheer will he has preserved for himself a portion of the Great Merchant economy which itself is detached from the nation's interests. To him art means acquisition; religion connotes an amoral unitarianism; and morality means doing the things to which he is accustomed. Yet, facing him at all times is the knowledge that if he once steps from the curb of Beacon Street in the wrong direction, he will be plunged into the nether world of South Boston.

Nathaniel's gentility is tinkling and comic beside the stout and vulgar gentility of Harriet Bumstead Alden of Great Falls, Connecticut. Outside of Boston, away from any center of art and thought, gentility is a mere accretion of all that is bad in the tradition upon an effete pioneering spirit. Harriet had neither the supernaturalism of Caleb nor the New England heritage of Nathaniel on which to regulate her life. In her the genteel tradition becomes vitiated and crude. For in order to make her claim to that tradition, she must continually remind others of her right to it. She surrounds herself with pseudo-cultured friends like the spinster librarian Letitia Lamb, marries Peter Alden in order to rebuild her family mansion overlooking Great Falls and gain a respected name for herself, and then sets out to fashion the world in her own image through her son, Oliver. By the time Oliver rebels, she has become insensate enough to gather the folds of her black gown around her and retire into comfortable isolation, convinced that the world is hopelessly corrupt for not acclaiming her right to legislate for it.

Both Nathaniel and Harriet find contentment in living as parasites off the fruits of the past. Their liberalism is completely anti-intellectual. Their intellectual contemporaries refuse to accept a similar role; but bred in the tradition of gentility they are not yet prepared to break away from it. Peter Alden and Harold Van de Weyer (the father of Mario, the Latin foil for Oliver) represent the incapacity to channel their mental enthusiasms outside of the genteel tradition. "Dear Harold" (who has died before the novel begins) is a type of that youth whom Santayana remembered seeing enter the *Lampoon* office, "flushed with the project of some comic illustration that had just occurred to him" but incapable of bringing it to a point. His despair of becoming a great painter led him to study genealogy, then heraldry, on which he was engaged at his death. He was never quite able to write the proposed monumental work on heraldry for which he had long before formulated the first principle: "heraldry held in a nutshell the secret of all the arts, which were nothing but self-exhibition upon the shield of self-defence" (pp. 4–5). Peter Alden, too, fails to produce anything but a sophisticated, adventurous life that is an escape from what he feels are his more important duties. Having tested life in all its forms, he makes no pretense of his unwillingness to cope with it. Like Santayana, he is content to view the world from a distance, remarking all the while the irony of its misdirection. But because of his heritage, Peter is not satisfied with solace from the Life of Reason. His disillusion becomes post-rational;[10] and only artificial escape through drugs allows infrequent relief. When life itself begins to tax him in Oliver's pend-ing failure and Harriet's callous interference, drugs provide him with a last way out.

III

Oliver Alden does not fail in the same way as do the other members of the genteel tradition. As early as 1924, Santayana wrote that Oliver's namesakes were Oliver Cromwell and John Alden, thereby implying that he would possess both the stout and tender aspects of puritanism.[11] But this in itself is ironic. Oliver knows that he is neither militant like his grandfather, a "ferocious Calvinist" who ground "the faces of the poor, . . . consigning them afterwards to hell-fire," nor gentle like his father, who was "limp, kind, lavish, and humorous; yet [with] force enough to choose his own way, and not to be roped in or annexed by anybody, not even by [his] mother." Nevertheless, Oliver denies that his family is right when it regards him as "just negative, just passive, turned out like printed wall-paper, the third sloppy wash in the family teapot" (p. 355). Oliver's stoutness comes from the conviction that he is always right, his tenderness from the lack of energy to make everyone agree with him. Each negates the other. He fails to act on his own convictions.

The difference between the gentility of Oliver and the early twentieth-century genteel tradition is that he still possesses the agonized conscience of Calvinism and the subjectivism of transcendentalism.[12] His is a "moral na-ture burdened and over-strung, and a critical faculty fearless but helplessly subjective" (p. 602). If the genteel tradition is ineffectual because it has successfully forfeited these things in favor of complacence, Oliver Alden is ineffectual because neither conscience nor subjectivism is compatible any longer with the age. The fact is that Santayana had made Oliver even more pure than the puritans. In the modern world he is an absolute anachronism. He possesses "the metaphysical austerity of the seventeenth century" without "the horrid uncertainity about the truth of traditional myths and dogmas."[13] Oliver has found the conditions for morality in the universe, disdaining man-made bases for it in art, religion or politics (p. 114). Yet Oliver's puritan conscience demands that he participate in the world. As he does so, his conscience wars against itself. For if his duty is to take part in the contempo-rary world, the conditions of that world force him to give up puritanism. Hence, the dilemma which Mario Van de Weyer describes for Santayana in the Prologue—that Oliver "thought it his clear duty to give puritanism up, but couldn't" (p. 6). His attempts to do so in sports, studies, love-making and friendships, all prove feeble. Santayana writes in the Preface to the Triton edition that Oliver goes against his essential nature: "His great error [is] that he [tries] to be commonplace." Without vocation or the ability to find a direction in life, he halts his own existence. "Not trusting his inspiration" he knows " 'the pity, not the joy, of love' the severity of intellect and not its glory."[14]

Santayana wishes the reader to think of Oliver as something more than the essence of puritanism in which the strength is exhausted.[15] Even with a certain hardness and egotism, which Santayana says "limited his comprehension even of the people and things that attracted him most," Oliver is a superior individual. Santayana writes that he meant to emphasize Oliver's ability to maintain integrity and sweetness in the face of social order that violated his instincts. He gives Oliver the Christlike virtues of humility, charity, forgiveness, and hatred of sham.[16] In the novel, Oliver is compared with Christ on three occasions: Caleb asks Peter where he found such a boy who can dispute against the doctors, putting them to shame by his insights (Oliver is talking about Goethe) (p. 194); Irma Schlote, Oliver's German governess, mistakes his sleeping form reflected in a mirror for a full-length portrait of Christ on the cross (p. 223); and the Vicar, father of Oliver's English friend Jim Darnley, reminds Oliver that Christ did not seek a vocation in the world (p. 254). Santayana increases the irony of Oliver's position by this comparison to Christ. He describes a youth whose forebears have created a world that now has no room for their kind. Santayana seems to ask, "Where is there a place for a divine vocation such as that which Oliver possessed?" His answer is that it does not exist—at least not in modern America.

Perhaps Santayana was too occupied with describing the genteel tradition to make clear that both it and practical America are at fault in denying to the individual the freedom of spirit and thought. He does suggest this, certainly. But Oliver is a little too precious, a little too much the Clarissa or Evelina for the reader to care that he is not wholly responsible for his own failure. In a letter to Mrs. George Sturgis, written shortly after the American edition was published, Santayana recognized that he may not have made America's part in Oliver's failure plain enough. Oliver, he says, is austere toward all conventions: the natural man, his mother, Harvard philosophers and the Vicar's religion. He is not shaken even by the example of Jim Darnley ("Lord Jim") or Mario, with whose participation in the world he sympathizes. The reason for this unwavering austerity, Santayana writes, is that Oliver is a mystic, "touched with a divine consecration, and *couldn't* give way to the world, the flesh, or the devil." His deepest tragedy is that although he should have been a saint,

> he lived in a spiritual vacuum. American breeding can be perfect in form, but it is woefully thin in substance; so that if a man is born a poet or a mystic in America he simply starves, because what social life offers and presses upon him is offensive to him, and there is nothing else. He evaporates, he peters out.— That is my intention, or rather perception, in Oliver.[17]

This is the most explicit condemnation Santayana makes anywhere of America. If Santayana obscures America's failure in the novel by preoccupation with the story of Oliver Alden, this failure is nevertheless as much a cause of Oliver's tragedy as is his own incapacity to act.

Oliver is not just an atavistic puritan. To Santayana, he represents the mind of the North. In childhood Oliver is tutored in the maxims of Goetheian romanticism by Irma Schlote; yet, he unconsciously anticipates the Faustian lesson and sacrifices "his heart to his self-development" (p. 112). To Mario Van de Weyer he is a "magnificent Nordic" (p. 428). Santayana establishes Oliver's northern affinities in the Prologue, arguing with Mario that Oliver could never forsake the Nordic monorail of sheer will for the Roman road of tradition—the latter having a paved middle way "for the militant faithful" and "broad grassy alleys on either side for the sheep and goats . . ." (p. 8). Oliver's sense of duty but incapacity to act, his knowledge of physical fact but distrust of human nature, and his integrity of purpose but lack of direction are common to the northern temperament of Hamlet and Lucifer, both of whom figure prominently in Santayana's criticism of northern culture.[18]

The antithesis of this temperament is found in Mario Van de Weyer. Mario, like Oliver, is late-born.[19] But he has Santayana's ability to see things in the perspective of the past, which in turn enables him to find humor in the world and in himself. In the Prologue Santayana tells Mario that the two of them differ from Oliver in that they were born clear and did not have to achieve clearness. Oliver, he says, while attempting to emerge from the darkness of his own conscience maintained his divine right to legislate for the world (pp. 9–10). Although Mario is the son of an American and is educated in the North—at Eton, Harvard and Oxford—he makes his home in Italy, his mother's country. Like Santayana, Mario is a wanderer who discovers that Rome links the past and the present in western civilization. Of the city itself, Santayana wrote in his autobiography, it is "inhabited by a people that more than any other resembles the civilised ancients."[20] "In Rome," he continues later,

> I feel nearer to my own past, and to the whole past and future of the world, than I should in any cemetery or in any museum of relics. Old places and old persons in their turn, when spirit dwells in them, have an intrinsic vitality of which youth is incapable; precisely the balance and wisdom that comes from long perspectives and broad foundations.[21]

Mario can confront the present because he knows the values of the past. If beside Oliver he appears somehow the fop, or the hedonist, or even otherworldly, it is because he lacks Oliver's austerity of purpose. Instead he has those Epicurean qualities Santayana prefers and mentions in the Prologue: abundance, intelligence and "the irony of ultimate truth." Nonetheless, he is stable. Participating in the experiences which life has to offer, he remains certain of his own goals. Mario can enter into the life of England, France, America, indeed of the whole world, and return to his natural self. It is not that he is unaffected by his experience; but he has a strong sense of his own culture and his place in it. Mario confronts the world frankly and honestly, all the while using the lessons of the past.[22] When Santayana says in the Epilogue that any future worth having will come from men like Mario, "not from weedy intellectuals or self-inhibited puritans," he means that Mario's is a modernism that carries with it the lessons of the past. He has not disowned, as Oliver has done, "the living forces of nature" (p. 600).

IV

Santayana's division of America into the genteel tradition and modernism, and of western civilization into the North and the South is, of course, dictated by his allegiance to the Mediterranean-Catholic ethos. If the past is still very much in the present in southern Europe, it is not a past whose values are maintained by the pretensions of a few self-appointed guardians. It functions in the lives of the people. In the North and particularly in America whatever can be called vital has forgotten the past. The past remains only in such places as the American Intellect, where it decays from want of activity. On the other hand, the American Will has been accustomed to think of the Mediterranean-South itself as decadent, because the South finds pleasure in the quality rather than in the quantity of its civilization. But if the North shows no decay in its production of things, it shows great fatigue in the uses of the mind. As late as the 1950s Santayana wrote that the North "has turned its back on the attempt and even on the desire to live reasonably." For half a century Santayana had been a witness to the fact that his northern hosts— intellectuals and barbarians alike—had ignored the conditions for living rationally: they lacked the Socratic principle of "self-knowledge" and a "sufficient knowledge of the world to perceive that alternatives are open to [them] and which of them are favourable to [their] true interests."[23] If the morally unenlightened North is to survive, Santayana wrote, "it will be only because it will have humanised itself, reduced its dogmas to harmless metaphors, and sunk down a tap-root, to feed it, into the dark damp depths of mother earth."[24]

The Last Puritan analyzes a failure in American culture. The life of Oliver Alden illustrates a serious but ineffectual attempt by sensitive young American intellectuals of the early twentieth century to provide a culture commensurate with the achievements of a mechanized society. Possessing the legacy of puritanism themselves, they were dissatisfied with its precipitant, the genteel tradition. But the conditions of that legacy prevented them from uniting with the vital American Will and redirecting that Will from preoccupation with the control of matter to reflection on the consequences of its control. In a "mechanized democracy" content with its physical successes, there was no function for young intellectuals who inherited the "agonized conscience" of their forebears. Santayana saw the atavistic puritan as a tragic figure—full of noble intentions but lacking the vigor to effect them. Ralph Barton Perry has written that Santyana's novel defines the death of the puritan creed in America. This death, he writes, "resembles the death of any creed when its subordinations have become negations, its conventions rigidities, and its surviving zealots monstrosities."[25] Even if this is true, Santayana does not discount the puritan contribution to both the Will and the Intellect in America. For him puritanism is the only identifiable tradition there is in America. But on the intellectual side in either genteel or pristine form, it has become effete. Like Hamlet and Faust, Santayana's puritan is a Nordic who suffers from self-delusion and lack of direction.

Santayana's view of America as a land divided is shared most notably by the early Van Wyck Brooks, who in *America's Coming of Age* (1915) described the bifurcation of American culture in terms of the *Highbrow* and the *Lowbrow*. Like Santayana, Brooks rejected the possibility that the descendants of puritanism could effect an organic culture. In *Letters and Leadership* Brooks called his contemporary American intellectuals a "race of Hamlets" who in a material and productive age, "acutely conscious of their spiritual unemployment and impoverished in will and impulse, . . . drift almost inevitably into a state of internal anarchism that finds outlet, where it finds outlet at all, in a hundred unproductive forms."[26] Brooks implies in this work that the solution to America's cultural stagnation lies outside the United States; that vital, productive, mechanical America will eventually discover in other nations the achievement of an organic life and realizing the gravity of its own situation, recreate "out of the sublime heritage of human ideals, a new synthesis adaptable to the unique conditions of our life."[27]

Like Brooks Santayana calls for an organic American culture, the matrix being the mechanistic society which is at present so insensate to cultural development. Santayana further maintains that the dialogue that will educate the American Will should not be between itself and the American Intellect but between the Will and the detached and contemplative mind of the South. In an essay entitled "Americanism," Santayana writes that physical domination over nature can yield only a primitive civilization. He exclaims, "What irony there would be in having learned to control matter, if we thereby forgot the purposes of the soul in controlling it, and disowned the natural furniture of the mind, our senses, fancy, and pictorial knowledge!" From his southern European heritage he has learned that "the greater part of human life, by a biological necessity, must always be carried on in terms of sense, passion, and language." If science and industry are to be useful, they must be made subservient to the Life of Reason that understands the value of the human soul. Otherwise, he concludes, it would be fatal for mechanized

America to dominate reason and substitute "blind work for free imagination." Out of its primitivism America has the potential to establish the arts "in such a way that they are practiced intelligibly and that they yield agreeable fruits."[28]

Yet, during his long life, Santayana never found evidence that the American Will and the American Intellect had united to form a common, organic culture. When speaking of modern America in 1951, Santayana does not even discuss the American Intellect, an indication that he felt it had faded from importance almost entirely. And he believes that in "manner and sentiment" the American Will is "so continuous and monotonous as to become automatic." Further, the post-World War II American psyche is unlike the "human psyche" of the "few and idealistic" pre-Civil War New England sages who had "a seminal bent, a spontaneous inner proclivity, often an originality and turn for invention." Santayana writes that these ancestors of Oliver Alden had been "overwhelmed by the major current, into which they themselves wished to pass; and they were increasingly subdued to the colour of what they worked in, and hailed as prophets of the brave new world that was taking shape in complete disregard of their private spirits."[29] Toward "modernism undiluted," of which he wrote with favor in 1927,[30] he has an ambivalent attitude in 1951. He praises America's quest for peace and universal trade; but he wonders about the consequences if American philanthropic liberalism should impart its culture to other nations along with its goods. American culture, he implies, having suffered from failure of its intellectuals, has not yet become organic. The American Will, "the ferocious 100%" America, has still not developed the life of the mind. In a final essay in *Dominations and Powers* entitled "The United States as Leader" he warns nations about submitting themselves unconditionally to the philanthropic zeal of the American Will:

> By the obvious well-being which they bring, they breed self-satisfaction and complacency. . . . The authority that controlled universal economy, if it were in American hands, would irresistibly tend to control education and training also. . . . The philanthropic passion for service would prompt social, if not legal, intervention in the traditional life of all other nations, not only by selling there innumerable American products, but by recommending, if not imposing, American ways of living and thinking.[31]

For Santayana, post-World War II America does not contain the puritan ethos of which Oliver Alden was the last and most essential representative. America has lost its cultural identity; or else its cultural identity has been vitiated and absorbed by an alien cultural force which has not yet learned to understand itself. The life of the mind ossified with the puritan conscience and disintegrated with Oliver's ineffectual attempts to meet the conditions imposed upon him by the American Will. What is left is the American Will still in its barbaric state, not yet aware of its own identity, and so far unable to realize its potential to cultivate that identity. It is from Mario Van de Weyer that the American Will can learn to liberate its "native potentialities." In the essay "Americanism" Santayana makes clear why Mario Van de Weyer rather than Oliver Alden is the hope for the future. He says that America must cease to be only physical—a condition of inorganic matter—and become both intellectual and moral. "Mechanistic democracy" can emerge from its primitive state only by becoming organic, by effecting a life that is "vital, perfect, and appropriate":

> [Life] should be *vital,* that is, fed by sap rising from its hereditary root, spontaneously, gladly, freely. A life should also be *perfect,* that is, harmonious with itself, and culminating in a distinct form or order in which all the parts are included without being distorted. Finally, life should be *appropriate;* that is, capable of maintaining itself and feeding on its surroundings, by adopting for its vitality a type of perfection which circumstances render possible at that particular time and place.[32]

Notes

1. *George Santayana* (Philadelphia, 1938), p. 262. See Santayana's opinion of American intellectual life in "The Genteel Tradition in American Philosophy" (1911), included in *Winds of Doctrine: Studies in Contemporary Opinion* (New York, 1913); and *The Genteel Tradition at Bay* (New York, 1931).

2. "That Smile of Parmenides Made Me Think," *A Gathering of Fugitives* (Beacon paperback; Boston, 1956), p. 157.

3. From Rome, May 22, 1927, in *The Letters of George Santayana,* ed. Daniel Cory (New York, 1955), pp. 225–26. Hereafter cited as *Letters.*

4. Letter to Warren Allen Smith, from Rome, Feb. 9. 1951, in *Letters,* p. 408.

5. In his preface to the Triton edition of the novel Santayana states that his hero Oliver Alden became the type for a number of his friends of the 1880s and 1890s who had in some way failed to fulfill their promise. See the Triton edition, XI (1938), ix–x. Elsewhere he writes that "an important element in the *tragedy* of Oliver . . . is drawn from the fate of a whole string of Harvard poets in the 1880s and 1890s—Sanborn, Philip Savage, Hugh McCullough, Trumbull Stickney, and Cabot Lodge: also Moody, although he lived a little longer and made some impression . . . as a playwright." They were "visibly killed by the lack of air to breathe" not having "an alternative tradition . . . to fall back upon." See letter to William Lyon Phelps from Rome, Mar. 16, 1936, in *Letters,* p. 306. Santayana makes about the same comment in "Marginal Notes on *Civilization in the United States,*" *Dial,* LXXII (June 1922), 563–64.

6. "The Education of a Puritan," *Saturday Review,* XIII (Feb. 1, 1936), 4.

7. "Santayana's View of America," *Saturday Review,* XIII (Mar. 7, 1936), 9.

8. See "The Appeal to Supernaturalism," *The Genteel Tradition at Bay,* Triton ed., VIII, 148–49, 153.

9. *The Last Puritan: A Memoir in the Form of a Novel* (New York, 1936), pp. 186–89. Hereafter cited in the text by page numbers.

10. See "Post-Rational Morality," *The Life of Reason, Reason in Science,* V (New York, 1906).

11. See letter to Henry Ward Abbott, from Rome, Jan. 16, 1924, in *Letters,* p. 207.

12. See "The Genteel Tradition in American Philosophy," *Winds of Doctrine,* Triton ed., VII, 128–29, 148. Santayana writes that the American momentum in matters economic and social had destroyed the vitality of both Calvinism and transcendentalism: in the one its "agonized conscience"; in the other its "radical subjective criticism of knowledge." The academic mind at the start of the century was left with a moral code and an emphasis on the human efficacy of discovering truth which had lost their only means of justification. By renouncing the conditions which made their philosophy vital, American intellectuals could not cope with the practical realities of their time.

13. Preface, *The Last Puritan,* Triton ed., p. xiii. Hereafter cited as Triton edition.

14. P. xv.

15. Trition ed., p. xiii.

16. Triton ed., p. xii.

17. From Rome, Feb. 5, 1936, in *Letters,* p. 302.

18. See Frederick W. Conner, *"Lucifer* and *The Last Puritan,"* *American Literature,* XXXIII (Mar. 1961), 1–19. Also see Howgate, *George Santayana,* p. 267.

19. Triton ed., xiv.

20. *My Host the World: Persons and Places* (New York, 1953), p. 56.

21. *Ibid.,* pp. 131–32.

22. In February 1951, the year before his death, Santayana wrote in the Preface to *Dominations and Powers,* "It is a hindrance to the free movement of spirit to be lodged in one point of space rather than in another, or in one point of time. . . . Seen from the form of eternity, all ages are equally past and equally future. Everything gently impels us to view human affairs scientifically, realistically, biologically, as events that arise, with all their spiritual overtones in the realm of matter." This is the vision of the pre-Platonic naturalist which Mario has and Oliver cannot attain.

23. *My Host the World,* p. 139.

24. *Ibid.,* p. 144.

25. *Puritanism and Democracy* (New York, 1944), p. 64.

26. (New York, 1918), pp. 52–55.

27. *Letters and Leadership,* p. 128.

28. *The Idler and His Works and Other Essays,* ed. Daniel Cory (New York, 1957), pp. 52–53. Daniel Cory writes that this essay was composed "sometime between 1935 and 1940" (p. v).

29. *Dominations and Powers: Reflections on Liberty, Society, and Government* (New York, 1954), pp. 356–57.

30. See footnote 3.

31. Pp. 458–59. Santayana always had a distinct distrust of what he called "The Higher Snobbery," that of "earnest liberals" like the philanthropist, the evangelist and the political idealist. In *Soliloquies in England and Later Soliloquies,* he condemned benevolence and philanthropy which required "everything else to produce it," and produced nothing itself. See the essays "The Higher Snobbery" (pp. 49–52) and "The Irony of Liberalism" (pp. 178–89).

32. Pp. 42–43.

Introductory

Douglas L. Wilson

I

At what now appears to have been precisely the right moment, George Santayana introduced into the American cultural dialogue a phrase and an idea that were destined to make a difference. They were destined to affect the tone as well as the substance of what was becoming, in the early years of this century, an increasingly urgent dialogue and to help focus the attention of a disaffected generation on the nature and character of that with which they were most deeply at odds in the culture they had inherited—the genteel tradition. Whether one should emphasize the peculiar appropriateness of the moment or the compelling aptness of the phrase and idea in accounting for their subsequent impact and influence is not altogether clear. However it may be, both are crucial, and the phrase has become so completely ingrained in the twentieth-century American conception of the immediate past that Lionel Trilling has asserted flatly: "what the historian of American culture would do without Santayana's term 'the genteel tradition' is impossible to imagine."[1]

Santayana came at his subject from an angle peculiarly his own, and how he came to make such an utterance at the moment that he did amounts to a cultural accident. He never accepted America or its culture as his own; he was truly an alien right from the time that his Spanish father brought him to the United States at the age of eight to remain and be reared by his Spanish mother, whose first husband had been born a Boston merchant. Neither Boston, where he was raised, nor Harvard, where he was educated and taught for over twenty years, was congenial to his Spanish temperament and he escaped their chafing effects by traveling in Europe whenever he could. Privately, Santayana was capable of scoring the institutions of American culture in bitter terms. In 1900, he wrote to William James, his former teacher and then colleague in the Philosophy department at Harvard: "You tax me several times with impertinence and superior airs. I wonder if you realize the years of suppressed irritation which I have past [sic] in the midst of an unintelligible sanctimonious and often disingenous Protestantism,

Reprinted from *The Genteel Tradition: Nine Essays by George Santayana* (Cambridge, Mass.: Harvard University Press, 1967), 1–25, with the permission of the publisher.

which is thoroughly alien and repulsive to me . . . ."[2] But publicly he either was too diffident or too polite to ruffle the feathers of Boston and Harvard with such plain speaking. It was, for example, a genuine relief to him to deliver a series of lectures in English at the Sorbonne in 1905, for he wrote to James: "The freedom of speaking in a foreign language among foreigners—I mean the intellectual room—is exhilerating. You can say what is *really true*. You needn't remember that you are in Cambridge, or are addressing the youth entrusted to your personal charge. I have never felt so grown up as I do at the Sorbonne; after our atmosphere, this is liberty."[3]

But Santayana's moment for speaking out in public eventually came. In 1911, at the University of California at Berkeley, where he had accepted a teaching position in the summer session, he was duly invited to address the Philosophical Union. As he indicated in a letter to a friend, he had accepted the California appointment as "probably the last chance I should have"[4] to see California and the Pacific; his mind seems already to have been made up not to return from his forthcoming sabbatical leave abroad. Separated from New England by the breadth of an entire continent and about to take permanent leave of America, Santayana was thus presented with the right time and place for saying, as he told his audience, "something I have long wanted to say which this occasion seems particularly favorable for saying."[5] What he said was apparently quite unexpected even among those who knew him intimately, for writing a few months later to his sister, to whom he had probably sent a copy or account of the address, he asked:

> Where did you get the impression that anything in California could have affected my opinions or sentiments? When there . . . I felt almost out of America, so much so that I once said inadvertently to someone in San Francisco that I soon had to go back *to America*. That is why, from [there], I felt like expressing myself: because when I am here [Cambridge] in the midst of a dull round, a sort of instinct of courtesy makes me take it for granted, and I become unconscious of how much I hate it all: otherwise I couldn't have stood it for *forty years*![6]

The address he delivered on August 25, the most incisive piece he was to write on the subject, was "The Genteel Tradition in American Philosophy."

Santayana's address, whose title phrase would shortly become famous, was thus an accident in space and time as well as personal circumstances; had he not found himself in California with an invitation to speak at that propitious moment, he would almost certainly have left the country having said nothing. "But accidents," as Santayana was to write in another connection, "are accidents only to ignorance; in reality all physical events flow out of one another by a continuous intertwined derivation . . . ."[7] In 1911, as Santayana was putting down his analysis of the malady of American intellectual life, a whole generation was awakening to the deficiencies of its literary and intellectual heritage—a generation that was to mount a critical onslaught that would precipitate a cultural revolution. It was the point in time that Van Wyck Brooks was a few years later to designate hopefully as "America's coming-of-age." A more recent analysis has seen it as the point that marked the beginning of "the end of American innocence."[8] The moment for Santayana's attractive phrase—and the theory that went with it—was ripe.

In spite of the "philosophy" in its title, Santayana's address was as much if not more concerned with the American tradition in literature. He had begun his career as a poet and had turned to philosophy—what he called his "alternative tradition"—only when circumstances, personal and cultural, conspired to deprive him of his muse, so that he was keenly sensitive to the shortcomings of the American literary milieu. He had been part of the Harvard school of poets in the nineties who had tried—and failed—to rejuvenate American poetry by a radical reversion to classical models and methods. Not able to recognize that his movement was actually the last gasp of an exhausted Romantic mode, Santayana persisted in thinking that its failure was due to the cultural environment, what he referred to as "a lack of air to breathe."[9] This was a crucial factor in focusing his attention on the nation's intellectual underpinnings in such a way that he came to regard gentility as the prime enemy of a vigorous and imaginative cultural life and to think that American thought and letters were plagued by a genteel tradition.

Santayana's strictures were welcomed by the younger, resurgent generation, once they became known, not only because they expressed something important and useful, but because they put the "custodians of culture"[10] on the defensive. Writing in the *Atlantic Monthly* a few years after Santayana's address appeared in book form, Randolph Bourne, the most brilliant spokesman of the younger generation, took note of "the guarded defenses and discreet apologies for the older generation which keep filtering through the essays of the *Atlantic*."

> It is always an encouraging sign [Bourne wrote] when people are rendered self-conscious and are forced to examine the basis of their ideals. The demand that they explain them to skeptics always makes for clarity. When the older generation is put on the defensive, it must first discover what convictions it has, and then sharpen them to their finest point in order to present them convincingly. There are always too many unquestioned things in the world, and for a person or class to have to scurry about to find reasons for its prejudices is about as healthy an exercise as one could wish for either of them . . . This always indicates that something has begun to slide, that the world is no longer so secure as it was, that obvious truths are no longer obvious, that the world has begun to bristle with question marks.[11]

Certainly one of the most valuable effects that Santayana's theory of the genteel tradition was to have was to make the established world less secure and the received views less obvious.

Toward the social smugness, the intellectual complacency, and the thorough-going gentility of this older generation, Bourne and the whole host of writers typified by him adopted an attitude of radical disaffection that was to have an important residual effect upon succeeding generations of young artists. So pervasive and important was this development that a recent commentator has seen it as the source in American literary history of the self-conscious posture that we are accustomed to call "alienation." In describing this phenomemon in the introduction to his book, *After Alienation,* Marcus Klein writes:

> "Alienation" I take to begin in that deliberate strategy of discontent, almost a program, which was enunciated just before World War I by Van Wyck Brooks and Randolph Bourne, which informed if it did not entirely account for famous episodes in our modern literature like the *Risorgimento,* and the Lost Generation, the Younger Generation, and Disillusion, which then was inherited and put to the uses of revolution by the proletarian 1930s, which finally was the dominant mode of our literature until just yesterday, some time after World War II. It is the theory, not necessarily enunciated, of something more than a generation of our *avant-gardes.*[12]

Mr. Klein's suggestion, that the attitude adopted by these writers continued to affect succeeding literary generations, however adequate or inadequate its formulation, serves to underline the importance of the movement for which Santayana's critique of the genteel tradition was welcome ammunition.

The groundwork for this movement, and much of the inspiration for it, came, of course, not from men like Santayana, who refused to believe in progress or democracy, but from the "liberal ideology" emanating from the work of men like John Dewey, Thorstein Veblen, and Charles Beard.[13] These writers, all professors, symbolized the arrival of a new spirit in the academy as well as the country at large. It was in this spirit and in this period that another professor, Vernon Parrington, began a monumental effort of cultural reappraisal which would eventually emerge more than a decade later as *Main Currents in American Thought.* A veritable avalanche of New Poetry was let loose, filling countless little magazines that had to be founded to accommodate it, just as the *New Republic,* the *Masses,* the *Seven Arts* and the new *Dial* had to be established to accommodate the critical prose. Recalling this period only a few years later in a memoir of Bourne, Van Wyck Brooks testified, "It was a tremendous moment. Never had we realized so keenly the spiritual inadequacy of American life: the great war of the cultures left us literally gasping in the vacuum of our own provincialism, colonialism, naiveté, and romantic self-complacency."[14] The time could not have been more ripe for a vivid and telling characterization of the genteel tradition.

II

Santayana's criticism of America has sometimes been discounted and even discredited by cultural historians as coming from a biased and unsympathetic quarter. Noting that he is no champion of democracy, they like to make him out, as Lionel Trilling has neatly put it, as "the Gilbert Osmond of their *Portrait of a Lady,* the Lady being America . . ." But while he was aristocratic in his outlook and openly critical of democracy, those who would cast Santayana in such a role, as Trilling points out, "are much mistaken . . . America, it is true, seemed to have affected him adversely in almost a physical way, making him anxious and irritable. But it was to a particular aspect of American life that he directed his antagonism, the aspect of its high culture."[15] Trilling's point is well taken and particularly apt, for it is important to bear in mind above all else that Santayana formulated his theory of the genteel tradition preeminently as an attempt to diagnose the shortcomings of American intellectual life and its feeble creation, American high culture.

Santayana's theory of the genteel tradition begins in an attempt to account for a certain doubleness in the American mind, "a curious alternation and irrelevance," he once called it, "as between weekdays and Sabbaths, between American ways and American opinions."[16] Other important elements figure into his analysis, as the reader of these essays will discover, but the idea of doubleness, of a split in the national mind, of a kind of separation of mental powers, is central to his whole conception of the American intellect and its works.

Santayana was well aware that he was not the first to point out this doubleness, nor is it as a *discovery* that his formulation has become influential and important. It is perhaps a small irony that the man who was in many ways the personification and voice of the genteel tradition, Theodore Roosevelt, had delivered a series of lectures, also in Berkeley and also in 1911, only a few months before Santayana's address, in which he remarked: "I chose as the opening lecture this address on realizable ideals, because the longer I have lived the more strongly I have felt the harm done by the practice among so many men of keeping their consciences in separate compartments; sometimes a Sunday conscience and a week-day conscience: sometimes a conscience as to what they do and like other people to do; sometimes a conscience for their private affairs and a totally different conscience for their business relations."[17] Had Santayana had no more to say than this, his address, like the ex-president's, would have been quickly forgotten, and the "revolt against gentility," as Malcolm Cowley was to call it, would have had to proceed without the benefit of his incisive mind. Santayana's contribution was far more considerable than merely pointing out what many other people had already observed. His contribution, appropriate to his position and stature, was to give a philosophical account of the origin, development, and character of a serious defect in American cultural and intellectual experience.

Near the beginning of the Berkeley address, Santayana summarizes the theory of the genteel tradition as succinctly as he was ever to do:

> America is not simply, as I said a moment ago, a young country with an old mentality: it is a country with two mentalities, one a survival of the beliefs and standards of the fathers, the other an expression of the instincts, practice, and discoveries of the younger generations. In all the higher things of the mind— in religion, in literature, in the moral emotions—it is the hereditary spirit that still prevails, so much so that Mr. Bernard Shaw finds that America is a hundred years behind the times. The truth is that that one-half of the American mind, that not occupied intensely in practical affairs, has remained, I will not say high-and-dry, but slightly becalmed; it was floated gently in the back-water, while, alongside, in invention and industry and social organization the other half of the mind was leaping down a sort of Niagara Rapids. This division may be found symbolized in American architecture: a neat reproduction of the colonial mansion—with some modern comforts introduced surreptitiously—stands beside the sky-scraper. The American Will inhabits the sky-scraper; the American Intellect inhabits the colonial mansion. The one is the sphere of the American man; the other, at least predominantly, of the American woman. The one is all aggressive enterprise; the other is all genteel tradition. [18]

It might be said that this is, to some extent, an enlargement of Emerson's remark that "our people have their intellectual culture from one country and their duties from another."[19] But Santayana's distinction is much finer and it carries the idea of a good deal further, insisting as it does on the magnitude of the disparities and dramatizing their deep-seated presence in the life around us. Moreover, Santayana's distinction emphasizes that the two mentalities constitute a single mind and suggests the interrelationship between the weaknesses of the American mind and its strengths. Once this point has been grasped, its consequences in terms of dangers and shortcomings in American life can be readily discerned. Malcolm Cowley, following Van Wyck Brooks, has demonstrated how this divided mentality might manifest itself in the behavior of a single man. The example is Andrew Carnegie, "who made a fortune by manufacturing armor plate and then spent it in promoting peace by impractical methods and in building libraries where the men in his rolling mills, who worked twelve hours a day and seven days a week, would never have time to read the master-works. Culture was something reserved and refined for the Sunday people: women, ministers, university professors and the readers of genteel magazines."[20]

A close look at Santayana's summary of the dualities in the American mind reveals that the poet-philosopher's imagery not only establishes the tone but quietly passes judgments: a "survival" rather than an "expression," a "back-water" alongside a "Niagara," a nostalgic "reproduction" over against a towering modern structure, and finally the feminine and passive as opposed to the masculine and aggressive. The characteristic vividness of Santayana's images and the deftness with which they delineate the antinomies of American life are of course important factors in the attractiveness and success of his thesis. Santayana's metaphors, like those of any good poet, are considerably more than so much decorative bric-a-brac; they radiate implications, they breed meanings. But in addition to this, Santayana's imagery relentlessly seeks out the most vulnerable aspects of his subject, quickening in the responsive reader his awareness of the sources of his own discontent and confirming and justifying his sense of alienation from the proprietors of the genteel establishment. A prosaic account of equal validity would have been incapable of attracting the interest or exerting the influence that Santayana's actually did. Passing on from the original address, let us consider some illustrations of Santayana's strategic imagery in essays that were to appear subsequently.

The identification of the genteel tradition with a predominantly feminine sensibility—one that is passive, decorous, delicate, apart from the ongoing business of society—is comic yet serious and pervasive. Consider his description, for British audiences, of American public schooling: "The child passes very young into a free school, established and managed by the municipal authorities; the teachers, even for the older boys, are chiefly unmarried women, sensitive, faithful, and feeble; their influence helps to establish that separation which is so characteristic of America between things intellectual, which remain wrapped in a feminine veil and, as it were, under glass, and the rough passions of life."[21] Also, the genteel tradition at its most entrenched is usually represented, in keeping with his theory of the old and young America, as a superannuated mentality, or as outright senility. The opening of *Character and Opinion in the United States* (1920) is an example: "About the middle of the nineteenth century, in the quiet sunshine of provincial prosperity, New England had an Indian summer of the mind; and an agreeable reflective literature showed how brilliant that russet and yellow season could be. There were poets, historians, orators, preachers, most of whom had studied foreign literatures and had travelled; they demurely kept up with the times; they were universal humanists. But it was all a harvest of leaves; these worthies had an expurgated and barren conception of life; theirs was the purity of sweet old age."[22]

Accordingly, Santayana's description-indictment is at its most devastating when these two images, the feminine and the superannuated, are fused and the genteel tradition is personified as a kind of senile femininity. Thus, his description of "genteel American poetry": "It was simple, sweet humane, Protestant literature, grandmotherly in that sedate spectacled wonder with which it gazed at this terrible world and said how beautiful and how interesting it all was."[23] In a single blow, the mindless cheer, the intellectual myopia, and the spiritual complacency of an entire tradition in American poetry is rendered ridiculous. Part of the genius of Santayana's method and the success of his grandmotherly personification, it should be noted, lies not in its severity but in its guileless comic nature. Though he may have had private cause for it, he exhibits publicly no bitterness. His words are calculated to provoke humor, though not humor alone.

The value of Santayana's theory of the genteel tradition can probably be counted as much in inspiration as in insight. The phrase served not only to focus attention on the most vulnerable chink in the Establishment's armor, but it also served the "literary radicals" as a rallying cry in their insurgent war on intellectual poverty. Gentility, as a consequence, continued to draw sniper fire long after is had been permanently disabled. Meanwhile, Santayana's personification—the bespectacled grandmother—continued to reappear in a multitude of incarnations. She is featured, for example, by one of Santayana's earliest admirers, Wallace Stevens, in the title-role of his poem, "A High-toned Old Christian Woman." She is also enshrined in an early poem of E. E. Cummings, whose father, like Santayana, was a Harvard professor.

> The Cambridge ladies who live in furnished souls
> are unbeautiful and have comfortable minds
> (also, with the church's protestant blessings
> daughters, unscented shapeless spirited)
> they believe in Christ and Longfellow, both dead,
> are invariably interested in so many things—
> at the present writing one still finds
> delighted fingers knitting for the is it Poles?
> perhaps. While permanent faces coyly bandy
> scandal of Mrs. N and Professor D[24]

"Furnished soul" and "comfortable minds" are precisely what the genteel tradition is all about: the unexamined life, the empty allegiance to whatever custom prescribes, the smug complacency (the "permanent faces" of the poem), the meaningless activity that buzzes, like Emily Dickinson's fly, in the presence of the death of the mind.

III

When Santayana left America in January of 1912, he was on an extended leave from his teaching duties at Harvard, part of an arrangement with President Lowell whereby he was obligated, after a year's absence, to teach only the first term of each session. He resigned when his mother's death, less than a month after he sailed, left him free of family attachments in America, and he never returned. By 1913, when "The Genteel Tradition in

American Philosophy" became available to the general public in book form, Santayana was permanently settled abroad. The outbreak of war a year later may have obscured somewhat his observations of the kind of impression his genteel tradition thesis was making, though he was much in demand, in both the British and American press, as a commentator on the American scene. He appears to have been aware, to some degree at least, of the currency and force that his phrase was acquiring, as evidenced by his use of *genteel* and *genteel tradition* in subsequent essays. In "Genteel American Poetry," published in 1915, he was still expounding what he meant by a tradition of gentility, using nineteenth-century American poetry as his example. But by 1918, he could say in an address to the British Academy, "Philosophical opinion in America is of course rooted in the genteel tradition,"[25] a remark which clearly takes for granted that the audience may be expected to know that *the* genteel tradition is. A review written for the *Dial* in 1922, "Notes on Civilization in the United States," reveals that Santayana is aware of the powerful potential that his phrase has acquired as an epithet of opprobrium, as he speaks of witholding the charge of gentility lest it enrage the authors of the book too much. Finally, in "The Genteel Tradition at Bay" (1931), we find him yielding to what had become by then a common temptation to use the phrase as nothing more than a stick with which to beat one's adversaries—in this case, the New Humanists.

Some varied examples of the use that was made by others of Santayana's genteel tradition may serve to suggest the range of its utility and appeal. The literary and cultural historian, Vernon Parrington, who had been at work on his ambitious treatise, *Main Currents of American Thought,* since approximately the time Santayana coined the term and whose discovery of it was apparently early (he cites the Berkeley publication), saw in the genteel tradition the explanation behind the enfeebled culture of the seventies. He wrote: "The inevitable fruit of such thin soil was the genteel tradition, the excellence of which in the seventies New England maintained in the face of all frontier levelling and romantic liberalism—a timid and uncreative culture that lays its inhibitions on every generation that is content to live in the past . . . Yet to the generation of the seventies the inhibitions of the genteel tradition were all-powerful, and the little Boston group set themselves up as a court of final jurisdiction over American letters. New England parochialism had become a nation-wide nuisance."[26]

Another example of the use to which Santayana's genteel tradition was put, very different yet not far removed in time from Parrington's, is found in the Nobel Prize acceptance speech of Sinclair Lewis in 1930. This is an incident so indicative that Malcolm Cowley builds a whole essay, the introductory to his *After the Genteel Tradition,* around it. In his speech, Lewis not only labels his literary enemies in the American Academy of Arts and Letters as the representatives of the "genteel tradition," he cites them as an "example of the divorce in America of intellectual life from all authentic standards of importance and reality."[27] This is of course, precisely the keynote of Santa-yana's concept of the genteel tradition.

A very much later and very different example of the use of Santayana's genteel tradition, and one that demonstrates the enduring utility of the concept, is Leo Marx's use of the term in a well-known essay on *Huckleberry Finn*. Marx is concerned in his essay with the unsatisfactory conclusion of Mark Twain's great novel, and he finds in a passage from "The Genteel Tradition in American Philosophy" the key to its failure. "The unhappy truth about the ending of *Huckleberry Finn*," he says, "is that the author, having revealed the tawdry nature of the culture of the great valley, yielded to its essential complacency." This way of loooking at the novel he goes on, "confirms the brilliant insight of George Santayana, who many years ago spoke of American humorists, of whom he considered Mark Twain an outstanding representative, as having only 'half escaped' the genteel tradition. Santayana meant that men like Clemens were able to 'point to what contradicts it in the facts, but not in order to abandon the genteel tradition, for they have nothing solid to put in its place' . . . Clemens had presented the contrast between the two social orders but could not, or would not, accept the tragic fact that the one he had rejected was an image of solid reality and the other an ecstatic dream."[28]

These examples from Parrington, Lewis, and Marx are ones in which the indebtedness to Santayana is either openly acknowledged or otherwise direct enough to be fairly obvious. They all explicitly use his phrase genteel tradition, and many similiar examples could be presented. Yet the most important debt to Santayana with respect to his idea of the genteel tradition is one that has gone unacknowledged and virtually unrecognized. This is the indebtedness evident in the early writing of Van Wyck Brooks, particularly in the very influential essay, "America's Coming-of-Age." For while Brooks felt no personal or intellectual attraction for Santayana and views, the effect of Santayana's Berkeley address on his own thinking and writing is demonstrably distinct and unmistakable.

In the first volume of his autobiography, *Scenes and Portraits*, Brooks characterized Santayana, one of the luminaries of his years at Harvard: "He was repelled by everything that characterized American life, preferring a World 'run by cardinals and engineers' rejecting as 'all a harvest of leaves' the New England Renaissance and its best essayists, historians, romancers and poets. His smiling contempt for the efforts of men to better the world and humanity was reflected in a host of Harvard minds that were reversing the whole tendency of the great New England epoch, dismissing its faith in progress as 'the babble of dreamers.' "[29] This passage suggests rather vividly the distance between Brooks and Santayana, but it further suggests what innumerable references in Brooks's other volumes bear out, that he was quite familiar with what Santayana had written about American life; and the evidence makes it pretty clear that, as a young man, Brooks was able to profit immensely from the ideas of his former teacher, while groping for ways to diagnose and prescribe for the malady of American cultural life.

In the summer of 1911, Brooks was married in California and accepted an instructorship at Stanford University. He had close friends across the bay in Berkeley and he may well have been in the audience when, in August, Santayana delivered his celebrated address before the Philosophical Union. Or, not having been present, he almost certainly would have heard about the address and read it when it was published a few months later in the *University of California Chronicle*. That he was familiar with it and that it profoundly affected the characterization of our intellectual tradition that he was to offer a few years later in "America's Coming-of-Age" (1915), no one who has compared the two essays will want to deny. To review the points of comparison which reflect Brooks's indebtedness to Santayana's essay is to recount a series, not of borrowings and much less of thefts, but of modulations of phrases, metaphors, and ideas. The most telling of these points of comparison are found in the initial section, " 'Highbrow' and 'Lowbrow,' " the best known section of the essay, which was printed separately in the *Forum*. There Santayana's notion of the split in the American mind is appropriated by Brooks, modulated, and presented as the key to an understanding of the crisis in American culture. Using the vernacular "highbrow" and "lowbrow" to designate the two "attitudes of mind" one finds in America, he asks "What side of American life is not touched by this antithesis? What explanation of American life is more central and more illuminating? In everything one finds this frank acceptance of twin values which are not expected to have anything in common: on the one hand, a quite unclouded, quite unhypocritical assumption of transcendent theory ("high ideals"), on the other a simultaneous acceptance of catchpenny realities. Between university ethics and business ethics, between American culture and American humour, between Good Government and Tammany, between academic pedantry and pavement slang, there is no community, no genial middle ground."[30]

This is considerably more substantial than Teddy Roosevelt's commonplaces and somewhat different, in tone and emphasis, from Santayana, but as a description of a state of affairs, it is at one with Santayana's and begins at precisely the same point: a single America with a divided mentality. Brooks then goes on to give an account of the origin of this division, and here again we note the closeness to Santayana's account, including an echo, in the image of "main currents" (later picked up by Parrington), of Santayana's metaphor of the "back-water" and the "Niagara Rapids." But Brooks turns the idea to his own purposes and, in so doing, brings forth the now familiar comparison of Edwards and Franklin:

> So it is that from the beginning we find two main currents in the American mind running side by side but rarely mingling—a current of overtones and a current of undertones—and both equally unsocial: on the one hand, the

transcendental current, originating in the piety of the Puritans, becoming a philosophy in Jonathan Edwards, passing through Emerson, producing the fastidious refinement and aloofness of the chief American writers, and resulting in the final unreality of most contemporary American culture; and on the other hand the current of catchpenny opportunism, originating in the practical shifts of Puritan life, becoming a philosophy in Franklin, passing through the American humorists, and resulting in the atmosphere of our contemporary business life.[31]

Brooks's tone, it should be noted, unlike Santayana's, which is comparatively detached and disinterested, is that of one very much disturbed by the state of affairs he is describing. Indeed, one of the main purposes of the essay is to suggest a program for improvement, something at best incidental to Santayana's purpose. But what the one owes to the other is clearly discernible, nonetheless, at point after point.

Another telling parallel between Brooks's essay and Santayana's Berkeley address is their treatment of the situation of the genuinely talented writers of the nineteenth century. Santayana had said that such writers—he specifically named Poe, Hawthorne, and Emerson—were in "great straits" because they could not "retail the genteel tradition," being "too keen, too perceptive, and too independent for that."[32] "They were fastidious," he said, and, because of their situation, their writing had a "starved and abstract quality." Pointing to the same three men, Brooks says that they turned from the rudeness of actuality to a "disembodied world . . . a world fastidiously intellectual . . ." In the same section of his essay, one also finds Brooks speaking of "two publics" in America, "the one largely feminine, the other largely masculine."[33]

Throughout his essay, Brooks can be seen to be using Santayana's ideas or phrases as points of departure, but the point of documenting this indebtedness at such length is not simply that Brooks himself does not acknowledge it, but that what Brooks had to say was to have a tremendous influence on the younger writers, the same men who would precipitate the literary and cultural revolution of the twenties which effectively broke the hold of the genteel tradition on American high culture. The Brooks of this period, Edmund Wilson has written, was "probably, for the writers of these years, the principle source of ideas on the cultural life of the United States. People got from him, not only, as they did also from Mencken, a sense of the second-ratedness of recent American writing and a conviction of the need for something better, but also an historical perspective and an analysis of the causes of what was wrong."[34]

In 1937, Malcolm Cowley edited the book of essays, previously referred to, entitled *After the Genteel Tradition,* in which, in addition to the important introductory essay, Cowley contributed a "literary calendar" which recorded the important events in the unseating of the genteel tradition from 1911 to 1930. The entries under 1911 do not include the Berkeley address nor is it mentioned elsewhere in the volume. But under 1915, Cowley writes, "Van Wyck Brooks sets the tone of the era in *America's Coming-of-Age*"[35] There is, of course, nothing surprising in this, nor has any conscious injustice been done. Cowley and his generation knew that Santayana had coined the term "genteel tradition," but they had little reason to think that they were actually and effectively in the debt of someone so unlike themselves in point of view as he. Nonetheless, Santayana's essay played a more important role in the movement than has been realized and deserves a significant place at the beginning of Cowley's calendar.

Gradually, the term genteel tradition began to wear out its initial welcome, being constantly invoked in a variety of contexts and in the service of various causes. By 1942 Alfred Kazin could justifiably complain in *On Native Grounds* about the mechanical application of "Santayana's well-worn phrase, the 'Genteel Tradition,' to everything Mencken's iconoclastic generation disliked in late nineteenth-century life"; it had become, in his view, a "dead horse."[36] But less than ten years later, F. O. Matthiessen brilliantly demonstrated that its original, incisive meaning had not been entirely lost in the shuffle of almost forty years. In his book on Dreiser he warned against the tendency at midcentury to develop a "nostalgic longing" for the genteel tradition and reminded his readers that

> Santayana coined the phrase "the genteel tradition" to describe what he considered was the most dangerous defect in American thought. Observing our dominant New England culture, Santayana believed that its deep-rooted error was that it separated thought from experience. Among the legacies of a colonial culture is the habit of thinking of creative sources as somehow remote from itself, of escaping from the hardness and rawness of everyday surroundings into an idealized picture of civilized refinement, of believing that the essence of beauty must lie in what James Russell Lowell read in Keats rather than what Walt Whitman saw in the streets of Brooklyn. The inescapable result of this is to make art an adornment rather than an organic expression of life, to confuse it with politeness and delicacy.[37]

This was indeed what Santayana had tried to convey, and his writings on the genteel tradition stand as a vivid reminder of the divergent tendencies within the American mind and of the dangers that attend their seemingly inexorable presence.

Notes

1. " 'That Smile of Parmenides Made Me Think,' " *A Gathering of Fugitives* (Boston: Beacon Press, 1956), p. 157.

2. *The Letters of George Santayana,* ed. Daniel Cory (New York: Charles Scribner's Sons, 1955), p. 62.

3. *Letters,* p. 80.

4. *Letters,* p. 105.

5. "The Genteel Tradition in American Philosophy," *University of California Chronicle,* XII:4 (October 1911), 357. Recently, this address has been described as "fully as important a document in the study of American culture as Emerson's 'The American Scholar' or Frederick Jackson Turner's 'The Significance of the Frontier in American History.' " Joe Lee Davis, "Santayana as a Critic of Transcendentalism," *Transcendentalism and its Legacy,* ed. Myron Simon and Thornton H. Parsons (Ann Arbor: University of Michigan Press, 1966), p. 160.

6. *Letters,* p. 110.

7. *Persons and Places: The Background of My Life* (New York: Charles Scribner's Sons, 1944), p. 2.

8. Henry F. May, *The End of American Innocence: A Study of the First Years of Our Own Time 1912–1917* (New York: Alfred A. Knopf, 1957). This far-ranging work cannot be recommended too highly to anyone interested in the period.

9. *Letters,* p. 306.

10. See May, pp. 30–51.

11. "This Older Generation," *The History of a Literary Radical and Other Essays,* ed. Van Wyck Brooks (New York: B. W. Huebsch, 1920), pp. 107, 108–109.

12. *After Alienation* (Cleveland and New York: Meridan Books, 1965), p. 17.

13. See Morton White, *Social Thought in America: The Revolt Against Formalism* (Boston: Beacon Press, 1957).

14. "Introduction," *History of a Literary Radical,* p. xix. Reprinting this essay later in *Emerson and Others* (New York: E. P. Dutton and Co., 1927), Brooks silently toned down "tremendous" to "interesting." For an account of the period from the point of view of literary history, see Robert E. Spiller et al, *Literary History of the United States,* 3 vols. (New York: The Macmillan Company, 1948), particularly chapters 67 and 68, "Creating an Audience" and "The Battle of the Books."

15. Trilling, pp., 156–57.

16. "The Moral Background," *Character and Opinion in the United States* (New York: Charles Scribner's Sons, 1920), p. 6.

17. *Realizable Ideals* (The Earl Lectures), *The Works of Theodore Roosevelt,* National Edition, 20 vols. (New York: Charles Scribner's Sons, 1926), XIII, 616. These lectures are referred to in May, p. 17.

18. "Genteel Tradition in American Philosophy," *University of California Chronicle,* pp. 358–59.

19. Cited in Van Wyck Brooks, "America's Coming-of-Age," *Three Essays on America* (New York: E. P. Dutton and Co., 1934), p. 22.

20. "The Revolt Against Gentility," *After the Genteel Tradition* (Carbondale: Southern Illinois University Press, 1964), p. ii. For this reissue of a book originally published in 1937, Cowley revised this essay which appears as a foreword to the book.

21. "The Academic Environment," *Character and Opinion,* p. 44.

22. "The Moral Background," *Character and Opinion,* p. 1.

23. "Genteel American Poetry," *New Republic,* III:30 (May 29, 1915), 94.

24. Copyright, 1923, 1951, by E. E. Cummings. Reprinted from "the Cambridge ladies who live in furnished souls" in *Poems 1923–1954* by E. E. Cummings by permission of Harcourt, Brace and World, Inc.

25. "Philosophical Opinion in America," *British Academy: Proceedings,* VIII (1917–1918), 300.

26. *The Beginnings of Critical Realism* (New York: Harcourt, Brace and Company, 1930), pp. 52–53.

27. "The American Fear of Literature," *Why Sinclair Lewis Got the Nobel Prize* (New York: Harcourt, Brace and Company, 1931), p. 17. An unpublished doctoral dissertation by

Danforth Ross ("The Genteel Tradition: Its Characteristics and its Origins," University of Minnesota, 1954), which cites this source, also includes a useful survey of the occurrences of Santayana's phrase.

28. "Mr. Eliot, Mr. Trilling, and *Huckleberry Finn,*" *The American Scholar,* XXII:4 (Autumn 1953), 432.

29. *Scenes and Portraits: Memories of Childhood and Youth* (New York: Dutton, 1954), p. 106.

30. "America's Coming-of-Age," pp. 17–18. May perceptively notes that Brook's highbrow-lowbrow distinction was "essentially Santayana's" (p. 324). Sherman Paul has pointed out the California juxtaposition of Brooks and Santayana in unpublished material.

31. "America's Coming-of-Age," p. 19.

32. "Genteel Tradition in American Philosophy," p. 362.

33. "America's Coming-of-Age," pp. 78–79.

34. "Van Wyck Brook's Second Phase," *Classics and Commercials* (New York: Farrar, Straus and Company, 1950), p. 11.

35. *After the Genteel Tradition,* p. 187.

36. *On Native Grounds* (New York: Reynal and Hitchcock, 1942), pp. vii, 56.

37. *Theodore Dreiser* ([New York]: William Sloane Associates, 1951), p. 62.

Santayana on Autobiography

JAMES C. BALLOWE

In 1940 at the age of seventy-six George Santayana reaffirmed his allegiance to the life of reason at a time when the world once again abandoned its opportunity to live reasonably. Having just published the last volume of his philosophical treatise *Realms of Being* (4 vols., 1927–1940), he began the task of finishing his autobiography *Persons and Places* (3 vols., 1944–1953) and his "political testament" *Dominations and Powers* (1951), both of which had been gestating for years.[1] The choice of these projects, typically, is ironic. He thought of these last works as "elastic and endless": the autobiography because he could not describe his own death and the politics because "there are always new wars and revolutions to give one fresh food for thought."[2] The irony becomes universal when one realizes that for the most part both books were written during World War II while Santayana was living in Rome, first under Fascism, then under Allied occupation. Both works—the first a politics of the self, the second a politics of societies— testify to the potential for order in a world gone mad.

These books are also examples of two apparently distinct modes of ideation. The autobiography is literary or "poetic." *Dominations and Powers,* in a qualified sense, is scientific or "academic." As Santayana explains in "The Idler and His Works" (an essay written at the time he was composing the autobiography and *Dominations and Powers*), a dual investigation of experience had become habitual with him.[3] He believed that for a complete expression of the life of reason, one must evoke its essence as well as describe its function. Earlier in *Scepticism and Animal Faith* (1923) he defined these two modes of thought under the terms "literary psychology" and "scientific psychology." In assuming the role of the literary psychologist Santayana felt that he was able to describe the "novelesque" aspect of his universe, something that he could not do as a scientific psychologist. Scientific psychology, he explains in *Scepticism and Animal Faith,* "is addressed to the bodies and the material events composing the animate world," whereas "literary psychology restores the essence intervening in the perception of those material events, and re-echoes the intuitions aroused in those bodies. This visionary stratum is the true immediate as well as the imagined ultimate. Even in the simplest

Reprinted from *American Literature* 41 (May 1969): 219–30, with the permission of the publisher; © 1969 by Duke University Press.

perceptions on which scientific psychology, or any natural science, can be based, there is an essence present which only poetry can describe or sympathy conceive."[4] Of course Santayana's autobiography is a more personal, responsive account of himself and his relation to the civilization in which he lived than is the more academic *Dominations and Powers*. When he wrote to William Lyon Phelps of his novel *The Last Puritan* (1935) that "this is something nobody else could do, since it gives the *emotions* of my experiences, and not my thoughts or experiences," he described the emphasis to be found in the autobiography.[5]

As literary psychology the autobiography divines the human condition from a frankly subjective point of view by assuming what Santayana calls "knowledge of discourse in other people, or of [the self] at other times."[6] This assumption implies its own dual value. In the first place, Santayana felt that literary psychology offers "virtual truth": "The literary psychologist," he writes in *Scepticism and Animal Faith*, "is like some antiquary rummaging in an old curiosity shop, who should find the score of some ancient composition, in its rude notation, and should sit down at a wheezy clavichord and spell out the melody, wondering at the depth of soul in that archaic art, so long buried, and now so feebly revealed." In the second place, he considered literary psychology to be illusory in a special sense: "The illusion of projecting one's own thoughts into remote or imaginary characters is only half an illusion: these thoughts were never there, but they were always here, or knocking at the gate; and there is an indirect victory in reaching and positing elsewhere, in an explicit form, the life which accident denied me, and thereby enjoying it *sub rosa* in spite of fate." Both virtual truth and illusion, Santayana suggests, are blessings, virtual truth because it reveals the minds of others, illusion because it expands one's own mind.[7]

Essentially, the literary psychologist offers a mythopoeic version of his own and other's experience. Concluding his chapter on "Literary Psychology" in *Scepticism and Animal Faith*, Santayana explains that discourse "is a living, a perpetual creation; and the very fatality that forces me, in conceiving my own past or future, or the animation of nature at large, to imagine that object afresh, with my present vital resources and on the scale and in the style of my present discourse—this very fatality, I say, reveals to me the nature of discourse everywhere, that it is poetry."[8] It is clear that Santayana thinks of discourse as an extension of nature as well as a means of apprehending experience. Comparatively, science, as an artificial construct, has a built-in defect. In *The Life of Reason* Santayana said that science is "abstract," that its accounts of things is not "full and sensuous enough."[9] Thus, there is a necessity for man to dramatize his experience. In his "Apologia Pro Mente Sua" (written for the Library of Living Philosophers in 1940), Santayana indicates that in fact science and literature are functionally complementary: that if science "ceased to investigate things by experiment and lapsed into description of experience as drama, it would cease to be science and would become autobiography. Science . . . is the study of *nature;* the description of *experience* is literature."[10]

II

Shortly before the Second World War, Santayana was sent the autobiographies of two of his lifelong friends, Logan Pearsall Smith and William Lyon Phelps. Both men were two years younger than Santayana; both had attended Harvard (Smith as an undergraduate with Santayana and Phelps as a graduate student); and both had waited until they were in their seventies before publishing their autobiographies. In America and Europe their paths often crossed Santayana's, and inevitably many of the same experiences are recalled by all three men. Santayana's reaction to the autobiographies of his two friends tells much about what he intended to accomplish in his own autobiography; and in particular, his reaction describes his point of view toward America, a point of view not attained, as Santayana makes clear, by the indigenous Americans, Smith and Phelps.

A descendant of a distinguished Philadelphia Quaker family, Smith left America in 1888, destined to become an expatriate in England and a member of the English intelligentsia. (His sisters became the wives of Bertrand Russell and Bernard Berenson.) His autobiography, *Unforgotten Years* (1937), in which he characterizes Santayana as "the wisest man I know," received Santayana's alloyed praise. In giving his impressions of the book to Smith, Santayana is cautiously complimentary, saying that the "reminiscences" will be successful because they are "interesting and humorous," and that Smith's account of Walt Whitman is worth the book. But Santayana concludes with the criticism that Smith's recollections ignore reality and Smith's place in it. The book offers no *details* of Harvard and Oxford nor of his friends and their philosophies. Santayana regards the omission as being particularly unfortunate since as a representative of "intellectual and fashionable Anglo-America" Smith was "exceptionally well placed and qualified to record the mental fashions of our times, and the relations then existing between 'cultured' England and America." Santayana suggests that Smith's very position in this aesthetic Anglo-American community (one "not attractive" to Santayana himself) caused Smith to ignore the issues. With a seriousness not obscured by the friendly tone of the letter, Santayana accuses Smith of the faults of "all Americans in print," particularly of Henry James and Henry Adams: all are "too gentle, too affectionate, too fulsome." Even Adams's impression of having a "a most terrible bitterness" and of being an "utter misfit with reality" in "*Saint Michel,* etc." does not satisfy Santayana. Reality, he writes, "requires a satirist, merciless but just." And in closing he implies that his own "materialism" can give just the "buoyant" tone that is needed.[11]

Though eccentric and expatriate, Smith was an intellectually genteel

American. Santayana was more at ease with William Lyon Phelps, a lifelong resident of New Haven, who, Santayana claimed, "converted" him "to charity even towards muscular Americanism." Because Phelps was a *barbarian*— "all Browning in a nutshell, and better for that compression"[12]—he was "irresistible" to Santayana as a representative of an America that he once referred to as "youthful, sporting, [and] ingenuous."[13] He satisfies Santayana's materialism better than does Smith. But where Smith is overrefined intellectually and morally, Phelps is simply raw. His *Autobiography with Letters* (1939) is enthusiastically indiscriminate. In a letter to Phelps, Santayana reacts to the *Autobiography* (he calls it an "avalanche") as he did to young America: he seems to feel that he has been thrown into the stream; and though enjoying the goodnatured fun, he makes his way gasping back to the bank where he can look on with amusement at the other swimmers splashing about in all directions. Choosing Phelps's description of Barrett Wendell to criticize (obviously because he himself planned to use Wendell in *The Middle Span,* Volume II of *Persons and Places*), Santayana complains that Phelps has not gone beyond "impressions"; he has failed to "pry," to "analyze," to "penetrate," to "sum up":

> If I were to mention him in my autobiography [he says to Phelps] the first thing I should ask myself would be: How far was Wendell a fool and how far was he a martyr? That he was a mixture of both seems to me certain. But you make no such beginning. You describe his voice . . . and mention the peculiar character of his learning and of his academic position. Externals, my dear friend; just what a casual stranger might report about him, and you knew him intimately. . . . Now I ask again: *Why* did Barrett Wendell talk like that? It was not an attempt to be English. . . . Wendell loved New England, but the N.E. before the Revolution. He would have wished to be a Cavalier, all courage and elegance. His speech was a failure as a mark of elegance but it was a success as a proof of courage. . . . Then, saturated with that pathos of distance, and being warm-hearted and affectionate, he was intensely sentimental, yet heroically kept his sentimentality in check, and put up with things as they were. That was his martyrdom. And he married Mrs. Wendell.[14]

Santayana prefers to show the relationship between the personality and its environment. Elsewhere, in *Soliloquies in England* (1922), he acknowledges his admiration for Charles Dickens, whose characters reflect their cultural origins: "one turn of the screw, one flash of reflection, and we have understood nature and human morality and the relation between them." Significantly, he continues by saying:

> The spirit of Dickens would be better able to do justice to America than was that of Walt Whitman [and obviously Browning, whom Phelps extolled]; because America, although it may seem nothing but a noisy nebula to the impressionist, is not a nebula but a concourse of very distinct individual

bodies, natural and social, each with its definite interests and story. . . . Walt Whitman, in his comprehensive democratic vistas, could never see the trees for the wood, and remained incapable, for all his diffuse love of the human herd, of ever painting a character or telling a story; the very things in which Dickens was a master. It is this life of the individual, as it may be lived in a given nation, that determines the whole value of that nation to the poet, to the moralist, and to the judicious historian. [15]

For Santayana *persons* and *places,* not marshaled fact, signify a culture. Failing to understand this point, Phelps achieved neither the truth nor the illusion of literary psychology. He only catalogued. [16]

If Smith remained an antiquary who uncovered a composition that he had better have left buried, Phelps dusted the composition, but could not read the notes. Knowing only that they were notes, he possessed neither the capability nor the desire to sound them. Santayana wanted to avoid the failures of both autobiographers. He was looking for a special point of view from which his discourse would impose coherent form on the disparate facts of his past. Even those years which hardly remain in his memory—from age eight to sixteen—become meaningful and fresh when looked at from the perspective of his "present resources and on the scale and in the style of [his] present discourse." In *The Background of My Life,* Volume I of *Persons and Places,* Santayana comments on this phenomenon of memory: "Even what we still think we remember will be remembered differently; so that a man's memory may almost become the art of continually varying and misrepresenting his past, according to his interests in the present. . . . Things truly wear those aspects to one another. A point of view and a special lighting are not distortions. They are conditions of vision, and spirit can see nothing not focused in some living age." [17] A bit later, while speaking of his participation in the social life of Harvard College, he explains, "I have a very short memory, except for such things I absorb and recast in my own mind; so I am a good observer and critic, but a bad historian: let the reader of this book take warning." [18]

III

Santayana's years of selecting a final residence coincided with the years in which he refined his perspective on the world, sharpening his point of view at the expense of historical accuracy. Increasingly, the realm of ideas displaced the realm of actual persons and places from the foreground of his interest. In the 1940's he even came to cherish the circumstance of failing eyesight which gave common objects "a second often merciful atmosphere" [19] elevating them immediately to essences that can be contemplated only by the mind and spirit. And the major philosophical works of his "retirement"—*Scepticism and*

Animal Faith and *Realms of Being*—testify to the intensity of his preoccupation with the life of the mind. It is from this perspective that the autobiography and other accounts of his youth are written. Persons and places become meaningful, he implies in *My Host the World,* the last volume of the autobiography, only insofar as they can be subsumed under the realm of ideas. A thematic corollary holds for the entire autobiography: to complete the process of living reasonably one must be able and willing to sublimate his past by an act of the imagination. "Never," he writes, "have I enjoyed youth so thoroughly as I have in my old age. In writing *Dialogues in Limbo, The Last Puritan,* and now all these descriptions of the friends of my youth and the young friends of my middle age, I have drunk the pleasure of life more pure, more joyful, than it ever was when mingled with all the hidden anxieties and little annoyances of actual living."[20] (He had anticipated this fortunate state thirty years earlier in "A Minuet on Reaching the Age of Fifty" when he wrote,

> Let wanton girls and boys
> Cry over lover's woes and broken toys.
> Our waking life is sweeter than their dream.)[21]

Warning against "irrational worship" of material persons and places, a worship which hopes to prolong the sensations of the passing moment, Santayana claims to have been held only by "the picturesque or moral suggestions" in experience and to have loved only its "*numen.*"[22] The solitude and timelessness of Rome proved a propitious environment in which to bring his life into perspective, a fact that he acknowledges in a paean to the age and wisdom it nurtured: "Old places and old persons in their turn, when spirit dwells in them, have an intrinsic vitality of which youth is incapable; precisely the balance and wisdom that comes from long perspectives and broad foundations."[23]

Because Santayana dwelt on the commonplace in the autobiography, his reader may view it as overly personal and inconsequential to the world at large. Santayana himself insisted to Edmund Wilson that the persons and places he chose for recollection are not those which exhibit the great themes of the century, but only those which consoled him in his old age.[24] Yet the same paradox which characterized his desire to live spiritually in a material world also characterizes the intention and scope of the autobiography: although *Persons and Places* focuses on the intimate events of his life, "all picturesque and aerial," it also suggests what he calls "the vast obscure inexorable world" behind them.[25] In the epilogue to the autobiography Santayana speaks of the circumstance of existence which fostered in him a dual vision, a uniquely sympathetic perception of what it is to be a rational being in an irrational world. The epilogue asks the reader to see the autobiography as a dramatic commentary on the struggle made by Santayana himself to retain his spiritual identity in a society that would absorb him. But these final comments are also a prelude to Santayana's analysis of this society in *Dominations and Powers* where he discusses the themes of liberty, society, and government in Western civilization. The chapter bridges the two final works of his career by emphasizing the necessity of the individual to take account of a world that is at once responsible for his existence and extraneous to his quest for self-identity.

Mindful of his descent from a "blue sea family" of colonial officials and great merchants, Santayana writes that he learned to regard the world as "inhuman: not meant for man, but habitable by him, and possible to exploit." In such a world mankind is occasionally decimated by nature but never dehumanized. Like the currents of the sea, the conditions for living change suddenly, often violently. But, Santayana writes, "the great question is not what age you live in or what art you pursue but what perfection you can achieve in that art under those circumstances." He was himself almost totally estranged from the given conditions of his world: "an ugly town, a stinted family, a common school." He describes his paradoxical existence in such a world in terms similar to those used by Emerson to distinguish between the self and nature. The "I," a "happy and free ranging" spirit, was held "troubled and captive in its close biological integument," the animal "Me." This, Santayana syas, "is the double conflict, the social opposition and the moral agony, that spirit suffers by being incarnate." Yet Santayana speaks of this spiritual bondage with the resignation of a pre-Platonic naturalist, acknowledging that his own spirit owed its existence and its function to nature which posited it in a particular time and place.

Even if he regarded his own spirit as doubly alienated by abnormal circumstances of exile, he rationalized the situation as favorable to a vocation that was "more speculative, freer, juster, and . . . happier" than it might have been otherwise. He relished the "voluntary, interested, appreciative rôle of the traveller" in a world which functioned as his host. And even though this host was preoccupied with mechanical progress, Santayana was not displeased. "Matter," he writes, "had been kind to me, and I am a lover of matter." (He even attributes his own productivity to the pleasure he took in the physical activity of reading and writing.) What bothered him was that the culture benefiting from mechanical progress had become "*vicious*," forming "habits destructive of its health and of its ability to prosper in its environment." Although his contemporary society knew how to use nature for its purposes, those purposes, according to Santayana, showed a "positively insane abandonment of its [own] true interests." The culture was nurturing a massive proletariat which had no freedom of movement or vocation. Santayana declared that "to be proletariat is an inhuman condition." They were unaware of the two conditions for living reasonably: "First, self-knowledge, the Socratic key to wisdom; and second, sufficient knowledge of the world to perceive what alternatives are open to you and which of them are favourable to your true interests." In the 1940's Santayana came to deplore "the monstrous growth of cities, made possible by the concentration of trade and the multiplication of industries, mechanized, and swelling into monopolies," which had encouraged a proletariat to rise in capitalist as well as Communist countries. The dream of the modern—that science would make man rich, free, and wise—was false. It did not spring as did the cultural dreams of the ancients from natural sources, "from domestic arts or common knowledge spontaneously extended." Instead the dream was that of barbarism calling for "vacant freedom and indeterminate progress." Santayana writes that his contemporary society "lacked altogether that essential trait of rational living, to have a clear, sanctioned, ultimate aim."

Santayana did not ask to live in such a culture; nor was he invited to do so. Facing his world with the equanimity gained from years of practiced detachment and amused by the life nature offered to him, he took solace in turning "into glimpses of eternal truth" the myriad "virtues and sorrows of nature" which passed before him. His vision brought forth a warning to his host. He speaks of the inevitability of conflict and ruin in civilizations as being "fundamentally internal to each society." But he warns, too, that political or militant rashness against perversities of the established order may be destructive of the total culture: "the blind in extirpating the mad may plant a new madness." Before contemporary civilization heals itself, Santayana says in anticipation of *Dominations and Powers,* the fanaticism of all parties must have "humanized itself, reduced its dogmas to harmless metaphors, and sunk down a tap-root, to feed it, into the dark damp depths of mother earth."

Santayana shows in the account of his own life that there is an order to be had in the most awkward of times. But the individual or society which tries to legislate that order without understanding the conditions necessary for its healthy growth will never achieve it. For Santayana, who "learned to think of the earth as a globe with its surface chiefly salt water, a barren treacherous and intractable waste for mankind," the very effort to find order gives man his dignity. But it is humility, Santayana reiterates, that man must have if he is to avoid insanity in his effort to make this world habitable. This is the glimpse of "eternal truth" with which Santayana leaves us in the autobiography: "The economy of nature . . . never diverts its wider processes to render them obedient to the prescription of human rhetoric. Things have their day, and their beauties in that day. It would be preposterous to expect any one civilization to last forever."

Notes

1. See Santayana's letter to Logan Pearsall Smith, January 22, 1938, in *The Letters of George Santayana,* ed. Daniel Cory (New York, 1955), p. 319. Santayana had been contemplat-

ing the autobiography for some time: see his letter to George Sturgis, July 29, 1924, *Letters,* p. 216. Also, like the autobiography, *Dominations and Powers* was conceived much earlier, in fact before the War of 1914–1918: see *Dominations and Powers* (New York, 1951), p. 22.

Of course Santayana had written of his life in various places. The most notable are "A Brief History of My Opinions," in *Contemporary American Philosophy* (New York, 1930), and the prefaces to Volumes I and VII of the Triton edition of *The Works of George Santayana* (New York, 1936–1937). These three essays were later collected under the title "A General Confession" and published as Santayana's introduction to *The Philosophy of George Santayana,* Library of Living Philosophers, ed. Paul Arthur Schilpp, II (Evanston, 1940).

2. See the letter to Lawrence Smith Butler, July 3, 1941, *Letters,* p. 347. In 1946 Santayana also published *The Idea of Christ in the Gospels,* "a theological book."

3. *The Idler and His Works and Other Essays,* ed. Daniel Cory (New York, 1957), pp. 5 ff.

4. *Scepticism and Animal Faith* (New York, 1955), pp. 256–258.

5. July 10, 1933, *Letters,* p. 282.

6. *Scepticism and Animal Faith,* pp. 173–174.

7. *Ibid.,* pp. 259–260.

8. P. 261. In *The Examined Self* (Princeton, 1965), Robert Sayre has treated the autobiographies of Benjamin Franklin, Henry Adams, and Henry James as the authors' imaginative efforts to inform their pasts with the eloquence of their present discourse. For the autobiographer to do otherwise would be to compose a fictionalized biography, that is, to indulge in sentimentalization. Such a work, Santayana says in *Scepticism and Animal Faith,* would proceed from a "defect of imagination," not from a mind intent upon comprehending the past by employing the wisdom of succeeding experience (p. 259).

9. (London, 1954), p. 376.

10. *Ibid.,* p. 507.

11. October 11, 1938, *Letters,* pp. 321–322. In a letter to Smith written almost twenty years before, Santayana expressed hope for a new culture rising out of the barbarous, wilful America Smith thought of as deteriorating, alien, and fallow. The letter is printed in *Unforgotten Years,* pp. 283–288, and in *Letters,* pp. 192–195.

12. See *The Middle Span,* (New York, 1945), pp. 175–176. In his remarks about Smith and Phelps in *The Middle Span,* pp. 37–39 and 174–177, respectively, Santayana reveals his preference for the "muscular" America over the genteel.

13. "Apologia Pro Mente Sua," p. 501.

14. April 16, 1939, *Letters,* pp. 332–333. Santayana follows this prescription explicitly in his discussion of Wendell in *The Middle Span,* pp. 170–172.

15. *Soliloquies in England* (New York, 1923), pp. 63–64. Phelps could not understand Santayana's admiration of Dickens and distaste for Browning, even though Santayana once tried to explain it to him: "My disgust at Browning is not because he loves life or has it abundantly, but because he doesn't love it (as Dickens does, for instance) for what is *good* in it, but for what is base, tawdry, and pretentious. I protest against being called a snob; what I love is what is simple, humble, easy, what ought to be common, and it is only the bombast of false ambitions and false superiority, that I abhor." See letter to Phelps, September 8, 1920, *Letters,* p. 187; also in *Autobiography with Letters,* p. 342.

16. Even Phelps's portrait of Santayana as "an atheist or pessimist" misfires because it is external; Phelps has not tried to see from Santayana's perspective. He labels Santayana as being "what people would call an atheist or a pessimist. In reality," Santayana protests, "I have never been either." But this subtlety escapes Phelps, just as do the distinctions of language among people he recalls when he relies, as Santayana writes, on "the second or third edition of [his] stories as edited by [his] own memory." See note 14.

17. (New York, 1944), p. 149.

18. *Ibid.,* p. 199.

19. *My Host the World* (New York, 1953), p. 129.

20. *Ibid.*, p. 131.

21. *Poems* (New York, 1928), p. 130.

22. *My Host the World*, p. 130.

23. *Ibid.*, pp. 131–132.

24. Edmund Wilson recalls Santayana's protest to a reviewer of *Persons and Places* who had objected to his writing at length on rather obscure figures. Santayana replied, "I wrote about them not because they were public figures but because they were important to me!" See *Europe Without Baedeker* (New York, 1966), p. 53. Like Dickens, Santayana found that nations expressed their essence most clearly in the common man, even though their history might—as Carlyle would have it—be nothing more than the biographies of great men.

25. *My Host the World*, p. 133. The remaining quotations are from the "Epilogue: My Host the World," pp. 133–144.

Oliver Alden and Studs Lonigan:
Heirs to Spiritual Poverty

EDWARD L. SHAUGHNESSY

America has produced an impressive body of fiction about youth, especially boys. The spate of elaborate theories evoked to account for this phenomenon might suggest that the greater part of wisdom is not to add yet another notion to the lot. However, since certain self-evident characteristics of the genre are everyone's to observe, one can feel reasonably secure in building on the common knowledge. Youth is treated by American writers since Cooper as a subject worthy of serious attention. And the one "given" of nearly all such literature is youth's moral dilemma in confronting the values of its world. The hero's conscience becomes a major factor in his fate. Again and again our fiction records this phase of the boy's crucial experience in becoming.

Yet a tragic condition frequently attends this fate. The youthful protagonist suffers not a want of values, but an insufficiency of values. Conditioned by the very norms which can abet the cultural evils, he possesses no articulate code to substitute for the conventions and mores he finds hollow. All readers recall the classic instance of this—Huck Finn's assumption that he will be damned for his "betrayal" of Christian morality in giving succor to Jim. Such a protagonist can wring neither satisfaction nor significance from his actions, no matter what course he chooses. He has no philosophy worthy of his humanity.

To catch this dilemma perfectly is to portray youth's essential tragedy. So long as the grim adult actuality has not taken place, youth retains her greatest privilege, that of a limitless potentiality. But American fiction relentlessly chronicles the loss of idealism and innocence to later contracting expectations. In the transition from youth to a bogus maturity, the hero senses that he has begun to compromise his better nature. His tragedy is his acculturation. James T. Farrell meant nothing less when he wrote: "*Studs Lonigan* was conceived as the story of an American destiny in our time. It deals with the making and education of an ordinary American boy."[1] It deals, in other words, with a pervasive and tragic spiritual poverty.

Reprinted from *Markham Review* 4 (October 1973): 48–52.

I

From their differing points of view, George Santayana and James Farrell provide separate bases of authority for an indictment of American values as spiritually lethal. *The Last Puritan* (1936) and *Studs Lonigan: A Trilogy* (1935)[2] are investigations into the conditions of spiritual poverty. Each traces the destruction of a young man's soul in a withering ambience. Both writers condemn a culture that, in its philistinism and unabashed materialism, freezes the individual's sacred potential to grow.

Santayana's point of vantage, of course, was that of the outsider. Yet his detached observations of life among the New England élite constitute a shrewd assessment of American manners and high culture. *Studs Lonigan,* on the other hand, offers an insider's view of a tragically limited system of values which dooms any hope for achieving genuine human growth and development. In each story the boy's spiritual potential is destroyed before he has achieved maturity. So, while *Studs Lonigan* has been looked upon as the literature of ethnicity and *The Last Puritan* as a history of the starved Brahmin soul, each deals at bottom with the broader effects of cultural impoverishment wherever it may occur.

The sterility of the genteel tradition, which Santayana first analyzed in 1911, is the theme of *The Last Puritan.* Although this tradition operates at the uppermost levels of American Protestant culture, Santayana saw it shot through with philistine preconceptions. Oliver's inheritance is portrayed as a kind of moral anemia, a cluster of duty-centered mores which, in their very gentility and distance from the *élan vital,* constitute mere pretensions to high culture. The genteel manner smothers spontaneity and muffles any articulation of life values in its best young men. A puritanism no longer accepting the doctrine of natural depravity but still burdened under "an agonized conscience," it retains only a moral chill. In accepting the authority of position based on heritage and wealth, in the mindless assumption of its ethical propriety and aesthetic perfection, genteelism retards the natural capacity of the spirit to rebel. The puritan's natural response becomes a reaction against nature.

Studs Lonigan enjoys no such privileges or high station as Oliver Alden. His world and life are the hurly-burly of the modern midwestern city. In their Southside Chicago neighborhood the Lonigans, the O'Neills, and the Reilleys strive for what their parents never possessed. As Farrell says of the first wave of American-Irish: "They came from the shores of that island whose history is one of the most bitter of all nations. Most of them were poor immigrants. Some of them could not read or write. They belonged at the bottom of the American social and economic ladder."[3]

The world of Studs Lonigan is but one arid corner of the modern wasteland. In its representativeness, therefore, the novel does not merely depict American-Irish provincialism; it focuses upon a microcosm of American life. Studs's experience provides one dismal chapter in the education of the American boy.

II

Santayana put the plight of his hero this way:

> [Oliver] ought to have been a saint. But here comes the deepest tragedy in his lot: that he lived in a spiritual vacuum. American breeding can be perfect in form, but it is woefully thin in substance; so that if a man is born a poet or a mystic in America he simply starves. . . . He evaporates, he peters out.[4]

The Last Puritan continues Santayana's critique of "The Genteel Tradition in American Philosophy" (1911). It portrays New England ambience of death-in-life. Santayana sees down the road of genteel traditionalism to its logical end. There, in its final reaches, he discovers frustration and a trailing off into oblivion. As he wrote later to William Lyon Phelps: ". . . poor Oliver, ready for every sacrifice, had nothing to pin his allegiance to. He was what the rich young man in the Gospel would have been if he had been ready to sell his goods and give to the poor, but then had found no cross to take up and no Jesus to follow."[5]

Oliver Alden is the last—that is, the ultimate—Puritan. He carries the principle of puritanism, the inner law of renunciation, to the end of its possible development. Such a principle is negative. Santayana held that renunciation and detachment alone cannot animate life. The organism itself operates on laws of unfolding and healthy flux. A perpetual movement backwards could never signify a natural metamorphosis, human or other. Oliver's fate is to possess no objects worthy of his renunciation; thus, his potential as mystic or saint is frustrated: "The trouble wasn't that he wouldn't be commonplace: there are plenty of people to be commonplace: the trouble was that *he couldn't be exceptional, and yet be positive.*"[6]

Santayana pictures a culture that is sedately righteous. Oliver's mother and his Uncle Nathaniel are its paragons. They derive their money from the world of commerce but never descend into it to oversee the pedestrian matters of business management. In such a culture as the author portrays one has position, wealth, and privilege. Yet one never utters an ostentatious word about these matters. He is detachedly conservative in matters of religion, politics, and the commonweal. He is not directly responsible for the misery of others. Therefore, he neither hates nor pities the masses: he simply fails to recognize their existence.

These genteel souls suffer an agonized conscience about everything.

Nathaniel, Santayana's philistine, is a kind of cultural specimen. He acts only out of a rigid and moralistic sense of duty. Nathaniel buys paintings, for example, as he performs any other exercise: "Nor that he liked pictures or frequented the society of artists: but once a month he would go into Doll & Richards' shop in Park Street, and inquire if they had anything new. It was a public duty, he declared, for those who could afford it to encourage art in a new country."[7] Men like Nathaniel do all things with equal enthusiasm— celebrate feasts, attend funerals, vote the Republican ticket. The archetypal genteelist is prudent and solid, a model of the chary and abstemious virtues. But these virtues demonstrate an entirely negative spirit, unproductive of joy and inner peace. Happiness has no place in the scheme of things. Indeed, to be happy would betray a frivolous irresponsibility. To Santayana, of course, a denial of happiness was a denial of reason.

The unworldly Oliver, the potential mystic, is capable of true virtue. So complete is the puritan's commitment that he achieves an ideal. Santayana had no love for Oliver's tradition, but he respected courage and honesty wherever he found them. Young Alden is a clear-burning flame: "The old Calvinists, Oliver felt, hadn't been puritan enough: you were not pure at all, unless it was for the love of purity: but with them it had all been a mean calculation of superstition and thrift and vengeance—vengeance against everybody who was happier and better than themselves" (318).

A frigid sense of duty was alive in the child from the beginning: he "had been born punctually." Here Santayana suggests that the agonized conscience infuses puritanism and that an individual born into a genteel milieu will be an inheritor of an anemic and crippled philosophy:

Philosophy possessed the soul of this child from his first breath: inarticulately, of course, as it was destined, at bottom, to remain always; because the words which his education supplied were not capable of uttering it truly. But in action, in determination, and by a sort of inner blind fortitude, his faith was distinctly in him from the beginning. There were good things and there were bad things, and there was an equal duty to pull through both and come out somehow on the further side of all trouble (76).

Such a philosophy, Santayana makes clear, lacks the capacity for inner free-dom. It must labor under the moral onus of continual responsibility. A tradition of duty, if duty is the only end, leads to meaningless action. All natural impulses are checked and the spontaneity of life is stifled. The consequences are automatic and mindless responses to duty. Natural anima-tion of the organism can no longer be recognized for what it is. This theory undergirds Santayana's criticism of the genteel tradition. A traditionalist himself, he never believed in any system for its own sake or in a program which failed to combine reason with natural éclat of performance.

Trained in a genteel ethic, Oliver learns to shun what is in any manner uninhibited. He learns to prefer things that are "sane" and chastened. But this sanity, Santayana shows, actually opposes health. It becomes effete, incapable of bringing forth anything in joy. Thus, life could never become a charming dream. Life tended instead to become a sad phantasm, refined yet tinged with melancholy.

Oliver's motivation is the key to his character. As he develops, his attitude toward group activities offers a striking insight into his psyche. For example, Oliver's early attitude toward athletics is boyish and enthusiastic. In time, however, his exuberance is displaced by a solid sense of duty. He plays because he is talented and therefore *must* lead: "So he led his football squad with a cold heart" (382). This development parallels the history of his spontaneity's dying out. Discovering responsible criteria for action becomes his major philosophical problem. Yielding to a sense of constraint, he develops the ethic of duty which chills his natural zest for life. The insufficiency of his values precludes any rational alternative to his *modus vivendi*. As his cousin, Mario Van de Weyer, puts it, Oliver "convinced himself on puritan grounds that it was wrong to be a puritan" (6).

Puritanism becomes an extreme demand for purity and an absolute denial of everything else. Ultimately, it must deny itself. It must seek to be consumed as it wishes all things to be consumed for their impurity. Its very human limitations commend its own end. Oliver achieves the limits of his philosophy and has nothing more to accomplish. His imagination is burdened under the weight of rigid moral duty.

Santayana condemns the tradition that consigns his hero to death in life. Oliver, unpretentious and far juster than the other genteelists, becomes the evolutionary pole of a worn-out tradition. The others are simply less absolutist than he. They are willing, therefore, still to traffic with the world. His accidental death is not the novel's tragedy; his earlier spiritual succumbing constitutes Santayana's version of an American tragedy:

> Oliver at least hadn't had his young life cut short cruelly, as the old ladies were sure to say in their letters of condolence to his mother. He would have gained nothing by living to a hundred, never would have found better friends, or loved women otherwise. His later years would only have been pallid copies of his earlier ones. He had come to the end of his rope. He was played out (584–585).

In Oliver Alden's story Santayana sees the demise of his culture. In that milieu the concept of life for itself is forced to wither. (This was the plight, Santayana said, experienced by his fellow Harvard poets—Savage, Stickney, and Lodge—who "were visibly killed by the lack of air to breathe.")[8] The life of material action is killed in a slow, unnatural way. Simultaneously, the life of reason is similarly silenced and the act of imagination becomes incapable of performance.

Finally, the genteel traditionalists could no longer renew themselves. As

Mario puts it, "He was the child of an elderly and weary man, and of a thin-spun race. . . . A moral nature burdened and over-strung, and a critical faculty fearless but helplessly subjective—isn't that the true tragedy of your ultimate Puritan" (602)? Oliver's inheritance was rich in all things except those of the spirit, but the spirit alone has value for the mystic.

III

Farrell's hero accepts the world as it is given to him:

> Studs Lonigan was conceived as a normal American boy of Irish-Catholic extraction. The social milieu in which he lived and was educated was one of spiritual poverty. . . . He is a normal young American of his time and his class. His values become the values of the world.[9]

Farrell perceived that the institutions undergirding Studs's life, potential spiritual reservoirs, had in fact run dry. When the sons and daughters of an impoverished and exploited land arrived in America, "Their spiritual resources were meager. They believed in the American myth of success and advancement. They believed in the teachings and dogma of their faith. They believed that with homilies, platitudes about faith and work, and little fables about good example, they could educate their children."[10] Farrell, of course, rejected these simplistic and damaging formulae, but he did not mean to criticize only the values ascendant in a sub-culture; he saw in the institutions of Chicago's South Side Irish a paradigm of the greater American culture.

Irish-American culture fostered a variety of puritanism and carried on a limited but certain Jansenist legacy.[11] Like the earlier American Puritans, the American Irish accepted the doctrine of man's fallen nature, the evil of the flesh, and the easy corruptibility of the spirit. They embraced a work ethic and looked with suspicion upon intellectual adventuring. At St. Patrick's, the Lonigan's parish church, Father Gilhooley preaches the dangers of the corrupting public schools which lead the good children from the faith. During the parish mission of 1927, Father Shannon defensively argues against the contemporary intellectualism. He castigates the diabolism of Mencken and Sinclair Lewis and the "enemies of the faith" at the University of Chicago. After the services young Danny O'Neill (a thin disguise for Farrell himself) seeks the priest out. "He had asked the priest if he could talk with him about the faith, because he was a University student who had lost his religion. Father Shannon had curtly replied that he was, for the present, very busy."[12] The incident drives Danny further from the Church and causes him to look upon religion as superstition or hypocrisy.

Studs's parents believe they offer their children important advantages and elevated prospects. Paddy Lonigan, the father, had struggled as an ordinary worker but finally has achieved independence as a painting contractor. Paddy and his wife, Mary, feel a certain smugness in their accomplishments and derive a sense of the rightness of their values. They can give their children a good education. It is a deserved prosperity as judged by the approved cultural canons of success built on work. The elder Lonigan reflects:

> Life was a good thing if you were Patrick J. Lonigan and had worked hard to win out in the grim battle, and God had been good to you. But then, he had earned the good things he had. Yes, sir, let God call him to the Heavenly throne this very minute, and he could look God square in the eye and say he had done his duty, and he had been and was, a good father. They had given the kids a good home, fed and clothed them, set the right example for them, sent them to Catholic schools to be educated, seen that they performed their religious duties, hustled them off to confession regularly, given them money for the collection . . . done everything a parent can do for a child (I, 21).

As Farrell shows, these complacent values are fatally narrow and founded upon the crassest materialism, unconsciously rationalized in vague pieties. The institutions which hold Studs's world together are but extensions of the institutions of the culture at large.

A crushing tribal insularity limits the vision not only of the Lonigans and the parishioners of St. Patrick's but of all the ethnic groups of South Side Chicago. Each group tends to taunt and look down upon the others. Negroes "encroach" on the inner sanctum of the parish neighborhood around 58th and Prairie Streets. The "niggers" and the "kikes" who sell real estate to blacks become the target of fierce prejudice and even physical assault. Although the parents of Studs and his friends do not explicitly encourage their sons' attacks on the Negro youths, they have passed along all their own stereotypes and benighted hatred to their children.

Here Farrell points to a classic instance of intolerance, seamy values, and "toughness"; and he shows their catastrophic results when taken as educative norms. The book is a classic, an *exemplum*, but it avoids all the fusty solemnity of the conventional didactic fable. The tale with a moral in the usual sense cannot be a tragedy, because the point of view from which it is told is complacent and assumptive of moral superiority. Farrell felt no superiority to Studs Lonigan. As he wrote later: "My attitude toward . . . my character here is essentially a simple one. 'There but for the grace of God go I.' "13

It is well to point out here that certain misconceptions attend *Studs Lonigan*. Studs is not simply a victim of poverty and slum life like Crane's Maggie Johnson. On the contrary, young Lonigan grows up in a gaining middle-class family establishing itself in financial security. The author thus escapes what many critics wrongly see in the novel: a narrow sociological tract designed to illustrate an economic thesis. Furthermore, because Studs is not without some power of will and therefore some responsibility for his fate, Farrell cannot be said to rely upon a simplistic determinism characteristic of classical naturalism.

The models which Studs accepts stand in place of a genuine model of manhood. He submerges his idealism in order to achieve a "manhood" that will be the envy of his peers. As he moves toward the street, the gang, pool rooms, brothels, speak-easies, he forces down the better impulses of his nature. He leads in punishing the "niggers" who are moving into St. Patrick's neighborhood; his prejudice towards Jews is a notion he takes from adults who believe the "kikes" are unworthy to live with them. In fine, Studs believes he must distrust his tender feelings in order to gain acceptance as a superior man, "the real stuff."

The trilogy chronicles Studs's forcing down of his own finer nature. By the end his soul has been so brutalized that he has lost nearly all spiritual promise. Early in *Young Lonigan,* when he is about to be graduated from St. Patrick's grammar school, Studs experiences a conflict between his desire for tenderness and his need to be thought of as tough. "And he goddamned himself, because he was getting soft. He was Studs Lonigan, a guy who didn't have mushy feelings! He was a hard-boiled egg that they had left in the pot a couple of hours too long" (I, 8).

Like most normal boys his age, Studs is coming alive to the first thoughts of love. He tends to idealize one girl, whose sweetness and tenderness appeal to his budding manhood. Lucy Scanlan makes him feel that she is "something beautiful and vague, something like a prayer sprung into flesh" (I, 115). But this "softness" causes him to feel vulnerable. He knows that his friends will ridicule his attentions to a nice girl. If he persists in showing affection to Lucy, he will lose his tough-guy status.

As a boy Studs naturally looks to the future. At various points he sees himself as war hero, athlete, celebrity, and priest. But as he undergoes the calcification that Farrell relentlessly documents, Studs loses his hopeful forward vision and is forced to live in the memory of what he might have been. His mental life turns to a melancholy nostalgia. As Farrell puts it: "He has as many good impulses as normal human beings have. In time, because of defeat, of frustration, of a total situation characterized by spiritual poverty, these good impulses are expressed more and more in the stream of his reverie."[14] Thus, the theme becomes one typical of modern American literature: the theme of lost opportunities.

The ravages of debauchery take a massive physical and spiritual toll: the drinking bouts with bootleg gin and worse, the whoring, fighting, the work on his father's painting gang, and sieges of pneumonia wreck his constitution. He never loses the guilt feelings related to his lusts and so develops an attitude toward confession which borders on compulsiveness: "He saw himself saying his penance, saw himself kneeling in the confessional, talking through the screen to Father Doneggan, running through the catalogue of his sins, commandment by commandment. He tried to put himself into a contrite mood. He wanted his act of contrition tonight to be a perfect act of contrition, as if it were his last confession" (II, 109). But Studs gains no capacity for true introspection or an analysis of the forces that drive him.

His demise is predictable, not from the point of view of linear determinism but in terms of the complex dynamics of human nature. He thinks, as he is dying: "If he had never gone to that New Year's Eve party in 1929. If he hadn't drunk as much as in the old days. If he had only let himself get an education" (III, 382).

Read from one point of view, the theme of *Studs Lonigan* is, as John Chamberlain has pointed out, that "The wages of sin is death."[15] However, Farrell is anything but the self-righteous moralist. It is true that in the character of Danny O'Neill he moved away from the values of Studs and the other boys. Yet his compassion for all those around whom his youth revolved reminds us of Eugene O'Neill's in *Long Day's Journey Into Night*. That is why *Studs Lonigan* is cast as a tragedy, as the later autobiographical Danny O'Neill "pentalogy" is not. Like Santayana, Farrell loved in his hero what he was in his boyish potential. And the artist despised the cultural impoverishment that robbed Studs of the power to grow into genuine maturity.

IV

These separate accounts of the stangled human spirit derive from essentially different philosophical attitudes. Farrell's literary practice is part of a modern phenomenon called Naturalism. Moreover, he was influenced importantly by John Dewey, whose philosophy appeared grotesque to Santayana. For his part the author of *The Last Puritan* claimed a classical naturalism founded by the pre–Socratic Greeks and running through Lucretius to Spinoza. Such a philosophy will always celebrate the life of reason, that kind of austere and highplaned life embraced by Oliver Alden. Such heroes must see existence as tragic, and they accept that truth unflinchingly.

No doubt we are confronted with a greater irony in *The Last Puritan* than we are in *Studs Lonigan*; our normal expectations are that Oliver's inheritance equips him with unlimited opportunities for spiritual fulfillment. Yet each novel tells the story of a young man who suffers a moral atrophy brought on by cultural desolation, a culture built upon a kind of spiritual quicksand.

The questions posed by Farrell and Santayana relate to social values in America. Santayana wrote of this problem elsewhere in more explicitly philosophical terms. He wondered how we can account for the zeal and industry— the near religion—that characterize the American preoccupation with things. Identifying the principle which animates this frenzy, Santayana called the American "an idealist working on matter."[16] Such idealism, he seemed to say, tends to be very hard on the human spirit.

Notes

1. James T. Farrell, "How *Studs Lonigan* Was Written," in *The League of Frightened Philistines and Other Papers* (New York: Vanguard Press, 1945), p. 89.

2. It is interesting to note that *Studs Lonigan: A Trilogy* and *The Last Puritan* were published within months of each other. Santayana's novel, his single attempt at fiction, won second place among the best-sellers of 1936. *Studs Lonigan,* although its early sales were modest, has become a classic of modern American fiction. It is perhaps worthwhile to ponder what disparate literary tastes these writers appealed to, while at the same time undeniably striking a positive response from a broad cross section of American readers. For certainly, although each book has had its coterie of admirers on the ideological extremes, there exists a vast middle group to whom both novels have been important.

3. "How *Studs Lonigan* Was Written," p. 87.

4. *The Letters of George Santayana,* ed. Daniel Cory (New York: Scribner's, 1955), p. 302.

5. *Ibid.,* p. 305.

6. *Ibid.,* p. 302 [italics his].

7. *The Last Puritan: A Memoir in the Form of a Novel* (New York: Scribner's, 1936), p. 20. Further page references appear in text.

8. *The Letters of George Santayana,* p. 306.

9. "How *Studs Lonigan* Was Written," pp. 86, 88.

10. *Ibid.,* p. 87.

11. An excellent history of this background is available in *The American Irish* by William V. Shannon (New York; MacMillan, 1963).

12. *Studs Lonigan: A Trilogy* (New York: Vanguard Press, 1935), p. 369, II. Further page references appear in the text, preceded by a Roman I, II, or III. The Roman numerals indicate which novel of the trilogy is being cited: *Young Lonigan, The Young Manhood of Studs Lonigan, or Judgement Day.*

13. "How *Studs Lonigan* Was Written," p. 89.

14. *Ibid.,* p. 88.

15. John Chamberlain, "Introduction" to *Studs Lonigan: A Trilogy,* p. xii.

16. George Santayana, *Character and Opinion in the United States: With Reminiscences of William James and Josiah Royce and Academic Life in America* (New York; Scribner's, 1921), p. 175.

Imagination as Value

Lucy Beckett

Arnold's true successor was not Pater or any other English writer of the generation immediately following his own but George Santayana, the Spanish philosopher and critic who lived in America from his ninth to his forty-ninth year, and was for the last twenty-three of those years on the Faculty of Harvard University. After his resignation in 1912 he never returned to America. He lived in England during the war and later in Paris; in 1924 he settled in Rome and died there in 1952. All his writings were in English. As a critic, or, rather, a philosopher who frequently turned his attention to literary questions, he was certainly not Arnold's successor in any conscious or deliberate sense. Like Eliot (whom perhaps Santayana influenced in this as in other, more fortunate directions) he attributed to Arnold the highflown vagueness that should have been laid at Pater's door. He launched, against Arnold's famous verdict, a defence of Shelley as a poet[1] which not only reveals a distorted and unjust view of Arnold, but also defies the critical principles that he himself had earlier laid down in substantial agreement with Arnold. And in a note on 'Liberalism and Culture' published in 1915, he attacked Arnold without mercy and with very little understanding:

> Liberalism does not go very deep; it is an adventitious principle, a mere loosening of an older structure. For that reason it brings to all who felt cramped and ill-suited much comfort and relief . . . It opens to them that sweet, scholarly, tenderly moral, critically superior attitude of mind which Matthew Arnold called culture . . . Piety and learning had their intrinsic charms, but, after all, they had been cultivated for the sake of ulterior duties and benefits, and in order to appropriate and hand down the revealed wisdom which opened the way to heaven. Culture, on the contrary, had no ulterior purpose, no forced unity. It was an aroma inhaled by those who walked in the evening in the garden of life.

Santayana is here as unfair to Arnold as Eliot was later to be: Arnold's view of culture, for instance, was always informed by precisely the 'ulterior purpose'

Reprinted from *Wallace Stevens* (Cambridge, England: Cambridge University Press, 1974), 23–45, with the permission of the author and the publisher.

which Santayana denies. But Santayana's unfairness is more expected than Eliot's, since his own best writing on literature, and particularly on its relation to religion, shows such striking and complete concordance with Arnold that, but for such passages as this, one might guess him to have read all Arnold's works with care and enthusiasm.

For Santanyana's critical idealism is as strong as Arnold's, if more rigorous; it is formulated and substantiated by his study of literature in very much the same way; and it is seen as subject to very much the same threats and dangers, though these looked even direr to the younger man. Arnold, visiting America at the end of his life could see that its faith in "the *average man*" was a menace to the standards that he had passionately preached. Santayana, who could have heard Arnold's lecture "Literature and Science" as an undergraduate, was revolted by the prevailing values of the university in which he lived and worked. In *Character and Opinion in the United States*, he tells this story:

> The president of Harvard College, seeing me once by chance soon after the beginning of a term, inquired how my classes were getting on; and when I said I thought they were getting on well, that my men seemed to be keen and intelligent, he stopped me as I were about to waste his time. 'I meant' said he, "*what is the number* of students in your classes?'

Santayana's refusal to knuckle under to this atmosphere was unqualified: "I object to and absolutely abhor," he wrote to William James, who had accused him of 'impertinence and superior airs,' "the assertion that all the eggs indiscriminately are good because the hen has laid them." And, in another letter:

> While I wish to be just and to understand people's feelings, wherever they are at all significant, I am deliberately minded to be contemptuous towards what seems to me contemptible, and not to have any share in the conspiracy of mock respect by which intellectual ignominy and moral stagnation are kept up in our society.

It is not surprising to find that when Santayana applied his unpopular principles of moral and intellectual excellence to contemporary literature, he found nothing to satisfy him. For one who felt as he did, and as Arnold had, that: "The sole advantage in possessing great works of literature lies in what they can help us to become," the literary scene in America and England in the 'nineties was not encouraging. Surveying it in 1896 he wrote: "The crudity we are too distracted to refine, we accept as originality, and the vagueness we are too pretentious to make accurate, we pass off as sublimity." And in his critical essays collected and published in 1900 under the title *Interpretations of Poetry and Religion* he presents as it were the firm conclusions about the poet's task in the modern world towards which all Arnold's work had tended but which Arnold himself had never definitely stated.

In his Preface Santayana summarises the idea which connects the essays in terms which show how closely his view approached Arnold's:

> Religion and poetry are identical in essence, and differ merely in the way in which they are attached to practical affairs. Poetry is called religion when it intervenes in life, and religion, when it merely supervenes upon life, is seen to be nothing but poetry. It would naturally follow from this conception that religious doctrines would do well to withdraw their pretension to be dealing with matters of fact . . . For the dignity of religion, like that of poetry and of every moral ideal, lies precisely in its ideal adequacy, in its fit rendering of the meanings and values of life, in its anticipation of perfection.

Santayana may have thought that he was attacking Arnold in this passage later in the Preface: "The liberal school that attempts to fortify religion by minimizing its expression, both theoretic and devotional, seems . . . to be merely impoverishing religious symbols and vulgarizing religious aims." But Arnold's constant insistence on the fundamental value of the Bible itself, and his leaning towards the liturgy (though not the theology) of the Catholic Church absolve him from such a charge; and he would have agreed with every word of Santayana's conclusion to the Preface:

> Not to see in . . . rational activity the purpose and standard of all life is to have left human nature half unread . . . In comparison with such apathetic naturalism, all the errors and follies of religion are worthy of indulgent sympathy, since they represent an effort, however misguided, to interpret and to use the materials of experience for moral ends, and to measure the value of reality by its relation to the ideal.

Just as Santayana shared, though apparently without realising it, Arnold's view of the relation between poetry and religion and of the nature of religious language and symbolism, so he shared with Arnold a vision of the enormous imaginative and intellectual responsibility confronting the modern poet, and a despairing perception of the failure to meet it. In the well-known essay "The Poetry of Barbarism," of which Whitman and Browning are the particular targets, he diagnoses this failure in these words:

> We find our contemporary poets incapable of any high wisdom, incapable of any imaginative rendering of human life and its meaning. Our poets are things of shreds and patches; they give us episodes and studies, a sketch of this curiosity, a glimpse of that romance; they have no total vision, no grasp of the whole reality and consequently no capacity for a sane and steady idealization. The comparatively barbarous ages had a poetry of the ideal; they had visions of beauty, order and perfection. This age of material elaboration has no sense for

those things. Its fancy is retrospective, whimsical, and flickering; its ideals, when it has any, are negative and partial; its moral strength is a blind and miscellaneous vehemence . . . This poetry should be viewed in relation to the general moral crisis and imaginative disintegration of which it gives a verbal echo; then we shall avoid the injustice of passing it over as insignificant, no less than the imbecility of hailing it as essentially glorious and successful.

This passage, like the whole essay from which it comes is most remarkable for its date (1900). It not only crystallises, in terms stronger and clearer than Arnold's own, the situation as Arnold had seen it; it also looks forward across the chasm of 1914–18 to the Yeats of "The Second Coming"—"The best lack all conviction"—to *The Waste Land* and the "imaginative disintegration" of the *Cantos*, and also to *Four Quartets* and Stevens's later poetry which are the only fully-achieved victories in this century and in English of poetry against barbarism.

Santayana had a closer and more accurate appreciation than Arnold of the way in which the poetic imagination actually works. In "The Elements and Function of Poetry," the essay which concludes *Interpretations of Poetry and Religion*, he says:

The great function of poetry . . . is . . . to repair to the material of experience, seizing hold of the reality of sensation and fancy beneath the surface of conventional ideas, and then out of that living but indefinite material to build structures, richer, finer, fitter to the primary tendencies of our nature, to the ultimate possibilities of the soul.

And a little further on he coins a concept, a celebrated shorthand description of the poetic process, for which Eliot has taken the credit. The poet's imagination, he says, operates like the day-dreaming child's: "The glorious emotions with which he bubbles over must at all hazards find or feign their correlative objects." This is, as far as I know, the first appearance in criticism of the objective correlative. But whereas Eliot leaves the causal relationship between object and emotion undefined, so that one suspects him of suggesting that the poet, like the child, sets out to find or feign a correlative in the real world. Santayana makes it clear that it is "the seed of sensation" which comes first.

The passions are naturally blind, and the poverty of the imagination, when left alone, is absolute. The passions may ferment as they will, they can never breed an idea out of their own energy. This idea must be furnished by the senses, by outward experience, else the hunger of the soul will gnaw its own emptiness for ever.

Both Eliot and Stevens were undergraduates at Harvard while Santayana was teaching there. Eliot took two of Santayana's courses of lectures, in 1908 and (as a graduate student) in 1909. Stevens, who was at Harvard from 1897 to 1900, took no courses in philosophy and was therefore never officially one of Santayana's pupils. But he knew him, was often invited by Santayana to come and see him, and read him his early poems. Both poets were influenced by him to a very considerable degree. To anyone who has read *Interpretations of Poetry and Religion* and *Three Philosophical Poets* (1910), ideas first organised by Santayana are plainly visible in Eliot's early criticism, though their derivation, as with the objective correlative, is usually not acknowledged. It is above all a toughness, an intellectual rigour in thought about poetry and an unwillingness to tolerate emotional self-indulgence that Santayana strengthened in the young Eliot. But Santayana's fundamental view of poetry, his vision of its relation to religion, and the consequent vast reach of his hope for it—all so like Arnold's—were ultimately to prove, of course, far from sympathetic to Eliot. One can hardly imagine him, at least after the late 1920s, agreeing with this pronouncement in "The Elements and Function of Poetry":

> Where poetry rises from its elementary and detached expressions in rhythms, euphemism, characterization and story-telling, and comes to the consciousness of its highest function, that of portraying the ideals of experience and destiny, then the poet becomes aware that he is essentially a prophet, and either devotes himself to the loving expression of the religion that exists, or like Lucretius or Wordsworth, to the heralding of one that he believes to be possible. Such poets are aware of their highest mission; others, whatever the energy of their genius, have not conceived their ultimate function as poets. They have been willing to leave their world ugly as a whole, after stuffing it with a sufficient profusion of beauties. Their contemporaries, their fellow-countrymen for many generations, may not perceive this defect, because they are naturally even less able than the poet himself to understand the necessity of so large a harmony . . . Such insensibility to the highest poetry is no more extraordinary than the corresponding indifference to the highest religion; nobility and excellence, however, are not dependent on the suffrage of halfbaked men, but on the original disposition of the clay and the potter; I mean on the conditions of the art and the ideal capacities of human nature.

The irony and the paradox of Eliot is that, although in *Four Quartets* he fulfilled the "ultimate function" of the poet as Santayana here defines it, as a critic he consistently evaded the admission that such a function exists even for the Christian poet, let alone for the non-Christian.

The challenge that Santayana formulated for the modern poet, more cogently and carefully than Arnold had done, though less optimistically, was essentially post-Christian. It was connected, that is to say, to a view of religion incompatible with orthodox Christianity, in so far as orthodox Christianity imposes upon its poets the service of specific and unquestionable truths. When Santayana uses phrases like "the loving expression of the religion that exists," he is speaking of the past. He sees the present, his own period, as a time of "general moral crisis and imaginative disintegration," and nowhere does he envisage a return to the orthodoxy of the past as the modern poet's proper response to this crisis. It was thus inevitable that Eliot, the convert to Anglo-Catholicism, should move altogether away from the influence of a man whose theology he would presumably have considered as juvenile as that of Arnold which it so closely resembles. "That fallacy," wrote Santayana in a characteristic passage,

> from which the pagan religion alone has been free, that πρῶτον ψεῦδος of all fanaticism, the natural but hopeless misunderstanding of imagining that poetry in order to be religion, in order to be the inspiration of life, must first deny that it is poetry and deceive us about the facts with which we have to deal—this misunderstanding has marred the work of the Christian imagination and condemned it, if we may trust appearances, to be transitory.

It is hardly likely that Eliot would have regarded such an observation with enthusiasm, still less all in Santayana's critical thought which depends directly upon such a conception of religion.

Santayana's influence on Stevens was altogether different, in kind, in duration, and in intensity. It was not only that Santayana's critical ideas, some of them much elaborated, remained permanently at the centre of Steven's thought, so that the vision of the poet's task sketched by Santayana comes to seem a bright unbroken thread reappearing again and again throughout Stevens's work. It was also that the figure of Santayana himself, whom after 1900 he never saw again, assumed for Stevens over the years a strangely symbolic, almost a numinous quality. In a passage from the very difficult and important essay "Imagination as Value," which Stevens delivered as a lecture in 1948, Santayana appears as the single illustration illuminating a whole complex of ideas essential to the understanding of Stevens himself. I quote at length because the force of Stevens's peculiar prose, at once tentative and dense with integrity, is lost in the short extract. The neat and quotable conclusion is not the object of his method of thought; as he wrote elsewhere,[2] of Santayana: "His pages are part of the *douceur de vivre* and do not offer themselves for sensational summary." The following passage from "Imagination as Value" is part of a meditation exploring and defining the suggestion contained in these two sentences: "To regard the imagination as metaphysics is to think of it as part of life, and to think of it as part of life is to realize the extent of artifice. We live in the mind."

> The discussion of the imagination as metaphysics has led us off a little to one side. This is justified, however, by the considerations, first, that the operation of the imagination in life is more significant than its operation in or in relation to . . . arts and letters; second, that the imagination penetrates life; and

finally that its value as metaphysics is not the same as its value in arts and letters. In spite of the prevalence of the imagination in life, it is probably true that the discussion of it in that relation is incomparably less frequent and less intelligent than the discussion of it in relation to arts and letters. I suppose that the reason for this is that few people would turn to the imagination, knowingly, in life, while few people would turn to anything else, knowingly, in arts and letters. In life what is important is the truth as it is, while in arts and letters what is important is the truth as we see it. There is a real difference here even though people turn to the imagination without knowing it in arts and letters. There are other possible variations of that theme but the theme itself is there. Again in life the function of the imagination is so varied that it is not well—defined as it is in arts and letters. In life one hesitates when one speaks of the value of the imagination. Its value in arts and letters is aesthetic. Most men's lives are thrust upon them. The existence of aesthetic value in lives that are forced on those that live them is an improbable sort of thing. There can be lives, nevertheless, which exist by the deliberate choice of those that live them. To use a single illustration: it may be assumed that the life of Professor Santayana is a life in which the function of the imagination has had a function similar to its function in any deliberate work of art or letters. We have only to think of this present phase of it,[3] in which, in his old age, he dwells in the head of the world, in the company of devoted women, in their convent, and in the company of familiar saints, whose presence does so much to make any convent an appropriate refuge for a generous and human philosopher. To repeat, there can be lives in which the value of the imagination is the same as its value in arts and letters and I exclude from consideration as part of that statement any thought of poverty or wealth, being a *bauer* or being a king, and so on, as irrelevant.

What is being aimed at in this remarkable paragraph, as in the whole of the essay, is nothing less than a definition of the human qualities and human powers by which man is able to confer value on his life and on his relation to the world. The definition is not arrived at by the ordinary process of consequential statement but evoked, as it were, by an accumulation of suggestions lit by Stevens's incandescent caution. The large words "by which men long lived well" but which in the modern world have lost the firmness and credit that vanished structures gave them, words like "goodness," "freedom," "nobility," even "meaning," are consistently avoided. Yet it is precisely towards the conviction such words used to carry that Stevens moves with due and elaborate care both in his poetry and in this prose. Within the convolutions of the passage above lurks the proposition that the freedom to create significance, a commonplace of perception and discussion in the aesthetic sphere, can be related to the freedom from which a man may choose to create the significance of his own life. And within even this proposition there is the suggestion, made with the subtlest circumspection, that Santayana is a good man, and that his goodness has to do with just such created significance as is usually thought of in connexion with the arts. These large words belong, of course, to "sensational summary." Stevens knew what he was about when he denied himself the use of the easy classification. "Your use of the word nobility causes some difficulty," he told a critic[4] who had thus labelled a recurrent theme of his poetry. "Not long ago I wrote to John Crowe Ransom and told him that I thought that while the word was essentially the right word it was a most impolitic word to use." But by evading the dangers referred to in the phrase "a most impolitic word," Stevens took on the simpler danger of not being understood. If what he was saying is to be heard, it must in the end be said in the old, large words, sharpened and strengthened a little, perhaps, by his own refusal to rely on them.

On the basis of this passage alone it would seem extravagant to claim that the figure of Santayana came, towards the end of both their lives, to represent for Stevens the saving goodness, the emblematic victory over life, that in another age would have been represented by the figure of a saint. The claim is substantiated, however, by the poem "To an Old Philosopher in Rome" which Stevens wrote four years later (it was published, by coincidence, in the month that Santayana died, September 1952). The subject of the poem is not only Santayana himself, the old philosopher dying "in the head of the world"; it is also "the imagination as value." Stevens sees Santayana's life as a representative and sufficient answer to the question posed elsewhere in the essay of that name: "What, then, is it to live in the mind with the imagination, yet not too near to the fountains of its rhetoric, so that one does not have a consciousness only of grandeurs, of incessant departures from the idiom and of inherent altitudes?" The question implies an insistence on the normal, on the tethering of the imagination to reality, which is highly characteristic of Stevens. The imagination, in his view, is not to transcend, to leave behind as worthless and despised, what he called the poverty of human life. On the contrary, it is this inescapable poverty which the imagination, as only the imagination can, must inform with significance. The point is clearly made in these sentences from the closing passage of "Imagination as Value":

> My final point, then, is that the imagination is the power that enables us to perceive the normal in the abnormal, the opposite of chaos in chaos. It does this every day in arts and letters. This may seem to be a merely capricious statement; for ordinarily we regard the imagination as abnormal per se . . . It is natural for us to identify the imagination with those that extend its abnormality. It is like identifying liberty with those that abuse it. A literature overfull of abnormality and, certainly, present-day European literature, as one knows it, seems to be a literature full of abnormality, gives the reason an appearance of normality to which it is not, solely entitled . . . Those that insist on the solitude and misery and terror of the world . . . will ask of what value is the imagination to them; and if their experience is to be considered, how is it possible to deny that they live in an imagination of evil? Is evil

normal or abnormal? And how do the exquisite divinations of the poets and for that matter even the 'aureoles of the saints' help them? But when we speak of perceiving the normal, we have in mind the instinctive integrations which are the reason for living. Of what value is anything to the solitary and those that live in misery and terror, except the imagination? . . .

The chief problems of any artist, as of any man, are the problems of the normal and . . . he needs, in order to solve them, everything that the imagination has to give.

The possible triumph suggested here, the triumph of human value achieved by the imagination, is the triumph described and saluted in "To an Old Philosopher in Rome." An essential constituent of any such triumph, as Stevens sees it, is the ordinariness, the poverty and the sadness inseparable from human existence, and here it is exemplified by the ordinary objects surrounding Santayana's, as any man's, deathbed. It is hard to quote from this poem: the long sentences move through the sixteen stanzas with such mastery of measure that quotation seems more than usually like mutilation. The two worlds, reality and imagination, are established at the beginning:

> On the threshold of heaven, the figures in the street
> Become the figures of heaven, the majestic movement
> Of men growing small in the distance of space,
> Singing, with smaller and still smaller sound,
> Unintelligible absolution and an end—
>
> The threshold, Rome, and that more merciful Rome
> Beyond, the two alike in the make of the mind.
> It is as if in a human dignity
> Two parallels become one, a perspective, of which
> Men are part both in the inch and in the mile.

The mind, in it "making," unites the two worlds by endowing the bare particulars of reality with the imagination's value, inventing nothing and exaggerating nothing, always acknowledging the nakedness and poverty of the human condition.

> Be orator but with an accurate tongue
> And without eloquence, O, half-asleep,
> Of the pity that is the memorial of this room,
>
> So that we feel, in this illuminated large,
> The veritable small, so that each of us
> Beholds himself in you, and hears his voice
> In yours, master and commiserable man,
> Intent on your particles of nether-do,

> Your dozing in the depths of wakefulness,
> In the warmth of your bed, at the edge of your
>   chair, alive
> Yet living in two worlds, impenitent
> As to one, and, as to one, most penitent,
>
> Impatient for the grandeur that you need
> In so much misery; and yet finding it
> Only in misery, the afflatus of ruin,
> Profound poetry of the poor and of the dead . . .

After the long sentence comes the simple statement:
"It is poverty's speech that seeks us out the most," and then the stanza
which forms the summit, as it were, of the whole poem:

> And you—it is you that speak it, without speech,
> The loftiest syllables among loftiest things,
> The one invulnerable man among
> Crude captains, the naked majesty, if you like,
> Of bird-nest arches and of rain-stained vaults.

After this stanza the emotional intensity of the poem dies away towards the
serenity of its close:

> It is a kind of total grandeur at the end,
> With every visible thing enlarged and yet
> No more than a bed, a chair and moving nuns,
> The immensest theatre, the pillared porch,
> The book and candle in your ambered room,
>
> Total grandeur of a total edifice,
> Chosen by an inquisitor of structures
> For himself. He stops upon this threshold,
> As if the design of all his words takes form
> And frame from thinking and is realized.

This was the last long poem that Stevens published (though not the last
he wrote). In the year of its composition he was 73, and had not seen
Santayana for more than half a century. It is obvious that mixed with his
veneration for a figure who had become for him a symbol of certain kind of
victory, is reflection, meditation, perhaps even hope almost amounting to
prayer, about his own approaching death. The religious connotations of the
poem, which certainly exist, we shall examine later. For the moment the
point is only to demonstrate how deeply Santayana, alone among all the
people he had known and all the writers he had read, became involved in the

innermost texture of Stevens's intellectual and emotional life, in this poem to the point of complete imaginative identity. The root of this relationship of the mind was clearly a strong sympathy between the two men as individuals when both were at Harvard, together with a close similarity of aim. They shared an aloof and lonely determination of spirit which each may have detected in the other; and they also shared an ambition for poetry which Santayana was formulating at the time and which Stevens spent the rest of his life attempting to put into practical effect. Beneath the extreme reticence of a passage in one of Stevens's letters it is possible to detect a sense of his having assumed a role that Santayana abandoned when he gave up writing poetry.

> I doubt if Santayana was any more isolated at Cambridge than he wished to be . . . He invited me to come to see him a number of times and, in that way, I came to know him a little. I read several poems to him and he expressed his own view of the subject of them in a sonnet which he sent me . . . This was forty years ago,[5] when I was a boy and when he was not yet in mid-life. Obviously, his mind was full of the great projects of his future and, while some of these have been realized, it is possible to think that many have not. It would be easy to speak of his interest and sympathy; it might amuse you more to know that Sparklets were then something new and that Santayana liked to toy with them . . . I always came away from my visits to him feeling that he made up in the most genuine way for many things that I needed. He was then still definitely a poet.

With the hints of this passage in mind, one wonders whether it is Santayana the old philosopher or Stevens the old poet who is the more strongly referred to in the lines:

> He stops upon this threshold,
> As if the design of all his words takes form
> And frame from thinking and is realized.

The ideas expressed with odd elliptical precision in "Imagination as Value" are very close to much that Santayana had expounded in a more orderly, but nevertheless a less definite, manner many years before. This is by no means to suggest "influence" in any crude or careless sense. "Imagination as Value," like all his prose, is most clearly the fruit of Stevens's own experience and thought. Its ideas are related to Santayana's ideas in the same way that the two men are related in the one's poem about the other: by an identity of feeling and of aim. "It is as if . . . two parallels become one, a perspective." We have observed Stevens's insistence on the normal, on the tethering of the imagination to reality. Here, in another passage from the essay, is this insistence pitched at its highest:

The world may, certainly, be lost to the poet but it is not lost to the imagination. And I say that the world is lost to him, certainly, because, for one thing, the great poems of heaven and hell have been written and the great poem of the earth remains to be written. I suppose it is that poem that will constitute the true prize of the spirit and that until it is written many lesser things will be so regarded, including conquests that are not unimaginable.

Santayana several times expressed the same hope, with the same lack of confidence. In *Three Philosophical Poets*, published in 1910, he wrote:

It is time some genius should appear to reconstitute the shattered picture of the world. He should live in the continual presence of all experience, and respect it; he should at the same time understand nature, the ground of that experience; and he should also have a delicate sense for the ideal echoes of his own passions, and for all the colours of his possible happiness. All that can inspire a poet is contained in this task, and nothing less than this task would exhaust a poet's inspiration . . . But this supreme poet is in limbo still.

And in *Reason in Art* (1905) there is a passage describing the relation between reality and the imagination which might serve as an epigraph, not only for "To an Old Philosopher in Rome," but for the whole of Stevens's work:

Literary art in the end rejects all unmeaning flourishes, all complications that have no counterpart in the things of this world or no use in expressing their relations; at the same time it aspires to digest that reality to which it confines itself, making it over into ideal substance and material for the mind . . . [The writer's] art is relative to something other than its own formal impulse; it comes to clarify the real world, not to encumber it; and it needs to render its native agility pertinent to the facts and to attach its volume of feeling to what is momentous in human life. Literature has its piety, its conscience; it cannot long forget, without forfeiting all dignity, that it serves a burdened and perplexed creature, a human animal struggling to persuade the universal Sphinx to propose a more intelligible riddle. Irresponsible and trivial in its abstract impulse, man's simian chatter becomes noble as it becomes symbolic; its representative function lends it a serious beauty, its utility endows it with moral worth.

There is much in Santayana's hope for poetry, and in Stevens's, that seems reminiscent of Emerson. Among the hazy rhetorical paragraphs of, for instance, Emerson's essay "Poetry and Imagination," one finds remarks that seem to anticipate the two later writers:

Poetry must be affirmative. It is the piety of the intellect . . . The poet who shall use Nature as his hieroglyphic must have an adequate message to convey thereby.

> The poet is rare because he must be exquisitely vital and sympathetic, and, at the same time, immoveably centred . . . The poet is representative,—whole man, diamond merchant, symboliser, emancipator; in him the world projects a scribe's hand and writes the adequate genesis.
>
> We must not conclude against poetry from the defects of poets.

But Emerson's ideas about poetry, as about other things, are vitiated by a vagueness, a lack of respect not only for the discipline of organised thought but also for the hard facts of reality and for plain commonsense, that Santayana himself exposed in a devastating essay in *Interpretations of Poetry and Religion*. The object of his attack is Emerson's tendency towards the elevation of the imagination, as some sort of faculty of the absolute, above the real world and ordinary human understanding of it. This tendency Santayana calls 'mystical'. Of Emerson's 'alternately ingenuous and rhapsodical' reliance upon the imagination alone Santayana writes:

> By attacking the authority of the understanding as the organon of knowledge, by substituting itself for it as the herald of a deeper truth, the imagination . . . prepares its own destruction. For if the understanding is rejected because it cannot grasp the absolute, the imagination and all its works—art, dogma, worship—must presently be rejected for the same reason.

On this issue, which is really the issue of a satisfactory definition of the imagination, Stevens, though some critics have linked him with Emerson in an escapist realm of pure wishful thinking, is unequivocally on the same side as Santayana.

Again and again Stevens insists, in full accord with Santayana, that the imagination divorced from reality is nothing. His view of it, unlike Emerson's, is never transcendental or absolutist. Emerson, defining the imagination, says:

> Whilst common sense looks at things or visible nature as real and final facts, poetry, or the imagination which dictates it, is a second sight, looking through these, and using them as types or words for thoughts which they signify . . . The very design of imagination is to domesticate us in another, in a celestial nature. This power is in the image because this power is in Nature. It so affects, because it so is . . . Or, shall we say that the imagination exists by sharing the ethereal currents.

He believes, in other words, with whatever degree of optimistic imprecision, that there exists a rival reality, beyond or above mundane reality, to which the imagination alone has access. Stevens's view of the imagination could not be more firmly opposed to such a belief. "To be at the end of fact is not to be at the beginning of imagination but it is to be at the end of both," he wrote in his notebook. And here is a typical pronouncement:

Poetry is a passion, not a habit. This passion nourishes itself on reality. Imagination has no source except in reality, and ceases to have any value when it departs from reality. Here is fundamental principle about the imagination. It does not create except as it transforms . . . Imagination gives, but gives in relation.

These crisp sentences, from a letter of 1940,[6] are part of a gloss on section XXII of "The Man with the Blue Guitar," the long and difficult poem about his theory of poetry that he had written three years before. Nothing could better illustrate the distance that separates Stevens from Emerson's soft woolliness of thought than these dry lines, pared to the very bone of accuracy:

> Poetry is the subject of the poem,
> From this the poem issues and
>
> To this returns. Between the two,
>
> An absence in reality,
> Things as they are. Or so we say.
>
> But are these separate? Is it
> An absence for the poem, which acquires
>
> Its true appearances there, sun's green,
> Cloud's red, earth feeling, sky that thinks?
>
> From these it takes. Perhaps it gives,
> In the universal intercourse.

The unexpectedness both of the colours and of the sudden pathetic fallacies in the penultimate couplet, particularly in their close proximity to the word "true," are a swift and subtle indication of the part played by the poet himself in the process described. As Stevens was to put it, concluding "Effects of Analogy," a lecture delivered in the same year as "Imagination as Value": "Poetry . . . is a transcendent analogue composed of the particulars of reality, created by the poet's sense of the world, that is to say, his attitude, as he intervenes and interposes the appearances of that sense." The "transcendent analogue" is quite unrelated to Emerson's "celestial nature": Stevens insists always that "The imagination is the faculty by which we import the unreal into what is real." And Stevens's parallel insistence on the essential role of the creative individual in any act of the imagination is equally remote from Emerson's neoplatonist visions of the world-soul common to all men. Whenever Stevens in his prose writings moves towards a tentative definition of poetry, his stress is, as above, on "the poet's sense of the world." In "The

Noble Rider and the Sound of Words" (written in 1941), the first of the lectures in *The Necessary Angel*, the emphasis takes this form:

> The pressure of reality is, I think, the determining factor in the artistic character of an individual. The resistance to this pressure or its evasion in the case of individuals of extraordinary imagination cancels the pressure so far as those individuals are concerned . . . The role of the poet . . . is paramount. In this area of my subject I might be expected to speak of the social, that is to say sociological or political, obligation of the poet. He has none . . . What is his function? Certainly it is not to lead people out of the confusion in which they find themselves. Nor is it, I think, to comfort them while they follow their leaders[7] to and fro. I think that his function is to make his imagination theirs and that he fulfils himself only as he sees his imagination become the light in the minds of others. His role, in short, is to help people to live their lives . . . He has had immensely to do with giving life whatever savour it possesses. He has had to do with whatever the imagination and the senses have made of the world. He has, in fact, had to do with life except as the intellect has had to do with it and, as to that, no one is needed to tell us that poetry and philosophy are akin.

It is worth remarking that in the middle of this passage Stevens makes an observation whose realism sharply limits the apparent extravagance of his argument: "Time and time again it has been said that [the poet] may not address himself to an élite. I think he may. There is not a poet whom we prize living today that does not address himself to an élite."

In "The Figure of the Youth as Virile Poet" (1943)—his bizarre titles reflects the luxuriance of his care for accuate speech—he approaches the same theme with the same emphasis, but from a humbler direction. He suggests "that we define poetry as an unofficial view of being," and continues:

> This is a much larger definition of poetry than it is usual to make. But just as the nature of the truth changes, perhaps for no more significant reason than that philosophers live and die, so the nature of poetry changes, perhaps for no more significant reason than that poets come and go.

In the light of this use of the word "truth" the puzzling firmness of a sentence in the long passage quoted above from "Imagination as Value" begins to quiver. "In life what is important is the truth as we see it." It becomes clear that "reality" rather than "the truth" is what is meant here, as, indeed, the rest of the passage suggests. Meanwhile "The Figure of the Youth as Virile Poet" circles for a little round the question of defining poetry and then settles on a conclusion of resilient exactness.

> Since we have no difficulty in recognizing poetry and since, at the same time, we say that it is not an attainable acme, not some breath from an altitude, not

something that awaits discovery, after which it will not be subject to chance, we may be accounting for it if we say that is a process of the personality of the poet . . . There can be no poetry without the personality of the poet, and that, quite simply, is why the definition of poetry has not been found and why, in short, there is none.

On this conclusion Stevens comments: "One does not have to be a cardinal to make the point." Possibly one had to be a poet: at any rate, those who write about poetry as if it had some mysterious life of its own, and, worse, those who write it as if it had, should be healthily embarrassed by the sanity of these remarks. Stevens adds:

We are talking about something a good deal more comprehensive than the temperament of the artist as that is usually spoken of. We are concerned with the whole personality and, in effect, we are saying that the poet who writes the heroic poem that will satisfy all there is of us and all of us in time to come, will accomplish it by the power of his reason, the force of his imagination and, in addition, the effortless and inescapable process of his own individuality.

It might seem unnecessary to say things about poetry and the poet which are so obviously true were it not for the vast quantities of pretentious absurdity that are perpetrated in the name of criticism. Stevens knew that there was not only room, but a great need, for some central sense to be spoken about poetry. He wrote, in 1951, in the short Introduction to *The Necessary Angel*:

The theory of poetry, as a subject of study, was something with respect to which I had nothing but the most ardent ambitions. It semed to me to be one of the great subjects of study. I do not mean one more *Ars Poetica* having to do, say, with the techniques of poetry and perhaps with its history. I mean poetry itself, the naked poem, the imagination manifesting itself in its domination of words. The few pages that follow are, now, alas! the only realization possible to me of those excited ambitions.

The pages of the essays that follow, with all their fine and elaborate affirmation, imply several targets for attack. One is what Leavis has called, with scorn, the upholding of "purely literary values"—"Nor are [these] merely literary pages," says Stevens in his Introduction, "They are pages that have to do with one of the enlargements of life." Another target as we have seen, is the wishing of a "social obligation" upon the poet. Between these two, the idea that imaginative literature is useless and the idea that is should be deliberately and specifically useful, lies a path which Stevens (like Leavis) devoted much time and thought to charting. A third target of Stevens's essays, and perhaps the one that was to him the most important, is the idea to which Emerson among many others was prone, that the imagination is some sort of involuntary absolute power involving the existence of some sort of alternative reality. It is above all to counter this idea, or any variant of it, that he repeatedly dwells upon both the interdependence of reality and the imagination and the creative responsibility of the poet in the whole of his personality. A passage towards the end of "The Figure of the Youth as Virile Poet" shows how inextricably the two themes are related:

> It is important to believe that the visible is the equivalent of the invisible; and once we believe it, we have destroyed the imagination; that is to say, we have destroyed the false imagination, the false conception of the imagination as some incalculable *vates* within us, unhappy Rhodomontade. One is often tempted to say that the best definition of poetry is the sum of its attributes. So, here, we may say that the best definition of true imagination is that it is the sum of our faculties. Poetry is the scholar's art. The acute intelligence of the imagination, the illimitable resources of its memory, its power to possess the moment it perceives—if we were speaking of light itself, and thinking of the relationship between objects and light, no further demonstration would be necessary. Like light, it adds nothing, except itself.

The imagination "adds nothing, except itself." Behind such a statement is Stevens's constant devotion to reality, his belief that the phrase "the truth of the imagination" has a meaning only with respect to the imagination's relation with reality, his descriptions of metaphor, of poetry itself, in terms of "accuracy," "appositeness," "rightness." All these ideas involve to the highest degree the responsibility of the poet himself. When Stevens, as he does in this same essay, makes a gnomic pronouncement like: "The morality of the poet's radiant and productive atmosphere is the morality of the right sensation," one should not dismiss it as a piece of wilful and question-begging obscurantism. Stevens's essays have frequently, particularly in England, provoked such reactions. But, to take only this instance, the thought is fully achieved, the support for the use of the word "morality" is there. What Stevens is proposing to the poet is a discipline from which the moral element cannot be abstracted. "The poet," he says, two sentences later, "must get rid of the hieratic in everything that concerns him and must move constantly in the direction of the credible." When he comes to explain what he means by "the credible," we begin to see also what he means by "the morality of the right sensation."

> Desiring with all the power of our desire not to write falsely, do we not begin to think of the possibility that poetry is only reality, after all, and that poetic truth is a factual truth, seen, it may be, by those whose range in the perception of fact—that is, whose sensibility—is greater than our own? . . . What we have called elevation and elation on the part of the poet, which he communicates to the reader, may be not so much elevation as an incandescence of the intelligence and so more than ever a triumph over the incredible.

These ideas are put forward in the form of suggestions. But the suggestions derive from the mature experience of a poet of unassailable integrity whose own work displays unassailable quality. They should be tested not against some vague and misleading notion of "poetry-in-general" but against the best poetry that we have. From Johnson on, the critical theories that have crashed on the rock of Shakespeare have been legion. It is an indication of the value of what Stevens has to say about poetry that Shakespeare is the name that most frequently occurs to one as vindicating proof when one is reading Stevens's prose. This is true for instance of a passage from "Effects of Analogy" where Stevens, who is discussing the poetic image and "the discipline that comes from appositeness in the highest degree," makes finally clear his case against "the false imagination," above all against what he saw to be the widespread and dangerous tendency "to identify the imagination with those that extend its abnormality." Again it is necessary to quote at length:

It [the discipline of the imagination] is primarily a discipline of rightness. The poet is constantly concerned with two theories. One relates to the imagination as a power within him not so much to destroy reality at will as to put it to his own uses. He comes to feel that his imagination is not wholly his own but that it may be part of a much larger, much more potent imagination, which it is his affair to try to get at. For this reason, he pushes on and lives, or tries to live, as Paul Valéry did, on the verge of consciousness. This often results in poetry that is marginal, subliminal. The same theory exists in relation to prose, to painting and other arts. The second theory relates to the imagination as a power within him to have such insights into reality as will make it possible for him to be sufficient as a poet in the very centre of consciousness. This results, or should result, in a central poetry . . . The proponents of the first theory believe that it will be a part of their achievement to have created the poetry of the future. It may be that the poetry of the future will be to the poetry of the present what the poetry of the present is to the ballad. The proponents of the second theory believe that to create the poetry of the present is an incalculable difficulty, which rarely is achieved, fully and robustly, by anyone . . . The adherents of the imagination are mystics to begin with and pass from one mysticism to another. The adherents of the central are also mystics to begin with. But all their desire and all their ambition is to press away from mysticism toward that ultimate good sense which we term civilization.

This passage—which sums up much of what is said throughout *The Necessary Angel*—should be borne in mind by those who believe that Stevens was, in more than incidental ways, either Emerson's heir or a French Symbolist in everything but language. "To an Old Philosopher in Rome" was written by an "adherent of the central," as were the very few English poems of this century that can be compared with it, "The Dry Salvages" perhaps, and "Among School Children." And of these three, each in its way a masterpiece, Stevens's poem has moved the furthest away from "mysticism" in

Stevens's and Santayana's sense and "toward that ultimate good sense which we term civilization." To put this in another way, the quality which Stevens's poem has more of than either Eliot's or Yeats's is the kind of wholeness or complete integration of creative personality indicated by Santayana in a pessimistic passage in *Winds of Doctrine*:

> How, then, should there be any great heroes, saints, artists, philosophers, or legislators in an age when nobody trusts himself, or feels any confidence in reason, in an age when the word dogmatic is a term of reproach? Greatness has character and severity, it is deep and sane, it is distinct and perfect. For this reason there is none of it today . . . The master's eye itself must be single, his style unmistakable, his visionary interest in what he depicts frank and supreme. Hence this comprehensive sort of greatness too is impossible in an age when moral confusion is pervasive, when characters are complex, undecided, troubled by the mere existence of what is not congenial to them, eager to be not themselves; when, in a word, thought is weak and the flux of things overwhelms it.

There are phrases here which catch briefly but exactly some of the fallings from a "comprehensive sort of greatness" that mark the work of the three "modern" poets who have been awarded the status of English classics: Eliot, "troubled by the mere existence of what is not congenial," Yeats, "eager to be not himself," Pound, "thought is weak and the flux of things overwhelms it." There are other phrases here that have their relevance to Stevens, to the best essays in *The Necessary Angel* as well as to the best of his poems: "greatness has character and severity, it is deep and sane . . . The master's eye must be single, his style unmistakable, his visionary interest in what he depicts frank and supreme."

Notes

1. "Shelley: or the Poetic Value of Revolutionary Principles," *Winds of Doctrine,* 1913.
2. In 'A Collect of Philosophy,' *Opus Posthumous,* p. 187.
3. In 1948 the octogenarian Santayana was living in the convent in Rome where, in 1952, he died.
4. Letter to Robert Pack, 14 April 1955.
5. This letter was written in 1945 (to José Rodríguez Feo, 4 January 1945).
6. To Hi Simons, 19 August 1940.
7. Misprinted as 'readers', *The Necessary Angel,* p. 29.

Santayana's Emerson:
Ultimate Puritanism

JOEL PORTE

When George Santayana came to write his "Preface" to the Triton Edition of *The Last Puritan* in 1937, he claimed that he had lived with the book's characters for forty-five years.[1] He was undoubtedly referring to his friendships, in the 1890's, with the Harvard undergraduates who served as models for Oliver Alden and Mario Van de Weyer.[2] But in view of the true underlying subject of the book, Santayana might have extended his time span for the genesis of that "Memoir in the form of a novel" back at least to 1886, when he submitted his own undergraduate essay, "The Optimism of Ralph Waldo Emerson," in an unsuccessful bid for Harvard's Bowdoin Prize. *The Last Puritan,* one student of the subject notes, "is really a novel about Santayana's own . . . semitranscendental ambivalence toward Emerson and transcendentalism"; and he suggested that someone ought to write a chapter in Santayana's life entitled "*The Last Puritan* and the Ghost of Emerson" or "*The Last Puritan* as an Exercise in Loving Exorcism."[3]

If such was Santayana's intent, then he seems to have failed in laying the ghost to rest. At the end of his life, writing the last volume of his autobiography, Santayana invoked both the spirit and the letter of Emerson to explain the *metanoia,* or "change of heart," which led him "through darkness . . . into the pure starlight that transports without dazzling" of his disillusioned mature philosophy.[4] The Emerson that Santayana quotes is represented by the best lines from "Threnody" ("This losing is true dying, / This is lordly man's down-lying, / This his true and sure declining, / Star by star his world resigning"),[5] but the drama of renunciation enacted here recapitulates another Emersonian moment—Oliver's last chapter in Santayana's novel. His proposal of marriage turned down by Rose Darnley, "his earthly person . . . rejected, his earthly plan defeated," Oliver feels "wonderfully liberated" as he walks away from "the burning city of our vanity." Love is finished, and both the Vicar and his son Jim, the two people Oliver cared about most, are dead, yet Oliver thinks: "The strain is relaxed. The play is over, the doors open, and after all those unnecessary thrills and anxieties, I am walking out into the

Reprinted from *Representative Man: Ralph Waldo Emerson in His Time* (New York: Oxford University Press, 1979), 16–31, with the permission of the publisher.

night, into my true life . . . . I am falling back upon my deeper self. I may hardly be able to see the stars, after the blinding light of the theatre, but there they are; and gradually they will become visible again, I shall recognize them, I shall call each of them by its name."[6] And the name that Oliver gives to the feeling that exalts him is pure Emerson: "self-recovery."[7]

Santayana's attitude toward Emerson has usually been measured by the essay he wrote for *Interpretations of Poetry and Religion* in 1900, which is largely informed by the same tone of ironic detachment that James had employed in 1887. In Santayana's case, the note of gentle satire struck at the beginning of the piece served to undercut the hagiographic tradition which was already firmly in place in the Harvard of Santayana's day:

> Those who knew Emerson, or who stood so near to his time and to this circle that they caught some echo of his personal influence, did not judge him merely as a poet or philosopher, nor identify his efficacy with that of his writings. His friends and neighbours, the congregations he preached to in his younger days, the audiences that afterward listened to his lectures, all agreed in a veneration for his person which had nothing to do with their understanding or acceptance of his opinions. They flocked to him and listened to his word, not so much for the sake of its absolute meaning as for the atmosphere of candour, purity, and serenity that hung about it, as about a sort of sacred music. They felt themselves in the presence of a rare and beautiful spirit, who was in communion with a higher world.[8]

That Santayana himself was not disposed to speak in only reverent tones of New England's saint is clear from other evidence of the period. In some comments recorded in the back of a copy of Santayana's *Lucifer,* Wallace Stevens describes an evening spent with Santayana in the spring of 1900 when, over whisky and cigarettes, they "discussed the Emerson essay" in *Interpretations* (as well as a "decidedly unpleasant—and shallow" criticism in the *Nation*) and "laughed at Emerson's habit of eating pie for breakfast etc."[9] Another student of Santayana's, Baker Brownell, reports on Santayana's reaction to the statue of Emerson that presides over Harvard's philosophy building:

> Once on his way down the hall, he paused before the bronze, seated Emerson for whom the hall is named. He looked at it a moment and turned to me standing nearby. "How do you like it?" he asked me; and to my rather indefinite reply, he said, "The upper part is all right, but those shanks are too prominent."[10]

If Santayana was suggesting that the statue made Emerson look more like a long-legged Yankee preacher or schoolmaster, such as Ichabod Crane, than a candidate for canonization, such a debunking view might have adumbrated Jim Darnley's acerbic response to Oliver Alden's calling Emerson a "saint" who loved nature and humanity: "An old barebones like Emerson doesn't *love;*

he isn't a *saint*. He's simply a distinguished-looking old cleric with a sweet smile and a white tie: he's just honourable and bland and as cold as ice."[11]

Such a prouncement, decidedly not characteristic of Santayana's later attitude toward Emerson, does in fact capture some of the sharpness of tone discernible in the "Emerson" of 1900:

> A Puritan whose religion was all poetry, a poet whose only pleasure was thought, he showed in his life and personality the meagerness, the constraint, the frigid and conscious consecration which belonged to his clerical ancestors, while his inmost impersonal spirit ranged abroad over the fields of history and Nature, gathering what ideas it might, and singing its little snatches of inspired song.[12]

Santayana's animus is obvious, and the reason for it should be equally so— and familiar in Emerson criticism. Beneath Emerson's "occasional thin paradoxes and guileless whims," Santayana thought he detected a cruel indifference, or imperviousness, to pain and suffering.[13] Granting—importantly—that imagination was clearly Emerson's "single theme," Santayana nonetheless felt that Emerson's insistence on the power of imaginative thought "first to make the world, then to understand it, and finally to rise above it" was rather too facile and chillingly mystical, though it moved in the direction of a philosophical attitude which Santayana himself was ambivalently attracted to:

> While the conflict of life and the shocks of experience seem to bring us face to face with an alien and overwhelming power, reflection can humanize and rationalize that power by conceiving its laws; and with this recognition of the rationality of all things comes the sense of their beauty and order. The destruction which Nature seems to prepare for our special hopes is thus seen to be the victory of our impersonal interests. To awaken in us this spiritual insight, an elevation of mind which is at once an act of comprehension and of worship, to substitute it for lower passions and more servile forms of intelligence—that is Emerson's constant effort. All his resources of illustration, observation, and rhetoric are used to deepen and clarify this sort of wisdom.[14]

This was the sort of wisdom which Santayana was almost—but not quite—prepared to accept in 1900, as he contemplated renouncing his youthful impulses in the name of spiritual peace. But in 1886, when he wrote his Bowdoin essay, Santayana was even less disposed to accept an optimism based on "indifference to circumstances"—one, that is, which feels that all things are well because it has taken refuge in a frigid aestheticism that habitually, and heartlessly, distances itself from the inconveniences and tragedies of experience. "From optimism of this kind," Santayana notes (exposing, perhaps unconsciously, one of the darker paradoxes of Emerson's thought), "pessimism differs only in name."[15] In the second paragraph of his essay, calling Emerson a "champion of cheerfulness," Santayana claims that "he does not hesitate to surrender the field of experience to the weeping philosophers" because of his idealistic armor; whereupon Santayana, interestingly and significantly, quotes this passage from "Love":

> Each man sees his own life defaced and disfigured . . . . Let any man go back to those delicious relations which have given him sincerest instruction and nourishment, he will shrink and moan. Alas! I know not why, infinite compunctions embitter in mature life the remembrances of budding joy, and cover every beloved name. Everything is beautiful seen from the point of view of intellect, or as truth. But all is sour, if seen as experience . . . . In the actual world, the painful kingdom of time and place, dwell care, and canker, and fear. With thought, with the ideal, is immortal hilarity, the rose of joy. Round it all the Muses sing. But grief clings to names, and persons, and the partial interests of today and yesterday.[16]

The passage evidently broached issues that touched the young Santayana nearly; and we shall notice very shortly how he himself, struggling to clarify his own feelings, would turn Emerson's sentences and metaphors to good use as he developed the central figure of *The Last Puritan.*

But one other point is worth mentioning in a consideration of this early piece on Emerson. As he reached his conclusion, Santayana admitted that he still, somehow, found the "mystic turned dilettante" charming, even occasionally "delightful" in his "very indifference." Turning to his final paragraph, Santayana then made a pregnant concession: "To do justice to the personal element in Emerson's optimism we should have to study his whole life. We should have to inquire whether he ever felt an emotion stronger than delight in the landscape, and decide whether his serenity was the result of discipline or of insensibility." Santayana, of course, did not have at his disposal the materials that would have enabled him to conduct such an investigation. But he did put his finger on *the* crucial issue in modern Emerson studies and presciently suggested the direction they might take. "He is never a philosopher," Santayana noted, "but always Emerson philosophizing."[17]

Beginning perhaps with Henry Nash Smith's essay, "Emerson's Problem of Vocation," in 1939, a highly influential group of scholars and critics, notably sensitive to Emerson's human complexity, would return to his writings with the hope of discovering a living personality beneath the bland (or pompous, or smug) official portrait. An unfamiliar Emerson thus would begin to emerge—one whose painful struggle for self-realization belied that older image of an optimistic aphorist appropriately cherished by captains of industry, genteel professors of literature, and hopeful preachers in search of suitably uplifting remarks. Like other great writers of the American Renaissance—Hawthorne, Melville, Dickinson—Emerson was on the way to being considered a richly evasive and enigmatic figure whose interest would more and more turn on that "personal element" which Santayana had pointed to in his Bowdoin essay.

Santayana's third significant piece of writing on Emerson in his own Harvard period, delivered on May 22, 1903, during the centennial celebrations, is entitled "Emerson the Poet" and marks a dramatic departure in Santayana's continuing effort to clarify his own philosophy by struggling with Emerson's. The tone and posture of this address are markedly different from those of the essays that precede it. For one thing, Santayana had now moved away from clichéd references to Puritan "constraint" and begun to talk about Emerson's ancestral religion in more nearly tragic terms: "The dogmas which Calvinism had chosen for interpretation were the most sombre and disquieting in the Christian system, those which marked most clearly a broken life and a faith rising out of profound despair." What despair, Santayana goes on to ask, could a young American of Emerson's hopeful time have felt to justify sharing such "spectral traditions"? Emerson, indeed, was one of the first fully to throw off the "incubus" of this "ancestral dream" and spring wholeheartedly into "the world of nature."[18]

Associating Emerson with Spinoza, Shakespeare, and Goethe, Santayana argues that this "born master at looking deep and at looking straight" discovered that the generative order of nature is not inclined to respect human feelings and inspire "transcendental conceit."[19] Although Santayana had claimed only a few years earlier that "reality eluded [Emerson],"[20] he now insists on precisely the opposite, namely, that Emerson "saw [nature] as she really is and loved her in her indomitable and inhuman perfection":

Not the least of his joys was the self-effacing one of being able to conceive, and therefore to share, a life which creates, animates, and destroys the human. He was charmed and comforted, quite without technical apparatus, by universal beauty. He yielded himself insensibly and placidly to that plastic stress which in breeding new forms out of his substance would never breed anything alien to those principles of harmony and rhythm which stand like sentinels at the gates of being and challenge the passage into existence of anything contradicting itself or incongruous with its natural conditions. His best lyric flights express the honest and noble acceptance of destiny, this imaginative delight in innumerable beauties which he should never see, but which would be the heirs of those he had loved and lost in their passage.[21]

As a kind of secular analogue to the Puritan faith's "rising out of profound despair," Santayana now posits Emerson's delight in the *forms* and *structures* which underlie human experience and persist despite the destruction of individual expressions of that "plastic stress." Particular lives may be "broken," but the glorious principles of metamorphosis move on unharmed.[22] Caught up by his own excited exegesis of the true Emersonian philosophy, Santayana now announces that he has arrived "at the frontiers of

that province in Emerson's kingdom into which it is hardest to penetrate—
the forbidden Thibet, with its Grand Lama, behind his Himalayas," namely,
Emerson's religion. It is not at bottom, Santayana claims, "an account of
credible facts producing, when duly reported, saving emotions in the soul. It
is rather an expression of the soul's native emotions in symbols mistaken for
facts, or in facts chosen for symbols." Emerson's interest, we are being told,
has shifted to the *process* by which the soul generates its own symbols of belief.
And "all the unction and sanctity of religion" that Emerson has salvaged from
his discarded dogmas he is now free to invest in a new, ultimate religion—
the worship, not of particular existent *beings,* but of the multiform energy
itself that perpetually builds new *shapes* of being. Santayana's exposition of
this notion is filled with a true Emersonian afflatus:

> All ideas, we presently perceive, are fluid; and we are on the point of venturing
> the assertion that it matters very little what things exist or how long they
> endure, since the only reality is the perpetual motion that creates, transforms
> and exchanges them. We have seen how this perpetual motion, observable in
> nature, fascinated Emerson; but while the poet could justify and communicate
> his delight by dwelling on the forms and beauties of things in transition, the
> metaphysician would fain sink deeper. In his desperate attempt to seize upon
> the real and permanent he would fain grasp and hold fast the disembodied
> principle of change itself.[23]

This idea is "loaded with religious passion," Santayana tells us. And he
goes on to cite the conclusion to "Threnody," Emerson's lamentation and
testament of acceptance in the face of the abject tragedy of his young son's
death. Emerson's poems, Santayana concludes, "proclaim the divinity of
nature, her kinship with man, and her immortal fecundity in all things
which the human spirit might recognize to be beautiful and good if keyed to
heroism and rapt in contemplation." Such beauty, Santayana concedes, "involves cruelty" and the optimism preached by Emerson's poetry is a difficult
one that "demands abnegation." The ability to sing "nature's fluid harmonies" is not given to all—indeed, only to that man with "a long civilization
behind him who has learned to love nature for her own sake."[24] James had
claimed, in writing of Hawthorne, "that the flower of art blooms only where
the soil is deep, that it takes a great deal of history to produce a little
literature, that it needs a complex social machinery to set a writer in motion."[25] The claim that Santayana now seemed prepared to make for Emerson
was perhaps more fundamental and obviated the need to apologize for America: only a man with a long experience of reality could truly come to accept
that deeper soil out of which spring the forms of both society and art.

The Last Puritan represents Santayana's most serious and sustained engagement with Emerson's ultimate refinement of Puritanism. On the surface, at least, the presence of Emerson is not difficult to detect in the book.

Oliver Alden's mentality is more than once described as "transcendental," and he is frequently associated with Emerson (stopping one day to feed his "idealism" on Concord's meagre sights, Oliver finds that "unseen things loomed all the larger and nearer in that visible desolation"; he subsequently takes up residence in Emerson's room in Divinity Hall, and when he moves on to Oxford his lodgings remind him somehow of that room).[26] Verbal echoes of Emerson's writings abound in the book, and may be sufficiently exemplified through a glance at the first chapter of Part V. Oliver's "journey round the world had taught [him] little except how inevitably centered and miserably caged he was in himself" ("Travelling is a fool's paradise" [W, II, 81]). Meditating on Goethe (Oliver had been taught in school that "Emerson served up Goethe's philosophy in ice-water"), he follows Emerson in pronouncing the great man insufficiently idealistic and asserts, "I won't be the slave of my circumstances" ("You think me the child of my circumstances: I make my circumstance" [CW, I, 204]). Whereupon, Santayana tells us, Oliver felt "confirmed in his spiritual self-reliance."[27]

But such allusions really constitute the least of Santayana's Emersonianism in *The Last Puritan*. A much more complex and significant instance may be seen in the many pages Santayana devotes to an exposition of "the vision of Jacob's ladder," which is presented to us in the form of a debate between Oliver and his father, Peter. The notion, we are told, is a favorite one of Peter's (meaning of Santayana's), and the father tries to explain:

> "Jacob's ladder, you will say, what do I mean by that? Let me try to tell you. Do you remember Cousin Caleb Weatherbee and his opinion about Goethe? Yes, and you naturally continued to think Goethe a great, wise, and good man, even if a heathen and not a gentleman. Well, Jacob's ladder is the fabulous moral order imposed on the universe by the imagination of Cousin Caleb and Plato and conservative Anglican gentlemen; but the heathen imagination in Goethe and Emerson and you and me, and in your liberal British intellectuals and philosophers, has outgrown that image. Instead, either we impose no moral order on the universe at all—which I think would be safer—or else a moral order such as we expected to find in our own lives when we were young and romantic. I suppose, as a matter of fact, there is an obscure natural order in the universe, controlling morality as it controls health: an order which we don't need to impose, because we are all obeying it willy-nilly. But this half-deciphered natural order leaves us, morally, in all our natural heathen darkness and liberty: and we are probably little inclined to devote ourselves to ascending and descending the particular Jacob's ladder imagined by Platonists and Catholics and Conservative English Gentlemen."[28]

Santayana is here offering us, in terms of the familiar fable, a continuation and amplification of the central issue which he had isolated in his discussions of Emerson—an issue of crucial importance in his own philosophy: namely, the extent to which a disillusioned thinker, having jettisoned all the traditional (Platonic, Judeo-Christian) "machinery" of transcendence, may reasonably place his reconstituted faith in a moral order which is purely naturalistic. It is fundamentally a question of adequately defining a spiritual life, and spiritual discipline, which might truly be called humanistic as opposed to the supernaturalistic systems symbolized by the traditional idea of Jacob's ladder. Is Emerson really in the dark, morally, Santayana seems to be asking; or is his passionate belief in the unshakable natural structures of the universe—"the spires of form" (CW, I, 7)—a credible substitute for the discarded harmonies of Jacob's ladder?

Oliver responds that he believes in Jacob's ladder even less than his father does, rejecting all hierarchical systems, social as well as metaphysical. Peter continues:

> "Why have we free Americans a certain sneaking tendency to be snobs? Proud, romantic heathens that we are, like Nietzche, or like Walt Whitman, why do we feel an unavowed inclination to worship the archangel in a light blue cap— or a pink one, if he is elderly—standing at the top of Jacob's ladder? Because, my dear Oliver, our heathenism is still green and bashful. We are imperfectly weaned from feudalism and Christianity. Our pride in freedom is a mere affectation: we put it on in order to stifle our deeper conscience which still believes in Jacob's ladder."[29]

It is as if Santayana were saying that Emerson can afford to be so defiantly antinomian in his naturalism only because in his heart he still half believes in the Christianity he claims to have discarded. Some lingering vestiges of faith still buttress his heathen pride or console him in his moments of self-doubt. Peter, in fact, goes on to argue that the elements of traditional religious discipline (humility, penance, suffering, mortification—and the thrashing practiced at Eton!) may actually function as "rungs in Jacob's ladder" to lead the soul to a higher state, even though the religious system of which they form a part can be considered an illusion.

> All of this seemed to Oliver rather in the air. Why dwell on the consequences of a false hypothesis? Or was the hypothesis possibly true? And he broke in rather impatiently:
> "But do you believe in Jacob's ladder yourself?"
> "Believe?" Peter answered, as if bewildered. "Dear me, I don't believe in anything nowadays, if I can help it. Didn't I say that Jacob's ladder was a myth? It's a picture of what the universe would be if the moral nature of man had made it. I suppose in the universe at large the moral nature of man is a minor affair, like the moral nature of the ant or the mosquito. But our moral nature is everything *to us*; to us the universe itself is of no consequence apart from the life we are able to live in it. Jacob's ladder is a picture of the degrees which this moral life of ours might attain, in so far as we can imagine them. It is a poetic image. Those who mistake it for an account of the universe or of

history or of destiny seem to me simply mad; but like all good poetry, such an image marks the pitch to which moral culture has risen at some moment. To the morally cultivated, Jacob's ladder shines distinct and clear: it becomes vague and broken to the morally barbarous."[30]

Peter Alden is speaking now in the accents, not only of Santayana, but of Emerson and Wallace Stevens. All knowledge and experience—and especially the moral side of life—are mediated to us by means of poetic symbols, the fictions which enable us to imagine our lives. And though we may lose Jacob's ladder as literal religious truth, it can still—perhaps *must* still—be retained as a viable part of our imaginative vocabulary. It is what Stevens calls a "transcendent analogue."[31] A life in which transcendence has ceased to be possible, a life without *degrees,* is morally bankrupt. And we shall see more precisely, in the case of Emerson, how his own "vague and broken" mood in "Experience" is figured in the collapse of Jacob's ladder; whereas to the ultimately reconstituted self of "Threnody," the ladder begins again to shine "distinct and clear." As Daniel B. Shea has argued well, and as Santayana intuited, Emerson's career may be viewed in terms of an "alternation between regressive and progressive metamorphosis."[32]

Oliver Alden's own ultimate lesson in the possibility of self-transcendence is emblemized by Santayana in the conflation of two symbols, everywhere to be found in *The Last Puritan,* which seem clearly to recall the Platonic ladder of love, in Emerson's essay "Love," with the ideal "rose of joy" perched at its top.[33] Even before he had been denied by the crimson rose— his cousin Edith—and the white one—Rose Darnley—Oliver senses that he has a sterner destiny reserved for himself:

> All these images are shifty and misty and treacherous. What endures is only this spirit, this perpetual witness, wondering at these apparitions, enjoying one, suffering at another, and questioning them all. If I keep this spirit free, if I keep it pure, let roses be red or white as they will, let there be no end of wars of the roses; let me wear the rose of Lancaster or the rose of York; neither will taint my soul or dye it of a party colour.[34]

He turns away from the worldly advice he finds in an old volume of verse ("Stripling, rifle now the rose, / tempt the perils of a kiss"), and ultimately walks by choice into the heaven that Santayana has prepared for him, believing that the feeling he had of being in love was only a mirage created by his own aspirations:

> They may drop out, they may change, they may prove to be the sad opposite of what I thought them: but my image of them in being detached from their accidental persons, will be clarified in itself, will become truer to my profound desire; and the inspiration of a profound desire, fixed upon some lovely image,

is what is called love. And the true lover's tragedy is not being jilted; it is being accepted.[35]

Though this may strike modern ears as representing a rather chilly brand of Platonism, it is unquestionably characteristic of both Santayana and Emerson in their most exalted moods.

Perhaps, however, one can respond more sympathetically to the philosophical point that "Santayana has embodied in his theme of "pure" love whereby we come closer to the speculative essence of this story of the "purification of puritanism." The holocaust which Oliver suffered, Santayana tells us, was "real enough":

> . . . it was the endless fire of irrational life always devouring itself: yet somehow the spirit rose from that flame, and surveyed the spectacle with some tears, certainly, but with no little curiosity and satisfaction. Oliver hardly got so far as to feel at home in this absurd world: I could never convince him that reason and goodness are necessarily secondary and accidental. His absolutist conscience remained a pretender, asserting in exile its divine right to the crown.[36]

We note in this adumbration of his theme in the "Prologue" how the verbal texture of Santayana's symbols informs his abstract formulation. Leaving its earthly flowers behind, Oliver's spirit itself "rose," as it inevitably had to, up the ladder of being from suffering to the vantage point of pure idea. And we may be sure that that which Santayana claims he could not convince Oliver of continued to pain him also as the central problem of existence: the thwarting of every rational ideal in the mixed currents of experience. The only true satisfaction that remains for the human spirit, according to Santayana, is the possibility of surveying "the spectacle" from the level of pure contemplation. This notion is stated more eloquently on the last page of the book, where Mario is allowed to paraphrase Santayana's very own sentiments from *Platonism and the Spiritual Life:*

> After life is over and the world has gone up in smoke, what realities might the spirit in us still call its own without illusion save the form of those very illusions which have made up our story?[37]

Ultimate Puritanism, then, is equivalent to total disillusionment, the ability to see that what persists through every disappointment and death in a world of incessant and inexorable change, the only reality, is the form or principle which *creates* our illusions. That divinity, which might be called the *order* of created things, informs the human imagination no less than it does the natural world which generates human beings. Such a formulation returns us directly to Emerson's "religion" and suggests, perhaps, that Santayana's text for his novelistic sermon might well have been the concluding paragraph of Emerson's *Conduct of Life*:

There is no chance and no anarchy in the universe. All is system and gradation. Every god is there sitting in his sphere. The young mortal enters the hall of the firmament; there is he alone with them alone, they pouring on him benedictions and gifts, and beckoning him up to their thrones. On the instant, and incessantly, fall snow-storms of illusions. He fancies himself in a vast crowd which sways this way and that and whose movement and doings he must obey: he fancies himself poor, orphaned, insignificant. The mad crowd drives hither and thither, now furiously commanding this thing to be done, now that. What is he that he should resist their will, and think or act for himself? Every moment new changes and new showers of deceptions to baffle and distract him. And when, by and by, for an instant, the air clears and the cloud lifts a little, there are the gods still sitting around him on their thrones,—they alone with him alone. (W, VI, 325)

Notes

1. See *The Works of George Santayana*, Triton Edition, XI (New York: Scribner's, 1937), pp. vii ff.

2. Many illuminating comments about the Harvard background of Santayana's novel are scattered throughout his *Letters* and autobiographical volumes, especially *Persons and Places*. See also Maurice F. Brown, "Santayana's American Roots," *New England Quarterly*, XXXIII, 2 (1960), 147–63, and my article, "Santayana at the 'Gas House,' " *New England Quarterly*, XXXV, 3 (1962), 337–46.

3. Joe Lee Davis, "Santayana as a Critic of Transcendentalism," in *Transcendentalism and Its Legacy*, ed. Myron Simon and Thornton H. Parsons (Ann Arbor: University of Michigan Press, 1966), p. 166. Davis provides useful bibliographical references in his notes.

4. George Santayana, *My Host the World* (New York: Scribner's, 1953), p. 13.

5. Ibid., p. 13. The lines are slightly misquoted. Cf. W, IX 153. Santayana had already cited the same lines, correctly, in his *Three Philosophical Poets* (1910).

6. George Santayana, *The Last Puritan: A Memoir in the Form of a Novel* (New York: Scribner's, 1936), pp. 579–80.

7. Ibid., p. 580. Cf. Emerson, EL, III, 262; CW, I, 39, 57; W, II, 309; W, III, 81.

8. George Santayana, *Interpretations of Poetry and Religion* (New York: Scribner's, 1900), p. 217.

9. Holly Stevens, *Souvenirs and Prophecies: The Young Wallace Stevens* (New York: Knopf, 1977), p. 68.

10. *The Philosophy of George Santayana*, ed. Paul Arthur Schilpp (New York: Tudor, 1951), p. 35.

11. Santayana, *The Last Puritan*, pp. 200–201.

12. Santayana, *Interpretations of Poetry and Religion*, p. 231.

13. Ibid., pp. 220, 228.

14. Ibid., pp. 220–21.

15. "The Optimism of Ralph Waldo Emerson," in *George Santayana's America*, ed. James Ballowe (Urbana: University of Illinois Press, 1967), pp. 73–4.

16. Ibid., p. 72.

17. Ibid., p. 83.

18. "Emerson the Poet," in *Santayana on America,* ed. Richard Colton Lyon (New York: Harcourt, 1968), p. 270.

19. Ibid., pp. 271, 273.

20. Santayana, *Interpretations of Poetry and Religion,* p. 218.

21. Lyon, *Santayana on America,* pp. 273–74.

22. Ibid., pp. 270–74.

23. Ibid., p. 278.

24. Ibid., p. 282.

25. *The Shock of Recognition,* p. 428.

26. Santayana, *The Last Puritan,* pp. 92, 171, 552, 404, 416, 518.

27. Ibid., pp. 507, 126, 509.

28. Ibid., pp. 313–14.

29. Ibid., p. 315.

30. Ibid., p. 316.

31. Wallace Stevens, *The Necessary Angel* (New York: Vintage Books, 1951), p. 130.

32. Daniel B. Shea, "Emerson and the American Metamorphosis," in *Emerson: Prophecy, Metamorphosis, and Influence,* ed. David Levin (New York: Columbia University Press, 1975), p. 46. Santayana's abiding interest in the figure of Jacob's ladder is attested by its presence in *Platonism and the Spiritual Life* (1927) and *Dominations and Powers* (1951).

33. Apart from the obvious Platonic source of the ladder of transcendence (Oliver Alden's essay on Plato in *The Last Puritan,* written for Santayana's philosophy course, deals with love in the *Phaedrus* and the *Symposium*), it is likely that both Santayana and Emerson were recollecting Dante in general and, in particular, his use of Jacob's ladder in *Paradiso* XXII. Santayana had discussed Dante at length in his *Three Philosophical Poets,* and Emerson was manifestly interested in Dante throughout his life. Kenneth Walter Cameron has given evidence of the presence of the *Paradiso* in Emerson's sermons (*Emerson Society Quarterly,* 12 [3rd Quarter, 1958], p. 8), and Emerson himself quotes from *Paradiso* in one of his early lectures (EL, II, 351). A very careful survey of Emerson's experience of Dante is Joseph Chesley Mathews, "Emerson's Knowledge of Dante," *University of Texas Studies in English,* July 8, 1942, pp. 171–98.

34. Santayana, *The Last Puritan,* pp. 400–1.

35. Ibid., pp. 561, 580.

36. Ibid., p. 10.

37. Ibid., p. 602.

George Santayana and Ezra Pound

John McCormick

Few literary friendships can have been so unlikely as that between George Santayana and Ezra Pound. Their difference in age was considerable; their difference in temperament ranged from the amusing to the alarming. Santayana was Pound's senior by twenty-two years. In 1937, when Pound first approached Santayana, Pound was a volatile fifty-two, while Santayana at seventy-four was leading an intellectually active but socially retiring existence. In 1912 he had resigned from his professorship in Philosophy at Harvard and had left the United States, never to return. In France, in England during the 1914–1918 war, in his native Spain, and in Italy he had lived on a small inheritance from his mother, and eventually on his earnings as a writer. From 1920 on, Santayana habitually spent his winters in Rome, then moved to Cortina d'Ampezzo in the Dolomites to escape the hot Roman summers, returning in the fall to Rome, often by way of Venice or Fiesole to visit the Bernard Berensons, or his old friend and Harvard classmate, Charles Strong. Pound had settled in Rapallo in 1923, where Daniel Cory, Santayana's confidant and literary executor-to-be, had encountered Pound during a holiday residence in 1937.

A lifelong student of the subject, Cory talked philosophy to Pound, particularly Santayana's, and reported by letter to Santayana upon his conversations in Rapallo. Santayana replied that it was "Capital that you should have come to know so characteristic a man as Ezra Pound. Will you tell me, or can you draw from him, how he connects his sympathy with Eliot and Mussolini with his otherwise extreme romantic anarchism?"[1] Thus at the outset, Santayana registered his often stated distrust of romantic egotism and raised the agitated question of his own and Pound's attitudes toward the Italian Fascist movement.

As was his habit, Pound took it upon himself to move in on Santayana, not so frontally as on others, but vigorously, suggesting to Cory that he wanted to send to Santayana one of his books. Santayana's response is printed only in part in Cory's *Santayana: The Later Years:*

Reprinted from *American Literature* 54 (October 1982): 413–33, with the permission of the publisher; © 1982 by Duke University Press.

For heaven's sake, dear Cory, do stop Ezra Pound from sending me his book. Tell him that I have no sense for true poetry, admire (and wretchedly imitate) only the putrid Petrarch and the miserable Milton; that I don't care for books, hardly have any, and would immediately send off his previous volume to the Harvard Library or to some other cesspool of infamy. That is, if he made me a present of it. If he sent it only for me to look at and return, I would return it unopened; because I abhor all connection with important and distinguished people, and refuse to see absolutely anyone except some occasional stray student or genteel old lady from Boston.[2]

Because Pound was still alive, Cory omitted the second paragraph of Santayana's letter:

I shouldn't mind helping Ezra Pound if he were hard up, through you, for instance, if he wasn't to know where the money came from: but I don't want to *see* him. Without pretending to control the course of nature or the tastes of future generations, I wish to see only people and places that suggest the normal and the beautiful: not abortions or eruptions like E.P.[3]

This letter encapsulates Santayana's first attitude toward Pound: he is politely rude at the thought of meeting the man; he is genuinely self-effacing, aware that Pound is a figure to reckon with, and he is characteristically generous in his offer to contribute to the support of a poet, even though he disliked his work. That dislike is apparent not only from the correspondence but also from Santayana's marginal notes in Pound's *Quia pauper amavi,* which Santayana neither sent to the Harvard Library nor returned unopened to its sender. A close reader and a demanding craftsman, Santayana shows an ambivalent then a negative response to Pound's volume (containing an early version of the first three Cantos). At the line: "Hang it all, there can be but one 'Sordello,' " Santayana wrote, "*Fert* [sic] *animus* to imitate Browning." And at ". . . I dump my catch, shiny and silvery/As fresh sardines flapping and slipping . . ." Santayana noted, "Good image of catch what comes." His ear was offended by a passage in "Langue d'Oc":

> When the nightingale to his mate
> Sings day-long and night late
> My love and I keep state
> 　In bower,
> 　In flower,
> 'Till the watchman on the tower
> Cry: "Up! Thou rascal, Rise, . . ."

Santayana underlined the preposition "on," and noted, "This is unintentional? Otherwise guitar-like." He corrected the accent marks in the printed

Greek at the end of "Stele," and made an X at Pound's "True, it was Venice/ And at Florian's, under the *North* arcade" [Santayana's emphasis]. In "Homage to Sextus Propertius," Santayana wanted Pound's "Wherefore father Ennius . . ." to read "wherefrom. . . ." And at

> Back once again in middle Indiana,
> Acting as usher in the theatre,
> Painting the local drug-shop and soda bars,
> The local doctor's fancy for a mantle-piece:
> Sheep! jabbing the wool upon their flea-bit backs.

Santayana wrote, "1890: Americans gone to seed."

A most telling comment occurs in the margin to Pound's lines in the first Canto in the volume:

> I stand before the booth (the speech), but the truth
> Is inside this discourse: this booth is full of the
> marrow of wisdom.
> Give up the intaglio method?

Santayana's marginal note: "Vomit, don't write." efficiently summarizes Santayana's attitude to Pound's verse and helps to account for a distinct wariness, despite increasing cordiality, in his letters to Pound over the course of the next fifteen years. As it has survived, Santayana's library contains only one other publication of Pound: an issue of *Pharos* (No. 4, Winter, 1947) entitled *Confucius: The Unwobbling Pivot & The Great Digest.*[4] Because Santayana did not annotate the little book, as was his almost unvarying habit, therefore he probably did not read it.

Pound's response to Santayana's snub appeared in a letter to Cory, written in Pound's characteristic rib-nudging, American backwoods punning style:

> Rapallo
> 4 Lug/or
> the natnl hollerday

Waaal; me dear Dan'l, I caynt say wot ole Jarge sounds like he fly/loserfy had done his digestion much good/but he haint troubled my sleep for the past 30 years, and I reckon I wunt lose much now.

Humsumever; sensitivity iz rare in dis woild/and 25 years at Hawvud is enugh I should/think to turn any blokes liver.

Mebbe you better let it alone/on the other hand you can, if you like, tell Jarge I don't believe it/and I bet he haint seen no more old ladies from Bastun than I have/and I don't believe he agrees with ole Sprague, the hawvud sheconomist. Waal, mebbe you better let it alone/
regards to the missus. EZ.P.[5]

When Pound's *Guide to Kulchur* was published in 1938, he wanted Cory to review it, but wrote to T. S. Eliot that Cory would have to write "over a pussydonym cause Santyyanner would sack him" if he praised the book.[6] The comment indicated ignorance of Santayana's disposition toward Cory, for he urged Cory to embark on a professional literary career and was always delighted when Cory published articles and reviews.

Although Pound's "Santyyanner" suggests that the snub rankled, in 1939 he resumed his courtship with an unannounced personal visit, the first of several. The year 1939 was momentous for Santayana. In New York, Scribner's began to bring out the fifteen-volume Triton edition of his works, an elegant, limited edition which, although less elegant than he had hoped, still pleased him considerably. G. W. Howgate published a biography ("as if I were already dead") Santayana noted wryly;[7] his philosophy would be the subject of volume II in the Library of Living Philosophers, a series that even he respected; and a new edition of *Egotism in German Philosophy,* first published in 1915, was in press in London. Rumors of the war so soon to come had caused his hotel in Cortina to close earlier than usual; thus, when the war actually began in September, Santayana was living in the Danieli, Venice, where, he wrote to Cory, "We are at peace here, and quite cheerful, although keeping a sort of Lenten vigil: two days a week without meat, moderate lighting, no shrill motor-boats (Deo gratias!) and shorter newspapers (Deo gratias again)." Of his room he noted that it "is *intime* and yet gay, almost in the very midst of the passing crowd, gondoliers, children, and pigeons flocking on the quay."[8] Into Santayana's noisy yet pleasant retreat came a louder noise, late that fall. Pound and his daughter, Mary, turned up in Venice "and made me a series of long oracular visits [;] I don't know why. I couldn't hear or understand half of what he said, but carried on as well as I could, by guesses and old tags."[9]

An odd inconsistency in Santayana's attitude toward Pound occurs at this point. Santayana, the most honest of men, forgets or ignores in his letters to Cory that he had exercised his customary courtesy to Pound and was partially responsible for the resulting intrusions. On a post card of 30 November 1939, to Pound, Santayana remarked that Venice suited him; that he had thought of going to Rapallo "with the prospect of seeing you," but that if his hotel in Rome were to be re-opened following reconstruction, he would return there in 1942. The card concludes, "but I shall be glad to see you anywhere."[10] Pound wrote to Santayana in a letter of 8 December concerning his first visit,

> The venbl Corey [sic] so put the fear of gawd into me re yr. wanting to be left in peace to finish the Opus that I had the decency not to introduce serious subjects into our first conversation.
>
> Do give notice if same is likely to be henceforth permissible. There are

one or two gropings of my notes to Cavalcanti and one or two Chinese texts whereupon sidelight wd. be welcome.[11]

In a second postcard of 12 December 1939, Santayana assures Pound that he will be in Venice assuredly, short of "physiological cataclysm" on the 26th and 27th of the month. Then follows a cutting remark: "But you must not count on my philosophy to answer your questions, because questions are apt to imply a philosophy and don't admit of answers in terms of any other; so that you had better find your answers for yourself." Santayana wants no part of Pound's amateur philosophizing. Courtesy returns, however, as Santayana concludes: "But you might show me some of the beauties of Venice, which I have very likely missed all my life. The other day Thomas Whittemore showed me the Treasury of St. Mark's: very Byzantine, *Aurevoir* G.S."[12]

Six letters exist from Santayana to Pound of the early war years, 1940–1942, three from Venice and three from Rome, to which city Santayana returned in October, 1940, for what proved to be the final dozen years of his life. Pound, the literary executor and enthusiast of the orientalist, E. F. Fenollosa, conveyed to Santayana an article by Fenollosa on what Santayana described as "Chinese hieroglyphics." Santayana enjoyed himself in gentle satire on the ideogram: "instead of classic Sol we have a sort of broken rail fence," and showed his preference for the syntax and inflection of Greek and Latin. "Your Confucius," he wrote to Pound, "makes me think that the Chinese are . . . only highly refined prosaic sensualists. What could be more platitudinous, as an abstract thought, than 'be good and you will be happy'? So much does this proverbial eloquence dominate, that truth itself is sacrificed to moral monition." The letter ends, "You see I am floundering in your philosophy, badly but not unpleasantly. I am sending you Fenollosa back in the same envelope."[13] Santayana, in short, remained unimpressed by Pound's nascent affair with the ideogram. More on ideograms and on Pound's "philosophy" occurs in Santayana's response of 20 January 1940, to a letter from Pound that seems to be lost (Santayana kept few letters):

Dear E.P.
This mustn't go on for ever, but I have a word to say, in the direction of fathoming your potential philosophy.
When is a thing not static? When it jumps or when it makes you jump? Evidently the latter in the case of Chinese ideograms, you being your thoughts.
And these jumps are to particulars, not regressive to general terms. Classifications are not poetry. I grant that, but think that classifications may be important practically; e.g. poisons: how much? What number?
. . . .
When you ask for jumps to other particulars, you don't mean (I suppose) *any* other particulars, although your tendency to jump is so irresistible that the

bond between the particulars jumped to is not always apparent. It is a mental grab-bag. A *latent* classification or a *latent* genetic connection would seem to be required, if utter miscellaneousness is to be avoided.[14]

Santayana was neither the first, nor the last, to observe the grab-bag quality of Pound's work, in verse and in prose; Santayana's comment in a casual letter stands out for accuracy and lucidity.

The tarnish on Pound's intellectual brass is apparent in his account to Eliot of his dealings with Santayana. Now, according to him, he is *instructing* Santayana in the outlines of his views of the place of usury in the world:

> Wot wiff ideograms and all, George *is* trying to *see* the connection. I have fed him the Cavalcanti and all is nice and cordial at the Hotel Daniele [sic]. In fact, if you were still an American I might propose a triumvirate. As *copain* I prefer him to some of yr. tolerated.[15]

Pound's various approaches to Santayana concealed guile. What he was after was Santayana's collaboration with Eliot and him in a "new Paideuma," a book in which the three would set about the task of reforming American education. Pound had indeed sold the idea to Eliot, and Eliot had got a sympathetic response from his editorial board at Faber and Faber. In a letter of 6 February 1940, Pound wrote to Santayana that the idea of including him had arisen from Santayana's account of a conversation with Henry Adams: " 'So you are trying to teach philosophy at Harvard,' Mr. Adams said, . . . 'I once tried to teach history there, but it can't be done. It isn't really possible to teach anything.' "[16] Pound wrote that Eliot was also aware of Santayana's having said that it did not matter "*what* so long as they all read the *same* things."[17] In his long letter, Pound tried to convince Santayana of the opportunity before him by saying that the book would be a good place in which to answer critics of his philosophy and a forum from which to display his philosophy before readers who normally might never encounter it. It would be

> a chance to blast off some of the fog and fugg. . . .
>
> Have I been clear? Faber invites a volume or triptych or however you spell it: G.S. T.S.E. and myself on the Ideal University, or the Proper Curriculum, or how it would be possible to educate and/or (mostly or) civilize the university stewd-dent (and, inter lineas, how to kill off bureaucratism and professoriality). . . .
>
> I don't know what more I can say other than one more citation of Eliot's letter re the Faber committee: 'They say it ought to be a very queer book and it appeals to them.'[18]

Despite, or because of Pound's fevered pitch, indicating lack of intuition about his man, Santayana's negative response left no possibility of misinterpretation:

No. it is impossible for many reasons that I should accept the honour of collaborating with you and T.S.E. on a subject about which I have no ideas. It is impossible materially at this moment because I have seven critical essays about my philosophy to reply to, nine more coming, and the proofs of the *Realm of Spirit,* in two editions, to read. And it would always be impossible morally because you and T.S.E. are reformers, full of prophetic zeal and faith in the Advent of the Lord; whereas I am cynically content to let people educate or neglect themselves as they may prefer. Would your ideal education be for the U.S. or for all mankind? And would it be identical say up to the age of 16 for all Americans? Or are you contemplating only an ideal that you might like for a son of yours, or might have liked for yourselves? I can't frame even that conception. I should like to have learned Latin and Greek better; but a Spanish proverb says that is impossible without the rod, without blood—*la letra con sangre entra*—and I don't like blood. And it is so with all Utopias.

I don't remember my Henry Adams anecdote further than that he said history couldn't be taught. If I have embroidered on that, you or Eliot are welcome to use my fancy-work as a text. But you, you must preach the sermon.

G.S. [19]

Santayana's letter to Pound of November, 1940, that ominous time in our history, brings up the entire matter of Santayana's unorthodox, disturbing, and to a large majority of readers' minds, unsatisfactory views of war and Judaism. That letter begins innocuously with an account of his new residence in the Grand Hotel, Rome; he notes that he is working on "a sort of autobiography," then compares Mencius to Hume on causation. The ending of the letter, however, contains a paragraph to chill the blood of survivors of the Battle of Britain, then very much in progress, to say nothing of survivors of the Holocaust, also very much in progress: "How much pleasanter this war, seen from Italy, than the other one seen, as I saw it, from England! I feel as if I were living in great days, and witnessing something important. Or is it a mere sequence with no causes and no promises?"[20] Santayana's unsettling comment about Mussolini's war, rather like his apparently anti-Jewish attitudes, must be balanced against his several utterances on war and on Judaism. In *Reason in Society* (1905) he had written an anticipatory self-refutation to the comment in the letter to Pound: "the panegyrist of war places himself on the lowest level on which a moralist or patriot can stand and shows as great a want of refined feeling as of right reason. For the glories of war are all blood-stained, delirious, and infected with crime; . . ."[21] And again, "It is war that wastes a nation's wealth, chokes its industries, kills its flower, narrows its sympathies, condemns it to be governed by adventurers, and leaves the puny, deformed, and unmanly to breed the next generation."[22]

In *Dominations and Powers* (1951), Santayana considered war and its implications at great length. He perceives modern wars as failures of government, as exercises in unreason, and possibly as inevitable, given our failures in social organization. He is philosophical, remote, and inhuman when he alludes to the death in war of common men: "Death as it overtakes the unwilling, is ignominious; and it is ignominious even in war for the herded rabble, who are not spontaneously or personally soldiers, but poor conscripts with a blank mind. This makes the unmixed pitifulness of many a casualty."[23] Santayana characteristically sees all sides of the matter simultaneously, but he finally rejects war, while pessimistically registering doubt that efforts to outlaw war can succeed. That they might succeed under a central, universal government he grants, but such universal peace, he thinks, might lead to "the peace of moral extinction. Between two nothings there is eternal peace; but between two somethings if they come within range of each other, there is always the danger of war."[24]

By May, 1941, Santayana had moved from his hotel to the Blue Nun's Hospital in Rome, partly because of currency regulations, partly because of his advanced age. Pound had begun his notorious radio broadcasts. On 22 May, Santayana wrote to Cory, "Ezra Pound was here yesterday, quite mad; I offered him some tea, not very good, which he drank uncomplainingly to the dregs, without milk and sugar, although both were provided. He complains of the people's utter ignorance of economics, and says that is the root of all the trouble. I wonder if he is understood when he speaks through the radio. Why does he talk in that way? Is it incapacity, or inspiration? Perhaps nine tenths of one and one tenth the other."[25] One of Pound's lifelong misapprehensions about Santayana was that the two of them indeed were intellectual "copains." It is a measure of Pound's remoteness from certain human truths that he mistook Santayana's astonished politeness for cordiality and even for approval of his ideas, quite ignoring Santayana's anguished "I can't reply to your suggestions and diagrams because I don't understand them."[26]

Pound's misapprehension, nevertheless, gave rise to the view among later commentators on his career that he and Santayana in truth were political and intellectual bedfellows during the Fascist years, and particularly during the years of the war in Italy. In four of his broadcasts from Rome, Pound referred to "George Santayana" as though they were intimates, and in a broadcast of 1943 on "Materialism," he moved counter-chronologically from the Russians to Santayana to Aristotle, in his best auto-didactic manner:

> George Santayana calls himself a materialist. It rather shocked old William James. Ole William told young George, he was younger at the stage of world history, that his, Santayana's philosophy was organized rottenness. I can not agree with fuzzy old James. It appears to me that George Santayana rather agrees with Thomas Aquinas. I mean the materialist Santayana ends up by writin' a book called The Realm of Spirit. I occasionally plunge into the work to calm my heated mind. I mean when I am not up to Confucius and Mencius. And Thomas Aquinas says somewhere that the soul is the first ACT of an organic body. Well, I ask George Santayana what THAT means. And he says

entelechy, which seems to me to be dodgin' behind a Greek word. But anyhow, a materialist definition of the soul seems to be that it is the first act, or first action, or first condition of an organic body.[27]

Working only from sources having to do with Pound, biographers have repeated the canard that Santayana and Pound saw the world identically. In *Ezra Pound: the Last Rower,* C. D. Heyman writes that Cory had introduced Pound "to the Spanish philosopher and former lecturer at Harvard George Santayana, who, like Pound, was a fervent fan of Mussolini."[28] Pound's German biographer, Eva Hesse, includes Pound in a strongly conservative intellectual group consisting of "Mencken, Santayana, Yeats, Hulme, Eliot, Lewis— . . . "[29] Frau Hesse also finds an anti-semitic strain in a second list of writers: Yeats, Wyndham Lewis, Eliot, D. H. Lawrence; while Claudel, Colette, Maurras, Morand, Giraudoux, Marinetti, Belloc, Gentile, d'Annunzio, Chesterton, Pirandello, Rilke, and Santayana are alleged to be followers of Mussolini. That lengthy group in turn is linked to those writers who had inclined towards Hitler early in the Fascist day: Céline, Hamsun, Hauptmann, Henry Williamson, Gottfried Benn, and Ernst Jünger.[30]

When Edmund Wilson, visiting Santayana in Rome shortly after the war, remarked that he thought the atmosphere showed "it had really picked up the people to get rid of the Fascist machine," Santayana replied that at its best, the regime had displayed admirable aspects. It had helped the young,

And they had been helpful—to him, I gathered—in a way that was characteristic of Americans, but completely unknown in Europe. And then his irony began to creep in. He had received a letter one day inviting him to become a Roman citizen. He had gone to the bureau indicated and explained that he was a Spanish subject and that that was what he preferred to remain. They told him being a Roman citizen would not interfere with this. What were the obligations involved? he asked. Very simple: you paid so many lire. So, he said, he had declined the honor and had not availed himself of this chance "to become *civis Romanus.*"[31]

Wilson further noted that Santayana's "weakness for Mussolini" may have been owing to his approval of displays of "virility," and that although unsympathetic to the Germans, he had admired the officers in uniform during his student-days in Berlin.[32]

The allegation of Santayana's "Fascism" and anti-semitism is comprehensible but finally unjust, for it is too simple-minded to account for the many factors involved. He was never politically active; his attitudes were philosophical, aristocratic, and completely illiberal by any modern definition of the word. Santayana himself took up the matter of his "Fascism" in a letter of 1950 to Professor Corliss Lamont. A passionate admirer of Santayana and an impeccable liberal, Lamont wished to preserve Santayana from the allegation of sympathy for the Italian regime or any taint of Fascism. Santayana found Lamont's defense off the point: "Of course I was never a Fascist in the sense of belonging to that Italian party, or to any nationalistic or religious *party*. But considered, as it is for the naturalist, a product of the generative order of society, a nationalist or religious *institution* will probably have its good sides, and be better perhaps than the alternative that presents itself at some moment in some place. That is what I thought, and still think Mussolini's dictatorship was for Italy in its home government." The socialism that preceded Mussolini's regime and the chaos that has followed, Santayana wrote, need only be compared: "But Mussolini personally was a bad man and Italy a half-baked political unit; and the *militant* foreign policy adopted by Fascism was ruinous in its artificiality and folly. But internally, Italy was until the foreign militancy and mad alliances were adopted, a stronger, happier, and more united country than it is or had ever been. Dictatorships are surgical operations, but some diseases require them, only the surgeon must be an expert, not an adventurer."[33]

Although Santayana's rationale for Fascism in Italy may still offend the liberal mind, it is far from Pound's rant, and further to be understood according to Santayana's theory of naturalism. With Lucretius, he disdained God or the gods, and found man absolutely lodged in nature, rooted in matter, an animal gifted with spirit, capable of aspiration, and equally capable of appalling barbarity. Disdainful of politicians and contemptuous of their actions, he was always prepared for the worst and unsurprised when it came to pass. Nor was he a dogmatist of the far Right. At Easter, 1946, he was reading Togliatti's two-volume translation of Stalin's Russian, *Questioni del Leninismo,* which he found "excellent, and refreshingly dogmatic."[34] Santayana's extensive marginalia to the volumes show both a sympathy and a criticism of the USSR completely consistent with his remarks about Mussolini's Italy. Santayana in his age saw both Italian and Russian dictatorships from the same perspective as Rome had of the Goths, in the aspect of eternity.

As for the charge of anti-semitism, it is quite wrong to believe that Santayana shared Pound's ravings about "yids" and "goyim." From the published work and from the correspondence, published and unpublished, it is clear that Santayana accepted the conventional antisemitism of the Boston and Cambridge of his youth, that "socially habitable Boston" that he described in his novel, *The Last Puritan* (1935). It is probable that his early Catholic training and his strong Spanish inheritance reinforced the mindless, cruel, dangerous, all-but universal American prejudice. That attitude may also have lent protective coloring to the Spanish, exotic-looking young man, cast by fate and choice upon the narrow, high-minded society (Saul Bellow's "upper depths") which he would later so effectively satirize. Anti-semitism in any degree is surprising in so intellectually unconventional, perceptive, and sensitive a man as Santayana. The best that can be said of it is that it was not of Pound's stripe, and that it is modified by evidence in the marginalia in several of his books that he reconnoitered and skirmished with the tendency.

Despite Pound's mateyness in his radio broadcasts, no evidence has come to light to indicate that the two men were in touch between July, 1942, the date of the last letter to Pound of the period, and spring, 1945, when Santayana learned through a young U.S. Army medical orderly that Pound had been arrested by the U.S. Army and incarcerated at Pisa. Santayana was shocked at the news, expressed admiration for Pound as a poet and for his performance as a " 'poor man's Maecenas' . . . . He hoped that Pound would be judged as a poet, artist, and helper of artists, and that his 'confusing entry into alien disciplines would be understood and forgiven.' Pound in turn was delighted to learn that Santayana was in health and had a good word for him."[35]

Pound's subsequent imprisonment, in November, 1945, in St. Elizabeth's hospital for the criminally insane, Washington, D.C., produced a sequence of sixteen letters from Pound to Santayana in Rome. Only one of Santayana's letters to Pound in response has come to light, but often one can infer from Pound's letters the nature of Santayana's. Pound wrote his letters on a typewriter, either on air-letter forms, or on brown stationery headed by the printed legend, "ezra pound J'AYME DONC JE SUIS." The sequence begins with Pound's letter of 16 September 1946. Santayana had directed Scribner's to send Pound *The Middle Span,* the second volume of his memoirs, which had appeared in April, 1945, and *The Idea of Christ in the Gospels* (1946). Pound had not yet received the latter, but Santayana apparently had written to him about some of the matters considered in it. Pound remarks that "yr. stuffy old pub. prob. not consider me suitable recipient for yr. last vol." In *The Idea of Christ in the Gospels,* Santayana discussed the idiom of the several gospels, particularly the mystical and symbolic language of the Gospel of John. Pound amusingly condenses that discussion to a vision of illiterate fishermen worrying about Greek pronounciation, and adds, "I simply suspect that you confuse mere antispepsis with la *purezza.* I don't see how you are goin' to handle the incarnation on yr. base or as stated in yr. ultimate epistula. if you aint keerful you'll end as a Manichean and find yrself on the hot spot."[36]

By 30 September 1946, Pound had been reading *The Middle Span*: "p.6 Midl Span a great page and I nearly missed it—having opend bk. in midl and thought it chit-chat." On that page, Santayana traces the origin of his own views on ethics to lectures he had heard in Berlin in 1886–87, in which the attitudes of the Greeks and of Spinoza were discussed. Santayana writes that the Greeks were

> saved from littleness and arrogance . . . . The Jews, on the contrary, and even Spinoza with them, fell into both littleness and arrogance: into the littleness of being content with anything, with small gains and private safety; and into

arrogance in proclaiming that, in their littleness they possessed the highest good, heard the voice of absolute truth, and were the favourites of heaven. Undoubtedly if you renounce everything you are master of everything in the ideal sense, since nothing can disturb you: but the Jews never renounced anything that was within reach; and it was rather the Greek hero who renounced half of what he might have possessed, in order that the other half should be perfect.[37]

Whether the view here expressed is correct or incorrect, it is the result of a great deal of reading and meditation. It distinctly is not a casual, anti-semitic conclusion. Pound, however, appears to have read it as such, and at the end of his letter begged Santayana for more:

> For those who like me can't read I wish you wd inmercy do 20 pages like p.6 of simple proposition—as guide to what you @ greater span have elaborated.
> hang it I am prob. not clear. Ep

On the overleaf, Pound added,

> I mean in chaps I and II you've got a concise simplicity—chiarezza—different from what you have when *trying* to make philosophic (professionals) understand.
> forgive this.
> EP

By 2 November Pound had received *The Idea of Christ in the Gospels,* for he wrote to Santayana, "Yr. stuffy old pubrs have—rather to my surprise—, obey'd you." Mary, Pound's daughter, had just married Prince Boris de Rachelwitz: "Wonder if my brat and her marito (of 2 days or so) will eventually bring you Confucius? I shd like em to have philosophic as well as ecclesiastic or civil benediction." On the overleaf is a probable swipe at Bernard Berenson (with whom Santayana had broken off relations in about 1925), "by. didja see Behrensohn's Mahrrrrrvelous obit of Placci con Titolo!!" A page of gibberish follows, in which Pound seems to confuse *The Idea of Christ in the Gospels* with his own Chinese research. The letter ends with

> they just haven't a nice tone if compared with the civil literature of gks., chinks, or Frobenius' africans.
> I spose by gks. I mean Homer and a few poets. ma che!!
> the Seneca quote has a suavity.

Pound resumed something like epistolary rationality in his letter of 20 February 1947:

It is qu fun to be reading Persons and Places [the first volume of Santayana's memoirs] @ same time as by odd chance reading Galdos 'Dona Perfecta' (which was out of print in Spain and unprocurable in Italy 9 yrs. ago when a young wop wanted to know what Spanish to read and translate.)
You may have got more of yr philosophy into it than into the Treatises. or at least in form more communicative to my ruins.

Pound seems to revert to *The Idea of Christ in the Gospels* in his letter to Santayana of 14 June 1947, which I quote in full:

> Trouble with yr————xianity is that it is a slum cult cut off from agriculture.
>
> ———————
>
> Steam roller no substitute for plow
>
> ———————
>
> all fanaticisms came from general (abstract) statements.
>   yrs EP
> bestiality due to not facing Time and vegetation

A gap of eighteen months in the correspondence was closed with Pound's air-letter of 22 December 1949, wishing Santayana season's greetings, and including a Chinese character that Pound defines as "respect for the kind of intelligence that enables the cherry-stone to make cherry; or grass seed to make grass." This cryptic remark, together with his next letter of 1 February 1950, to the effect that there had been no philosophy in the occident for 2300 years, "nothing but philo-epistemology," is explained by Santayana's letter to Pound of 7 February 1950:

> Dear Pound
>   Two messages from you awaiting an answer. The first, besides being a compliment to my materialism, or to the generative order of nature (as I call it in my new book [*Dominations and Powers*], now nearing completion) exemplified it in a cherry-stone able to produce cherries, after going a long way round, and facing a good many risks of perishing on the way. And it would be fussy to object to your word 'intelligence' to describe that potentiality in the cherry-stone; somehow it possesses a capacity to develop other cherries under favourable circumstances, without getting anything vital wrong. That is 'intelligence' of an unconscious sort. I agree in respecting it.
>   The other message comes today with the observation that there has been no philosophy in the West, at least since Pythagoras, but only philoepistemologia. That is true of English and even in part German speculation, but not of the traditional philosophy which has never died out, in the Church and in many individuals. My friends Lucretius and Spinoza were not especially epistemologists but had theories of the measure of things, putting human 'knowledge' in its place.

It was good of you to remember me. I have not been very well, but hope to last long enough to finish my book . . . .

Yours

G Santayana

Pound responded in his slightly surreal, paratactical fashion on 13 February:

Revered G.S.
OK intellectus agens? and Leibnitz 'gristly bits' . . . . didn't the blokes mostly call 'em selves theologians? (awful mess, of trying to hitch gk. and lat. horse-sense to epilepsy from alien source.) Fred. Mannings's 'How much mist could a mystic stick, if a mystic could etc?'

Hope you last longer than long enough to get to 'fang', T-square, Epistemology? the science of annoying others. I quote yr. 'coral insect' simile @ least 2° weekly. If only for swank, I ought to have excepted Ocellus? O'Kelly in private life.

The above exchange remained on Pound's mind, for he reverted to it in an undated letter to Daniel Cory in which he alludes to Santayana's words about the "unconscious" nature of the cherry-stone, "How the HELL does he KNOW it's 'unconscious'?" and to his Ocellus-O'Kelly pun, "Za matter of act, I think I sd/Ocellus and not Pythagoras but dont spose G.S. kept my letter, so impos/verify."

On 2 March 1950, Pound was not thinking about epistemology but about economics. Writing to Santayana (without a salutation, not even an ironic one), he declares that

a system which does not reach into the means of exchange is defective

----

an indefinite middle is as accursed in material exchange as in logic

respectfully EP

By 15 April Pound had turned to a critique of Aristotle, "the old twiddler":

Two reasons why the GODDAM occident is a bdy/nuisance, staring at you in the very opening of Ari's metaphysics.

1. the old twiddler speaks of everybody having senses etc.
        aesthanesthai.   koinon
as if they had 'em equally. Good painter or syrian rug-maker sees 100 times as much as a stockbroker whenever he looks at form or colour.

2. nasty definition of sophia/knowledge of etc.
        instead of 'having sense to ACT on and with knowledge of nacherl process.'

> hence the occidental SKIZ
> flatchested highbrows etc.

Obviously something phoney in all his sequelers or he wdnt hv/been knocked out, i.e. classics etc. wdn't have been knocked out by the epileptic filth from the bubbylonian bugwash basin.

For "epileptic filth from the bubbylonian bugwash basin" we are of course to read Judaism; again Pound assumes agreement on Santayana's part as a sequel to his mis-reading of Santayana's views on the origins of Christianity and his interpretations of Judaism.

Six weeks later, Pound changed targets from Aristotle to the Adams family, "Hen. and his kid bro/and superior Brooks." After a few lines of impenetrable free association, Pound ends the letter on a comic note, "Wonder was not why Hen. A sd/yu 'couldn't/teach at Harvard/=probably just snobbism or plain iggurance?" One remembers the prominence of the Adams-Santayana anecdote in the *Cantos* and in the earlier correspondence. At such times Pound seems like a very old person repeating his favorite stories to any and all listeners, indifferent to his own repetition.

Four of Pound's letters to Santayana of 1951 exist; one in March to ask about *Dominations and Powers*;[38] one to send the Confucian character for "love, duty, propriety, Wisdom"; then on 15 April his acknowledgment of *Dominations and Powers*:

> Thanks v. much it is very good of you to send 'Dom and pow' guided by index opened to p. 249 and have enjoyed 252–4
>
> _____
>
> whether I hv. strength to anallyze and comment I doubt
> or whether yu want to be bothered with comment.
>
> _____
>
> this just to express gratitude and say Scrib has sent it. Wishing you best possible Roman Spring
>
> ever E.P.

Pound's praise was for Part Two, chapter 3 of Santayana's new book, "The Middleman in Trade." Page 249 discusses barter versus money as a medium of exchange. Santayana appears to prefer barter, for then "there is no dominance of any party over the other. Each knows his own positive interest and need, and closes the bargain willingly, with open eyes . . . ." Such a view accords with Pound's in the *Cantos,* the letters, and the radio broadcasts during the war. Particularly in agreement is Santayana's statement that while money is convenient, it "introduces a middle term pregnant with terrible dangers." With the convenience of money, the middleman arises, commerce among nations becomes possible, and (on pp. 242–54, which Pound praised) a cosmopolitan upper class emerges. "Or a cosmopolitan middle class, like the Jews, already diffused throughout the world and dedicated to commerce, may rise to the top, and may undertake to subordinate all nations and religions to international cooperation and prosperity." That middle class takes over the arts, sciences, and literary activities of older societies "and often manipulates them cleverly, with an air of superior enlightenment; but this is merely the subjective superiority of the incurable foreigner, who has no roots in the society he studies or has cut himself off from his own roots."

Again, Santayana's words would seem, given Pound's disposition, to affirm Pound's own views of Judaism. Read fully and in the context of his ideas about society, Santayana himself would have argued the quoted passage is a passing, if hostile footnote to an elaborate discussion of the contribution of industrialism and trade to what he saw as the decline of civilization in the nineteen and twentieth centuries. He tried, one may conclude, to direct his animus against trade itself rather than against Jewish trade, with indifferent success. As ever, he wrote from above the fray, he believed, neither surprised nor alarmed at what he saw beneath.

In the last two letters of the sequence from St. Elizabeth's Pound returned compulsively to the "cherry-stone" episode, and to Henry Adams' exchange with Santayana about teaching at Harvard. On 8 December 1950, Pound wrote, "coming back to yrs. of 1950—instead of 'how do you know' etc can I put it what save habit causes you to assume it is 'unconscious'?" Then about what Pound called the "uni worst ities" in the U.S.,

> Did they conserve (or use in their classic brawls) in your time, Agassis or was there nothing left but glass flowers in a mouseum for Christian endeavour conventing?
>
> benedicions of the season. EP

The final letter of 8 January 1952, is a four-line jest:

> Speaking of HOPE
> a friend (in fact a prof @ cat. Univ.) has just left after stating that he was (verbatim) 'going to teach @ Harvard'.
> I sd I wd report the matter to you
> Benedictius for '52
> EP

Pound's "benedictius" was ineffective, for his friend? acquaintance? correspondent? George Santayana died of cancer of the liver on 26 September 1952. He would have turned eighty-nine on 16 December of that year. What are we to make, finally, of the relationship between the two men? Because of the one-sidedness of the correspondence as we have it, one might be tempted to see Santayana as an approving spectator of Ezra Pound's floor-show. One quality of Santayana's, however, that might not be immediately obvious in the few letters to Pound was his punctiliousness in responding to readers whom he recognized as serious but somehow wrong in their interpretations of his published ideas. Several of the letters to Pound have that tone of the professor *malgré-lui* expounding his thought, letters which Pound in his increasing disarray interpreted as expressions of sympathy, and agreement with his own extraordinary outlook. That Santayana felt compassion for Pound imprisoned and hospitalized is clear from the reports of others and is true to his nature.

Whether Pound's letters to Santayana constitute proof for or against his mental balance is a question not for the biographer but for medical analysts. His brashness at the outset, his frequent silliness relieved by occasional humor, his compulsive single-mindedness, all constitute a kind of intellectual can-can, against which Santayana's courtesy and formality seem like the ritual movements of a Greek chorus. Whatever one's view, no reader can ignore the pathos of Pound's "forgive this" (letter of 30 September 1946), a pathos that may help to counteract his mis-judgment of Santayana's positions on Italian Fascism and on Judaism.

Notes

1. Daniel Cory, *Santayana: The Later Years: A Portrait with Letters* (New York: Braziller, 1963), p. 187.

2. *The Later Years,* p. 188.

3. Autograph letter, Santayana to Cory, 1 July 1937. Ms. Collection. Butler Library, Columbia University. Printed with permission of Mrs. Margaret Cory, literary executrix of Santayana's estate, and of the Butler Library.

4. Marginalia reproduced with the permission of Mrs. Margaret Cory, literary executrix, Santayana's estate. Some 350 volumes of Santayana's library are on deposit in the rare book room, University of Waterloo, Waterloo, Ontario. Annotations cited from Erza Pound, *Quia pauper amavi* (London: The Egoist, [19—]).

5. Daniel Cory, "Ezra Pound: A Memoir," *Encounter,* 30, No. 5 (1968), 32–33.

6. "Ezra Pound: A Memoir," p.33.

7. Autograph letter, Santayana to John Hall Wheelock, 16 July 1939, Scribner Archive, Firestone Library, Princeton University. Particular thanks are owing to Mr. Charles Scribner III, for making his entire Santayana archive available to scholarship.

8. Autograph letter to Cory, 9 September 1939. Butler Library, Columbia University. By permission.

9. Autograph letter to Cory; Venice, 11 March 1940; Butler Library, Columbia University. By permission.

10. Autograph post-card to Pound; Venice, 30 November 1939. From the personal collection of Mrs. Margaret Cory.

11. D. D. Paige, ed., *The Letters of Ezra Pound:* 1907–1941 (New York: Harcourt, Brace, 1950), p. 331.

12. Autograph post-card to Pound; Venice, 13 December 1939. From the personal collection of Mrs. Margaret Cory.

13. Typescript letter to Pound; Venice, 15 January 1940. From the personal collection of Mrs. Margaret Cory.

14. Autograph letter to Pound; Venice, 20 January 1940. From the personal collection of Mrs. Margaret Cory.

15. *The Letters of Ezra Pound,* p. 335.

16. Thus in George Santayana, *Persons and Places: The Background of My Life* (New York: Scribner's, 1944), p. 234.

17. *The Letters of Ezra Pound,* p. 338.

18. *The Letters of Ezra Pound,* pp. 338–39.

19. Autograph letter to Pound; Venice. 7 March 1940. From the personal collection of Mrs. Margaret Cory.

20. Typescript letter to Pound; Rome, 19 November 1940. From the personal collection of Mrs. Margaret Cory.

21. George Santayana, *The Life of Reason: Reason in Society* (New York: Scribner's 1922), p. 85.

22. *Reason in Society,* p. 82.

23. George Santayana, *Dominations and Powers* (New York: Scribner's 1951), p. 217.

24. *Dominations and Powers,* p. 449.

25. Autograph letter, Butler Library, Columbia University. By permission.

26. Autograph letter to Pound: Rome, 4 January 1941. From the personal collection of Mrs. Margaret Cory.

27. *"Ezra Pound Speaking": Radio Speeches of World War II,* ed. Leonard W. Doob (Copyright © 1978 by the Trustees of the Ezra Pound Literary Property Trust), published by Greenwood Press; used by permission of New Directions, agents for the Ezra Pound Literary Property Trust. Pp. 353–54.

28. C. David Heyman, *Ezra Pound: The Last Rower* (New York: Viking, 1976), p. 93.

29. Eva Hesse, *Ezra Pound: von Sinn und Wahnsinn* (Munich: Kindler Verlag, 1978), p. 183.

30. *Ezra Pound: von Sinn und Wahnsinn,* n. 21, p. 500.

31. Edmund Wilson, *Europe without Baedeker* (New York: Doubleday, 1947), p. 57.

32. *Europe without Baedeker,* p. 62.

33. Daniel Cory, ed., *The Letters of George Santayana* (New York: Scribner's), p. 405. Santayana's emphasis.

34. Autograph letter. Santayana to Cory; Rome, 9 March 1946. Butler Library, Columbia University. By permission.

35. Charles Norman, *The Case of Ezra Pound* (New York: Funk & Wagnalls, 1968), pp. 71–72.

36. The sequence of sixteen letters from Pound to Santayana, and one from Santayana to Pound, is on deposit in the Humanities Research Center, University of Texas at Austin. Publication with permission of Mr. James Laughlin, Executor, Ezra Pound Literary Property Trust, and of the Humanities Research Center.

37. George Santayana, *The Middle Span* (New York: Scribner's, 1945).

38. The text reads, "What about that book
of yours? Are your ————ishers
trying to suppress yr/
indecorous opinions,?
   or only the usual
American tempo—molasses
flowing up hill below zero"

This letter is reprinted in "Bruno Lind" (pseudonym of Robert C. Hahnel), *Vagabond Scholar: A Venture into the Privacy of George Santayana* (New York: Bridgehead Books. 1962), pp. 65–66.

George Santayana and the Genteel Tradition

Daniel Aaron

When George Santayana delivered his lecture "The Genteel Tradition in American Philosophy" to a California audience in 1911, the word "genteel" had pretty well lost its original meaning. The adjective, a derivative of the French "gentil," was for a long time synonymous with "polite," "graceful," "decorous," "refined." It distinguished the manners, dress, and tone of the well-born from those of the commonality. That is the way Jane Austen, for example, understood it. Mr. Darcy in her novel *Pride and Prejudice* is "genteel." The smug and obsequious lower-class Mr. Collins is decidedly not. But by the middle of the nineteenth century, the term had become largely pejorative. "Do you call those genteel little creatures American poets?" Whitman rhetorically asks in *Democratic Vistas*. "To prune, gather, trim, conform, and ever cram and stuff, and be genteel and proper, is the pressure of our days" (Whitman, 1982, pp. 955, 961). Today "genteel" is an epithet contemptuously applied to persons (I cite the OED) "who are possessed with a dread of being taken for the 'common people', who attach exaggerated importance to supposed marks of social superiority." (Also see Tomsich, 1971, pp. 2–3.) To be "genteel" now is tantamount to being both ignoble and socially insecure.

Little of this sense of the word is implicit in Santayana's usage. For him the "genteel tradition" was a descriptive, not an abusive term. It connoted propriety, correctness, dogmatism and conservatism (Howgate, 1938, pp. 186–7)—and flaccidness, passivity, and complacence as well. "The subject," he wrote, "is complex, and calls for many an excursus and qualifying footnote" (Santayana, 1913, p. 212), but he did sketch its outlines. Indeed, it's possible to watch his conceptions of the "genteel tradition" taking shape in his consciousness long before he gave it a name. In time he came to see it as a kind of cultural malady that had afflicted the American mind since at least the end of the Civil War. A consecutive story of its birth, dominion, and decline could be pieced together from his random pieces and casual asides. If it had been, the plot might have run something like this.

The genteel tradition originated abroad like so many other American phenomena but became pandemic in Protestant America after Calvinism had

Reprinted from *Overheard in Seville: Bulletin of the Santayana Society* 7 (Fall 1989): 1–8, with the permission of the publisher.

ceased to be a vital and dynamic faith and the transcendentalism of an Emerson or Thoreau had atrophied. By mid-century, the citizens of the republic were totally absorbed in building and expanding and accumulating while at the same time internalizing a "hereditary philosophy" that no longer bore any relation to their quotidian activities. The religious and secular priests of a stale idealism represented one half of the national mentality. They were the custodians of a superannuated "high culture." The philistines, cousins of Emerson's Men of Understanding—calculating machines devoid of true emotion or "instinctive piety"—represented the other half. No third party of any size or dimension emerged to reconcile them. But science and intellectual and material progress created an unhospitable milieu for the genteel tradition, undermined its shaky foundations, and drove its proponents into academic enclaves. The consequences of this split between the spiritual and material cultures left the nation "half-formed," as Santayana put it, "and groping after its essence" (Santayana, 1986, p. 195)—a nation without a civilization.

Santayana's even-tempered if piecemeal diagnosis of a divided national mentality has been thoroughly aired, and so has the story of its aftermath: how the literary radicals in the early twentieth century made the genteel tradition the target of their antipathies just as it was about to peter out. Santayana had seen in 1911 that the Bohemian insurgents with their "poetry of crude naturalism" were the forerunners of a coming cultural revolution, but he didn't welcome them as allies. The confirmed Tory felt obliged to detach himself from the thirty contributors to Harold Stearns's *Civilization in the United States* when he reviewed that noisy book in 1922. He found the Young Turks "morally underfed" and "disaffected," and he learned more, he drily noted, "about their palpitating doubts than about America or about civilization" (Ballowe, 1967, pp. 161–2). Much of what they disliked about the United States he liked; the Americanism they deplored (the genteel tradition excepted) was "simply modernism." He even intimated that the "offended sensibility" emanating from Stearns's book was "itself genteel" (Ballowe, 1967, pp. 161–2).

Even so, he felt no hostility toward the young "barbarians," in his lexicon a term signifying "unevenly educated," "undisciplined," "rebellious against the nature of things." Barbarians were people who despised "that which exists, in language, vocabulary, or morals, and set up the sufficiency of their unchastened impulses." He wasn't put off by their rambunctiousness—that was youth's privilege—but he faulted them for expressing their demands for "self-expression" in appallingly muddy English. Still, no matter how "crude and unnecessarily wasteful" they were (Cory, 1963, pp. 29–30), he preferred them to the New Humanists, the last flurry of the New England genteel tradition, who had no wild passions to subdue for all their talk about the "inner check." In his youth he had resisted and resented the moral absolutism of Boston and Cambridge, the essence, he thought, "of the genteel tradition in America" (Santayana, 1931, p. 28). Perhaps this accounts for a certain animus detectable whenever the genteel tradition surfaces in his books and essays. It was more than a topic for the Tocquevillian commentator on American culture; it was a personal matter. Addressing it gave him an excuse to pay back some old scores.

I mention Tocqueville here as the prototypical outsider who came to the United States less than a half-century before Santayana arrived, stayed ten months, and wrote his classic study of a democratic state, the advanced guard of what he saw as an inevitable tendency. He carried his presuppositions with him and left with most of them intact. He liked the country and its people, but American society didn't appeal to him. America had no literature, no music, and was destined by its political system and its social egalitarianism to produce at best a diluted culture.

It would never have occurred to Santayana to make a systematic survey of American ideas and institutions, but his conclusions about American civilization, such as they were, were not all that different from Tocqueville's even though his involvement with America was far more complex and ambivalent.

Both *Persons and Places,* a novelistic autobiography, and *The Last Puritan,* an autobiographical novel, are as much the productions of the insider as outsider as they are the reverse. In the former, Santayana makes his marginality the clue to his character and career. He presents himself as the stranger in America, the uneasy guest, the exotic, the spy, the Prince in Disguise. In his public role, he plays the laughing philosopher, the bemused observer of the human menagerie, the tolerant world citizen. Hardly discernible is the not-so-disengaged social critic embedded in the society he is criticizing. Many social critics, Stefan Collini reminds us, tend to dramatize their roles by representing themselves "as 'marginal.' But such a claim," he continues, "need not be naively taken as an accurate piece of social description: it serves functions of its own, including that of legitimating the criticisms by indicating the critic's special access to some standard of authority denied to those blinkered by or imprisoned in the assumptions of their own society" (Collini, 1988, p. 427). Santayana was such a critic, I think, and I suspect that he was more affected by the genteel culture he slyly spoofed than he ever let on.

He may have shared some of the traits Thorstein Veblen in a famous essay attributed to the renegade Jew—the hyphenate's "divided allegiance" and skepticism—that made him, in Veblen's terms, an "intellectual wayfaring man" and "a disturber of the intellectual peace" (Lerner, 1970. pp. 474–5). But unlike Veblen, an authentic outsider, Santayana managed to secure his place "in the scheme of conventions" and to remain safely and comfortably ensconced in the society of the well-heeled. He could do this in good conscience, because he had no quarrel with America's political and economic institutions and accepted (if not necessarily agreeing with) the social prejudices of the establishment, but also because he conveyed his unsubversive opinions with charm and urbanity. However foreign he felt himself to be, his "insider" credentials protected him from the retribution visited upon the genuine outsider.

Persons and Places, at once so revealing and evasive, so clearly written and abstract, is instructively different from the autobiographical books of Henry Adams and Henry James, authors with whom Santayana has often been compared. Both belonged to Old America. Both escaped the contagion of the genteel tradition by distancing themselves from it, Adams through science and historical back-tracking, James in what Santayana called "the classic way"—that is to say, by turning it "into a subject-matter for analysis" and "by understanding it" (Santayana, 1913, p. 204). Santayana professed to understand it too, but that did not keep him from coming almost obsessively to its spirit-chilling manifestations long after its knell had sounded. Significantly, he often associated it with his Boston youth.

Two Bostons figure noticeably in his memoirs: the Boston typified by his own shabby genteel household and the Boston of the rich. He made no bones about his preference for the luxurious households of the latter ("if most things were illusions," he decided, "having money and spending money were great realities"), but the Boston he abandoned with relief—the only part of America he knew at first hand—emerges in his recollections as the quintessence of the genteel tradition: a compound of tepid refinement and blatant commercialism. "In Boston but not of it." Thus he described his adolescence. His foreignness, his Roman Catholicism (such as it was), and what he refers to tiresomely in his autobiography as his family's "poverty," didn't bar him from fashionable and intellectual circles; it did keep him skirmishing "on the borders of the polite world." At Harvard there were no borders he had to cross, but both in Boston and Cambridge he occupied a middle ground somewhere between that of a native and a "visiting foreigner" (Santayana, 1986, pp. 85, 224, 354). So at least the older man remembered his younger self.

The Boston of *Persons and Places*—Santayana's America—is reflected through a glass tinted with sentiment, malice, and humor. His fondness for the "kind and correct Bostonians," those "highly moralised and highly cultivated" types, was unfeigned (Santayana, 1986, pp. 254, 354). But his memoirs were also punctuated with vignettes of drab people not unlike the cranks Henry James mischievously portrayed in his novel *The Bostonians.* There is something curt and a little spiteful in his recollections of Boston maidens drifting into spinsterhood and of a society left limp and exhausted in the aftermath of a civil war about which he had no feeling and little interest. He is particularly hard on Boston Unitarianism which seems to have epitomized for him the hollowness and complacency of the genteel tradition. He associated it with congratulatory sermons that neither discouraged believers nor antagonized agnostics; with solemn ill-humored and unappetizing breakfasts—"the improved Unitarian substitute for morning prayers," and bland cultural uplift (Santayana, 1937, p. 27).

The personal note that slips into these animadversions and belies the pose of the bemused outsider he assumes in *Persons and Places* is even more noticeable in *The Last Puritan*. I read this memoir in the form of a novel as a sequel to the autobiography and a sustained soliloquy (as so much of his writing is) in which the voice of the author resounds not only in the pronouncements of the narrator but also in the conversation of the disparate characters, mouthpieces for his *obiter dicta*. Here the meaning of "genteel" is dramatized rather than spelled out. It is as if under the guise of fiction, he could touch on matters he was disinclined to probe in his memoirs and essays.

Oliver Alden, the luckless hero of *The Last Puritan*, bears a certain resemblance to the type Henry Adams labeled "*bourgeois-bostonien*" (Arvin, 1951, p. 239). He is prefigured in Santayana's *Character and Opinion in the United States* as one of those gaunt solitary American idealists who "either folds up his heart and withers in a corner" or flees to foreign shores "to save his soul—or perhaps not to save it" (Santayana 1967, p. 170), and who exhibit, in the words of William Dean Howells, "that anti-Puritan quality which was always vexing the heart of Puritanism" (Howells, 1964, p. vii). Oliver Alden is a throwback to his Calvinist forebears and lacks, like Captain Ahab, "the low enjoying power." Having convinced himself that it's wrong to be a Puritan, he's still unable to stifle his "agonized conscience." Neither can he accommodate himself to the "shams and mummeries" of the genteel tradition (Santayana, 1937, pp. 6–7). Santayana admires Oliver's integrity and blames him only for not adhering "to his own standard" (McCormick, 1986, p. 329) and not breaking through to "live victoriously in the spirit" (Singer, 1956, p. 251). There's a good deal of Santayana in Oliver, but as he wrote to a friend, the novel "gives the *emotions* of my experience and not my thoughts and experiences themselves" (McCormick, 1986, p. 330). The author was far readier to compromise "with the mixed loose world" (Singer, 1956, p. 252) than his inflexible protagonist.

Oliver's father, Peter Alden, is more a Santayanan than his son. A rootless traveler—urbane, skeptical, ironic—he fancies handsome young men, good food, agreeable travel, and is instinctively the gentleman for all his unconventional habits and ideas. Peter's marriage to Oliver's mother seems out of character despite the labored authorial explanation, but the settlement he makes with Harriet Bumstead, the genteel tradition incarnate, is analogous to Santayana's strategy vis-a-vis America. Peter restores the Bumstead house to its former stateliness and gives over the arrangement of its rooms to his wife while insisting that one upstairs room—a "Chinese room," he calls it, symbolic of his world elsewhere—be reserved for himself. Peter Alden soliloquizes:

In walking up and down these dignified stairs, we shall have time to recompose ourselves for the change of atmosphere, in passing from solitude to society, or *vice versa;* I don't mean from sincerity to pretence, but from the illusions with which each probably cheats himself, to the deceptions with which he probably doesn't deceive other people. Let us endeavour to preserve our genteel traditions for one generation more. If I have a son, I should like him to start from there. God knows where he will end. (Santayana, 1937, pg. 63)

As long as he lived in the United States, Santayana also lived on two floors, so to speak, with his "Chinese room" to retreat to. Like Peter Alden, he had been "thoroughly initiated in his youth into a particular native circle," had found it "too narrow and old-fashioned" to endure, and "in slipping out of it, he had also missed the general movement of national events and national sentiment" (Santayana, 1937, p. 113). Even so, he took pleasure in the company of an "inner circle" whose members retained something of the social flavor of the old merchant patriciate. He wasn't really of it, as Henry Adams was, or William and Henry James, or Oliver Wendell Holmes, Barrett Wendell, and John Jay Chapman, but he felt a kinship with Europeanized Boston cosmopolites, however "genteel" their culture, and enjoyed their cultivated talk and good dinners.

He felt much closer to the scions of these old families, especially the gifted minority among his Harvard classmates and students, and brooded over their wasted lives. Underdeveloped and dissatisfied, gasping for breath in the thin New England air, they lacked the power of mind to dominate their circumstances. He differentiated himself from this traditionless remnant (he could fall back, he claimed, on Old World resources unavailable to them in spite of their frequent sojourns abroad), yet they all vibrated to the same aesthetic string. Santayana succeeded where they failed, because he was driven by practical necessity and more skilled in the arts of survival. He was also tougher and smarter.

Martin Green in his book, *The Problem of Boston,* has analyzed the tastes and temperaments of the aesthete-exiles with particular attention to what Santayana, Bernard Berenson, Henry James, and Henry Adams had in common: an aesthetic idealism, a marked feminine component, a preference for the society of brilliant and mutually-enriching "chosen spirits," a fascination with Roman Catholicism, and a fondness for the manners and style of the English upper class (Green, 1966, pp. 142–63). Santayana was never more Bostonian than when playing the anti-Bostonian—ironic, humorous, gentlemanly, temperate, self-contained—observing the proprieties of dress, distrustful of the French character. The Boston aesthetes, Santayana included, were men of the world and tolerated the forbidden if it were presented elegantly and without grossness, but in shying away from the experimental, the confessional, the outré, they were no less genteel than their literary contemporaries.

Consider Santayana's life-long debate over Walt Whitman—one might almost say *with* Walt Whitman. In "Walt Whitman: a Dialogue" written in

1890, he plays the double role of defender and prosecutor. Van Tender, the tender-minded poet, hails Whitman as "the voice of nature crying in the wilderness," the celebrator of "the beauty of common things." His tough-minded friend, McStout, comes down hard on the vague and indecent pantheist, the "fashionable mountebank" (Ballowe, 1967, pp. 97–104). A decade later, Santayana grants Whitman "a wonderful gift of graphic characterisation and an occasional rare grandeur of diction" but sees him as an inspired tramp and poetic demagogue wallowing "in the stream of his own sensibility" (Singer, 1956, p. 157). He appears to have grown more critical of Whitman as he aged, if Peter Alden speaks for the author in *The Last Puritan.* Alden calls Whitman a "speechifying" rhetorician "as superficial as Rousseau," not a true poet. "He pretends" (Alden continues) "to turn—for it is largely affectation—only from the more refined devices of mankind to a ruder and more stupid existence. He is like Marie Antoinette playing the shepherdess" (Santayana, 1937, pp. 180–1). By disregarding the genteel tradition, he concedes, Whitman performed a valuable service, but because he was lazy and self-indulgent and undiscriminating, and because he "renounced old forms without achieving a new one" (Ballowe, 1967, p. 149), he laid no foundation for its amendment.

So, Santayana pigeon-holed the patron saint of the bohemians. And they, having appropriated the "reverberant name" (as Van Wyck Brooks referred to the "genteel tradition") conducted a crusade against it and its alleged priests, unaware that they were attacking some of Santayana's cherished values—order, discipline, integration—and encouraging in themselves and others what was for him a sloppy subjectivism. Initially he had confined the word "genteel" to a philosophical tradition. The social and literary iconoclasts of the teens and twenties stretched its meaning to cover the whole of American milk-and-water Anglo-Saxon culture and its (until roughly 1910) influential missionaries. Santayana was no democrat. He accepted class distinctions as a matter of course, along with the social prejudices and preferences of the genteel bookmen. He didn't anticipate an American renaissance. It would have seemed to him an oxymoron.

The radicals did. What is more, they advocated a melting-pot culture which to Santayana was no culture at all. Van Wyck Brooks's little book, *America's Coming-of-Age,* published a few years after Santayana left the United States for good, is an expression of this cultural nationalism. Brooks is the link between Santayana and the unharnessed apostles of the New who came of age during the presidency of Woodrow Wilson. In his Harvard years (1904–7) Brooks had belonged to the company of college aesthetes, some of them Santayana's friends and protegés, and had shared (in the words of his biographer) their "weary languor and mild *fin-de-siècle* pessimism" (Hoopes, 1977, p. 47). Brooks's *The Wine of the Puritans* (1908), written in the form of a dialogue, was published one year after his graduation and three years before Santayana's "The Genteel Tradition in American Philosophy." Its title and theme are embodied in the remark of one of the speakers: "You put the old wine in new bottles . . . and when the explosion results, one may say the aroma, or the ideal, turns into transcendentalism, and the wine, or the real, becomes commercialism. In any case, one doesn't preserve a great deal of well-tempered wine" (Sprague, 1968, p. 6). Brooks's metaphor of a transported culture and of a country deprived of a cultural childhood is echoed in Santayana's observation: "The country was new, but the race was tried, chastened, and full of solemn memories. It was an old wine in new bottles" (Hoopes, 1977, p. 62).

Eventually Brooks discovered treasures in America's "usable past," enthusiastically espoused a cultural nationalism, and grew testy with expatriots like Eliot and Pound. Santayana never changed his mind about a country he was delighted to leave and about which he came to know less and less. When he quit the United States in 1913, the genteel tradition was virtually defunct, doomed, he believed, by an unlovely modernist counter-culture—itself the product of a triumphant industrialism. Like Matthew Arnold, G. Lowes Dickinson, and H.G. Wells—but perhaps with fewer misgivings—he beheld America as a promise or threat of what was to come. He took a lot of America with him when he left, especially the genteel New England he had anatomized and laughed at and half despised. For this New England he retained the kind of respect and a covert affection one has for a persistent and familiar enemy.

Works Cited

Arvin, Newton, ed. *The Selected Letters of Henry Adams* (New York: Farrar, Straus and Young, 1951).

Ballowe, James, ed. *George Santayana's America: Essays on Literature and Culture* (Urbana, Ill.: University of Illinois Press, 1967).

Collini, Stefan. "Speaking from Somewhere," *The Times Literary Supplement*, April 15–21, 1988, p. 427.

Cory, Daniel. *Santayana: The Later Years. A Portrait with Letters* (New York: G. Braziller, 1963).

Green, Martin. *The Problem of Boston: Some Readings in Cultural History* (London: Longmans, Green & Co., 1966).

Hoopes, James. *Van Wyck Brooks: In Search of American Culture* (Amherst, Mass.: University of Massachusetts Press, 1977).

Howells, W.D. *The Landlord at Lion's Head* (New York: The New American Library, 1964).

Howgate, G.W. *George Santayana* (Philadelphia: University of Pennsylvania Press, 1938).

Lerner, Max, ed. *The Portable Veblen* (New York: Viking Press, 1970)

McCormick, John. *George Santayana: A Biography* (New York: Alfred J. Knopf, 1987).

Santayana, George. *Winds of Doctrine: Studies in Contemporary Opinion* (New York: Charles Scribner's Sons, 1913).

———. *The Genteel Tradition at Bay* (New York: Charles Scribner's Sons, 1931).

———. *The Last Puritan* (New York: Charles Scribner's Sons, 1937).

———. *Character and Opinion in the United States* (New York: W. W. Norton, Inc., 1967).

————. *Persons and Places: Fragments of Autobiography* (Cambridge, Mass.: MIT Press, 1986).

Singer, Irving, ed. *Essays in Literary Criticism of George Santayana* (New York: Charles Scribner's Sons, 1956).

Sprague, Claire, ed. *Van Wyck Brooks, The Early Years: A Selection from his Works, 1908–1921* (New York: Harper Torchbooks, 1968).

Tomsich, John. *A Genteel Endeavor: American Culture and Politics in the Gilded Age* (Stanford, California: Stanford University Press. 1971).

Whitman, Walt. *Complete Poetry and Collected Prose* (New York: The Library of America, 1982).

The Significance of the Subtitle
of Santayana's Novel
The Last Puritan:
A Memoir in the Form of a Novel

WILLIAM G. HOLZBERGER

Santayana's only novel, *The Last Puritan,* was first published in 1935 when the author was almost seventy-two years old,[1] but he had started it forty-six years earlier in 1889 when he was a young man of twenty-five and a philosophy instructor at Harvard. Santayana worked on the novel for six years until 1895 when he apparently felt stymied and could not devise an effective plot. The first World War gave him a means for developing the plot; his interest in the project revived, and he resumed work on it in 1920. He continued to work on the book intermittently during the twenties and then regularly in the late twenties and early thirties to its completion on 31 August, 1934.[2] The original idea for the novel was a story of college life centered on two young men, "a good boy and a bad boy," who are both members of a club like the Delta Phi at Harvard (familiarly known to its members in the 1890s as the "Gashouse" and later officially renamed the Delphic Club) of which Santayana was an honorary member. The two young men were to have an interesting and salutary effect on one another.[3] None of the handwritten manuscript materials for *The Last Puritan* has survived, and we do not know how far Santayana progressed with this original conception of the work.[4] We do know, however, that as the author's experience of persons and knowledge of the world increased through travel, the original conception of the novel changed. Numerous characters and events were added and the central characters of the two young men, who became Oliver Alden and Mario Van de Weyer, were deepened and developed. Several other principal characters were included as well as a number of interesting minor ones. In fact two of the added major characters—Oliver's father, Peter Alden, and the captain of Peter's yacht, Jim Darnley—may well have eclipsed Mario in importance. All of the characters and events of the eventual novel, though, had their origins in Santayana's experience of persons and places, and, like many first

This essay was written specifically for this volume and is published here for the first time by permission of the author.

novels, *The Last Puritan* is highly autobiographical. This autobiographical quality is made evident by the subtitle: "A Memoir in the Form of a Novel."

Although much of the personal experience that Santayana called upon to create *The Last Puritan* occurred during the forty-five years of its composition, the circumstances and events of Santayana's early childhood and adolescence also contributed greatly to the work, and the novel is fundamentally a story of youth. (The life of the protagonist, Oliver, ends when he is only twenty-eight.)[5] It is a novel of youth in that it traces the infancy, early childhood, adolescence, and young manhood of Oliver and the adolescence and young manhood of Oliver's father, Peter Alden (as well as Peter's later life), and of Oliver's cousin Mario; however, it is also a story of youth because much if not most of the experience that Santayana draws upon in creating the novel derives from his own younger days. Thus, the motto from the French philosopher Alain is particularly apt: "On dit bien que l'expérience parle par la bouche des hommes d'âges; mais la meilleure expérience qu'ils puissent nous apportez est celle de leur jeunesse sauvée."[6] The experience preserved from Santayana's youth that he brings to us through the novel includes that of his childhood spent in unusual and often difficult circumstances (including his separation from his mother from the age of five through almost nine, the permanent separation of his mother and father, and his own transferal at an early age from his native Spain to the linguistically and culturally foreign United States), his school days in Boston, his undergraduate years at Harvard, and his two years of graduate study in Germany. Also significant are his almost twenty-three years as a teacher and observer of youth at Harvard. As Santayana himself put it, "If you have actually read *The Last Puritan* you must have perceived that I had put everything I know into it. . . ."[7] And in a letter to Otto Kyllmann of Constable Publishers in London, he wrote: "The book is really 'a Memoir in the Form of a Novel,' and perhaps it might have been wiser not to publish it until everything and everybody concerned, including the author, had ceased to exist. Without being an autobiography, the narrative is rooted at every point in my personal recollections. . . ."[8]

A few of the characters of *The Last Puritan* are portraits of individual real-life persons, but most of them are composites of several persons whom Santayana had heard about, met, or known well. To attempt to trace all of the major characters and events of the novel would require a book-length study. We must confine ourselves in this essay to only one principal character and to the experiences of Santayana's life that led to his creation. By doing so, we can observe quite clearly from this single example how Santayana used the persons, events, and various experiences of his own life to constitute the cast and develop the plot of his remarkable novel. The reader of *The Last Puritan* familiar with Santayana's life knows that there is something of the author in each of his major characters and even in some of the minor ones. Surely there is much of him in his protagonist, Oliver Alden. But the character who is in many essential ways (though obviously not in all) very much like Santayana himself is Peter Alden. Peter—a non-practicing medical doctor, absentee husband and father, millionaire yachtsman, and (though he denies it [143] a philosopher—is the chief spokesman in the novel for Santayana's own views and experience of the world.

Peter's early life is in many ways similar to Santayana's. The unprepossessing Boston house owned by his brother Nathaniel is Santayana's mother's house at number 302 Beacon Street: one of "a pair of old brick houses, flatter and plainer than the rest. They were evidently twins and had been identical at birth, but life had developed them in different directions" (15).[9] Peter lived in the Beacon Street house with his half-brother Nathaniel and cousin, Hannah Bancroft, the housekeeper, as did Santayana live in the number 302 Beacon Street house as a boy with his mother, his half-brother Robert Sturgis, and Robert's sisters, Susana and Josephine. Robert Sturgis was by no means a Nathaniel Alden: he evidently had neither Nathaniel's puritanical prudishness nor his definiteness of character. But from what Santayana says about his half brother in his autobiography, there was scarcely more sympathy, understanding, or affection between Santayana and Robert than between Peter and Nathaniel.

There was a difference of one child between Santayana's family and the Alden family: Nathaniel's widowed (and afterward murdered) father had married the widowed mother of Caroline, when Nathaniel and Caroline were both thirteen, making Caroline Nathaniel's stepsister; the union of Nathaniel's father and Caroline's mother produced Peter, who was therefore half brother to both Nathaniel and Caroline (43–44). Santayana's father lived only a few months with the family in Beacon Street, after bringing eight-year-old George from Avila in 1872, before returning to Spain; Nathaniel's and Peter's father, a merciless slum landlord, was murdered by an outraged tenant (though we do not know exactly when this occurred). We discover from Santayana's letters that the character of Nathaniel Alden is "a recognisable caricature of two real persons, long since dead, & both old bachelors."[10] The two old bachelors, we learn, were George Parkman and Thomas Wigglesworth. In a letter to his nephew, George Sturgis, Santayana refers to "my 'Nathaniel' (George Parkman),"[11] and in a letter to George Sturgis's former wife Rosamond, Santayana refers to "old murdered Parkman" (the real-life counterpart of Nathaniel's father) and adds: "And I gave George Parkman some traits of Mr. Thomas Wigglesworth, and a younger brother, Peter, to peter out."[12] In this letter to Rosamond, Santayana refers to "Amory's book on The Proper Bostonians" in which the murder of old Parkman figures in the story.[13]

The presence of Caroline (Mrs. Erasmus Van de Weyer when we first meet her [45] in the Alden household has many parallels to the presence and influence of Santayana's half-sister Susana in the Santayana household. Caroline and Nathaniel were both thirteen when their parents married (44, 47), and Caroline expresses great affection for Peter and speaks of playing with him on her lap when he was a baby. There were, therefore, perhaps fourteen or fifteen years between Caroline and Peter in age. This is very similar to the relationship between Santayana and his beloved elder half-sister Susana, who was twelve years older than he.[14] Susana, though doubtless not so ebullient as the vivacious Caroline, was a young woman of spirit and character and devoted to her young half brother. It was she who took over his education when he arrived in America and introduced him to religion and architecture, two of Santayana's greatest interests. It was Susana, the twelve-year-old godmother who named him George after her own dead father, George Sturgis, and who gave the boy the attention, care, love, and nurture that his mother never did. Similarly, the mature Peter Alden, contemplating marriage to Harriet Bumstead, reflects that he has "never really known a mother, never enjoyed the voluminous soft protection of a wise woman" (64). Caroline tells Nathaniel that her mother (and Peter's) "was so beautiful that she had to neglect us: all very beautiful women are slaves to their looking-glass" (47). Santayana's mother was not beautiful, but she evidently invested little emotion in her children (except perhaps for Pepín, her first-born, who died at the age of two and a half) (*P&P*, 41–42). The relationship between Santayana and Susana was strong and very deep, and the humorous banter of Caroline when she tells the prudish and astonished Nathaniel that they had been in love with one another as children (47) has perhaps a deeper significance if we momentarily merge Nathaniel and Peter and identify them with the young Santayana who in old age said that his sister Susana was "certainly the most important influence in my life, psychologically my mother, and one might almost say, my wife. Not that an incestuous idea ever entered my mind or hers; but Freud might have discovered things unsuspected by ourselves."[15]

Peter, like Santayana, attends the Boston Public Latin School until his brother Nathaniel decides that the place has too much degenerated since he had been a pupil there because of the continual influx of persons of "alien" origin (36). (This xenophobia in the form of resentment against persons not of English ancestry is something of which the young Santayana must himself have been painfully aware; it no doubt contributed significantly to the "alienation" that he felt and described in *Persons and Places* and elsewhere.) The sensible physician in the novel, Dr. Hand—called in together with the lawyer, Mr. Head, and the Rev. Mr. Hart to advise Nathaniel on the problem of dealing with young Peter who shamelessly associates with young men and women of the working class in Boston—expresses one of Santayana's fundamental convictions when he says that "most of us would prefer circles we can't frequent, and must frequent circles we never chose"(35). Though there is no real-life parallel in Santayana's life to the rustication of Peter by his brother to the Rev. Mark Lowe's camp for "backward lads" in Wyoming, the fresh and wholesome air of such a place must have been something for which Santayana often longed in his Boston days. The simple wisdom of one of the Rev. Mr. Lowe's five-minute sermons to the boys before supper seems more characteristic of the naturalistic philosopher than the Episcopalian minister: "Don't be ashamed . . . of being backward lads. We are all backward lads in God's sight. Be good fools, and brave enough to be humble, and you will be wiser than most learned men. Put away human respect. Man is only one of God's many creatures; here in the wilds you see how little the pride or the welfare of man counts in the universe"(41). Peter's realization, acquired from cowboys visiting the Rev. Mr. Lowe's camp and from two neighboring Englishmen ranchers, that Beacon Street was not universally known and impressive is a great consolation, and like the young Santayana he begins to dream of foreign travel (43). Upon young Peter's return from Wyoming, Nathaniel and his stepsister Caroline Van de Weyer arrange for him to live with Caroline and her family in New York City and to attend Exeter school. Though Santayana never attended a private boarding school like Exeter, there is at least an imaginary parallel because Santayana observes in *Persons and Places* that, if his mother could have afforded the cost of sending him to a private school, she would have done so. We also get the impression from the autobiography that Santayana himself might have preferred the social exclusivity and more intensive instruction and concentration on study of a prestigious private school. He seems to have been content at Boston Latin, but he emphasizes that the school was a place for the

> ambitious poor—Irish boys wishing to be priests, lawyers, or doctors, Jews wishing to be professors, and native Americans, like Warren and Smith [school chums of Santayana's], whose families were in reduced circumstances. It was my mother's straitened means that caused her to send me there, instead of to some private school; and I should perhaps have seemed an entirely different person and had an entirely different life, if this genteel poverty, and this education in a public day school, among the children of humble parents, had not fortified in me the spirit of detachment and isolation. Not that the most luxurious American surroundings—such as I afterward had some contact with—would ever have made an American of me. America in those days made an exile and a foreigner of every native, who had at all a temperament like mine. (*P&P* 174)

Peter Alden had a temperament like Santayana's and was made "an exile and a foreigner" by the America of his time.

Peter spends two years at Exeter and Harvard before a college prank turned tragedy forces him to leave college and the country. The brief description of those two years given in the novel shows a number of parallels with Santayana's Boston Latin School and Harvard undergraduate years. "He didn't study very much; a little, with his intelligence, was more than sufficient for the tasks assigned; but he acted in the school theatricals, wrote for the school and college paper, became the wit of his class, and even played a little base-ball" (49). Except for the baseball—Santayana was hopeless at sports—this could well be a description of Santayana's last year or two at the

Latin School and his four years at Harvard College. Santayana hated having to peg away at subjects like Greek and mathematics that required diligent application and rote memorization of inflections and formulas. In his freshman year, he failed a half-course in algebra that he was obliged to repeat later, and he also did poorly in his Greek studies with Louis Dyer (*P&P*, 229, 231). His remarkable intelligence and knowledge of the great philosophers, however, enabled him to graduate *summa cum laude* from Harvard in 1886. Like Peter, Santayana also took part in college theatricals, playing the role of a girl in a Hasty Pudding production. While at the Latin School, he had published several poems in the school paper, the *Latin School Register,* and beginning in his freshman year, he drew cartoons for the *Harvard Lampoon.*

Peter Alden's Harvard undergraduate career is cut short after only a year by his unfortunate purloining of the College Bible which results in the death of a watchman. While pledging a secret society, Peter is required to steal the Bible from the College Chapel. As he is taking the heavy tome from its resting place on the high pulpit, he is interrupted by the night watchman. Instinctively, "like a staunch Israelite, he brought down the whole weight of the Holy Scriptures upon his adversary's head" (50). The watchman falls senseless from the blow, and Peter escapes through the window by which he has entered. The following day the watchman's dead body is discovered at the foot of the pulpit. Peter's half-sister Caroline's husband, the New York banker Mr. Erasmus Van de Weyer—himself a Harvard man who had belonged to the same secret society—comes to Boston "to advise Peter, and to exert a friendly influence in the inner circles" (50). It turns out that the presiding magistrate had also been a member of the society, and the upshot of the affair is that the night watchman is declared to have met death by misadventure. It is decided, rather casuistically, that the blow from the soft flat Bible could not have killed him, but rather he had been killed in his fall against the "sharp edge of the brass railings, which had dislocated the vertebral column at the neck" (50). No charges are brought against Peter, but "it was thought best that Peter should temporarily disappear, not only from the college but from the country" (50–51).

We learn from Santayana's letter of 23 December 1935 to his old friend and college classmate, Boylston Adams Beal,[16] that the debacle of the purloining of the Bible from the Harvard College Chapel evidently had its real-life origins in the experience of a member of the prominent Forbes family. W. Cameron "Cam" Forbes, grandson of Ralph Waldo Emerson, Harvard student, athlete, and sometime coach of the football team, had been a particular friend of Santayana's in the 1890s and had contributed several essential characteristics to Oliver Alden, the protagonist of the novel.[17] His father, William Forbes, was, in some fundamental ways, the principal model for Peter Alden. In the letter to Beal,[18] Santayana writes: "I hope the Forbes's won't mind the story about the college Bible. I tell it as it reached me, or as it shaped itself years after in my own mind. Perhaps it is transformed enough not to be recognisable, and in any case it is such ancient history now that I suppose it may be printed without offence." There is nothing in the letter to Beal (or elsewhere to my knowledge) to indicate that William Forbes was himself involved in the actual attempt on the College Bible. It may have been he or perhaps another member of the Forbes family.

The Harvard secret society that Santayana had in mind in composing this episode of the novel was the so-called "Dickey" or "Deeks," though in the book he does not mention the organization by name. In a letter of 20 February 1950 to Hamilton Vaughan Bail, Santayana writes that he had heard from the historian Samuel Eliot Morison regarding the episode of the purloining of the College Bible: "Mr. Morrison [*sic*] has informed me that the story of the Dickey initiation involving purloining the College Bible is not accurate. That it was not the Dickey but an earlier Med Fac that was concerned and that the watchman was not killed."[19] This is curious because in his *Three Centuries of Harvard 1636–1936,* Morison refers to "the D.K.E., 'Dickey' or 'Deeks' (the 'secret society' of Santayana's novel 'to which everybody of consequence belonged')."[20] Though Santayana does not mention the secret society by name in the novel, Morison, presumably upon reading the book, identified it as the D.K.E., "Dickey" or "Deeks," but then wrote to Santayana that in fact Santayana was mistaken and that the society that actually had made the attempt on the College Bible was not that one but rather the "Med. Fac.," a student organization notorious for the perpetration of numerous hoaxes. According to Morison, the "Med. Fac." was active during the 1880s and 1890s, but was finally suppressed in 1905 by Harvard authorities.[21] In an "O.K." Club[22] poem dated 5 June 1892, Santayana refers to both of these secret societies. The poem consists of a conversation that the poet ostensibly has had recently with the statue of John Harvard, the young Puritan divine after whom the college was named, and who is depressed and disgusted by current conditions. In stanza 9 the poet tells the statue:

> "To muckers and brass bands I make objection,
> I never lit a bonfire in the yard;
> The Med. Fac. never dreamed of my election
> Nor sought I to place anything, I swear,
> At your unveiling underneath your chair."[23]

In stanza 10 he says,

> "It wasn't I who went by night aprowling
> And did most mischievously paint you red,
> I have aversion to the Dickey's howlings
> Tho' Prexy hasn't; and when all is said,
> If the much mud and the conceit confounded
> Of Harvard grieve you, why then did you found it?"[24]

In response to Morison's rather confusing communication, Santayana wrote in the letter to Bail: "That, of course, does not change the dramatic propriety of my inaccurate version to explain the character and subsequent life of Peter Alden, in whom I was as much interested, and perhaps more successful, than in the case of my two young heroes. There were in my time several Harvard men living more or less in Europe who could supply models for that sort of helpless character. Neither Oliver nor Mario were 'Harvard men,' so that their respective passages through the place should be regarded as intrusions by outsiders."[25]

After a year at Harvard, Peter, like Santayana, felt a need to leave Cambridge. Peter sought to escape the potentially terrible consequences of the attempt to steal the College Bible. (Santayana yearned to visit his father, whom he had not seen for eleven years.) Peter makes his hasty departure from the country by sailing to Europe in the *Samaria,* the modest steamer in which Santayana, perhaps a decade later, came to America in 1872. He travels the world, but, for a rich young man, he does so rather frugally, and—as Santayana himself always did—spends only a fraction of his income. This practice enables Peter to grow ever richer and richer, as it enabled Santayana to amass enough money to retire from his professorship at Harvard at the age of forty-eight in 1912 and remove permanently to Europe, and eventually, at the time of his death in 1952, to bequeath a substantial fortune to his Sturgis relations.[26]

Peter's travels take him to the far east, and in China he charters a junk "in which to sail up those great rivers far into the interior, while living all the time, so to speak, in his own house" (52). Santayana was never in the far east, but as a young man, early in the summer of 1888, he did have the experience of spending several weeks sailing the inland rivers of France with his friend the young Earl Russell in the latter's small steam yacht, the *Royal.*[27] John McCormick, in his recent biography of Santayana,[28] makes an interesting connection between Peter Alden and Santayana's Harvard friend, Andrew Green. Green, who had been one of Santayana's students, evidently cared as little for business and the world of affairs as Peter or Santayana did, for *Persons and Places* mentions that Green "went into business in Chicago expressly to make money quickly and to escape from business, exactly as I went into teaching, but more successfully; for in a few years he had made his little pile, went alone to China, and hired a junk to live in, while he sailed leisurely up and down the great rivers and explored the wonders of that country" (*P&P,* 385). In the novel Peter "hated worse than poverty all the constraints to which your conventional rich man was subjected: pompous business, pompous society, pompous speeches, and a gold watch-chain heavily festooning a big paunch." Peter's impulse was to ramble, to observe, to follow up, not too hopefully, little casual adventures and acquaintances" (51). The free-spirited Green eventually settled in the West Indies where he married a black woman and became a fruit grower (*P&P,* 386). Peter, after leaving China, travels to

Japan where, like Lieutenant Pinkerton in *Madama Butterfly,*[29] he is "temporarily married" (52) to a Japanese woman. Also like Pinkerton, Peter eventually leaves his Japanese wife (though Santayana assures us that she does not commit suicide, but rather she and her grateful family shower blessings upon the generous Peter) and returns to his own country and makes a (disastrous) permanent marriage to an American woman (Oliver's mother, Harriet Bumstead of Great Falls, Connecticut). Green, however, remained married to his West-Indian wife. Both couples had a single child, a boy. McCormick also points to another source for the character of Peter Alden: "Sturgis Bigelow, like Peter, was a wealthy man who qualified as a doctor and spent years of wandering the world."[30]

The primary inspiration for the character of Peter, however, was supplied by the personality and life of Mr. William Forbes. In a letter of 21 December 1922 to his old Harvard friend, architect Robert Burnside Potter, in which he asks if Potter can provide a source of information about yachts so that he can authentically describe Peter's luxurious *Black Swan,* Santayana mentions "the day that I spent on Mr. William Forbes's yacht in Buzzard's Bay [off Cape Cod, where Oliver sails for a day on his father's yacht]—an occasion which is the more pertinent as Cam Forbes and his father are among the models of my personages."[31] In *Persons and Places,* Santayana describes William Forbes as "a rich father, a sportsman, and a man in whose life there was something vague and ineffectual" (347).[32] In the letter to Beal quoted above, Santayana says that "a certain element in his relation to his father" was significant in Cam Forbes's contribution to the character of Oliver Alden.[33] During the 1890s, there were evidently a good many rich Americans of Peter Alden's type. To his nephew's wife, Rosamond Sturgis, Santayana writes in 1936: "I don't wonder that you feel some sympathy with Peter Alden: he is an amiable type of failure; there were many such in my day;"[34] and to the poet Sadakichi Hartmann he writes: "His [Oliver's] father is the sort of person that was likely to be one's friend, or at least a familiar figure in one's world. . . ."[35]

Peter Alden's travels about the world, however, were not merely those of the international sportsman or member of the yacht-racing set (a type and society that Peter in fact detested).[36] Rather, Peter studied the countries and societies in which he lived; he knew their history and he acquired knowledge of their languages. In China, he studied Chinese (52–53); in Arabia he learned Arabic and made a serious study of the Mohammedan religion (53). He also traveled in Greece. Peter's travels in the middle east and in Greece parallel Santayana's own travels in this region during his sabbatical year abroad in 1904–1905. In July 1904, Santayana sailed from New York to Plymouth, England. The following fall he set out from Paris on what he called his "first real travels" (*P&P,* 45). He visited Rome and Venice with his Harvard friend and classmate, Charles Loeser. After spending a few weeks at Naples in December 1904, he visited Pompeii; then he went on to Sicily, where at Syracuse he read the first proofs of *The Life of Reason*.[37] He returned from Sicily to Naples and sailed for Greece. In January 1905, Santayana was in Egypt where he traveled by boat up and down the Nile. (One of his fellow travelers in Egypt and in Arabia was the American painter John Singer Sargent [*P&P*, 450], who is referred to by Peter in the novel in a telegram he sends to Oliver inviting him to spend a year with him in Europe, as one of the "two most creditable living Americans[,] John Sargent and Henry James [,] both expatriates" [218].)[38] From Egypt Santayana went to Palestine, where he spent three weeks at Jerusalem. He visited Damascus and Baalbeck and then traveled from Beirut to Athens and through Greece. Greece in its modern form was very disappointing to Santayana, as it was to Peter, who in a letter home to Cousin Hannah Bancroft (who reads the letter aloud to Nathaniel Alden) expresses Santayana's own disappointment with the remains of the once glorious Hellas: "I am at Nauplia. Near by are the ruins of Tiryns and Mycenae; a castle overhangs the port where was the ancient acropolis, and round the point is Epidaurus, with a steep cockpit of an ancient theatre, between the mountains and the purple sea. How forlorn is all that greatness! How squalid what remains!" (55).[39] Santayana then sailed from Athens to Constantinople, concluding his *Wanderjahr* in Budapest and Vienna. Never again would he be able to travel extensively "for the sake of travelling" (*P&P*, 467). While still in the middle east in 1905, Santayana was notified by Harvard that he had been appointed the Hyde lecturer at the Sorbonne for 1905–1906. He was thus enabled to extend his holiday abroad by another year and spent the period lecturing at Paris and at the provincial universities. By the time of his return to Harvard in September 1906, he had been abroad for twenty-seven months.

As Santayana had ended his sabbatical-year travels in Vienna, so does Peter wind up there at the conclusion of his odyssey in the far and near east. Peter studies medicine in Vienna and Paris, but more specifically he studies the new science of psychiatry that was being pioneered by the Viennese school. There is an analogue here to Santayana's graduate study in Germany in 1886–1888. At Berlin, Santayana was studying philosophy, but the concentration there at that time was on the developing science of psychology, and there was a physiological bias in theory that Santayana found falsely scientific and oppressive.[40] Also, just as Santayana came home to America to complete his doctorate in philosophy at Harvard,[41] so did Peter return to Harvard to complete his medical degree. At the age of thirty-five, Peter receives his M.D. degree from his old Alma Mater (56).

Peter never practices medicine but uses (and abuses) his privileges as a doctor to dose his own ailments, real and imagined, and to prescribe drugs for himself to which he becomes addicted. We are told in the novel that without actually becoming a hypochondriac, Peter "aggravated his real weaknesses by continually dwelling on them" (56). Here there is some similarity to Santayana's father, Agustín Santayana (1814–1893), who was similarly preoccupied with his ailments.[42] There is also, from the description we get of Agustín in *Persons and Places,* a distinct similarity in personality between him and Peter Alden. The elder Santayana, a lawyer by training and a Spanish colonial official in the Philippine Islands, loved to travel and had done so extensively; he was a portrait painter of considerable ability,[43] and a man of scholarly bent who had translated "all the tragedies of Seneca into Castilian blank verse: a pure work of love, since he could expect no advancement, perhaps rather the opposite, from such an exhibition of capricious industry" (*P&P,* 5) Agustín Santayana, like Peter Alden, was also a man of wit with an ironic turn of mind. His marriage was as ill-founded and unsatisfactory as Peter's. Santayana said that he never understood why his parents had married one another, that there seemed no basis for such a union either in passion or reason: "It was so ill-advised a union that only passion would seem to justify it; yet passion was not the cause. I say so with assurance because there is not only the fact of their ages, nearly forty and nearly fifty respectively,[44] but there are my mother's verses, kept in secret and sent to my father twenty-five years later, when it was likely that the two would never meet again; and there are also certain expressions of my father's about love and marriage, which it would not be proper for me to repeat, but which show that my mother, a widow who had had five children, could not have been the object for him of an irresistible love" (*P&P,* 50).

While a paying guest-patient in the psychiatrist Dr. Bumstead's house at Great Falls, Connecticut, Peter conceives of the idea of marrying Dr. Bumstead's daughter Harriet. Though no longer in her first youth, Harriet is nevertheless a very handsome woman a few years younger than Peter. Peter knows that Harriet is priggish and provincial, but he rationalizes the decision to marry her by concluding that it is wiser to marry Harriet who is a lady and a known commodity than to risk perhaps one day making a worse marriage to his landlady or laundress or some other woman for whom he might feel sorry (61). Peter concludes that happiness is not to be found: "I have sought everywhere for the kind of life that might really please me: I haven't found it; it doesn't exist; and I might as well accept anything decent that presents itself" (61). His remark to himself, "I don't ask to be happy; I want to be at peace," reminds us of the words of La Vallière, whom Santayana quotes in *Persons and Places:* when asked if she were happy in the Carmelite convent to which she had retired, she responded: "Je ne suis par heureuse; je suis contente" (*P&P,* 428).

The marriage of Peter Alden and Harriet Bumstead is, of course, a failure, and by the time Oliver is a teenager the relationship of his parents has taken a form not uncommon among wealthy mis-matched couples: Peter lives away from home as much as possible. He sails about the world in his luxurious *Black Swan,* coming home only for holidays. There is neither affection nor sympathetic understanding between him and his wife, only rivalry for influence over the shaping of the personality and destiny of Oliver.

In this contest, Harriet's Puritanism is more zealous and ultimately victorious; even though eventually Oliver consciously repudiates the fundamental tenets of the puritanical philosophy by which he lives, he cannot live otherwise. In a letter to Bruno Lind written nine months before his death, Santayana acknowledges the similarity between his own parents' marriage and that of Oliver's parents:

> The relation between Peter and his wife was *emotionally* based on that between my father and mother, but *historically* the two cases are contraries. He had money in the novel; she had it in real life, what little there was of it. But my father, if he had been very rich and yet independent of the world . . . would have lived much as Peter did, and would have behaved towards me as Peter did to Oliver. But I was more like my father (and like Peter) than Oliver was like his: for he really was more like his mother, only genuine and not sham in his virtue. And my mother was not like his. She was silent and indifferent in minor matters, and stoical. But the absence of affection all round was the same in both mothers and in both husbands and both sons. You will do right if you see the shadow of myself and my family in the book, but must not assimilate the circumstances. It was perhaps exactly a reversal, in a dream, of the circumstances of my life, while preserving the characters, that produced the novel.[45]

In an earlier letter of 1936, Santayana wrote: "The relations between my father and mother were not unlike those of Peter Alden and his wife in my book, although the circumstances and the persons were entirely different." Santayana also observes in this same letter: "My parents were not young when they were married and more like grandparents to me in many ways."[46]

Santayana's mother and father were married in Madrid in 1862 or early in 1863 (Santayana was born in Madrid on December 16, 1863). Agustín was forty-seven or forty-eight years old at the time of this marriage (his first), and Josefina was probably thirty-six or thirty-seven (this was her second marriage: her first had been to George Sturgis, of Boston and Manila, who had died five years earlier at the age of forty, leaving her a widow with five children, two of whom—José [called "Pepín"] and Victor—had died in infancy before her second marriage). Peter Alden receives his medical degree from Harvard "at the belated age of thirty-five" (56), and some time afterward (we are not told how long afterward, but the description [56–57] of the events of Peter's life suggests the passage of a few years at least) consults a psychiatrist, Dr. Bumstead, in Great Falls, Connecticut about his mental condition.[47] Some time later (the "next spring", "in May" [59]), "Peter Alden returns and establishes himself in the [Bumstead] family" (59). Dr. Bumstead says, in the conversation with his daughter Harriet in which he suggests that his wealthy patient might make her a very suitable husband, that Peter is then "hardly forty" (60). In light of a letter by Santayana to Otto Kyllmann of 3 September 1935, it might appear that Dr. Bumstead has exaggerated Peter's age, because Santayana writes: "I know a great deal about these people that is not set down in the book," and he says that "Oliver's father was born in Boston (in 1855) but he [Oliver] himself in his mother's house in Connecticut, on October 1st 1890."[48] If Peter were born in 1855 and his son Oliver in 1890, then Peter would have been thirty-five at Oliver's birth. But later the English physician, Mr. Morrison-Ely, who cares for Peter when he falls ill at Eton—shortly before Peter kills himself—might also appear to overestimate Peter's age when he says: "Curious how some men live to be sixty without ever having learned to exhale" (305).[49] For Dr. Bumstead and Mr. Morrison-Ely to exaggerate Peter's age by several years would not in itself be problematical because Peter was never in very good health or very vigorous and could, at both times, have looked several years older than he was. Nevertheless, Dr. Bumstead's remark is significant because, as Peter's physician, he would have ascertained Peter's precise age, and it would be somewhat unusual for him to refer to a man of thirty-five as "hardly forty."[50] In fact, Santayana's statement of Peter's year of birth as 1855 in the letter to Kyllmann is either a slip of the pen or a miscalculation. Perhaps he intended to write 1845, which would make the chronology come out about right. If Peter were born in 1845 he would be about sixty-three at the time of his death in 1908. But if Peter were born in 1855 and Oliver on 1 October, 1890, then Peter would have to be thirty-four or thirty-five when Oliver was born. If Peter receives the M.D. from Harvard at thirty-five and there is, as there appears to be, an interlude of some time between his receiving the degree and consulting Dr. Bumstead, then for Oliver to be born legitimate when Peter was thirty-five would necessitate Peter receiving his doctorate and meeting and marrying Harriet all in the same year. In fact, he would have had to woo, win, marry, and impregnate Harriet in the month of January 1890 for Oliver to be born on October first of that year. This is neither feasible nor possible in light of the above-quoted description that Peter returned and established himself in the Bumstead family "in May" (59). Thus, the 1855 birthdate for Peter must be an error.

About the same time that Harriet's father is considering Peter as an eligible husband for his daughter, Peter muses on the possibility of marrying Harriet, observing that he is only a few years older than she (64). This would make Harriet perhaps about thirty-five at the time of the marriage (her father refers to her as a "good-looking, strapping young woman" [60]), about the same age as Santayana's mother when she married Agustín.[51] Thus, Oliver's parents are considerably older than most persons when they first marry and are close to the ages of Santayana's parents at the time of their marriage (Agustín, forty-seven or forty-eight; Peter, between forty and forty-five; Josefina, thirty-six or thirty-seven; and Harriet, about thirty-five). There is also a similarity between Oliver's relation to his parents and the young Santayana's to his. Mrs. Alden is a cold, remote, opinionated, and self-centered woman. Oliver laughs when his cousin Mario asks him whether or not he had had a wet nurse or were given a bottle as a baby because after his birth he had been turned over to the scientific nurse, Miss Terkettle, who certainly was not prepared to suckle him (408), and his mother would have considered breast-feeding a subhuman activity. Indeed, Mrs. Alden regards all forms of close physical contact between mother and child as unhygenic and abhorrent, and Oliver grows up never having known the comfort of maternal affection. Santayana's experience in his relation to his mother was evidently similar to Oliver's in that Josefina was a cold, selfish, and egotistical woman who thought all of her children rather poor stuff and showed them little affection.[52] Though Peter Alden and Agustín Santayana were both warm-hearted men, their sons were separated from them for long periods. Santayana's father returned permanently to Spain after bringing his son to Josefina's house in Boston in 1872,[53] and Santayana was nineteen years old when he again saw his father in 1883. Thus, during their childhood, both Santayana and his character Oliver Alden saw little of their fathers for long periods at a time; and, given the remoteness and coldness of their mothers, both can be conceived as regarding their parents as Santayana says he regarded his, as more like grandparents.

Yet another connection between Santayana's father, Agustín, and Oliver's father, Peter, is that they were both suicides.[54] Peter is suffering from a heart condition and recuperating from a sort of attack. He and Oliver are occupying rooms belonging to an absent master at Eton, and Peter is being looked after in his convalescence by the capable nurse, "Little Mildred." He is comfortable in the rented rooms, which are furnished with a choice supply of rare books, and enjoys the company and conversation of his exceptional son. Suddenly, word is received that Mrs. Alden is on her way; she has learned from Oliver's letter that Peter has been seriously ill and plans to come and superintend matters herself lest Oliver be lured by sympathy into too close an attachment to his father and to a desertion of his plans and responsibilities in America. Peter, appalled at the prospect of his wife's imminent arrival—but not strong enough to flee in the opposite direction—and depressed over the inevitable defection of his son to his mother's puritanism and Oliver's own austere and puritanical personality, decides to make his own quietus with an overdose of drugs that he has kept on hand for the purpose when the time should be ripe. He dies five days before the dreaded arrival of his wife. Oliver, we are told (320), is "eighteen" at the time of Peter's death. If Oliver were indeed born in 1890 and is almost eighteen when his father dies, the year of Peter's death would be 1908.[55] If Peter were born in 1855, as Santayana says in the letter to Kyllmann, he would have to be only fifty-three years old when he dies. This would be strangely young for a man who at this time is referred to as an "old gentleman" (310) and, as we have seen above, this date for Peter's birth is not possible.[56]

Finally, Peter's last visit to London (presumably in 1908) reminds us of Santayana's reminisinces in *Persons and Places* about his own experiences in the great town. Like Santayana himself, Peter feels at home in London. "Here was the government of gentlemen by gentlemen and for gentlemen. Here the gentleman in Peter felt strangely at home"(243). Peter, like Santayana, loves the distinguished streets and park of St. James. He recalls the London of twenty years earlier, the 1880s, when he had had comfortable bachelor rooms in Jermyn Street in an establishment that now had ceased to exist (245). The Tory London of Peter's prime is that of Santayana's as well. For more than twenty-five years, Santayana was faithful to Miss Bennett's establishment at No. 87 Jermyn Street, St. James. Upon arriving one year, he discovered that his genial landlady had died and that her widowed younger sister had remarried and turned the place into a private residence. Henceforth, Santayana had to stay in London hotels where he never felt at home, and his visits to London became shorter and shorter (*P&P*, 270).

Like Santayana, Peter was more English than American in his speech and manners. There was the "testy old general" who would never admit that Peter was not an Englishman: " 'They pretend,' he would splutter, 'that this Alden chap is an American. Impossible. He doesn't look like an American, he doesn't talk like an American, he doesn't dress like an American, and he takes such *sound views*. Alden is not an American' " (244–45). Santayana's spoken English was evidently something like Peter's. Daniel Cory told me that Santayana had a pleasant baritone speaking voice and that his accent was more British than American. In *Persons and Places*, Santayana describes an incident of 1887 when his friend the young Earl Russell introduced him to his grandmother, Lady Stanely of Alderly, who observed that Santayana had not an American accent. "I reminded her of the culture of Boston, and protested that all my English was American, as I had been but three days in London. 'No,' she admitted, 'you haven't a *London* accent. You speak like Queen Victoria.' Let this stand as early testimony to my English speech: I spoke like Queen Victoria" (*P&P*, 134–35).

Other similarities between Peter Alden and the author who created him can here be only briefly summarized. Both liked good food and wines, but neither was very fond of women. Peter "liked the ladies without exactly loving them" (243), but he muses that he doesn't "need women at all sentimentally, to pet and to be petted, and socially they bore me to death; but physically and by a sort of reviving boyish curiosity, I still sometimes fall a prey to them; and I try to make a joke of what is hardly a pleasure" (61). Both took a dim view of marriage. Santayana's view of matrimony is expressed by Peter: "being duly registered and legally owned, in a word, married" (64). The difference is that while Peter was sexually attracted to women, Santayana was not. Both Peter and Santayana had the same view of Robert Browning: "Dr. Alden, indeed, didn't seem to think Browning a great poet at all" (69); and both had the same theory of poetry: "I [Peter] mean poetry in the deeper sense in which it merges with love and with religion. Poetry, I say, is like spray blown by some wind from a heaving sea, or like sparks blown from a smouldering fire: a cry which the violence of circumstances wrings from some poor fellow. This cry or spark or spray is flimsy in itself and playful, yet there's tragedy behind it" (318).[57] Both were at home in several languages; both acknowledged *useful* modern improvements: apropos of the modern bathroom aboard the *Black Swan,* Peter tells Oliver that he has "no prejudice against modern improvements when they simplify life" (144). Santayana agreed with this view, drawing the line at central heating: "Modern improvements seem to me in almost everything to be a blessing. Electricity, vacuum cleaning, and ladies' kitchens render life simpler and more decent; but central heating, in banishing fireplaces, except as an occasional luxury or affectation, has helped to destroy the charm of home. I don't mean merely the ancient and rustic sanctity of the hearth; I mean also the home-comforts of the modern bachelor. An obligatory fire was a useful and blessed thing" (*P&P,* 185). Both men used their bankers as a postal address when traveling (323); neither was fond of Germans generally ("Ideally he [Peter] might have preferred an English or even a French governess [for Oliver], for the sake of a certain refinement and soberness not to be expected of Germans" [91]); and both were bald.

Neither Peter nor Santayana was opinionated or argumentative: "Somehow," Peter muses, "I've escaped a weakness which seems to attach to the strongest characters, in that they can't bear it if anybody is not of their own opinion" (63). A rare quality in a philosopher, but Santayana did not care to argue anyone into agreeing with his views. If someone caught a spark from his ideas, fine; if not, not. Peter's reflection on his own personal character at the end of his life—"I haven't hated, I haven't feared, and I've preserved my intellectual liberty" (246)—is much like Santayana's estimate of himself, expressed toward the end of his life, in "The Poet's Testament": "All times my present, everywhere my place,/ Nor fear, nor hope, nor envy saw my face."[58] Peter muses that instead of marrying and producing a son, it might have been "easier to do the right thing by society at large, writing a book of travels, or one on ships in the sixteenth century, or collecting works of art and bequeathing them to the Boston Museum" (247). Santayana thought of his books as "children," his contribution to society, and several times refers to them as such in his letters. Peter hoped that the evening of his life would be more satisfying than the morning, and it was. (178) This is true also for Santayana who, concluding his autobiography in the summer of 1944, in his eighty-first year, wrote: "Never have I enjoyed youth so thoroughly as I have in my old age. In writing *Dialogues in Limbo, The Last Puritan,* and now all these descriptions of the friends of my youth and the young friends of my middle age, I have drunk the pleasure of life more pure, more joyful, than it ever was when mingled with all the hidden anxieties and little annoyances of actual living. Nothing is inherently and invincibly young except spirit" (*P&P,* 131).

It would doubtless be rewarding to study the origins of the other principal characters of the novel in the way we have studied Peter Alden, but it is only necessary to concentrate on the single character to perceive how Santayana used his own life and personality, together with the lives and personalities of his family and friends, to create the characters and events of *The Last Puritan*. In fashioning the remarkably complex, interesting, and thoroughly believable character of Peter, Santayana has drawn upon all of these sources. From William Hathaway Forbes, Peter derives his wealth and concomitant broad leisure and also—according to Santayana—his ultimately ineffectual personal character; from Andrew Green, Peter acquires a taste for the exotic in places, women, and food, and a general unconventionality in attitude and behavior; from Santayana's father, Agustín, Peter gets his subtle intelligence, ironic cast of mind, a propensity for making an irrational and unhappy marriage, and hypochondria; from Santayana himself come Peter's good humor, kindliness, love of travel, his naturalistic philosophy and resignation to the ineluctable laws of the universe and to the ways of human society, his opinions, and his love for a detached, reflective, and gentlemanly way of life amid beautiful and stimulating surroundings.

In creating the character of Peter Alden, and indeed all of the principal characters of the novel, Santayana, like all artists, has drawn upon the realm of the subconscious. That the characters and events of *The Last Puritan* derive not only from Santayana's conscious experience but also from his subconscious mind, personal fantasies, and desires for wish-fulfillment is manifested in the novel in various ways. Peter's great wealth and consequent freedom and independence; Oliver's physical stature, good looks, athletic ability and strength; Mario's warm, loving relationship with his mother, upperclass European cultural background and education, his charm, sophistication, sexual attractiveness and power—these all represent things that Santayana himself did not have but must have dreamed of possessing. Passages in *Persons and Places* imply that Santayana was dissatisfied with the Boston Public Latin School and Harvard College (with "the muddy paths and shabby grass, the elms standing scattered at equal intervals, the ugly factory-like buildings, and the loud-voiced youths passing by, dressed like shop-assistants" [291]) and would have preferred to have been educated, like Mario, at Eton and Christ Church College, Oxford. In sending Mario to these exclusive schools, Santayana was vicariously satisfying longings of his own. Indeed, the whole personality and career of Mario, like those of Peter and Oliver, are, in certain fundamental ways, projections of Santayana's own personality and life, both as they really were and as he wished they might be.

A letter that Santayana wrote in 1936 to the Yale English professor and influential literary critic, William Lyon Phelps, attests to the importance of Santayana's subconscious mind in developing the characters and events of *The Last Puritan*. Santayana describes a phenomenon not uncommon to novelists: the characters seem to have separate lives of their own that they are dictating to the author who serves as amanuensis. In the letter to Phelps, Santayana writes: "I have pictures, quite as distinct as memories; and my characters *speak* to me, I don't have to prompt them. This doesn't contradict the fact which you mention, and I point to in the *Epilogue,* that these characters speak my language, and are in some sense masks for my own spirit."[59] Characters of fiction, of course, have no existence apart from the work in which they appear and are necessarily emanations from the conscious and subconscious mind of the author. When the characters appear to the author to have an independent existence, the events of which the author is attempting to record, these characters are obviously drawing a significant portion of their being from the depths of the author's psyche, as was surely the case with Santayana in composing *The Last Puritan.*

While Santayana apparently made significant use of subconscious experience and fantasies in composing the novel, he also drew heavily, as we have observed, upon the personalities and lives of real persons. Thus, in creating *The Last Puritan,* Santayana merged the stuff of the subconscious and the imagination with autobiography and observation of real-life persons and events. In this respect, the work is certainly "a memoir in the form of a novel," and yet it is nevertheless much more than a memoir, more than autobiography. In the process of selecting from the rich specificity of his personal experience and from his knowledge of the personalities and experience of other real persons he knew or had known, and in merging these recollections with his own fantasies, Santayana transmuted these complex elements into a work of art with specific well-defined characters (one of whom represents Santayana himself) and an independent chronology of events.

In sum, the characters and events of *The Last Puritan* had their origins in the conscious and subconscious experience of the author, but in the process of creating the work of art the lived experience was transformed and transcended. The completed novel became a separate artistic entity, with its own *raison d'être,* with both a particularity and a universality independent of the author's life and of external sources. The way in which Santayana's book may indeed be said to be a "memoir in the form of a novel"—that is, a work of fiction having its origin in the remembered or "salvaged" experience of the author—but yet be recognized as an independent artistic entity, with an integrity and truth of its own, is an example of the mystery and triumph of art.

Notes

1. *The Last Puritan: A Memoir in the Form of a Novel* was first published in London on 17 October 1935 by Constable Publishers; a separate edition was brought out the following year in New York by Scribner's. All references to the text of the novel given parenthetically in this essay are to the Scribner's 1936 edition. A second two-volume Scribner's edition was included in volumes 11 and 12 of the Triton Edition of Santayana's works published in 1937. A new

single-volume critical edition of the novel, coedited by William G. Holzberger and Herman J. Saatkamp, Jr., is currently being prepared for publication as volume 4 of the MIT Press Edition of *The Works of George Santayana*.

2. Santayana gives this chronology of composition in a letter to Alfred L. Coester, 20 December 1938, University of Virginia Library, where he also says that he wrote the "New York scenes" in Toledo, Spain in 1920. He gives the completion date for the novel in a letter to George Sturgis of 3 October 1934, Collection of Robert S. Sturgis (Santayana's grandnephew, the son of George Sturgis), Cambridge, Massachusetts. (I have since 1972 been preparing a comprehensive edition of Santayana's letters, a project begun in the late 1960s by Daniel Cory, with whom I collaborated on the letters project for several months before his death on June 18, 1972. The letters will constitute volume 5 of the MIT Press Edition of *The Works of George Santayana* [although that volume will be composed of several individual books, as approximately 2,500 letters, the vast majority unpublished, have been collected and prepared for publication]. I shall make considerable reference to the letters—including several unpublished ones—in this essay, and I wish to express my gratitude to the following persons and libraries for their kind permission to quote from Santayana's unpublished letters: Mrs. Margot Cory, the Santayana literary executor; Mr. Robert S. Sturgis; the Library of the University of California at Riverside; the Rare Book and Manuscript Library, Columbia University; the William R. Perkins Library, Duke University; the Houghton Library, Harvard University; the Princeton University Library; the Temple University Library; and the Alderman Library, University of Virginia.)

3. Santayana briefly describes this evolution of the plot of the novel in a letter to Hamilton Vaughan Bail of 20 February 1950, Houghton Library, Harvard University.

4. A typescript of the first half of the novel, made from Santayana's handwritten manuscript and containing a few corrections and revisions in Santayana's hand, is in the University of Virginia Library.

5. Of Oliver's death, Mario tells Rose and Mrs. Darnley: "It was several days after the armistice" (585). The armistice ending World War I was signed on 11 November 1918. Oliver, born on 1 October 1890 (*per* Santayana's letter to Otto Kyllmann of 3 September 1935, Temple University Libraries), was just past his twenty-eighth birthday.

6. "It is indeed said that experience speaks through the mouths of old men, but the best experience that they can bring to us is that of their salvaged youth."

7. Santayana to Cyril Clemens, 14 December 1939, Duke University Library. Quoted by permission of the William R. Perkins Library, Duke University.

8. Santayana to Otto Kyllmann, 27 July 1935, Constable & Co. Directors' File Collection, Temple University Libraries. Quoted by permission of the Temple University Libraries.

9. The description of Santayana's mother's Beacon Street house is in George Santayana, *Persons and Places: Fragments of Autobiography,* a critical edition coedited by William G. Holzberger and Herman J. Saatkamp, Jr. (Cambridge, Mass.: MIT Press, 1986), 138–43, volume 1 of *The Works of George Santayana*. All further references to the autobiography are to this edition; they use the symbol *P&P* and are given directly in the text. The description of the house in *Persons and Places* is virtually identical to the one in the novel.

10. Santayana to John Hall Wheelock, 27 July 1935, Archives of Charles Scribner's Sons, Princeton University Library. Quoted by permission of the Princeton University Library.

11. Santayana to George Sturgis, 12 March 1940, Collection of Robert S. Sturgis.

12. Santayana to Rosamond Sturgis, 8 February 1948, Collection of Robert S. Sturgis. This letter is included in Daniel Cory's edition of *The Letters of George Santayana* (New York: Charles Scribner's Sons, 1955), 370–71. In the letter to George Sturgis of 12 March 1940, Santayana describes how an unidentified correspondent had sent him a dramatization of *The Last Puritan* in which Nathaniel and his old father "both try to rape the young Caroline, their step-sister and step-daughter, while Nathaniel beats his wife. I protested that these were not the manners of Beacon Street in my time, and that he mustn't use my

name or the title of my book for his production. He now says he is going to burn it! *Meno male!*"

13. Cleveland Amory, *Proper Bostonians* (New York: E. P. Dutton, 1947).

14. Peter recalls, however, that "Caroline was merry and kind, but at bottom too contemptuous. She hated sick children. A boy, especially, must look after himself. She just laughed at me, pushed me into the water, and told me to swim. I didn't quite drown, for here I am; but I swallowed a lot of salt water" (64).

15. Daniel Cory, *Santayana: The Later Years: A Portrait with Letters* (New York: George Braziller, 1963), 210.

16. Santayana to Boylston Adams Beal, 23 December 1935, Houghton Library, Harvard University.

17. Santayana describes William Cameron ("Cam") Forbes (1870–1959) as a young man of wealth and distinguished family who was spartan in his contempt for luxury and puritanical in his aversion to liquor, and indicates that physically, spiritually, and experientially he was a model (but by no means the *only* model) for Oliver (*P&P,* 346–48). In Santayana's letter to Beal of 23 December 1935, we learn that Oliver's discarding of his gold watch chain and instead using a bootlace for the purpose was a characteristic taken directly from Forbes. Cameron Forbes graduated from Harvard in 1892. He served as head football coach at Harvard from 1897–1899. His later career was quite distinguished: he became a financier and board member of a number of American corporations and served as Governor General of the Phillipine Islands from 1909–1913 and Ambassador to Japan from 1930–1932.

18. Santayana to Boylston Adams Beal, 23 December 1935, Houghton Library, Harvard University. Quoted by permission of the Harvard College Library. It is most unfortunate that Beal's letter to Santayana, to which Santayana's letter of 23 December 1935 was a response, has not survived, because in that letter Beal had identified many of the characters of the novel with their real-life counterparts. Santayana's letter to Beal begins: "You are of all persons the one who can read *The Last Puritan* most from the inside, and from the beginning to the end. The originals in most cases—where there are distinct originals—are known to you better than to me. Those you suggest are of course right in all cases, although I am inclined to put the centre of gravity sometimes in other quarters, less familiar to you." The loss of Beal's letter is one more disaster attributable to Santayana's unfortunate practice of destroying, with few exceptions, all letters received.

19. Santayana to Hamilton Vaughan Bail, 20 February 1950, Houghton Library, Harvard University. Quoted by permission of the Harvard College Library.

20. Samuel Eliot Morison, *Three Centuries of Harvard 1636–1936* (Cambridge.: Harvard University Press, 1936), 424.

21. Morison, 206.

22. The "O.K." or "Orthoepy Klub" (the word "orthoepy" means having to do with the pronunciation of a language or the study of the pronunciation of a language) was a Harvard literary society to which Santayana belonged during his undergraduate years and afterward and for which he served as secretary. The membership included men who, like Santayana, were on the staff of the *Harvard Monthly* and the *Lampoon.*

23. The idealized seated bronze figure of John Harvard by Daniel Chester French (1850–1931) was dedicated in 1884 and placed in the Delta, where it stood at the time this "O.K." poem was written. In 1909 it was moved to the front of University Hall in the Harvard Yard where it stands today.

24. *The Complete Poems of George Santayana,* Critical Edition, ed. William G. Holzberger (Lewisburg, Pa.: Bucknell University Press, 1979), 487.

25. Santayana to Hamilton Vaughan Bail, 20 February 1950, Houghton Library, Harvard University.

26. In 1945, seven years before his death, Santayana's net worth was six hundred thousand dollars. *Per* letter from Santayana to Francis H. Appleton, Jr. of 27 December 1945,

Houghton Library, Harvard University. (Appleton was the Boston attorney appointed by Santayana's nephew and financial manager, George Sturgis, to look after Santayana's property in the event of Sturgis's demise. George Sturgis died suddenly of heart failure on 20 December 1944 at the age of fifty-three.)

27. Santayana describes this journey with John Francis Stanley, the second Earl Russell, in *P&P,* 312–13. He joined Russell at Valence on the Rhône, early in June of 1888, and made a three-weeks' voyage to Paris, where Santayana disembarked. He then traveled to Avila to spend the rest of the summer with his father in Spain.

28. John McCormick, *George Santayana: A Life* (New York: Alfred A. Knopf, 1987), 330.

29. Santayana was a great opera fan and was quite knowledgeable on the subject. Opera plays a very significant part in the symbolism of *The Last Puritan.* Not only is Oliver's extended dream sequence, in which he plays the role of the betrayed and murdered Gilda in *Rigoletto,* a particularly impressive piece of dramatic writing, but it demonstrates Santayana's thorough knowledge of the Verdi opera. And there are several other references to operas and to the art of singing in the novel. For instance, it is not mere coincidence that Santayana chooses Rossini's *La Cenerentola* ("Cinderella") for Mario's mother to create a *furore* (411) in the title role: the gifted Maddelena was saved from a career as a "vulgar singer" (317) by her marriage to a "rich young American" (5–6), Harold Van de Weyer, Mario's father.

30. McCormick, 330.

31. Santayana to Robert Burnside Potter, 21 December 1922, Houghton Library, Harvard University. Quoted by permission of the Harvard College Library.

32. William Hathaway Forbes (1840–1897) married Edith Emerson, the second daughter of Ralph Waldo Emerson, in 1865. During the Civil War, Forbes served as a colonel in the Union army and was afterwards called by his military title. Despite Santayana's description of Forbes's life in *Persons and Places* and in his letters, Forbes seems to have had an active and successful business career: he was founder and president of the Bell Telephone Company and a director of several other companies.

33. Santayana to Boylston Adams Beal, 23 December 1935, Houghton Library, Harvard University.

34. Santayana to Rosamond Sturgis, 5 February 1936, Collection of Robert S. Sturgis.

35. Santayana to Sadakichi Hartmann, 3 January 1937, Library of the University of California, Riverside. Quoted by permission of the Library.

36. Aboard the *Black Swan,* anchored off Cape Cod, Jim Darnley tells young Oliver that "racing is the last thing your father would meddle with: he hates all that row and all those people" (157).

37. Published in five volumes by Scribner's in 1905–1906.

38. The text of Peter's telegram in the novel is all in capital letters, and in this excerpt I have inserted bracketed punctuation not included in the telegram.

39. Santayana says something very similar in *P&P,* 465–66: "The real Greece is dead, pulverised, irrecoverable. There remain only a few words and a few relics that may serve to suggest to us a rational ideal of human life" (*P&P,* 466).

40. On 3 July, 1888, Santayana wrote to his mentor at Harvard, William James; "Three terms of Berlin have fully convinced me that the German school, although it is well to have some acquaintance with it, is not one to which I can attach myself. After the first impression of novelty and freedom, I have become oppressed by the scholasticism of the thing and by the absurd pretension to be scientific. . . . when I came to Germany, I also lost my faith in psycho-physics, and all the other attempts to discover something very momentous. A German professor like [Wilhelm] Wundt seems to me a survival of the alchymist [sic]." Santayana to William James, 3 July 1888 (written from Avila, Spain), Houghton Library, Harvard University. This letter is included in Daniel Cory, ed. *The Letters of George Santayana* (New York: Scribner's, 1955), 30–31. This edition is hereafter referred to as *Letters.*

41. "I was wholly incapable of taking a Doctor's degree in Germany. The only thing for me to do was to return to Harvard and take my Doctor's degree there, where I was at home and sure of my ground. I knew German enough to write my thesis on a German subject, if I might write it in English" (*P&P*, 260).

42. " . . . the real drama was his health. He was a wiry and (for a Spaniard) a tall man, and lived to the age of seventy-nine; and long walks and long sea voyages in comfortless old sailing-vessels were nothing to him. Yet he was a hypochondriac, always watching his symptoms, and fearing that death was at hand" (*P&P*, 27).

43. John McCormick maintains, after an inspection of Agustín Santayana's surviving paintings, that his son George in *Persons and Places* "was unduly critical of his father's ability as an artist" (6).

44. At the time of their marriage in 1862 (or early in 1863), Josefina was probably thirty-six or thirty-seven and Agustín was forty-seven or forty-eight, Santayana says that Agustín died in 1893 at the age of seventy-nine (*P&P*, 423–24). This would make 1814 the year of Agustín's birth (not 1812 as in McCormick [51] who was probably calculating on the basis of Santayana's remark that his father was "nearly fifty" at the time of his marriage in 1862 or early in 1863 [*P&P*, 50]).

45. Santayana to Bruno Lind (pseudonym of Robert C. Hahnel, author of a biographical book about Santayana, *Vagabond Scholar: A Venture into the Privacy of George Santayana* [New York: Bridgehead Books, 1962]), 29 November 1951, Houghton Library, Harvard University. Quoted by permission of the Harvard College Library.

46. Santayana to Mrs. Theodore W. Richards, 18 May 1936, Houghton Library, Harvard University. This letter is included in Cory's *Letters*, 310–311.

47. Toward the close of chapter V of part 1 of the novel, Santayana tells us that at the age of thirty-five Peter received his M.D. degree from Harvard. Then he says, "He [Peter] picked up a few old acquaintances and even made a few new ones; sailed to Florida or the Bahamas in winter, to Mt. Desert or the Saint Lawrence in summer. The Atlantic Yacht Club elected him a member, and he ceased to be black-balled at the Somerset Club" (57). These events, presumably occurring after the receipt of Peter's medical degree, imply the passage of time, so that several years may have gone by before Peter decided to consult Dr. Bumstead at Great Falls and subsequently marry Harriet Bumstead. If this, as it seems, is indeed the case, then the various references in the novel to Peter being sixty (or older) at the time of his death are accurate. (In the case of Agustín Santayana, his death occurred in Avila, Spain in the summer of 1893, in the presence of his son George, who was thirty at the time. Agustín was "seventy-nine years old, deaf, half blind, and poor; he had desired his own death and had attempted to hasten it" [*P&P*, 423–24].)

In addition to being unhealthily preoccupied with his physical and mental condition at the time he decides to consult Dr. Bumstead, Peter may well be concerned about his potentiality for mental disease and even insanity because of the presence in his family of a madwoman: Nathaniel Alden's sister Julia (Peter's half sister) is sufficiently insane that Nathaniel at least would regard her death as a blessing (18). The parallel here to Santayana's own experience is to Lizzie Grew, a young woman related to Santayana's Sturgis siblings and "a howling maniac." As in the case of Nathaniel and his mad sister Julia, the attitude of the Sturgis-Grew family was "to hush, to suppress that unpalatable lesson [i.e., the "lesson" being "to recall their thoughts to ultimate realities"], and to go on living as if it were not true" (*P&P*, 60). Nathaniel, we read, "trembled at the possibility that some well-meaning aunt or insinuating cousin, perhaps a special friend of his mad sister, might draw him into a corner and whisper affectionately, "Tell me, *how* is poor Julia?" (18).

48. Santayana to Otto Kyllmann, 3 September 1935, Temple University Libraries. In a later letter to Kyllmann, Santayana writes that he has "long had a family chart with all the chief characters and dates carefully recorded." Santayana to Otto Kyllmann, 1 January 1936, Temple University Libraries. Unfortunately, the family chart has not survived. (The two letters

are in the Constable & Co. Directors' File in the Temple University Libraries and are quoted by permission of the Libraries.)

49. As Oliver knows, however, Peter is an expert exhaler: "Exhaling being one of Peter's hobbies" (305). It was evidently one of Santayana's hobbies as well. In a letter to Daniel Cory of November 13, 1929, Santayana writes that the breathing-exercises—called *"soufflez la bougie"* or "blow out the candle"—that he had been taught the previous summer by a doctor at the clinic at Val-Mont, Switzerland were helping to relieve the symptoms of his chronic bronchitis. In another letter to Cory of 4 December 1929, he again refers to "[Dr.] Hämmerli's *traitement,* which I follow religiously." These two letters are in the George Santayana Papers, Rare Book and Manuscript Library, Columbia University and are quoted by permission of the library.

50. In his autobiography, however, Santayana uses a similar expression in referring to his mother's age at the time she married his father: he says she was "nearly forty" (*P&P,* 50) when, according to what Santayana believed to be her actual date of birth (1826), Josefina could only have been thirty-six or thirty-seven. (She may, however, have been two years younger: Santayana says that although the official papers give his mother's date of birth as 1828, there is reason to believe that her real birth date was 1826. Josefina was born in Glasgow, Scotland and was not brought to Spain until 1835. Upon her arrival in Spain, she had not yet been confirmed in the Roman Catholic faith. Santayana believes that the family may well have falsified Josefina's birth date by two years—she was small for her age and could get away with the subterfuge—because it was something of a scandal for her at the age of nine not yet to have been confirmed in her religion. By changing her date of birth to 1828 she would make her confirmation at the age of seven, "the canonical age of reason . . . the right age for confirmation" [*P&P,* 8] If, however, Santayana was incorrect about the falsification of the date of his mother's birth and she actually was born in 1828, then she would have been thirty-four or thirty-five when she married his father in 1862 or early in 1863.)

51. Assuming, as Santayana does, that his mother was really born in 1826 rather than in the officially recorded 1828.

52. In the *Addendum* entitled "We Were Not Virtuous," inserted following chapter 16 at the end of the first part of the autobiography (*P&P,* 245–49), Santayana presents a forbidding portrait of his mother: "The sad fact was that, even when our intentions were good, none of us [children] could be satisfactory. None of us expressed to the eye all that our mother would have wished us to express" (*P&P,* 246). (This *Addendum* to the first part of the MIT Press Critical Edition of *Persons and Places* was suppressed during Santayana's lifetime and omitted from earlier editions of the autobiography.)

53. In the cases of both Santayana and Oliver, the houses that they grew up in belonged to their mothers. Mrs. Alden's house, the old Bumstead place, a colonial mansion of Empire style, is restored and bestowed upon her by Peter as a wedding gift; and Josefina's Beacon Street house, acquired in 1872, was probably purchased out of the ten thousand dollars given to her by her brother-in-law, Robert Sturgis, when after the death of her first husband she came to America to live (*P&P,* 47).

54. Peter Alden succeeds in killing himself by deliberately taking an overdose of drugs (330–31); Agustín Santayana "attempted to hasten" his death (*P&P,* 424).

55. *Per* Santayana's letter to Otto Kyllmann, 3 September 1935, Temple University Libraries. On page 379 of the novel, Oliver is in New York City "in the second September after his father's death"; and page 382 indicates that in "exactly thirteen months" Oliver will come into his money, i.e., presumably reach the age of twenty-one. Thus, Oliver's age at this time would be nineteen (it is September and on October first he will be twenty) and the year would be 1910. (Thirteen months later, on 1 October 1911, Oliver will be twenty-one.) If, therefore, we accept the birth date for Oliver given in the letter to Kyllmann, then Peter's death occurred two years earlier in (August [321]) 1908.

56. The idea of premature agedness is, however, interesting in light of what McCormick

says in his biography of Santayana about the attitude of Santayana's parents: "In the mid-Victorian period, or during the presidencies of Grant and Hayes, human beings were regarded as well on at forty, old at fifty, and if they survived, at death's door at sixty. . . . Despite their longevity, both of Santayana's parents believed themselves old and used up in what now would be considered their late prime" (9).

57. This is the theory of poetry developed in Santayana's book, *Interpretations of Poetry and Religion* (New York: Scribner's, 1900) and expressed essentially in the preface to his *Poems* (New York: Scribner's, 1923).

58. "The Poet's Testament," lines 11–12, in *The Complete Poems of George Santayana*, 268–69.

59. Santayana to William Lyon Phelps, 16 February 1936, Yale University Library. This letter is in Cory's *Letters*, 304–05.

Fiction, Philosophy, and Autobiography:
Santayana's *Persons and Places*

HERMAN J. SAATKAMP, JR.

Perhaps no major writer of the twentieth century has been more widely read and studied less than George Santayana. Santayana's prominence is well known: he is likely the only philosopher to appear on the front cover of *Time*;[1] his autobiography (*Persons and Places*) and one novel (*The Last Puritan*) were best sellers and Book-of-the-Month Club selections; and his literary and philosophical works were widely published throughout the Americas, Western and Eastern Europe, and Asia. Hence, nearly forty years after his death in 1952, it is surprising and disappointing that Santayana's life and work are not well researched and documented.[2]

The extent and the nature of Santayana's full literary corpus may account for some paucity of scholarship. It is a daunting task to read, understand, and evaluate Santayana the philosopher, poet, cultural critic, and novelist. His published works are great in number and broad in genres. Beginning with the pencil of a seven-year-old writing short stories, and closing with the blue crayon of an eighty-eight-year-old making corrections to philosophical manuscripts, Santayana produced works eluding easy academic classifications, works that reflect the complexity and festivity of his thought. He is a thoroughgoing materialist who places the highest value in aesthetic qualities, an atheist who counts religion as one of humanity's highest organizing and creative achievements, an anti-metaphysician who writes metaphysics, an academic who maintains that the worst environment for philosophy and literature is the university, a sage of elderly philosophers who remains best known for his earliest works, an American philosopher and writer who was never officially an American.

To make matters worse, the dearth of Santayana scholarship is maintained by a widespread but largely fictionalized account of Santayana's life. His biographical reputation has composted in a heap of praise mixed with innuendo, rumor, and falsehoods since his early retirement from Harvard in 1912 at the age of forty-eight. The ferment and lack of biographical studies

A portion of this essay appeared earlier in *Overheard in Seville: Bulletin of the Santayana Society* 4 (Fall 1986): 18–27 and is reprinted with the permission of the publisher. The expanded version of this essay was produced specifically for this volume and is printed by permission of the author.

have resulted in a version of Santayana's life that is widely accepted but false. Meager and sometimes mean, it renders Santayana as an outcast at Harvard, an aesthete in a practical world, distant and desultory, probably a practicing homosexual, who despondently left the academic scene in 1912 never to return because of his pariah status. This inaccurate understanding of Santayana's life extends to his post-Harvard years with the following summation: in the end, Santayana found a home in a convent in Rome where he died, isolated and unsympathetic to the horrors of both world wars.

The provenance of this account is not easily determined. It is surely based in part on the articulate difference in his lifestyle and outlook from that of his colleagues at Harvard, on his leaving Harvard to the dismay of his colleagues and despite the appeals and offers of the administration, on his convincing Bertrand Russell to spend a year at Harvard in Santayana's absence while agreeing with Russell that Harvard was hardly a place for the worldly philosopher, on his catholic (and Catholic) and European nature in a New England setting, on his being trapped on "foreign" land during both world wars and in enemy territory during World War II, on his having no graduate students to carry forward his views in the last and most productive forty years of his life, on the inadequacy of communication between Europe and the U.S. in the 1930s and 1940s, and, perhaps most significantly, on his unwillingness to correct misperceptions of his life and work. Commenting on the widespread Harvard legend that he was so eager to escape the United States that he walked out in the middle of class, Santayana said, "It's not true. My departure from America was long and deeply meditated. But the wrong story doesn't bother me. I like false tradition even better than the true kind, because the invention itself proves that it comes from the heart."[3]

Regardless of the origin of the fictionalized account of Santayana's life, it is time for it to end. At least the bare outlines of Santayana's life should be generally understood, and then perhaps one may expect a fair assessment of his work. The remainder of this essay is a short effort at both tasks. First, a capsulized version of Santayana's life is presented to counter some of the popular fictions about Santayana's life—recognizing that fiction is often more engaging than biographical detail. Second, the development of Santayana's philosophical outlook will be discussed based on newly discovered material in his autobiography.

OUTLINE OF THE LIFE OF SANTAYANA

Focusing on Santayana's principal residences, one can divide the geographical chronology of Santayana's life into three parts: nine years in Spain (1863–1872), forty years in Boston (1872–1912), and forty years in Europe (1912–1952). But Santayana's own account of his life, also divided into three parts for his autobiography,[4] more accurately describes the development of his person and of his thought: background (1863–1886); America and Europe (1886–1912); and Europe (1912–1952). The background of his life basically spans his childhood in Spain through his undergraduate years at Harvard. Santayana's transatlantic penchant for traveling led him to describe his years as a graduate student and professor at Harvard as "on both sides of the Atlantic, a description he suggested as a title for the second part of his autobiography. Likewise, the third part of his life, "all on the other side," indicates the forty years he spent as a full-time writer in Europe after retiring from Harvard in 1912. It was not until the late 1920s that Rome became his principal residence—Santayana was in his late sixties at this point. And it was not until 1941 that he entered a hospital-clinic where he spent the remaining years of his long and productive life. His age, health, and the inability to leave Italy for friendlier countries compelled him to take up his final residence in a hospital administered by an order of Catholic nuns.

FICTIONALIZED ACCOUNTS OF SANTAYANA'S LIFE

Santayana's long absence from the United States proved fertile ground for fictionalizing and dramatizing aspects of his life. Many of these inventions are intriguing and perhaps served to enhance Santayana's legend, but there are at least four such accounts that merit close scrutiny:

1. *Santayana was a recluse who withdrew from Harvard because of his cloistered nature and because he did not fit in.*

Santayana's Harvard years were remarkably active as an undergraduate, graduate, and professor. As an undergraduate he was a member of over twenty clubs, traveled to Europe each summer following his freshman year, and clearly enjoyed the adventures and frivolity of an undergraduate young man as is attested to by his letters to family—particularly his father—and to friends. Two of his graduate years were spent abroad, primarily in Germany and England, but his delight at being in academia began to dim with increasing restriction on his intellectual license. Josiah Royce, his dissertation advisor, assigned Santayana the philosophy of Rudolf Hermann Lotze as his dissertation topic rather than Santayana's preference of Schopenhauer. Royce noted that Schopenhauer might be an appropriate topic for a master of arts but not for a doctor of philosophy. This was a misdirection that Santayana regretted even in maturity and led to what he called his "dull thesis for the Ph.D."[5]

Santayana's career at Harvard was productive, active, and remarkable in achievement. In 1894 he began what he refers to as his *metanoia*, an awakening from somnambulism. At about the same time he began planning for early retirement, finding the university life unsuitable for his desire to be a full-time writer. He found faculty meetings, committees, and governance structures largely empty and their discussions mostly partisan heat over false issues, and the general corporate and business-like adaptation of universities not conducive to intellectual curiosity, development, and growth. He provides a general description of the Harvard faculty as "an anonymous concourse of coral insects, each secreting one cell, and leaving that fossil legacy to enlarge the earth."[6] But, in spite of this awakening outlook, his successes as a professor are well documented, and, indeed, these successes made possible his early retirement. At the same time, the new expectations and restrictions accompanying his achievements convinced Santayana that the academic environment was not the proper place for a serious philosopher with the desire to be a full-time writer.

After several books of poetry, Santayana, in his mid-thirties, published his first philosophical works: *The Sense of Beauty* (1896) and *Interpretations of Poetry and Religion* (1900). *The Sense of Beauty* was a natural outgrowth of his Harvard course on aesthetics. Contrary to the prevalent doctrines of the time, the work rooted esthetics in natural sensibilities—not in any refined qualities of mind—and placed beauty in the natural order of the world as a construct and response of human and animal activity. His boldness in writing was again affirmed in his second philosophical book where religion and poetry are viewed as imaginative by-products of the natural order, by-products that supervene on the natural order. Santayana's mentors and colleagues at Harvard were known for their views of muscular imagination; it was thought and imagination, according to them, that made possible the hope of pragmatic changes in the world. The offense was clear. Santayana's emerging view was that thought is meaningless in its consequence but eloquent in its expression. Its value is not practical, but celebrational and festive. This was a theme not well received in a department and university attempting to shape and structure future generations by its documented impact on the nation's governance and business. Santayana's five-volume *Life of Reason* (1905), however, was well received partly because it was misunderstood. Apparently Santayana had finally crossed the American line since it appeared to some that he now maintained the practical impact of mental constructs. Even though he expressed this in classical terms, it seemed to his American colleagues a welcome turn to practical affairs. Regardless of his reception, favorable and unfavorable, his notice as a serious philosopher was well established by the turn of the century.

Long before his retirement Santayana was a celebrated philosopher whose writings were widely read and who was a frequent guest lecturer at major universities. In his last years at Harvard, there is evidence he was being courted by Columbia, Williams, Wisconsin, and Berkeley. His resolve for early retirement, however, is confirmed in letters to his sister in 1909. When he announced his retirement in May 1911, President Lowell asked him to wait and agreed to provide Santayana with as much free time as he wanted. Santayana initially assented to teach only during the fall term with a full year's leave for 1912–13. However, in 1912 his resolve overtook his sense of obligation to Harvard and, at the age of forty-eight, he left Harvard to spend the remaining forty years of his life in such places as London, Oxford, Paris, Madrid, Avila, the Riviera, Florence, Cortina d'Ampezzo, and Rome. Harvard attempted to bring Santayana back several times and as late as 1929 offered him the Norton Chair in Poetry, one of Harvard's most respected chairs. In 1931 he turned down an invitation from Brown University, and Harvard later tempted him to accept for only a term the William James Lecturer in Philosophy, a newly established honorary post.[7] But Santayana never returned to Harvard, nor to America.

Santayana's distinctive nature is not to be denied. In background he was Spanish and Catholic, and Harvard with its protestant, puritanical, New England roots was hardly his native soil. He was the only classical American philosopher who was a classicist, and his lineage and allegiance to Europe made him an outsider in a university he considered more and more parochial. His numerous travels in Europe and Asia set him apart. His interest in art, poetry, and religion made his philosophy dubious in a department and university where practicality and action were becoming the principal marks of philosophical inquiry. But difference can both set one apart and also make one more interesting and more attractive. The latter was Santayana's fate, and his last years at Harvard brought trips to major universities, receptions and parties in New York, and widespread recognitions and friendships.

The death of Santayana's mother on 5 February 1912, released him from his family ties to America and also financially eased his planned retirement. His mother, Josefina Sturgis de Santayana, became ill in 1909, probably a victim of Alzheimer's disease. In May 1911 Santayana wrote to his half-sister, Susana (residing in Spain), that their mother was comatose most of the time. During his last months at Harvard, Santayana visited his mother frequently and, finally, daily. She was slowly dying. Upon her death he inherited $10,000 from her estate and made arrangements for his half-sister, Josephine (perhaps retarded), to be cared for in a home in Spain where Susana now lived and where Santayana first thought he would reside as a full-time writer. This inheritance plus Santayana's steady income from his publications made retirement easier. He asked his half-brother Robert to manage his finances (something Robert had done for their mother) with the understanding that Robert or his descendants would inherit the full capital upon Santayana's death. Hence, in January 1912, at the age of forty-eight, Santayana was free to write, free to travel, free to choose his residence and country, and free from the constraints of university regimen and expectations. Santayana welcomed the release.

2. Santayana was homosexual and this was a major factor in his leaving Harvard.

The evidence on this issue appears mixed and circumstantial. Some of Santayana's most-noted friends and associates were homosexual or bisexual, but he gives no clear indication of his own preferences. His life as a student certainly involved attraction to women as the letters from his travels indicate, and his family was drawn to express some concern over his attraction to Mrs. John Jacob Astor in 1909.[8] In 1929, however, in a remark to his long-time friend Daniel Cory, Santayana indicated he was perhaps a latent homosexual during his early years.[9] If Santayana was an active homosexual in his youth, this comment makes him a dissembler or perhaps makes Cory the dissembler since the remarks are recorded by him. Neither seems likely since there is no apparent reason why either Cory or Santayana would wish or need to disguise Santayana's youthful sexual activities, and furthermore the established integrity of Santayana tended toward a blunt truthfulness about himself and others.

Whether an active homosexual or not, Santayana held longstanding friendships with other men. The unusually high interest in the homosexual aspect of Santayana's life appears to be due less to factual information than to the North American attitude towards sexuality, and it is not clear what direct consequences follow from conclusions in either direction. Whatever the case, Santayana's courage in associating with and defending other men whose activities were deemed unnatural by many of Santayana's colleagues can be considered admirable from several perspectives and was certainly risky in the Harvard environment.

3. Santayana retired from Harvard to live in a convent.

Santayana retired from Harvard in January 1912, and only on 14 October 1941 did he enter the Clinica della Piccola Compagna di Maria, a hospital-clinic administered by a company of nuns better known as the Blue Nuns for the color of their habit. There he remained until his death in 1952. The thirty years prior to his residence in the nursing clinic began with twenty-odd trips between England and Europe from 1912 to 1914 to find a suitable place to live and write. Settling on Paris, he found himself in London at the outbreak of World War I and remained in England, mostly at Oxford, until 1919 when, rejecting offers for a lifetime membership at either Corpus Christi or New College, he returned to his chosen life as a traveling writer. Paris was no longer his settled choice of residence, and he then was truly the vagabond scholar until his established patterns began to center more and more in Rome.

4. Santayana sympathized with fascism.

There is no question that Santayana was politically conservative; in short, he believed that freedom derives from order and not order from freedom. Hence, he developed many criticisms of democratic liberalism that began with his youthful assessments of his father's political inclinations and ended with *Dominations and Powers* (1951). He viewed the whole of human behavior as natural, an outgrowth of material heritage and environment, and when asked about the atrocities of World War II, he, then in his mid-eighties, noted the historic atrocities of war as a natural occurrence. This seeming distance from the tragic horrors of war made him appear unfeeling to many, but his age, his family's diplomatic careers, his knowledge of human history, and his materialism provided a perspective not shaped by the usual commercial and governmental interests. He found even the historical materialism of Marx an attraction because of its materialist base. On the whole, his own remarks, the nature of his philosophy, and his *Dominations and Powers,* set him apart from the fascism that has brought such human misery into the twentieth century. Santayana's being trapped in Rome during World War II did much to further the rumor that he sympathized with fascism, but this is to overlook his propaganda-like piece, *Egotism in German Philosophy,* written during World War I, as well as his many efforts to disassociate himself from fascist sympathizers such as Ezra Pound.

Autobiography and the Development of Santayana's Philosophy[10]

The publishing history of Santayana's autobiography—the work recording the development of his life and thought—is tragic.[11] As Santayana wrote to Cory, "I regard this edition of *Persons & Places* as a mutilated victim of war and dream of a standard edition, which probably I shall never see, in which the original words, the omitted passages, and the marginal comments (not headings, as in the Triton Edition) shall be restored, and the portraits and other illustrations shall be well reproduced" (14 March 1945).[12] From composition to publication, few modern textual documents have suffered more than Santayana's autobiography. Intended as a one-volume work to be published posthumously, it was published instead as three individual works. Only the third book was published posthumously in 1953; the other two were published in 1944 and 1945 respectively.

The circumstances of the early 1940s caused Santayana, for the moment, to set aside his ambitions for his autobiography. After an unsuccessful attempt to leave Italy for Switzerland, Santayana lived in Rome for the duration of World War II trapped by circumstance and by his age. At the same time, Santayana's friend, Daniel Cory, was stranded in New York without any clear means of support. To assist Cory, Santayana arranged for the royalties of his autobiography, whenever it was published, to be paid directly to him. In addition, Santayana's publishers, particularly Scribner's, were eager to issue what would become a Book-of-the-Month Club's best seller, and they urged that the autobiography be published piecemeal rather than as a whole. Furthermore, there was an undercurrent of fear that the manuscript might be destroyed or lost during the war. These circumstances convinced Santayana to permit the publication of his autobiography in three parts and to allow the first two parts to be published before his death.

The typescript for book one was spirited out of Rome and delivered to Scribner's *sub rosa,* and likewise the typescript for book two was privately carried from Rome to the U.S. when official mail and official channels would not permit it to be brought to America.[13] Following these adventures, the fate of the first portions of his autobiography was fully in the hands of his publishers and editors since Santayana could not receive galleys or communication from the U.S. or England. These circumstances contributed to what Santayana termed the "mutilation" of his memoirs. Publishing was difficult and corners had to be cut. Some of Santayana's remarks seemed to his editors, and even to Santayana, too hard or too frank for the times. The publishers feared lawsuits, and Santayana was concerned that his friends and family might be upset. As a result, editors were charged with "softening" the text as well as deleting material difficult to print (for example, marginal notes) in restrictive times.

In 1941, Santayana, then nearly eighty years old and in the nursing clinic in Rome, was cut off by the war from the U.S., from his financial resources, and from his publishers. Not until the liberation of Rome did Santayana see a copy of the earliest book of his autobiography. Likewise, he saw the second book only after it was published in 1945. Not being able to read the galleys for any of the publications, he could only chide his publishers and editors for the state of his autobiography, and he did so with his usual ironic wit.[14] But in earnest, he repeatedly expressed his hope for a grander, unexpurgated edition.

The 1986 critical edition of *Persons and Places* restores significant passages that were omitted from all prior publications including lengthy sections on Spinoza, John Russell, Lionel Johnson, and members of Santayana's American family, as well as 644 marginal headings (or marginal comments as Santayana calls them). This material was previously purged for a variety of reasons: Santayana's wish that portions be published only after his death, publishers' sensitivity about Santayana's descriptions of his friend's marital and extramarital relations, printing and production convenience, and a general desire to deflect some of Santayana's cutting remarks. Restoring these passages renders the first unexpurgated version of Santayana's autobiography and thereby the first chance for Santayana to speak for himself. And what could be more important for an autobiography than that the author speak his own mind!

One extraordinary unpublished passage is particularly haunting. Imagine Santayana in his late seventies and early eighties composing his autobiography. He relies on his remarkably lucid memory, some miscellaneous notes, and four autobiographical notebooks drafted over several years. He is writing about Spinoza, who was his master and model concerning the natural basis of morality, but Santayana questions Spinoza's humane sense of the good. He does not think Spinoza "appreciates all the types of excellence toward which life may be directed."[15] Hoping to discard any ambiguity about his estimation of Spinoza, Santayana writes in his fine, clear hand "I will take this opportunity, *since I may not have any other,* of clearing my conscience of ambiguity in that respect" (emphasis mine). But even this opportunity was denied Santayana. This assessment of Spinoza only saw its first light of publication in the new critical edition of Santayana's autobiography. The passage ends as follows: "The saint and the poet are hardly sane or authoritative unless they embody a wide tradition. If they are rebels, disinherited and solitary, the world may admire but cannot follow them. They have studied human nature by looking at the stars."[16] This and many other passages are restored in the critical edition of *Persons and Places,* volume 1 of the *Works of George Santayana.*

Throughout the editing of *Persons and Places,* I could not help but reflect on the development of Santayana's philosophy and, in particular, on his own account of his philosophical thought. For Santayana, philosophy is not a methodology, nor a metaphysics, nor an ideology; it is an expression of the values and beliefs inherent and discoverable in living and acting. This perspective is derivative of Santayana's place, time, and ancestry, as well as of his creativity. In some marginal comments excluded from previous publications, Santayana describes three important stages in his thought. I shall use these comments as the basis for discussing the mature thought of Santayana and the manner in which his own life history serves as background and foundation for his reflections. The three stages are: first, his materialism; second, his moral relativism; and third, his sense of integrity or self-definition.[17]

1. *Materialism*

In chapter 11 of *Persons and Places,* "The Church of the Immaculate Conception," Santayana describes the development of his own thought. It is a journey from the idealisms of boyhood and from the intellectual materialism of a traveling student to the complete, materialistic outlook of the adult Santayana. Throughout this chapter he emphasizes the continuity of his life and beliefs, contrasting the seeming disparate tones of his developing thought to the overall unity of his outlook. He writes, "The more I change the more I am the same person."[18]

In a marginal heading he records that his boyhood idealisms were never his genuine beliefs.[19] These idealisms were not expressed in philosophical form, but they were "intensely felt by me to determine the only right or beautiful order possible for the universe. Existence could not be right or beautiful under other conditions."[20] Shortly thereafter he adds, "But those ideal universes in my head did not produce any firm convictions or actual duties. They had nothing to do with the wretched poverty-striken real world in which I was condemned to live. That the real was rotten and only the imaginary at all interesting seemed to me axiomatic. That was too sweeping; yet allowing for the rash generalisations of youth, it is still what I think. My philosophy has never changed."[21] Hence, he notes, in spite "of my religious and other day-dreams, I was at bottom a young realist; I knew I was dreaming, and so was awake. A sure proof of this was that I was never *anxious* about what those dreams would have involved if they had been true. I never had the least touch of superstition."[22] Santayana cites poems,[23] written when he was fifteen or sixteen, as revealing this early realism, and he quotes from memory one stanza of "At the Church Door" where the realistic sentiment is the same.

By the time he was a traveling student seeing the world in Germany, England, and Spain his "intellectual materialism" was firmly established with little change in his religious affections.[24]

> From the boy dreaming awake in the church of the Immaculate Conception, to the travelling student seeing the world in Germany, England, and Spain there had been no great change in sentiment. I was still "at the church door". Yet in belief, in the clarification of my philosophy, I had taken an important step. I no longer wavered between alternate views of the world, to be put on or taken off like alternate plays at the theatre. I now saw that there was only one possible play, the actual history of nature and of mankind, although there might well be ghosts among the characters and soliloquies among the speeches. Religions, *all* religions, and idealistic philosophies, *all* idealistic philosophies, were the soliloquies and the ghosts. They might be eloquent and profound. Like Hamlet's soliloquy they might be excellent reflective criticisms of the play as a whole. Nevertheless they were only parts of it, and their value as criticisms lay entirely in their fidelity to the facts, and to the sentiments which those facts aroused in the critic.[25]

The full statement and development of his materialism did not occur until later in his life. It was certainly in place by the time of *Scepticism and Animal Faith* (1923) but not fully so at the time of *The Life of Reason* (1905).

Within Santayana's fully cultivated materialism, the origins of all events in the world are arbitrary, temporal, and contingent. Matter (by whatever name it is called) is the principle of existence. It is "often untoward, and an occasion of imperfection or conflict in things."[26] Hence, a "sour moralist" may consider it evil, but, according to Santayana, if one takes a wider view "matter would seem a good . . . because it is the principle of existence: it is all things in their potentiality and therefore the condition of all their excellence or possible perfection."[27] Matter is the nondiscursive, natural foundation for all that is. In itself, it is neither good nor evil but may be perceived as such when viewed from the vested interest of animal life. Matter's nondiscernible, neutral face is converted to a smile or frown by latent animal interests. But "moral values cannot preside over nature."[28] Principled values are the products of natural forces: "The germination, definition, and prevalence of any good must be grounded in nature herself, not in human eloquence."[29] As he noted in his Preface, "From the point of view of origins, therefore, the realm of matter is the matrix and the source of everything: it is nature, the sphere of genesis, the universal mother. The truth cannot dictate to us the esteem in which we shall hold it: that is not a question of fact but of preference."[30] Even prior to the idealisms of boyhood and the intellectual materialism of the traveling student, the force of contingent, material events is evident in the background, birth, and early childhood of George Santayana. The lives of both his parents were based on the contingent patterns associated with the lives of diplomats. His father, Agustín Santayana, was born in 1812. He studied law, even practiced for a short time, and then entered the colonial service for posting to the Philippines. He was a remarkable man who, while studying law, served an apprenticeship to a professional painter of the school of Goya. To his credit, he translated four Senecan tragedies into Spanish, wrote an unpublished book about the island of Mindanao, had an extensive library, and made three trips around the world. In 1845 he became the governor of Batang, a small island in the Philippines. He took over the governorship from the recently deceased José Borrás y Bofarull, who was the father of Josefina Borrás, later to become Agustín's wife in 1861 and the mother of Jorge Agustín Nicolás Santayana y Borrás (George Santayana) on 16 December 1863.

In 1856, he again met Josefina while traveling on board ship from Manila for Spain. Josefina was then married to George Sturgis, a Boston merchant, and their three surviving children were traveling with them. This particular trip took Agustín to Boston, then to Niagara, then to New York City, and by steamer to England. His last diplomatic post was that of Financial Secretary to the Governor–General of the Philippines, General Pavía, Marqués de Novaliches. He retired early due to the ill effects of the tropics on his health. In 1861 he returned to Spain and there, once again, met Josefina Borrás Sturgis, now widowed, and they married.

George Santayana's mother's history is no less filled with contingent forces. Though Spanish, she was born in Glasgow, Scotland, in 1826 or 1828. She spent her girlhood in Virginia and Barcelona, Spain, and a portion of her womanhood in the Philippines. Her father left Spain for Scotland because of his political views. When they moved to the United States, he eventually became the American Consul at Barcelona. Later, when the fashion of the Spanish government turned more in his direction, he was appointed to a lucrative post in the Philippines. The voyage from Cadiz to Manila around the Cape of Good Hope lasted six months— through one of the worst storms the captain had ever experienced. On arriving in the Philippines, her father discovered there had been a change in the political climate back home and that the high-paying position in the

Philippines was no longer available to him, but a smaller post, the Governor of Batang, was his.

When her father died, Josefina remained on the island, establishing a moderately profitable export business, until Agustín Santayana arrived as the new governor. For whatever reasons, she left for Manila, met George Sturgis, married, conceived five children—two of whom died in early childhood—and then her first husband died. He was young when he died, his business was going badly, and his widow was once again stranded and this time with several children. A brother of her husband contributed a sum of money[31] to help her, and she moved to Boston.

In 1861 she made a trip to Madrid, met Agustín again—he was close to fifty years of age and she was probably thirty-five. George Santayana was born in 1863. The family moved from Madrid to Avila between 1864 and 1866. Josefina seemed determined to raise the Sturgis children in Boston, and, finally, in 1869 she left with her two daughters, the one surviving son from the first marriage having left earlier. From 1869 until 1872 Agustín and George lived together in Avila, and then in 1872 they traveled to Boston where George was left with his mother. The separation of mother and father was permanent. In 1888 Agustín wrote to Josefina: "When we were married I felt as if it were written that I should be united with you, yielding to the force of destiny . . . Strange marriage, this of ours! So you say, and so it is in fact. I love you very much, and you too have cared for me, yet we do not live together."[32] The contingent factors of his background, birth, and childhood form a backdrop for Santayana's mature materialism. Here are forces beyond one's reach, shaping one's destiny, and at the same time providing a chance for a reasonable and good life.

2. The forms of the good are diverse.

After materialism, two other important steps remained to be taken before Santayana's philosophy was "wholly clarified and complete." Santayana describes these steps as the two insights "that the forms of the good are divergent, and that each is definite and final." The first step enabled Santayana to overcome "moral and ideal provinciality, and to see that every form of life had its own perfection, which it was stupid and cruel to condemn for differing from some other form, by chance one's own."[33]

Santayana's moral relativism is consistent with his materialism. It is the neutral perspective of the naturalistic observer who, because he does not have the same commitments, can observe the behavior of others and value it for what it is, not because it coincides with his own interests.[34] No doubt this insight was influenced by the diplomatic careers and lifestyles of his parents, their distant and respectful marriage, the experiences of the young Santayana in Miss Welchman's kindergarten on Chestnut Street and in the Boston Latin School, the wanderings and deliberations of the traveling student, the personal and professional experiences of the young Harvard professor, and the success and travels of the mature, distinguished writer. It is clear that being Spanish, having a Catholic background, and perhaps being an "unconscious homosexual" set him apart in Protestant America. He nevertheless participated in and valued the American experience though he could never fully identify with it. Later, he chose Hermes the Interpreter as his god,[35] paralleling his mature insight as interpreter of views and values. Hermes is at home in the world of discourse—unraveling, decoding, and interpreting one perspective for another. Likewise, Santayana approaches philosophy as reflective discourse, understanding and interpreting many perspectives in his own dialect.

Materialism provides the naturalistic basis for morality while the chaotic realm of essence provides unlimited forms for imagination and interpretation. Santayana's naturalism projects a neutral, objective view towards the moralities, the vested interests, of animals. His realm of essence, likewise, is neutral to the realization or status of any possible form: "Any special system has alternatives, and must tremble for its frontiers; whereas the realm of essence, in its perfect catholicity, is placid and safe and the same whatever may happen in earth or heaven."[36] Santayana's insight that the forms of the good are divergent reveals a chaotic realm of possible goods not logically or morally ordered by animal interests or talents. An absolutely neutral perspective, however, is not possible. Perspectives derive from some living being in a particular place and time with latent interests originating from their physiology and physical environment. Santayana's naturalism is balanced by a polarity between the neutral, objective understanding of behavior and activity on the one hand and the committed, vested interest of the living being on the other hand. One may recognize that every form of the good has its own perfection, and one may respect that perfection, but "the right of alien natures to pursue their proper aims can never abolish our right to pursue ours."[37] Hence, Santayana's second insight: each form of the good is definite and final.

3. Each form of the good is definite and final.

Santayana's philosophy rests on his materialism and on his humane and sympathetic appreciation for the excellence of each life. From the perspective of autobiography, however, Santayana's clear notion of self-knowledge, in the sense of the Greeks, is his most distinguishing mark. For Santayana, "integrity or self-definition is and remains first and fundamental in morals."[38] Like his naturalism and his realm of essence, this insight establishes his thought in a wide tradition, and it marks his career and his personal life with distinction. Decided elements of his self-definition are found in his retirement from Harvard and his life as a roving scholar. After Harvard, his daily activities and long-term achievements were matters of his own direction. Free to choose his own environment and habitual practices, his life was festive and fruitful. Santayana was true to his own form of life to the end. Two days before his death Cory asked him if he was suffering: "Yes, my friend. But my anguish is entirely physical; there are no moral difficulties whatsoever."[39]

EPILOGUE

Santayana died of cancer on 26 September 1952 and is buried in the Campo Verano cemetery in Rome. The Spanish Consulate at Rome provided the Panteon de la Obra Pia Espanola as a suitable burial ground for the lifelong Spanish subject. Wallace Stevens memorialized Santayana in "To an Old Philosopher in Rome":

> Total grandeur of a total edifice,
> Chosen by an inquisitor of structures
> For himself. He stops upon this threshold,
> As if the design of all his words takes form
> And frame from thinking and is realized.

Somewhat like the fictionalized accounts of Santayana's life, these lines (especially the last two) miss the intent of Santayana's materialism. But there is drama in Stevens's account that focuses on the quality and strength of Santayana's chosen life, and certainly "Chosen by an inquisitor of structures / For himself" does accurately and poetically depict the decidedly clear form of Santayana's life.

Perhaps one can characterize the whole of Santayana's life in the manner he depicted his early boyhood: " . . . a passing music of ideas, a dramatic vision, a theme for dialectical insight and laughter; and to decipher that theme, that vision, and that music was my only possible life."[40]

Notes

1. *Time,* 3 February 1936, cover, 75–79.

2. The first full biography was only recently published, and it has decidedly helped to clarify and correct many of the misperceptions about Santayana's life. (See John McCormick, *George Santayana: A Biography* [New York: Alfred A. Knopf, 1987].) As more of Santayana's letters and other unpublished material come to light, however, there is a distinct need for a further biographical assessment.

3. "Spanish-American Philosopher Recalls Farewell to Harvard," *Independent,* Waterbury, Connecticut, 13 December 1950 (article in Santayana clipping file, Harvard Archives).

4. William G. Holzberger and Herman J. Saatkamp, Jr., eds., *Persons and Places,* (Cambridge: The MIT Press, 1986). All page references to *Persons and Places* are to this new critical edition.

5. Santayana, *Persons and Places,* 389; see also Paul G. Kuntz, ed., *George Santayana, Lotze's System of Philosophy* (Bloomington, Ind.: Indiana University Press, 1971).

6. Santayana, *Persons and Places*, 397.

7. McCormick, *George Santayana, 301–02.*

8. George Santayana to Susana Sturgis de Sastre, 19 April 1909. Daniel Cory, ed., *The Letters of George Santayana* (New York: Charles Scribner's Sons, 1955), 90–91.

9. Daniel Cory relates that Santayana, in 1929 after a discussion of A.E. Housman's poetry and homosexuality, remarked that "I think I must have been that way in my Harvard days—although I was unconscious of it at the time." Daniel Cory, *Santayana: The Later Years, A Portrait with Letters* (New York: George Braziller, 1963), 40.

10. An earlier version of this section appeared as "Santayana's Autobiography and the Development of his Philosophy," *Overheard in Seville: Bulletin of the Santayana Society* 4 (Fall 1986): 18–27.

11. *Persons and Places* (New York: Charles Scribner's Sons, 1944) *The Middle Span* (New York: Charles Scribner's Sons, 1945); and *My Host the World* (New York: Charles Scribner's Sons, 1953).

12. Cory, *The Later Years,* 251.

13 The first full accounting of the conveying of these transcripts from Rome to New York is given in *Persons and Places,* 591–92.

14. Santayana to Cory, 14 March 1945, "I see by your letter of Jan. 29th, that you have been officially debasing my pure and legitimate English to conform with the vernacular. . . ." On 8 April 1945, Santayana says that Wheelock of Scribner's has promised him "English spelling" in volume two and that "ultimately all three volumes will be bound in one." But that, he says, "is not at all my dream of the final illustrated and completed edition! . . . You must manage to have, some day, an *edition de luxe,* to appease my Shade." (Santayana's Letters to Daniel Cory are in Butler Library, Columbia University.) To Otto Kyllmann on 23 August 1947, Santayana says, "I wrote these memoirs intending them to be posthumous; when circumstances led me to publishing them, I made some excisions. . . ." (unpublished letter to Otto Kyllmann, housed in the Temple University Library). And throughout it all his ironic sense of humor had its say: " . . . I counted on dying, so that my indiscretions would all have acquired the impersonal authority of historical documents. I rely on Scribner to issue an edition eventually, if they think they can make money out of it. My idea had been, on the contrary, to help finance an edition that would have been a work of art" (unpublished letter of 3 October 1947, in the Harvard Archives).

15. Santayana, *Persons and Places,* 235.

16. Ibid., 235–36.

17. These three steps are described in marginal comments (headings) in the holograph of *Persons and Places.* These comments were omitted from publications prior to the 1986 critical edition of the autobiography.

18. Santayana, *Persons and Places,* 159mh.

19. Ibid., 166mh.

20. Ibid., 166.

21. Ibid., 167.

22. Ibid., 167.

23. Santayana, "To the Moon" and "To the Host," *Persons and Places,* 168.

24. Santayana, *Persons and Places,* 169.

25. Ibid., 169.

26. Santayana, *Realm of Matter,* v.

27. Ibid., v.

28. Ibid., 134.

29. Ibid., 131.

30. Ibid., xi.

31. A sum of $10,000. The same dollar amount Santayana would inherit when his mother died in 1912.

32. Santayana, *Persons and Places*, 9.

33. Ibid., 170.

34. This perspective is comprehensively discussed in Thomas Nagel, *The View from Nowhere* (New York: Oxford University Press, 1986), but, unfortunately, there is not a single reference to Santayana.

35. George Santayana, "Hermes the Interpreter," *Soliloquies in England* (Ann Arbor: University of Michigan Press, 1967), 259.

36. Santayana, *Realms of Being* (one volume edition) (New York: Charles Scribner's Sons, 1942), 82.

37. Santayana, *Persons and Places*, 170.

38. Ibid., 170.

39. Cory, *The Later Years*, 325.

40. Santayana, *Persons and Places*, 159.

Paternity and Patriarchy:
The Last Puritan and the 1930s

PETER CONN

> There is too much fathering going on just now. . . . There is father Mussolini and father Hitler and father Roosevelt and father Stalin and father Lewis and father Blum and father Franco . . . and there are ever so many more ready to be one.
>
> —Gertrude Stein, *Everybody's Autobiography*

1

George Santayana was seventy-two years old when his first novel was published, a circumstance that accounts for much of the considerable publicity attending the book's appearance. After nearly half a century of prolific metaphysical and aesthetic writing, an internationally distinguished philosopher had authored a work of fiction.[1] With the partial exception of Henry Adams, whose novels *Democracy* and *Esther* were published anonymously and much earlier in his career, Santayana's accomplishment was virtually without precedent in American letters.[2]

Deference to Santayana's perceived virtuosity explains at least a portion of the response *The Last Puritan* evoked upon its publication in January 1936. The book was widely reviewed, often in a leading position. Most of the reviews were favorable, and several were downright reverential. The popular press joined the more serious quarterlies in welcoming what the Boston *Transcript* called "a brilliant picture of New England life." Writing in the *New Republic,* Conrad Aiken announced that the "whole book is a delight," while Henry Hazlitt in the *Nation* wrote that the "merits of the book make up for everything, and sweep all its faults before them." The comparisons that reviewers routinely proposed between Santayana and such writers as Proust, Joyce, and Henry James suggest something of the esteem that was immediately conferred upon the novel.

Along with its good notices, *The Last Puritan* also earned a large commercial success. The book was in fact a bestseller. Santayana's picture

This essay was written specifically for this volume and is published here for the first time by permission of the author.

adorned the cover of *Time* magazine's 3 February 1936 issue—a notoriety that few writers have enjoyed—and his novel was chosen as a main selection of the Book-of-the-Month Club.[3] Christopher Morley contributed a long and intelligently supportive essay to the *Book-of-the-Month Club News* in which he acknowledged that the novel was "no great shakes" as a work of fiction; rather, Morley argued that the book's strengths lay in its remarkable prose and its satiric point of view. As a "study of a certain strain of New Englandism," Morley wrote, "as a sentimental-ironic dissection of a North American tradition . . . it is superb."[4]

For Morley, and for a good many other readers, the novel's relationship to American culture was mostly antiquarian. Such readers valued the book as an evocative backward glance, an expansive act of fictive reminiscence with little relevance to the issues and personalities dominating the American scene in the mid-1930s. Instead, *The Last Puritan* offered a demystified and disillusioned recollection of a vanished and rather picturesque social and intellectual world, the Brahmin society of Harvard and Cambridge, Massachusetts in the years around the turn of the century, and the cloistered eccentricity of prewar Oxford.

Similarly, Santayana's techniques, his indifference to both modernist experiment and to proletarian realism, helped to define the special and separate status of his book. In comparison to what Morley called "the novels of now fashionable currency," *The Last Puritan* was as "unreal as *Alice in Wonderland*—and as thrillingly true." In an admiring review in *Books,* Ellen Glasgow made much the same point, distinguishing Santayana's novel from what she termed "the flourishing cults in recent American letters." Implicitly defending her own fictional choices as well as Santayana's, Glasgow wrote that *The Last Puritan* would appeal "to all those who prefer to think while they read." On the other hand, the novel would affront readers she labeled disapprovingly as "the sentimental conservative, the new barbarian, or the earnest believer in social regeneration through literary violence."[5]

Whatever the merits of Glasgow's judgments, the categories that make up her invidious list do identify much of the fictional production of the 1930s. Six years of economic depression had encouraged writers and their audiences toward two antithetical responses, sentimentalized escapism or politicized (usually left-wing) literary engagement.

The unusually straitened realities of mid-depression America made escapism an especially valuable commodity, as pervasively in the screwball comedies and musicals of Hollywood as in literature. The decade's best sellers included a long succession of costume melodramas and romances. Hervey Allen's *Anthony Adverse* (1933), which sold nearly a million copies in three years, followed its swashbuckling title character from Napoleonic Europe to the West Indies and Africa. For twelve hundred pages, readers were lifted out of the intractably stagnant reality of depression America and transported into a distant world of glamorous adventure.

The Good Earth (1932), the novel that earned Pearl Buck international recognition and led eventually to the Nobel Prize she would receive in 1938, dramatized a deliberately simplified struggle between good and evil in China. Above all, *The Good Earth* was designed to demonstrate that political problems could be solved by moral integrity, that goodness and simplicity were inevitable allies, and that ordinary human beings would triumph in the end.

Most notably, in 1936, just a few months after the appearance of *The Last Puritan,* Macmillan published Margaret Mitchell's *Gone With the Wind,* a book that sold for a time at the unprecedented rate of 50,000 copies a day. The novel won the Pulitzer Prize, and the movie that followed took half-a-dozen Academy Awards. In both forms, Mitchell's saga of Civil War and Reconstruction combined sexual and military excitement with the reassurance that crisis could nurture heroism and survival.

As they have in decades before and since, these immensely popular romances, and others such as Kenneth Roberts's *Northwest Passage* (1937), Lloyd C. Douglas's *Magnificent Obsession* (1932) and *Green Light* (1935), and Walter D. Edmonds's *Drums Along the Mohawk* (1936) inscribed familiar consensual beliefs and ratified the received values of society. Beneath their exotic settings and costumes, the reductive moral vocabularies of these texts ultimately defended the ideological status quo. Their consolatory conservatism made them especially attractive diversions in a decade of unusual turbulence.

While the evasions of romance represented one important (and quite profitable) response to the depression's dislocations, the crisis also provoked a large body of more topical and politically engaged writing. The decade produced literary protest of all ideological shades, from pamphlets in support of authoritarian and fascist solutions to agitprop texts prophesying communist revolution.

Most of America's leading writers lined up somewhere on the left. In 1932, over fifty novelists, poets, and critics signed a statement called *Culture and Crisis,* which denounced the deformations of capitalism and endorsed William Z. Foster, the communist candidate for president. Sherwood Anderson, John Dos Passos, Lincoln Steffens, Langston Hughes, and Malcolm Cowley were among those whose names appeared on the document.

Protest writing was not as widely read as the historical romances, self-help books, and religious tracts of the decade, but it exerted a discernible influence on intellectual opinion. Among the novels that indicated capitalism and propagandized for a workers' revolution were Albert Halper's *Union Square* (1933), Clara Weatherwax's *Marching! Marching!* (1935), and Robert Cantwell's *Land of Plenty* (1934). The theater was pressed into radical service, especially in the work of Clifford Odets, whose *Waiting for Lefty* (1935) concluded with the shouted lines "STRIKE! STRIKE! STRIKE!"—the "birth cry of the 1930s," in Harold Clurman's famous phrase.

The work of these writers, and others whose views were more or less similar, was collected in the anthology *Proletarian Literature in the United States,* edited by Granville Hicks and others and first published in October, 1935. *Proletarian Literature* included stories by James T. Farrell, Michael Gold and Josephine Herbst, poetry by Kenneth Fearing, Muriel Ruykeyser and Richard Wright, reporting by John Dos Passos and Agnes Smedley, literary criticism by Malcolm Cowley, William Phillips and Philip Rahv. Here were sympathetic portraits of the unemployed and the dispossessed, angry denunciations of police and plutocrats, and demands for immediate and fundamental change.

In its subject matter, style, and attitudes, *The Last Puritan* seemed to stand outside the ideological welter of mid-depression literary debates. As the reviews of readers such as Christopher Morley and Ellen Glasgow suggest, the novel's partisans actually recommended the book because of its distance equally from "sentimental conservatism," as Glasgow called it, and revolutionary preachment. The well-known facts of Santayana's career reinforced this appraisal. Though he had lived for forty years in the United States, he had resigned his Harvard professorship in 1912 and moved permanently to Europe. When *The Last Puritan* was published, its author had not set foot in America for over twenty years. Furthermore, though the novel was published in the mid-1930s, Santayana had been intermittently at work on it for perhaps as long as forty years, since the 1890s—more evidence of the book's marginality to the America of dust bowl and New Deal.

For all these reasons, studies of *The Last Puritan* have seldom attempted to situate the book in the context of the nation's depression-era culture. Typically, the novel has been treated as a fictional footnote to Santayana's earlier work, in particular his essayistic analyses of America, among them "The Genteel Tradition" (1913), and the articles and lectures gathered in *Character and Opinion in the United States* (1920).[6] In the same vein though more ambitiously, Eliseo Vivas years ago elaborated points of likeness and difference between *The Last Puritan* and Santayana's multi-volume *Life of Reason* (1905).[7] Beyond that, several critics have searched out the probable models for the story's characters among Santayana's Harvard students and friends.[8]

In short, the novel has been treated as a document in Santayana's intellectual career, an elegant and moderately entertaining allegory exemplifying its author's argument with a long-vanished gentility. Consequently, since Santayana is less visible today than he was a half-century ago, his novel seems less central to cultural inquiry. Once praised for its resistance to the categories and sortings that define critical discourse, *The Last Puritan* has subsequently seemed merely anomalous—a fictional sport. Separated from the events and the ideological crosscurrents of the 1930s, the book has virtually disappeared from America's literary history. It has retained its small visibility as a minor instance of what James D. Hart many years ago called "Americana," a latter-day local color tale of little cultural significance.[9]

Nonetheless, with all that qualification by way of preface, a case can be made that *The Last Puritan* was indeed a timely novel in the 1930s, that its action dramatizes issues salient to that decade and that the book will therefore repay investigation within the context of America's turbulent depression debates. To anticipate my conclusion, *The Last Puritan* recapitulates a contest over authority in terms particularly relevant to the 1930s, using puritanism as a mechanism to investigate the problematic nature of America's patriarchal politics and mythology.

To begin with, insofar as Santayana's subject was an assault against puritanism—and specifically the destructive consequences of repression, secular asceticism, and misplaced moral absolutism—his ideas confirmed widely shared attitudes. The Puritan was a popular bogeyman in the 1930s, a satiric target for writers of quite varied political and intellectual persuasions, and Santayana's meditation on the deformations of the puritan conscience found a welcoming echo among many of his contemporaries.

Warren Susman has demonstrated, in a useful survey, that the reputation of the Puritan has shifted several times over the past century, always in response to shifting ideological needs.[10] Up to the end of the nineteenth century, the Puritans were regarded with a nearly universal admiration, venerated as founding fathers who had virtually invented law and industry and democracy on the American continent.

The blacklash began as early as 1886, in Brooks Adams's *Emancipation of New England,* but filial piety continued to characterize the prevailing response to puritanism for another generation. It was only in the years just before World War I, and especially in the twenties and thirties, that the noble Puritan was dismantled and replaced by a sanctimonious, grim-visaged successor, the caricature which H. L. Mencken lampooned when he defined "puritanism" as "the haunting fear that somewhere, someone may be happy." The attacks of Van Wyck Brooks, Lewis Mumford, Randolph Bourne, and especially of Mencken and V. L. Parrington had a cumulatively devastating effect.[11] Santayana himself made an early contribution to this collective demythologizing in his much-noted essay, "The Genteel Tradition," in which a vestigial puritanism is linked with the sterility of American culture.[12]

The indictments of the 1920s were directed principally against the perceived intolerance and sexual squeamishness that marked puritanism as indifferent to human needs. Writers who were attracted by the insights of Freud found the Puritan a convenient oppositional figure. In the 1930s, the resistance to puritanism remained intact, but the focus of anti-puritan sentiment shifted. The economic order which had collapsed in 1929 had been rooted in capitalist-acquisitive values that could allegedly be traced directly back to Puritan antecedents. As prosperity had ratified those values, so bankruptcy challenged them, and the Puritan became a commonplace emblem of failed arrogance and the harm that a narrowly conceived sense of duty can inflict. Since this is precisely the thematic burden of Santayana's novel,

The Last Puritan can be understood at least in this respect as a representative text.

According to the novel's narrator, Oliver Alden's "namesake" is Oliver Optic, an allusion that splendidly summarizes the specific terms of Santayana's argument with puritanism.[13] In the first volume of the autobiographical *Persons and Places*, probably written at about the same time as his novel, Santayana recalled reading the "boy's books" of Oliver Optic during his Boston childhood.[14] The fictional formulas he encountered there codified the ideological system against which he reacted in *The Last Puritan*. In over a hundred novels and a thousand stories, William T. Adams (Oliver Optic was his pseudonym) celebrated the rise of impoverished but talented boys from deprivation to respectable comfort.

Like his protégé and even more popular successor, Horatio Alger, Adams linked partriotism, piety, and prosperity in countless demonstrations of America's unlimited opportunities. Material success, in turn, invariably implied moral integrity: respectability was the sign and proof of virtue.[15] The most frequently invoked historical figure in the work of both Adams and Alger, not surprisingly, is Benjamin Franklin, whose own life seemed at once to anticipate and ratify the pattern of self-fashioning that later generations would celebrate.

Adams and Alger both died in the last decade of the nineteenth century, but their work remained immensely popular for many years. Sales of Alger's books actually increased, quite substantially, in the early 1900s.[16] Indeed, it was only the sustained collapse of the 1930s that seemed definitively to deny the entrepreneurial evangelism of Alger's stories. In the depression, neither luck nor pluck led to comfort or even to security. Prudent industry and self-management might as easily bring failure as success, and the moral vocabulary that tied personal merit to the outcome of worldly venturing was turned upside down.

Thus, the depression appeared to confirm the unhappy counterassertions of philosophical naturalism by insisting on the undeniable gulf that separated effort from achievement. This was the sort of position that Santayana had long embraced, a point of view which for generations had been subordinated to more familiar protestations of America's inevitable progress. In the 1930s, a conspiracy of economic circumstance had made the accomplishments of earlier Americans unattainable; the American dream had shrunk to a mocking memory.

The Last Puritan can be read as a fable inscribing this same grim moral. Oliver Alden begins life with every material advantage, dedicates himself relentlessly to every obligation, and finds only self-doubt and unhappiness. Where his "namesake" had created characters like Bobby Bright in *Now or Never*, Buck Bradford in *Down the River*, and Jack Somers in *The Sailor Boy*, whose energy and smiling persistence leads to an affluence that is coupled with moral serenity, Oliver Alden falls from a state of initial material grace into irremediable misery. He does keep his money, but only because he is unable to give it away; for all practical purposes, he loses his soul and dies a failure. His death itself is tinged in ironic pathos: denied even the problematic heroism of dying in battle, Oliver is killed in a motorcycle accident a few days after the Armistice of November 1918.

Oliver is doomed by his emotional and spiritual inheritance, and while his mother is a major figure in the novel, he is principally the victim of his father, his grandfather, and the largely patriarchal legacy of his culture. Santayana's study of puritan pathology led him into a bitterly skeptical analysis of what might be called American paternity. Oliver Alden is a case study in the mortal consequences that the dead hand of the paternal past inflicts upon its heirs.

The murderous violence that shadows the Alden male line encapsulates this fatality. Oliver's pathetic death is preceded and foreshadowed by other deaths: his grandfather, a mean-spirited exemplar of the post-Calvinist entrepreneurial ethic, has been murdered by an abused and outraged tenant; Oliver's father, who as a student had killed a Harvard watchman with the heavy Bible in the college chapel, ultimately takes his own life. In each case, death represents some deep fissure in the bonds that link fathers and sons.

Santayana's discouraged rendering of family relationships had its first sources in his own experience. From his earliest awareness, his connection with his father was a compound of confusion and doubt. Near the end of the first volume of *Persons and Places,* he wrote: "A real father in my case was lacking" (248). His literal paternity was not in question, but the disruptions that marked his early life challenged the ideas of fatherhood and fatherland that he received as his legacy. Even a brief summary of the more familiar facts of his biography illuminates the ground of his uncertainty.

Santayana was born in Madrid and spent his early years in Avila; his first language was Spanish, and he never exchanged his Spanish citizenship for that of any other country. He spent forty years in the United States, however, and he did all of his professional writing in English, his second language. The last forty years of his life were spent in Europe, not in Spain, but in England, Paris, and Rome. In all these places, he felt himself an exile and a perpetual stranger. [17]

Santayana's alienation was not merely a matter of geography and language. His father was his mother's second husband. When they married in 1861, Agustín Ruiz de Santayana was nearing fifty, his wife, Josefina Sturgis de Santayana, was in her late thirties. George would be her sixth and last child. Josefina's first husband, dead many years before Santayana's birth, was the merchant George Sturgis of Boston. It was Sturgis, significantly, for whom George was named, and it was Sturgis who was the father of Santayana's half-sister Susana, his dearest relation. From the age of nine, young George lived in Boston with his mother and his Sturgis relatives, while his father continued to live in Spain. Further emphasizing his father's absence from his life, the financial support Santayana received from his mother, and the legacy that at her death in 1912 permitted him to resign from Harvard and leave the United States for good was the Sturgis money.

Agustín Santayana appears often in his son's autobiographical reminiscences, almost invariably as a figure overtaken by disappointment, or futility, or illness. He was unsuccessful in just about all his worldly pursuits. He traveled badly, bequeathing to George a propensity for seasickness. He was often invisible even in his own home. To give just one example among many, Santayana in *Persons and Places* includes a recollection of his father's behavior after the death of his daughter, George's sister Antoñita. Instead of moving out of the Santayana house, Agustín's son-in-law Rafael not only remained, he "became all-important . . . as if my father had not existed" (124).

A more sinister episode of paternal inadequacy involved Agustín's inability to speak English. He read English perfectly, but he could neither pronounce it nor understand it when others spoke it. In consequence, with English-speaking people "he was reduced to uttering single words, if they could be recognised as he sounded them, or to writing them on a piece of paper" (129). Struggling with individual words, in the face of George's growing fluency, Agustín was reduced, in effect, to an almost childlike linguistic incapacity in his use of English; the roles of father and son were reversed. Agustín's embarrassment merely emphasized the gulf that each year widened further between him and his son. In a concluding gesture of disdain, the first volume of *Persons and Places* ends with a patronizing comment on "Papa Santayana," who "positively *liked* to be limited and perhaps wasn't quite virtuous" (249).

The most definitive moment of filial rejection recorded in Santayana's memoirs occurs in his account of his father's death and involves what I am tempted to call an act of symbolic patricide. Agustín's death was the first that his son had witnessed, and he recalls the circumstances as "deeply pathetic. He was seventy-nine years old, deaf, half blind, and poor; he had desired his own death and had attempted to hasten it." (The possibility of his father's complicity in his own death obviously haunted Santayana for years.) Then, in an illuminating passage of self-revelation, Santayana offers a summary judgment of the meaning of his father's life by prophesying his own: "The fact that he was my father, whose character and destiny were strikingly repeated, with variations, in my own, called up a lurid image of what my life in the world was likely to be: solitary, obscure, trivial, and wasted" (424).

Santayana's contempt for his father—it is difficult to call it anything else—had its sources partly in a son's judgments of his father's ineffectual behavior, but even more in Santayana's distaste for Agustín's ideas. Agustín was a dogmatic, anticlerical liberal, a position against which George felt himself strongly reacting, even in his early years. "To be monotonous, sophistical, and utterly intolerant," Santayana wrote, "is the characteristic of the liberalism he [Agustín] seemed to have adopted as final and absolute: I belong to the next turn of the tide" (199).

Santayana's opposition to "liberalism" actually involved a multiple repudiation. In an idiosyncratic but typical act of assemblage, Santayana coordinated several of the ideologies and perspectives he most strongly rejected, making them more or less versions of each other. Specifically, he argued that liberalism, Protestantism, Judaism, and positivism "all have the same ultimate aim and standard. It is prosperity, or as Lutheran theologians put it, union with God at our level, not at God's level" (200).

This remarkable massing of mistaken creeds does not contribute much to the history of thought, but it clarifies the intensity of Santayana's denial of his father. Santayana constructs a kind of syllogism, indifferent to facts but true to his sense of paternal injustice and inadequacy.

> Major premise: liberals are Protestants, positivists, and Jews;
>
> Minor: but, Agustín is a liberal;
>
> Conclusion: therefore, Agustín is a protestant, a positivist, and a Jew.

Santayana's father thus represents much more than the liberal atheist and enemy of priests he thought himself to be. He becomes in this reckoning the logical if unlikely target of his son's anti-Protestant and anti-Semitic anger as well.

Santayana's anti-Semitism was among the least savory of his intellectual commitments, and its traces can be found throughout his work, including *The Last Puritan*.[18] In his recent biography of Santayana, John McCormick charts his subject's changing but lifelong affiliation with anti-Semitism. A chapter called "Moral Dogmatism: Santayana as Anti-Semite" gathers citations from early and late letters that disclose attitudes ranging from the casual snobbishness of Anglo-Amercian educated classes to a more vivid and inflammatory hatred. In a letter to his nephew George Sturgis in 1936, after the outbreak of war in Spain, Santayana wrote that the "Jews, for instance, aren't in the least like Abraham or King Solomon: they are just sheenies. . . ."[19]

Anti-Semitism reinforced his repudiation of his father, and the link was further strengthened by Santayana's view of Judaism as ferociously patriarchal. Furthermore, Judaism was symbolically linked with Protestantism in Santayana's mind, and specifically the puritanism whose fatality traps the main character of his novel.[20]

Many years before the publication of *The Last Puritan*, Santayana dramatized the conjunction between paternal authority, puritanism, and Judaism by appropriating a central biblical episode and applying it to American culture. In a remarkable letter of 1920 to Boylston Beal, he lamented the fate of Herbert Lyman, a young man whose writing he had once encouraged. Obliged to enter the family business, Lyman had suffered a complete breakdown. "I have always felt," Santayana wrote, "that he was a sacrifice on the altar of Bostonian superstition about work—a sort of Isaac that Abraham was ordered to slay, and no opportune angel or sheep came in at the last moment to save him." The letter ends with the remark: "What a curious tragedy Puritanism is!"[21]

In this Old Testament image the thematic design of *The Last Puritan* is summarized with the stark clarity of a morality play: Puritan patriarchy, clothed in the likeness of Judaic revelation, is imaginatively rendered at the moment of murdering its child. The main difference is that Herbert Lyman, unlike Isaac, did not escape destruction. Nor does Oliver Alden. The original story of Abraham and Isaac is to be found in the Bible with which Peter Alden murders the Harvard watchman; its allegorical enactment makes up the plot of Santayana's novel.

The debate over paternal authority lies at the center of Oliver Alden's story. Oliver's cultural antecedents encompass several historical and fictional characters, a network of reference that contributes to Santayana's complex commentary on the factual and symbolic relations between fathers and sons.

To return for a moment to Oliver's "namesake," the stories of Oliver Optic almost always make sentimental use of filial relations. Typically, the heroes of these tales (as of Horatio Alger's) are fatherless boys—indeed, it is often the financial peril created by a father's death that drives the boys toward their precocious achievements. Deprived of paternal support, they become "self-made men" in a somewhat literal sense. They are always kind to their widowed mothers (an archetypal figure in this genre), but their filiopiety is reserved for their dead fathers.

Oliver Alden's father, on the other hand, lives through the years of his son's childhood but effectively abandons him. Oliver's boyhood is punctuated by occasional reports of his father's travels, accounts that document Peter Alden's aimless wandering, moral evasion and indifference. Shortly after they are reunited, Oliver watches his father slip into a self-willed death, an event that schools him in human futility, further weakens his sense of purpose, and accelerates his decline.

The ironic purposes that Oliver Optic serves in *The Last Puritan* are reinforced by several of the other references and allusions with which Santayana surrounds his main character. At one point, for example, Jim Darnley summons Oliver Twist as another "namesake," invoking a further contrast between Dickens's orphaned boy, who wins through to good fortune, and Santayana's privileged young man, who collapses into the despair that comprises his destructive birthright (368).

The same conclusion is implied in Oliver's monogram, which compactly elaborates Santayana's analysis of patriarchal presence and absence in *The Last Puritan*. In one of Fraulein Irma Schlote's letters, she tells her family that Oliver's monogram is an A inside an O: Ⓐ. "Do you think," she writes, "Dr. Freud could explain that?" (222). For Fraulein Schlote, who reveres the young man, the meaning of the monogram is plain: it is "the Alpha and Omega of our Saviour." In a P.S. to the same letter, she tells of a "wonderful" experience she has had, in which she mistook the sleeping Oliver's reflected image in a mirror for a vision of the crucified Christ.

In other words, Oliver's monogram links him, in the pious imagining of his governess, to Christ at the moment of his death. Christ of course had no earthly father and, according to his own last words, was abandoned in death by his divine father as well. Significantly, Oliver does not resemble the well-groomed and peaceful Christ of neoclassical tradition but "one of those uncouth mediaeval images, haggard, lean, stiff and out of proportion" (223).

Aside from Fraulein Schlote's interpretation, Oliver's monogram may encode yet another of the novel's meditations on paternity. The "A" inside the "O" duplicates the heraldic blazoning of Hester Prynne's punitive symbol with which *The Scarlet Letter* concludes. The connection is altogether apt. The plot of Hawthorne's novel revolves around the efforts of both community and husband to discover the father of Hester's daughter. Hawthorne's fictional child is female while Santayana's is male, but the issues of paternal abandonment and the unwarranted debts that children pay are equally central to both novels. And, like Oliver Alden, Pearl is reunited with her father just in time to watch him die, in some measure through his own resigned cooperation.

The lineage that Santayana provides for Oliver reaches back, both genealogically and symbolically, to the seventeenth century. Oliver has what his mother considers "the inexpressible privilege" of direct descent from "those famous pilgrims, Priscilla and John Alden, immortalised by Longfellow in his household classic, *The Courtship of Miles Standish*" (72). Oliver, however, stands at the morally exhausted end of the history that his ancestors helped to found. His own courtships inevitably fail, he dies childless, and with his death his line flickers out.

In any case, Longfellow's story of Priscilla and John Alden represents, in Santayana's opinion, an act of saccharine misrepresentation. His own harder conception of the Puritan seventeenth century can be discerned in yet another of Oliver Alden's namesakes, Protector Cromwell.[22] By linking his young hero to English Puritanism's principal soldier and statesman, Santayana places further emphasis on his concern with paternity in the novel. Put summarily, American Puritanism had its origins in the political and spiritual ideology that led, in 1649, to regicide. Since the commonplace correspondences of the seventeenth century joined the king's patriarchal and paternal identities, regicide was universally understood to be an extreme form of patricide.

Oliver Alden is Cromwell's heir; or, to put it more precisely, Oliver is the vehicle through which Santayana dramatizes his inquiry into the ideas of paternity and patriarchy. The several cultures that constituted his heritage each inscribed patriarchal conceptions in different ways. The Catholic Spain of his early childhood, and the Italy of his later years, were dominated by a faith that radically centralized authority in a single figure. (The Catholic pope is known to his followers as the "Holy Father," and the religion's childless priests are called "Father.") Amid the political turmoil of the years after World War I, both countries reaffirmed patriarchy by installing fascist dictators who signified the triumph of patriarchal rule. Both Franco and Mussolini employed a rhetoric that coupled national survival with divinely sanctioned paternal power, and both devised social policies that enforced this view.

Santayana welcomed Mussolini in the 1920s, and he later supported the Falange in Spain.[23] To that extent, he may be said to have endorsed the continuing legitimacy of patriarchal models, at least within the context of European history and its postwar disorder.[24] *The Last Puritan,* on the other hand, enacts a more complex response to these issues, and thus discloses its conspicuous affinity with one of the major debates of the American 1930s.[25] With the exception of the Civil War, no domestic crisis engendered such intense uncertainty over the nature of political authority as the depression did. The economic collapse and its consequences, including multiplied unemployment and poverty, combined with acts of nature—especially the most severe drought of the century—to produce an atmosphere of unparalleled anxiety.

The very premises upon which American society was grounded were challenged and, in the view of many, discredited. The sharp division between ideological positions was sometimes acted out in the arenas of electoral politics and polemical journalism, but it also embraced the nation's familiar symbols and icons. In the 1930s, as throughout America's history, the most universally recognized iconic figure was George Washington, and his image became the site of the contest over patriarchy and authority.

The elevation of Washington to quasi-divine status, and his veneration as "Father of His Country," actually commenced during his lifetime.[26] Throughout the nineteenth century, the mythmaking process continued. Gilbert Stuart's "Atheneum" portrait (Figure 1) was the basis of countless reproductions, and became the most widely circulated likeness in the country. Mason Locke Weems's largely fanciful but immensely popular *Life* went through numerous editions and stayed in print for generations. The Washington Monument rose slowly through the century; when completed, it was and remains the tallest stone structure in the world. The portrait, the biography and the monument are just three instances of the central place Washington occupied in America's symbolic politics.[27]

Washington's iconic value was the subject of renewed attention in the 1930s, but the response was as often skeptical as celebratory. The bicentennial of Washington's birth occurred in 1932, and that event precipitated a great deal of worshipful commemoration. At the same time, precisely because he embodied the values that were so fundamentally tested in the depression, Washington also became a satiric target.[28] The nation's politics,

Figure 1. Gilbert Stuart, *George Washington* (1796) [the "Atheneum" portrait]. National Portrait Gallery.

Fig. 2. Grant Wood, *Parson Weems' Fable* (1939). Amon Carter Museum, Fort Worth, Texas.

285

and its patriarchal assumptions, could be attacked at a single stroke in the figure of Washington.[29]

One of the more interesting examples of the reaction against Washington in the depression decade can be found in Katherine Mayo's once-popular novel, *General Washington's Dilemma,* published in 1938. Mayo had become a figure of international notoriety in the 1920s with her sensational attack on Indian culture and Hinduism, *Mother India,* a book that was attacked and defended in newspapers, foreign offices, and legislatures around the world. *General Washington's Dilemma* recreates an actual though long-forgotten incident in which Washington cynically authorized the hanging of an innocent British soldier in retaliation for the lynching of a Revolutionary privateer. Basing her long narrative on a good deal of archival research,[30] Mayo presents a morally bewildered Washington—motivated by reasons of state to allow the execution of a man chosen by lot from a group of British officers—in violation of all existing rules of war.[31]

Grant Wood's painting of 1939, *Parson Weems' Fable* (Figure 2), also provocatively testifies to the ambiguous nature of Washington's position in the depression. The "fable" Wood refers to is, of course, the tale of six-year-old George Washington cutting down a cherry tree and then confessing the deed to his father. The story, widely known to be a fabrication, was first included in the fifth edition of Weems's *Life* (1806). Significantly, the moral intended by the edifying anecdote had less to do with young George's honesty than with his father's success as a parent. An enlightened father, Washington senior had never beaten his son, and George's confession proved the value of this liberal system of child rearing. When the young Washington confesses, his father answers (in Weems's invented dialogue): "Glad am I, George, that you killed my tree; for you have repaid me for it a thousandfold. Such an act of heroism in my son is worth more than a thousand trees."

Wood's painting offers an elaborate travesty of America's most familiar myth. The parson himself pulls back a curtain to reveal the scene within. The composition is derived from eighteenth and nineteenth-century portraits,[32] but the curtain also functions as a theatrical prop, framing the enclosed tableau in declarations of artifice. The moment of Washingtonian truth is farcically rendered, in particular because young George's body is surmounted by the elderly head of the "Atheneum" portrait.[33]

This is all good fun, but it also raises serious questions about the validity of American filiopietism. The picture's irony is not directed toward Weems himself but toward the self-deluding taste of a republic that prefers fairy tales to truth. (The anonymous, laboring slaves in the background of the painting reinforce the point.) Wood turns the revered Atheneum image into a comic mask, and in doing so ridicules the patriarchal myth. He renders Washington, impossibly, as older than his father, portrays him indeed as already the "Father of His Country," the role with which the Atheneum portrait was universally associated. By confronting

Washington's father with a son who has become the "Father," Wood reverses father-son relations and effectively denies the paternity of the Father's father. In short, patriarchal legitimacy is parodically annulled a generation before its establishment.

Making use of a different but related colonial vocabulary, *The Last Puritan* reaches similar conclusions.[34] Santayana coordinated the memories of his own father's inadequacies with his unflattering typological reading of American history to challenge the most cherished myth of American politics. Like latterday and unrescued Isaacs, sons and nations are alike betrayed by their "founding fathers," and history becomes the scene of patriarchal tragedy. Oliver Alden's death in the aftermath of World War I signifies the bankruptcy of the heroic assumptions through which an earlier America has domesticated ideas of ultimate authority. Thus, his death is also an acute and monitory comment on the ideological divisions that attended the collapse and subsequent upheavals of the 1930s. The international depression and the threat of another world war shook the foundations of authority with unprecedented violence; *The Last Puritan* records Santayana's skeptical contribution to the ensuing debate.

Notes

1. Santayana's first book of philosophy, *The Sense of Beauty* had appeared in 1896, his first essays a decade before that.

2. *Democracy* had been published in 1880, when Adams was forty-two years old, *Esther* four years later.

3. The novel's selection by the Book-of-the-Month Club permitted Scribner's to reduce the list price from $3.00 (the advertised price in advance publicity) to $2.75.

4. The citations are taken from the pamphlet, *Book-of-the-Month Club News*, n.p.

5. Ellen Glasgow's review appeared in *Books*, 2 February 1936, 1.

6. See, among other examples, Newton Stallknecht, *George Santayana* (Minneapolis: University of Minnesota Press, 1971), 35–36; Paul K. Conkin, *Puritans and Pragmatists: Eight Eminent American Thinkers* (Bloomington: Indiana University Press, 1976), 420ff.

7. Eliseo Vivas, "From *The Life of Reason* to *The Last Puritan*," in Paul Arthur Schilpp, ed., *The Philosophy of George Santayana* (Evanston: Northwestern University Press, 1940), 313–50.

8. Santayana himself identified several of the former acquaintances who suggested characters in *The Last Puritan;* the list included Edward Bayley, Ward Thoron, and Cameron Forbes. See *Persons and Places: Fragments of Autobiography* (Cambridge: The MIT Press, 1986), 178, 221, 347.

9. James D. Hart, *The Popular Book: A History of America's Literary Taste* (New York: Oxford University Press, 1950), 262.

10. Warren I. Susman, "Uses of the Puritan Past," in *Culture as History: The Transformation of American Society in the Twentieth Century* (New York: Pantheon, 1984), 39–49.

11. Some of the key texts include Van Wyck Brooks, *The Wine of the Puritans* (1908); Randolph Bourne, "The Puritan's Will to Power" (1917); William Carlos Williams, *In the American Grain* (1925); and V. L. Parrington, *Main Currents in American Thought* (1927–1930).

12. Santayana first presented "The Genteel Tradition" as a lecture to the California

Philosophical Union in August, 1911. The essay was reprinted in the *University of California Chronicle* later that year, and subsequently in *Winds of Doctrine* (New York: Charles Scribner's Sons, 1913).

13. George Santayana, *The Last Puritan: A Memoir in the Form of a Novel* (New York: Charles Scribner's Sons, 1936), 70. Subsequent quotations from the novel will be cited in parentheses.

14. George Santayana, *Persons and Places: Fragments of Autobiography*, 142. Subsequent quotations from this volume will be cited in parentheses.

15. As several critics have demonstrated, neither the heroes of Alger nor of Adams aspire to "riches." The trajectory that their careers follow leads to middling affluence and, above all, to respectability. Indeed, the novels of both men should probably be read as satires against the excessive wealth amassed by the most successful nineteenth-century plutocrats. See John G. Cawelti, *Apostles of the Self-Made Man* (Chicago: University of Chicago Press, 1965), especially chapter 2, "From Rags to Respectability"; and Michael Zuckerman, "The Nursery Tales of Horatio Alger," *American Quarterly*, 24 (May 1972), 191–209.

16. On the history of Alger's reputation, see Carl Bode, Introduction to Horatio Alger, Jr., *Ragged Dick and Struggling Upward* (New York: Viking Press, 1985), xxi.

17. Declarations of homelessness are among the central motifs in all of Santayana's several autobiographical essays and books.

18. On the trip back to America with Peter Alden's body, the narrator describes a group of cardplayers surrounding Jim Darnley as "rather rowdy company: some young, others fat and middle-aged and evidently of the Jewish persuasion, but all looking more or less sallow, bloated, and dishevelled . . . (362). Jim himself refers to "a chap in London" who might help him sell Peter's collection of books and curios, a man who is "the very devil of a sharp Jew, who palms off old masters on the American millionaires" (366). Mario Van de Weyer is the most outspokenly anti-Semitic character in the novel, describing a Jewish character as a "sheeny" (395), and later railing against governments as mere cliques of "politicians, Free Masons and Jews, more than half of them, parasites of the parliamentary farce" (525).

19. John McCormick, *George Santayana: A Biography* (New York: Alfred A. Knopf, 1987), 364.

20. In a sense, Santayana was merely taking Puritan self-characterization at face value. Typological strategies that identified the New England mission with that of the Old Testament Israelites was a commonplace of colonial histories and biographies.

21. Unpublished letter, cited in McCormick, 37.

22. The reference to Cromwell is not explicitly recorded in the novel, but a Puritan named Oliver will automatically suggest the link. George Howgate, who discussed the book with Santayana not long after its publication, made the connection fifty years ago, in *George Santayana* (Philadelphia: University of Pennsylvania Press, 1938), 264.

23. See for example, McCormick, 294–95, 322, 343–45, 355.

24. In the view of John P. Diggins, it is "difficult to explain George Santayana's respect for the Mussolini government." Fascism glorified action, including violent struggle, and preached the fundamental reform of human society. Santayana counseled contemplation, restraint, and the resigned acceptance of human limits. Diggins locates the reasons for Santayana's embrace of fascism in his "rejection of American civilization. Convinced that America was divided into two states of mind, Santayana saw in Fascism a higher organic Italian culture that appealed to his atheistic catholicism and his Mediterranean anti-puritanism. Thus . . . Santayana's support of Fascism also reflected a lifelong disenchantment with a stunted, bifurcated American culture frantic with motion and bereft of direction." *Mussolini and Fascism: The View from America* (Princeton: Princeton University Press, 1972), 209–10.

25. Given the failures and confusion that marked his own experience of paternity, the novel may render his ideological inclinations more subtly and accurately than the simpler political statements he made from time to time about European events.

26. A useful review of the early popular response to Washington is contained in Wendy C. Wick, *George Washington: An American Icon* (Washington, D.C.: Smithsonian Institution, 1982).

27. Even in the nineteenth century, Washington's symbolic significance was actually somewhat more complicated than his admirers may have realized. He was, to begin with, a curiously anti-patriarchal patriarch: the government he founded and virtually personified had been established in an act of rebellion against a legitimate king. Furthermore, though he was revered as the hero of the revolution, the cult of Washington tended to reaffirm the post-revolutionary status quo and to make any subsequent revolution illegitimate. See, among other sources, Jay Fliegelman, *Prodigals and Pilgrims: The American Revolution Against Patriarchal Authority, 1750–1800* (New York: Cambridge University Press, 1982), 199ff; and Gary Wills, *Cincinnatus: George Washington and the Enlightenment* (Garden City, N.Y.: Doubleday & Co., 1984).

28. Perhaps predictably, the decade's two most popular former presidents may have been Abraham Lincoln and Andrew Jackson. The final four volumes of Carl Sandburg's celebratory and Pulitzer Prize-winning biography of Lincoln, *The War Years,* appeared in 1939. That same year saw the production of John Ford's *Young Mr. Lincoln,* with Henry Fonda in the title role. The film ends with images of Lincoln statues, suggesting the president's translation into the symbolic figure he would become. Marquis James's two-volume *Life of Andrew Jackson* (1933, 1937) also celebrated its subject, and also won a Pulitzer Prize. In their different ways, Lincoln and Jackson represented the apotheosis of the "common man," and thus fittingly served as emblematic figures in the depression decade.

29. On the rise and fall of Washington's reputation, see, among others, Karal Ann Marling's chatty survey, *George Washington Slept Here: Colonial Revivals and American Culture, 1876–1986* (Cambridge: Harvard University Press, 1988).

30. With twenty-four pages of footnotes, *General Washington's Dilemma* is, in effect, a nonfiction novel. Though the genre had not yet been named in the 1930s, the mixture of documentary and fiction was a relatively common technique during the decade. Dos Passos's *U.S.A.* trilogy, Steinbeck's *The Grapes of Wrath,* Maxwell Anderson's *Winterset,* and Agee and Evans's *Let Us Now Praise Famous Men* are some of the more familiar examples.

31. The accuracy of Mayo's account is not at issue here, of course, but her version of the story is not incompatible with the briefer discussions in more scholarly treatments of Washington's career. See, for one authoritative example, James Thomas Flexner, *George Washington in the American Revolution* (Boston: Little, Brown and Company, 1968), 479–82.

32. The most important predecessor painting is Charles Willson Peale's *Artist in His Museum* (1822), in which Peale holds back a curtain and discloses the collections of art and natural history that filled his Philadelphia museum.

33. Among the more useful discussions of the sources and composition of *Parson Weems' Fable* are those in Wanda M. Corn, *Grant Wood: The Regionalist Vision* (New Haven, Conn. Yale University Press, 1983); 120–23, and James M. Dennis, *Grant Wood: A Study in American Art and Culture* (Columbia, Mo.: University of Missouri Press, 1987), 112–14.

34. Washington himself is mentioned just once in *The Last Puritan,* in an ironically glancing reference. An illustrated *Life* of Washington lies unread on a parlor table of the Bumstead home in Connecticut (221).

Index

◆